DATE DUE

DEMCO 38-296

The Emil and Kathleen Sick

Lecture-Book Series

in Western History and Biography

The Emil and Kathleen Sick

Lecture-Book Series

in Western History and Biography

Under the provisions of a Fund established by the children of Mr. and Mrs. Emil Sick, whose deep interest in the history and culture of the American West was inspired by their own experience in the region, distinguished scholars are brought to the University of Washington to deliver public lectures based on original research in the fields of Western history and biography. The terms of the gift also provide for the publication by the University of Washington Press of the books resulting from the research upon which the lectures are based. This book is the fifth volume in the series.

The Great Columbia Plain: A Historical Geography, 1805–1910,
by Donald W. Meinig

Mills and Markets: A History of the Pacific Coast Lumber Industry to 1900,
by Thomas R. Cox

Radical Heritage: Labor, Socialism, and Reform in Washington and British Columbia, 1885–1917, by Carlos A. Schwantes

The Battle for Butte: Mining and Politics on the Northern Frontier, 1864–1906, by Michael P. Malone

The Forging of a Black Community: Seattle's Central District, from 1870 through the Civil Rights Era, by Quintard Taylor

The Forging of a Black Community

Seattle's Central District from 1870 through the Civil Rights Era

QUINTARD TAYLOR

Foreword by Norm Rice

UNIVERSITY OF WASHINGTON PRESS

Seattle and London

Library of Congress Cataloging-in-Publication Data
Taylor, Quintard.
    The forging of a black community : Seattle's Central District
  from 1870 through the Civil Rights Era / Quintard Taylor ; foreword by
Norm Rice.
      p. cm. — (The Emil and Kathleen Sick lecture-book series in
Western history and biography)
    Includes bibliographical references and index.
    ISBN 0–295–97315–3 (alk. paper : cloth). — ISBN 0–295–97345–5
(alk. paper : pbk.)
    1. Central District (Seattle, Wash.)—Race relations. 2. Afro-
Americans—Washington—Seattle—History. 3. Seattle (Wash.)—Race relations. I. Title. II. Series.
F899.S49N475 1994
979.7′77200496073—dc20   93-49522
                                                                   CIP

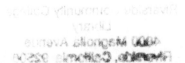

Contents

Illustrations

Maps

Photographs

Foreword

The Forging of a Black Community by Quintard Taylor is a powerful chronicle of the African American presence in Seattle over the last century. The result of years of painstaking research and dozens of interviews, it is a fascinating account of the social, political, and economic transformation of black Seattle through the city's formative frontier years, through two global wars and more limited military engagements, and through numerous cycles of depression and prosperity.

Professor Taylor's rich tapestry of the African American past in Seattle has captured the beauty, hope, aspirations, disappointments, and ongoing challenges of African Americans and other people of color in this diverse city. Furthermore, *The Forging of a Black Community* details the spirit and conviction of a people determined to defeat the legacy of racism, ethnocentrism, and discrimination that is, unfortunately, so much a part of our past as a nation. Taylor reminds us that African Americans who first came to Seattle in the nineteenth century found themselves in "a city deeply ambivalent about its commitment to racial equality." Drawing inspiration from their heritage, their faith, and their families, they fashioned a strong sense of identity that allowed these intelligent, gifted, hard-working newcomers to master the adversity they faced. From the arrival of the Massachusetts sailor, Manuel Lopes, in 1858, just six years after the founding of Seattle, to the African American newcomers joining our city today, African Americans continue to bring with them a variety of experiences. Yet those of us who, like myself, arrived from other cities and states, as well as those born here, continue to adhere to a common goal. We seek the freedom and opportunity that were, and remain, the promise of Seattle, that inspired prior generations of black newcomers to cross a continent or sail oceans to reach this small narrow isthmus of verdant land between Puget Sound and Lake Washington. Like them, we remain committed to join forces with all of the city's diverse peoples to ensure that freedom and opportunity will be available for all residents of our city.

As the first African American mayor of Seattle, I am proud to have a place in Professor Taylor's book. My 1989 election, as he notes, coincided with a number of other significant milestones in

African American political history, including Virginia's Lieutenant Governor Douglas Wilder's victory that same night which made him the first popularly elected African American governor of that or any other state.

Taylor's history recalls the deep roots of African American political activism in Seattle and the enormous debt we owe to heretofore unrecognized Seattleites whose struggles for social justice helped to provide the foundation for the contemporary politics of our city. Moreover, some of those struggles begun by the pioneers continue in various forms and in diverse forums of the city to this day.

Here in the 1990s, at the dawn of the twenty-first century, the United States continues to face racial intolerance and the consequences seen so often in political rivalry, economic competition, inter- and intra-ethnic estrangement, and residential confrontation. These challenges appear, unfortunately, to be a permanent fixture in American society. Yet the history of black Seattle illuminates how such challenges can be addressed in our age. *The Forging of a Black Community* is not simply a study of African American history in one city. It is above all else a guide for all of contemporary urban America. Our history recalls the long legacy of both confrontative and cooperative interaction between Euro-Americans, Asian Americans, Native Americans, and African Americans, ultimately illustrating the ability of people of good will to find common ground amid the often rancorous chorus of diverse voices. I believe Seattle's long history of racial interaction can serve as a model for other urban communities that are just now grappling with the consequences of their own growing ethnic and racial diversity. Thus I hope you will read, be inspired by, and learn from the history of African American Seattle as recounted in *The Forging of a Black Community*, not only for what we can learn about ourselves, our legacy, and our city, but also what significant experiences Seattleites can and must share with the wider world.

The Honorable Norman Rice
Mayor of Seattle

Acknowledgments

The Forging of a Black Community is the result of a decade of research and writing at three separate academic institutions on two continents. Over that period I benefited from the insights, critiques, and suggestions of numerous individuals. Space will not permit me to mention all of them, but there are many talented individuals whose crucial assistance at various stages of the manuscript's development warrant specific acknowledgment. They include my colleagues at the University of Oregon, Richard Maxwell Brown, Earl Pomeroy, Jack Maddex, Jeff Ostler, and Clarence Spigner, each of whom read all or parts of the manuscript, as well as Mavis Mate and James Mohr, my former and current department heads, who were particularly supportive with words of advice and wise counsel during the latter stages of my work.

Over the course of some years I had an ongoing dialogue with a number of scholars whose ideas are frequently represented in the pages of this book. During the research phase of the project I received advice, guidance, and suggestions from colleagues across the country, including George Cotkin, Daniel Krieger, Ed Mayo, Willi Coleman, Art Cary, my former colleagues at California Polytechnic State University; Ronald Coleman at the University of Utah; Malik Simba at California State University, Fresno; Emory Tolbert at Howard University; Shirley Moore at California State University, Sacramento; S. Frank Miyamoto and Richard Berner at the University of Washington; Douglas Daniels at the University of California, Santa Barbara; Allan Spier, Lancine Kaba, and Allen Issacman at the University of Minnesota; and Robert Fikes at San Diego State University. My thanks go to Albert S. Broussard at Texas A. & M. University, who shared his manuscript (since published) on black San Francisco, and to John McCann, a Ph.D. student at Oregon and already a published author, whose sensitive discussion of the complexity of labor union discrimination allowed me to revisit and revise my reading of black-white worker conflict. I also want to thank Esther Hall Mumford and Ralph Hayes, two Seattle-area historians who by example inspired my own work and who urged me to build upon their foundation. Although their influence on my scholarship predates this project, I also want to acknowledge the guidance and assistance of Joyce Suber, John Dawkins, and Talmadge Anderson. Clearly the colleague who provided the greatest help, support, and encouragement over the ten-year life of this project was Joe W. Trotter at Carnegie-Mellon University.

I also benefited from productive discussions about black Seattle in the larger context of race and culture during my year at the University of Lagos. Some of my Nigerian colleagues read parts of my manuscript and others forwarded comments and impressions based on their own experiences. I particularly want to thank Professors John Oriji, Kwame Serbeh-Yiadom, Lynn Nwuneli, and Hakeem Harunah among others at the university and in Lagos, Patrica Edremoda, Bruce Brown, Edwina Salako, and Richard Holmes.

My research was assisted by institutional support particularly at crucial periods when my own resources were marginal, allowing me to travel to Seattle and Washington, D.C., helping purchase books and computer equipment, and, most importantly, affording me time to think and write. California Polytechnic State University provided a Meritorious Performance grant in 1986. Two years later I received an NEH Travel to Collections Grant, and in 1990 I was awarded a California State Faculty Support Grant. Moreover, Professor Wilton Fowler of the Department of History at the University of Washington extended departmental privileges which allowed me full access to the wealth of information at Suzzallo Library.

A number of present and former Seattle residents helped me set up interviews or gain access to the community's rich array of human resources including Larry Gossett, Wilson Ed Reed, Terry McDermott, Henry Johnson, Juana R. Royster, and William H. Hodge. By far the most helpful person in that regard was Constance Thomas, my liaison with Seattle's black community for nearly two decades.

Particularly salient suggestions often came from my students or former students who were introduced to my work through the classes I taught and who often found ways to illuminate my discussion of African American Seattle. Again I cannot name them all but the following students assisted in innumerable ways: Billy Ray Flowers, Genevieve Gwynne, Richard James, Jennifer Cohen, Gary Murrell, Patricia Dawson, Saheed Adejumobi, and Bettie Sing Luke.

The staff at Suzzallo Library on the University of Washington campus was most helpful. I remember particularly the assistance from Karyl Winn at Manuscripts, Carla Rickerson at UW Special Collections, and Terry Kato in UW Microfilms. Similarly, Janice Stone and Jean Gordon at the Kennedy Library, California Polytechnic State

Introduction

Seattle:
The Urban
Frontier

Election day, November 7, 1989, was a political milestone for African Americans. Douglas Wilder of Virginia became the first elected black governor in the history of the United States, David Dinkins the first black to be voted mayor of New York City, and Norman Rice the first black mayor elected in Seattle. Wilder, Dinkins, and Rice – all elevated to these offices by an overwhelmingly white electorate – represented, according to conventional political wisdom, the dawning of a new age in African American politics where black office seekers could successfully appeal to nonracial issues and themes to garner support across the political spectrum despite their race. Nowhere was that more evident than in Seattle, where Rice's convincing victory paralleled the narrow defeat of a referendum on the city's controversial eleven-year program of crosstown busing to promote racial integration in the public schools.[1]

Rice's election was significant for Seattle and the Pacific Northwest, and it may indeed have reflected a new era in American politics. But his ascent from the city council to the mayor's chair came simultaneously with the success of a bitterly divisive antibusing initiative, thus underscoring a century-old paradox of race relations for black Seattle. Since the arrival of the first African American resident in 1858, the ideal of racial toleration and egalitarianism proudly espoused by the vast majority of the city's residents has been precariously juxtaposed against a background of racial fear, prejudice, and discrimination. Unlike their counterparts elsewhere in the nation, particularly in the South, who have until recently faced a clearly defined racial order placing African Americans in an unequivocally subservient position, African Americans in Seattle confronted the uncertainty generated by the public endorsement of equality and the private practice of discrimination. How they approached that dilemma in the northernmost and westernmost major city in the continental United States provides a model for understanding how contemporary America can address the contradiction between the professed ideal of equality in a political democracy and the stark reality of competitive, acrimonious intergroup dynamics in an increasingly multiracial and multicultural nation facing profound economic transformation as it enters the twenty-first century.

Ever since W. E. B. Du Bois investigated black Philadelphia and reported his findings in *The Philadelphia Negro* in 1899, social scientists have analyzed urban African American communities, searching for solutions to the complicated problem of race and class in our urban society.[2] Between the two world wars, for example, various monographs on urban black America appeared, building on the intellectual foundations provided by Du Bois's study. They focused on myriad issues including rural-to-urban migration, adjustment to the urban milieu, the reaction of white urbanites, and the paradoxical impact of urban life on African American families and social institutions. Like *The Philadelphia Negro*, these were largely sociological or anthropological surveys, but they were crucial in advancing the concept of a distinct African American urban culture evolving in the nation's cities.[3]

The civil rights movement of the 1960s gave the examination of urban black America new urgency. By the middle of the decade, that movement, born in the urban South ten years earlier, commanded center stage of national attention and reached a critical turning point in 1965 with the Watts rebellion in Los Angeles. More than any previous racial conflagration, Watts forced the nation to confront the disturbing reality of the black urban experience. Northern ghettos, bypassed by the civil rights legislation the nation so proudly embraced, remained angry, ignored, and alienated, and expressed their dissatisfaction in unfocused urban violence.

The black urban history case study, the model for most post-1965 writing on African American communities, emerged out of this sense of urgency. Historians turned to the past to provide salient insights

Thus blacks were drawn into intense competition with the city's Chinese, Japanese, and Filipino populations for employment and housing opportunities. Yet the virulent racism of the 1890–1940 era usually directed against blacks in urban communities was diffused among Seattle's Asian Americans, Native Americans, and African Americans. Consequently, Asians and blacks, admittedly uneasy neighbors, became partners in coalitions challenging racial restrictions while remaining competitors for housing and jobs. No study of western urban communities has adequately explored the impact of competition and cooperation among various peoples of color in urban America.[5] The implications of that exploration are important, for Seattle blacks are once again finding themselves the "third group" in a city that since 1970 has seen an influx of Southeast Asian and Taiwanese immigrants, and much of urban America is undergoing yet another wave of immigration, this time largely involving groups from Asia and Latin America.

The history of the Central District also affords an opportunity to analyze the forging of a black urban community ethos, "a guiding complex of beliefs," to borrow a phrase from urban historian Blaine A. Brownwell.[6] Urban history case studies have focused almost exclusively on residential segregation, employment discrimination, and political subservience in determining the social, psychological, and spatial limits of the black community. In short, the community has been defined by denial and exclusion. These forces are understandably important in shaping black urban life, but they have not exclusively determined the nature of the African American community. Black urban culture is not simply the distinctive food, dress, music, or language emanating from city streets; it is ultimately the infinite variety of interactions that allow a people to define their sense of collective identity and values. Thus it is crucial for the urban historian to examine how institutions and organizations service that process and forge it into a black urban ethos.[7]

The study of black Seattle affords such an opportunity. Its religious, cultural, and social institutions and organizations, its kinship networks, were a crucible of this new urban culture. They served the needs of the community in traditional ways, but they also help define the parameters of that community. Because of its distance from the rural South and its correspondingly small African American population, Seattle's churches, fraternal lodges, and social clubs loomed large in preserving the community's links both to the past and to the national black community.[8]

into contemporary African America's troublesome accommodation to the urban environment. Not surprisingly, most of these studies examined the largest African American communities shaped, as they were, by rapid growth during the World War I era "Great Migration," which brought 500,000 rural southern blacks to northern industrial centers in search of economic opportunity and racial justice. While these studies varied in style and approach, virtually all examined the urban experience between 1890 and 1930, the years when northern black communities emerged as a visible segment of the urban landscape.[4] These monographs broadened our knowledge of black urban communities but frequently failed to ask significant questions concerning the African American urban experience. The history of Seattle's black community provides numerous answers even as it raises important new questions about the dynamics of black life in the urban milieu.

Black Seattle through much of the twentieth century was synonymous with the Central District,* a four square mile section near the geographic center of the isthmus that constitutes the city. From the evolution of two small, disparate black neighborhoods at opposite ends of the city in the late nineteenth century through the seventh decade of the twentieth century, the Central District was home to the vast majority of Seattle's African Americans. This study delineates the spatial and institutional development of the Central District, stressing its origins in the Yesler-Jackson and East Madison neighborhoods and its employment and residential patterns over the century. Furthermore, it examines the community's civil rights and political struggles and the rapid growth of the district prompted by the massive influx of rural blacks beginning with World War II and continuing until the 1970s, as well as the profound changes in both the district and the city initiated by that growth.

While this survey is analogous to the urban case studies written over the past two decades, it places black urban history in a broader context. First it analyzes racial perceptions, attitudes, and expectations in light of the presence of another group of color, Asian Americans. In Seattle, in contrast to virtually all other cities in which an African American community has been surveyed, Asians rather than blacks constituted the largest racial minority until World War II.

---

* The term "Central District" came into currency in the 1940s, about the same time as the name "Central Area." Both terms were used interchangeably to describe the various residential neighborhoods between downtown Seattle and Lake Washington.

If the people of any race have no record of their past, or have no aspirations or achievements that they think worthwhile, that race becomes a drone in the community and is treated as a nonentity. Therefore it is the duty of each race to feel keenly the necessity of keeping some record in which are chronicled their past efforts to verify their statements, and show that they appreciate the part they have played as members of the body politic of the community in which they live. . . . We should learn to record our doings, or we will be unprepared for the future examination and remain a nonentity in the great universe in which we live. — Samuel DeBow and Edward Pitter, *Who's Who in Religious, Fraternal, Social, Civic and Commercial Life on the Pacific Coast* (1927)

The
Forging
of a
Black Community

Seattle's Central District

from 1870 through the Civil Rights Era

University, and Aimee Yogi and Joanne Halgren at the Knight Library, University of Oregon, proved invaluable in assisting me in locating rare documents. I also commend Judy Ugonna and A. Ogunbameru at the Ghandi Memorial Research Library, University of Lagos, who helped me maintained my links with this project while I was half a world away from my primary sources.

I owe a special debt of gratitude to Julidta Tarver, my editor at the University of Washington Press who guided me through the mental minefield of preparing this manuscript for publication, and Leila Charbonneau, the copy editor who transformed ambiguous and uncertain text into clear and lucid language. The photos and illustrations came from a variety of institutional and private sources. I particularly want to thank Al Smith for allowing access to his extensive private collection of photographs, as well as Ruth Vincent at the Wing Luke Museum, Marilyn Phipps at the Boeing Archives, Susan Pelton and Terry Ross, at the *Seattle Times* Photo Archives, Carolyn J. Marr at the Seattle Museum of History and Industry, and Richard Engeman at the University of Washington. Also acknowledge my appreciation to David Cutting, one of the University of Oregon cartographers, for producing the maps which appeared in this text, and to William Loy and his staff in the Geography Department at the University of Oregon, for much of the background research.

My deepest appreciation goes to my wife, Carolyn, and my children, Quintard III, Jamila, and William, who observed with amused bewilderment a husband and father's frantic search through dozens of texts for the appropriate quotes or models and understood and accepted my sacrifices of time and attention to family matters in order to complete this project, and to my sister, Diane Taylor Brown, who through the years consistently asked when the project would end in both anticipation and relief.

Finally, I dedicate this book to the memory of my parents, Grace and Quintard Taylor, the first historians who engaged my mind and my heart.

Quintard Taylor
Eugene, Oregon
June 9, 1993

The history of black Seattle should also prompt a rethinking of generalizations concerning the rise of the pre–World War II African American ghetto. Mounting racial tension in the nation's largest cities, which invariably followed the rapid influx of African Americans and their growing percentage of the urban population, was virtually absent in pre-1940 Seattle. The city's African Americans never comprised more than one percent of the total population before 1940, and the entire African American community grew by fewer than 1,500 persons between 1910 and 1940. While the largest northern black communities witnessed, in varying degrees, the rise of urban ills such as fragmented families, segregated education, and social anomie, Seattle blacks avoided most of these problems. Poverty was widespread among Seattle's African Americans, particularly during the Great Depression, but it did not automatically result in family disintegration and community disruption, which would unfortunately become commonplace in other black communities. That the Central District experienced such a significant variation in family structure, residential segregation, educational attainment, and housing conditions from black communities in New York, Chicago, Cleveland, and other cities suggests that the northern black urban experience prior to World War II was far less monolithic than historians previously assumed.[9]

Black Seattle also varies from the northern pattern of African American urban communities in the impact of its labor force. Pre–World War II black workers posed a competitive threat to organized labor in many northern cities. Their sheer numbers mandated their role as a significant segment of the emerging urban proletariat. Black Seattle's unskilled labor force, however, was never large enough to constitute a major challenge to the city's powerful labor unions or dominate any industrial employment category. Consequently black workers in prewar Seattle made only slight progress in eroding union barriers or in upgrading their occupational level. Furthermore, unlike their counterparts in Chicago, Pittsburgh, Milwaukee, and other industrial cities, Seattle's African American workers remained concentrated in domestic service occupations. Those occupations were, to be sure, unlike the agriculturally related work common to most Seattle blacks before their migration to the city, but the nature of the economy, the resistance of most unions to the inclusion of black or Asian workers, and the city's minute African American population relegated black Seattle's female and male workers to the periphery of the city's economy at least until World War II.[10]

Virtually all extant black community histories trace the experiences of African Americans in one city between 1890 and 1930, the critical years of black community formation. This history of black Seattle, however, examines one community for an entire century (1870–1970), following not only the late nineteenth-century origins of black Seattle but also its growth and maturation through two world wars and the turbulent 1960s.[11] World War II in particular proved a major turning point in the history of the African American community as the demand for defense industry workers generated an unprecedented influx of newcomers who enlarged the city's black population from 3,700 to 10,000 in less than three years, and who joined the city's industrial work force for the first time. As this study will illustrate, changing occupational and housing patterns, and shifting racial attitudes generated by that influx, created profound consequences for black Seattle and the entire city.[12]

The transformation initiated in the Central District during the 1940s and 1950s would lead to the civil rights and black power movements of the 1960s, when Seattle African Americans challenged housing discrimination, employment bias, and school segregation. Inspired by the courage and commitment of black and white activists in the Deep South, but responding to local grievances, Seattle African Americans, supported by sympathetic whites and Asians, used direct action tactics – sit-ins, economic boycotts, protest marches – to challenge the continuing manifestations of bigotry in the city, and in the process forced the entire community to reexamine its long-cherished reputation for racial toleration and equality. The movements succeeded in energizing and empowering significant segments of the black community. But they also exposed a growing "underclass" whose ongoing plight suggested that the source of the most troubling contemporary urban crisis was located in the nexus of race and class.

Ironically, the question of race and class, although discovered by social scientists in the 1970s, is as old as the city's African American community, and it has been played out against a backdrop of intragroup conflict in the Central District. Black Seattle, despite its small size and outward appearance of unanimity, was never a single community. Class differences were expressed in neighborhood preference, in the objectives of community leadership, and often in the conflict between "old settlers" and newly arrived migrants. Such differences were evident in the black community as early as the 1890s. The rapid growth of black Seattle in World War II drew to the surface these differences, and they became the basis for the schism in the civil rights movement in the city in the 1960s. Such class differences reveal the fallacy of ascribing the worldview of the leadership cadre to the entire community, and serve to remind urban historians of their responsibility to extend their examination of the past beyond "representative" women and men and their organizations.

Although Seattle's black community from 1870 to 1970 is the primary focus of our examination, the history of the Central District also affords the opportunity to study nonblack racial attitudes and practices, and measure their impact on African American community development over an extended period. Despite Seattle's liberal reputation, racism and discrimination were widespread through much of the nineteenth and twentieth centuries. Yet both changed over time, subject to variables such as the industrial base of the city, the type of leadership in organized labor (particularly the influence of the Left) and in the business community, the relative size of the African American population in relationship to white Seattle and to other peoples of color, the level of economic prosperity, and, of course, national trends and legislation. Such variations prompted changes in the strategies and approaches of African Americans dedicated to the eradication of racial inequality in the city. They also say much about the vagaries and vicissitudes of the local racial order influenced by class, ethnic, economic, and political rivalries in the white and Asian communities.

If nothing else, the examination of Seattle should prompt comparable studies of other western black communities. Richard White's assertion that "without the special experience of its minorities, the West might as well be New Jersey with mountains and deserts" should be tested by the applicability of the model advanced here to other communities such as Los Angeles, Denver, Salt Lake City, San Francisco, Phoenix, and Portland, to determine if the themes highlighted in Seattle apply with equal saliency to other western urban locales.[13]

Ultimately, however, this history is a study of a distinct group of black people who, numbering no more than a few hundred in the late nineteenth century, a few thousand through World War II, and slightly less than forty thousand in 1970, attempted to fashion a better life for themselves, often pursuing across a vast continent their hopes, dreams, and aspirations. For them Seattle was, literally and figuratively, "the end of the line both socially and geographically. There was no better place to go."[14] These Seattleites chose to nurture a distinct African American culture and community, in a city and region that remain overwhelmingly white. They confronted a young urban society vastly different from the nation's great metropolises in the South and East, one deeply ambivalent about its commitment to racial equality. And it is within that setting that they forged their particular experience.

PART ONE

African Americans in a Frontier City, 1860–1899

The blood of slavery seeped deep into the American soil and cannot be easily removed. But here in Washington State, where the slave ships never docked, we have tended to believe ourselves safe from the curse of slavery's heritage. Yet more than an echo of the distant struggle has reached us here; a smaller-scale contention proceeds as our local society agonizes within itself, for we also are Americans and our ground is also stained. — Commission on the Causes and Prevention of Civil Disorder, 1969

Chapter 1

Origins and Foundations, 1860–1899

Seattle's nineteenth-century African American population grew from a single resident in 1858 to 406 women and men by 1900. Despite their small numbers, these early settlers created organizations and institutions that defined the character of this nascent community well into the twentieth century. These pioneers founded the city's first black churches, businesses, and community and civil rights organizations. They also shaped black Seattle's values and views on social, political, and economic issues – views that were refined and redefined by subsequent generations of Seattle residents but remained remarkably consistent until the 1960s.

The pattern of employment discrimination that relegated Seattle blacks to the periphery of the economy until the 1940s first emerged during this formative period. Seattle's African Americans were excluded from most of the occupations and industries that helped shape the city's economy. With rare exception nineteenth-century blacks did not work in lumber processing, shipbuilding, or the skilled trades such as carpentry and brick masonry, which provided employment for the vast majority of male workers. They accepted menial positions as janitors and hotel or railroad porters, or unskilled work in construction. Their occupational mobility was so restricted that early black residents considered themselves fortunate to obtain jobs as restaurant waiters or personal servants to wealthy Seattleites.

And for many nineteenth-century black males the most prestigious employment was to work as a barber or porter. African American women fared worse. Almost without exception they were confined to jobs as maids.[1]

Blacks gravitated toward these jobs not because of an inbred subservience, as many whites of that era believed, but because of the opposition of employers and a nascent local labor movement that grew increasingly powerful politically and more restrictive racially. Seattle's earliest unions initially focused much of their concern on Asians but in the process of establishing exclusionary policies erected barriers against African Americans as well. Thus the history of Seattle's nineteenth-century black community would be shaped by occupational constriction, which in turn discouraged black population growth and the concomitant development of black community-based institutions.

Seattle was a paradox for its nineteenth-century African Americans. The small numbers of blacks in the city allowed white Seattle to indulge in a racial toleration toward African Americans which, when compared with the segregationist policies sweeping the nation, led both blacks and whites to conclude that their city was fundamentally liberal and egalitarian. This toleration was particularly evident in the recognition of civil rights. Moreover, because Seattle's tolerant attitude was arbitrary – Asians and Native Americans, for example, were the objects of virulent hatred and sometimes even organized violence – the city's African Americans felt they had escaped the antiblack antipathy so prevalent in the South and in many eastern cities.[2]

But limited job opportunities prevented African Americans from fully enjoying their political freedom. They were simply too poor to effectively challenge racial restrictions. The struggle to make a living consumed all their energy and attention. Nineteenth-century black Seattle could occasionally solicit the support of Seattle's elite, many of whom maintained an idealistic commitment to black voting and civil rights growing out of their attachment to the abolitionist tradition of the Republican Party. This elite accepted the principle of equality before the law while believing blacks must remain in their own separate social sphere. Moreover, the city's small, overwhelmingly male population of artisans, laborers, and shopkeepers augmented by thousands of transient workers allowed a frontier egalitarianism in the social sphere even in an environment of limited employment options. This situation prompted black Seattleite Mattie Vinyerd Harris to remark that "there wasn't an awful lot of prejudice [or] an awful lot of opportunities either." Nineteenth-century white Seattle allowed itself to indulge in racial toleration toward working-class and middle-class blacks in large measure because the tiny African American population posed no major economic or political threat to the existing social order.[3] Consequently the select minority of African Americans who undertook the arduous, expensive migration to this remote city in the far northwestern corner of the nation came imbued with both the hope of a better life and scant specific assurance that they would find employment to support that life.

On November 13, 1851, twenty-two Euro-Americans – ten adults and twelve children – disembarked from the coastal steamer *Exact* at Alki Point, the tip of a small peninsula jutting out into Puget Sound at the south end of Elliott Bay. These settlers, named the Denny party after their leader, twenty-nine-year-old Arthur Denny from Illinois, built cabins and wintered at Alki Point as they prepared to claim and develop farmland in the vicinity. One month after the Denny party landed, a second steamer stopped at Alki Point and contracted for a load of logs to be used as pilings for San Francisco docks. Other ships followed, exchanging food and tools for timber, and in the process persuaded the settlers that the area's future lay not in farming but in the lumber it could supply California's rapidly growing cities. Within the year, Ohioan Henry Yesler joined this fledgling settlement, built a sawmill on the waterfront, and became the city's first employer. These two landings and Yesler's arrival symbolized the future of Seattle: the first landing brought settlers and the second, coupled with the construction of the sawmill, established the city's role as a processor of lumber and other raw materials.[4]

Yet Seattle's preeminence in the Pacific Northwest was by no means assured during the first three decades of its history. Described in the 1872 *Puget Sound Directory* as a place resembling a suburban New England town, were it not for the occasional burnt stumps and ungraded streets,[5] Seattle survived its first twenty years by providing San Francisco with lumber and coal from the nearby Cascade foothills and by becoming a service center for the fleet of sloops, steamers, and schooners that sailed Puget Sound. In 1870 the community had only 1,300 residents. Rather than the metropolis envisioned by its founders, Seattle was a small, struggling community economically dominated by Yesler's sawmill and a few hardware and mercantile stores, boarding houses, barbershops, saloons, and brothels — all catering to the loggers, miners, and sailors who regularly passed in and out of town. This rough-hewn frontier village was the Seattle black migrants discovered when they arrived in the 1860s and 1870s.[6]

Manuel Lopes, Seattle's first black resident, arrived in 1858, opened a restaurant, and became one of the town's first barbers. Born in the Cape Verde Islands off the coast of Africa in 1812, Lopes by 1840 had settled in New Bedford, Massachusetts, and worked as a sailor, the occupation that brought him to Seattle. William Grose (sometimes written Gross), the city's second black resident and eventually its wealthiest nineteenth-century African American, arrived in 1861, followed shortly thereafter by his wife, Sarah, and their two children. Born in Washington, D.C., in 1835, the son of a free black restaurant owner, Grose reached Seattle after brief periods in California and British Columbia. He opened a restaurant and hotel called Our House and later added a barbershop. When the hotel was destroyed in the Seattle Fire of 1889, Grose retired to his ranch on the northeastern outskirts of Seattle, which eventually became the nucleus of one of the city's two nineteenth-century black residential districts.[7]

By 1870, thirteen African Americans, all males, with the exception of Sarah Grose and her daughter, Rebecca, had settled in Seattle. Most of these settlers had reached Seattle by employing what historian Douglas Daniels called *travelcraft* skills — reliance on personal contacts, newspapers, and travelers' reports for business or employment opportunities in the Far West, and utilization of the network of black seamen and ship stewards and, after the transcontinental railroad reached Seattle in the 1880s, Pullman porters. Such migrants often worked their way from eastern states, stopping for a few years in various locations before moving on to Seattle. Robert Dixon and Archy Fox, for example, lived in British Columbia before they made Seattle their permanent home. George Riley and William Thorpe migrated from the California gold fields via Portland. These early settlers, all barbers, cooks, waiters, or café owners, who hardly perceived of themselves as a black "community," served a mostly white male clientele of loggers, sawmill workers, and sailors.[8]

Grose, Lopes, Dixon, and the other single men — black and white — created what Roger Sale calls Seattle's "bachelor society." The town's economy, tied to logging, coal mining, and fishing, and its distance from eastern population centers, produced a male, transient society. In 1870 single men comprised two-thirds of Seattle's population, and as late as 1900 Seattle men continued to outnumber women by almost two to one. Moreover, Seattle's population fluctuated seasonally as loggers from western Washington entered the town temporarily in August and December, slack times in the logging camps. But scarce job prospects often forced "permanent" settlers to move away after a few months or years. Lopes, for example, left town for Port Gamble in the early 1870s, during one of Seattle's frequent economic slumps, and never returned.[9]

Seattle's transient population shaped residential and political divisions well into the twentieth century. Much of the permanent population resided north of Yesler's pier, Seattle's first dock and the unofficial dividing line of the city. South of the pier stretched rooming houses, stores, shops, and saloons which catered to the transient population. The "pioneers," as Seattle's permanent settlers called themselves, were linked by commercial interests, marriage and family ties, and their length of residence in the city. Thus they dominated Seattle's economy and government despite their small numbers. Both black and white Seattleites recognized the distinctions based on permanent residency, which in fact were indicative of emerging social class formations. The entire community recognized blacks such as William Grose as pioneers, but many of Seattle's early black cooks, waiters, sailors, and ship stewards were transients.[10]

As late as 1880 Seattle resembled a dozen other Puget Sound towns. Its loggers cut trees on the surrounding hills and pushed the logs down Yesler Hill along its "skid road" (a term that eventually became a euphemism for all urban transient districts) to waterfront sawmills. However, the entire Puget Sound region was transformed by the completion of the first transcontinental railroad to reach the Pacific Northwest, the Northern Pacific, which extended its line to neighboring Tacoma in 1883. When the rival Great Northern Railway reached Seattle a decade later, its arrival ensured the city's primacy in the regional economy. With rail transportation assured, small factories emerged throughout the city, manufacturing dozens of items for regional consumption, while food processing plants produced bread, cheese, beer, and coffee.[11] The city's burgeoning population was simultaneously a consequence of the developing regional economy and a catalyst for additional economic growth. Between 1880 and 1890 Seattle grew from 3,553 to 42,837 inhabitants (Table 1) and became the fourth largest city on the West Coast, after San Francisco, Los Angeles, and Portland. And like San Francisco in the 1850s, and Los Angeles in the 1880s, Seattle was an "instant city" of transplanted

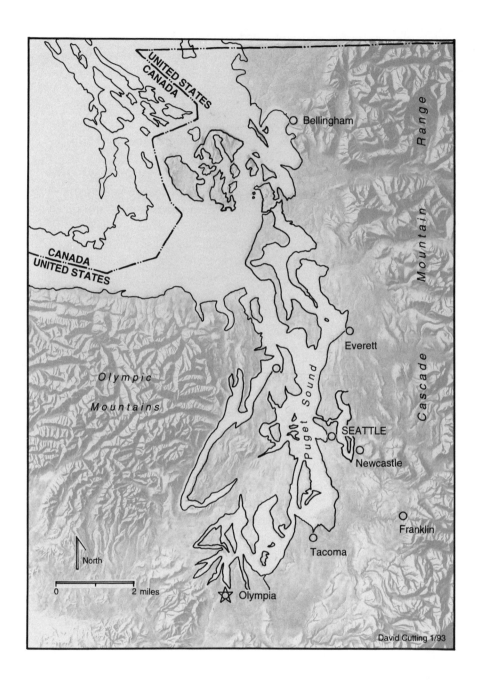

Map 1. Puget Sound region, 1890

Table 1
Growth of Seattle's Black Population, 1860–1900

Year	Black Population	Percentage Increase	Total Population	Black Percentage of Total Population
1860	1	–	182*	–
1870	13	1,200	1,107	1.2
1880	19	46	3,533	0.5
1890	286	1,405	42,837	0.7
1900	406	42	80,671	0.5

Sources: Clarence B. Bagley, *History of Seattle from the Earliest Settlement to the Present Time*, 3 vols. (Chicago: S. J. Clarke, 1916), 2:661; U.S. Bureau of the Census, *Negro Population, 1790–1915*, table 12.
*Special census by Clarence B. Bagley.

easterners and midwesterners; 92 percent of its 1890 population was born outside the state of Washington.

The overwhelming majority of Seattle's newcomers in the 1880s were native-born white migrants primarily from Minnesota, Illinois, Wisconsin, Iowa, and Michigan. The black population, composed mainly of southerners, grew from 19 at the beginning of the decade to 286 by 1890. These newcomers eagerly sought work on the railroads and in the restaurants and hotels of the city. The growing black population included for the first time a number of families. Elizabeth Grose, granddaughter of William Grose, recalled the era: "Times were good, everybody found work. Seattle was thriving. There was a steady stream of families arriving."[12]

Horace R. Cayton, who would soon become the city's most prominent African American, was part of this migration. The son of a black slave woman and a white planter, Cayton was born in Claiborne County, Mississippi, in 1859 and attended Alcorn College, where he studied with former U.S. Senator Hiram R. Revels. Moving first to Kansas and later to Utah, Cayton arrived in Seattle in 1889. After employment on the *People's Call* and briefly as a political reporter with the *Seattle Post-Intelligencer*, the city's largest newspaper, Cayton in 1894 founded the *Seattle Republican*, which for the next nineteen years coupled his staunch defense of black civil rights with fidelity to the Republican Party. Unlike the city's first African American newspaper, the *Seattle Standard*, which was specifically directed toward the small black community, Cayton's *Republican* carried general political news for all of Seattle and at one point had the second largest circulation in the city. The *Seattle Republican* made Cayton and his wife Susie, its associate editor, the most prominent African American couple in the Pacific Northwest by 1900.[13]

Most black migrants, however, were far less successful than the Caytons. James Orr arrived in 1883 after working as a steward in the Palace Hotel dining room in San Francisco. He sought similar employment in Seattle. John T. Gayton, a Mississippi coachman, arrived in 1889 with his white employer and by the mid-1890s was working as a waiter at the Rainier Club. John A. Coleman, born an Alabama slave in 1852, lived in New York, Chicago, and Duluth before arriving in Seattle in 1889 to take a porter's job. Occasionally artisans such as Georgia-born Seaborn J. Collins, a machinist and carpenter who arrived in 1885, pursued skilled occupations, but most blacks accepted the menial jobs available at the time.[14]

Black Seattle remained overwhelmingly male through the end of the nineteenth century, but the migration of the 1880s and 1890s brought families. In 1889, two years after their marriage in Fredonia, Kansas, Lloyd and Emma Ray moved to Seattle, as did Thomas and Margaret Collins, from Georgia. Dr. Samuel Burdett brought his family to Seattle in 1890 after retiring from the U.S. Army. John and Mary Cragwell arrived from Washington, D.C., in 1891, and Conrad Rideout, a former Arkansas state legislator, brought his family later that year.[15]

Clearly many black migrants arrived in Seattle in pursuit of economic opportunity. But many others were fleeing the oppressive political and economic conditions of the post–Civil War South. Indeed the line of demarcation between economic and political terrorism against the freedwomen and freedmen of the South was often irreparably blurred. To deny legitimacy to the racially integrated Republican governments in the ex-Confederate states, white Democrats waged a relentless propaganda campaign depicting those regimes as hopelessly corrupt, extravagant, and undemocratic. Moreover, ballot boxes were stuffed, polling places were capriciously changed at the last moment, and votes were coerced or miscounted. Southern white landlords and employers threatened tenants and workers with the loss of their homes and jobs if they challenged "white supremacy," the term which gradually became the symbol of political and economic domination of the ex-Confederates over the ex-slaves. There was also the seemingly ubiquitous violence of race riots, terrorist attacks by groups such as the Ku Klux Klan, rapes of black women, and, increasingly after 1880, lynchings of both men and women.[16]

Although they fled at different times and for different reasons, a small but growing number of blacks opted to leave the South, and some found their way to Seattle. Wade Hampton, an ex-slave, Union Army veteran, and delegate to the 1868 Mississippi Constitutional Convention, arrived in Seattle in 1888. Although his more famous namesake, the "redeemer governor" of South Carolina, symbolized the return of ex-Confederates to power after Reconstruction, Seattle's Hampton frequently addressed interracial Republican campaign rallies, vividly describing the violent tactics of Mississippi Democrats who excluded white and black Republicans from the political life of his native state. Brittain Oxendine, a former member of the North Carolina legislature, who arrived in Seattle in 1889, praised his adopted city despite numerous personal economic setbacks, including his inability to obtain a position other than as janitor at the *Seattle Post-Intelligencer* and his short-lived effort to publish the city's first African American newspaper, the *Seattle Standard*, in 1890.[17]

If migrants such as Oxendine faced employment restrictions, they also found a city with surprisingly few racial barriers in other spheres. Unlike neighboring Oregon with its "black laws" dating back to its territorial period, or segregationist legislation in the South, Washington Territory had no discriminatory statutes. In 1890 the first state legislature passed a public accommodation law which specifically prohibited racial discrimination. As Oregon, Idaho, and Montana enacted anti-interracial marriage measures in the 1890s, Washington's lawmakers resisted similar calls for their state. Oregon and Montana officials segregated their public schools, abandoning their efforts only when the small number of black students made the cost of a dual system prohibitive. Washington, however, never contemplated a segregated school system. Black male Washingtonians voted without restrictions, and when the Washington Territorial Suffrage Act of 1883 made it possible for women to vote for the first time, so did African American women. Seattle's African Americans testified in court as early as 1867, and after 1883 black women as well as men sat on juries, with African Americans occasionally serving as jury foremen. South Carolina native I. Israel Walker succinctly summarized the remarkable tolerance he found upon his arrival in 1889 when he spoke of Seattle's "free air." Robert O. Lee, the first African American admitted to the bar in Washington, declared in 1889 that he had chosen Seattle because he was seeking a place where "race prejudice would not interfere with his prosperity."[18]

Although the small number of African Americans in nineteenth-century Seattle contributed to the spirit of racial toleration, population size only partly explains the contrast with neighboring states that were much less tolerant, for they had even fewer black residents. Seattle blacks initially benefitted from the rapid growth of the city. As its population grew by 1,112 percent between 1880 and 1890 and another 88 percent the following decade, Seattle was filled with newcomers often unsure of their place in the social order. With few well-defined class or economic lines for all groups, many African Americans indeed felt they had found a place where they could breathe "free air." Moreover, the small black population was insulated from the more virulent expressions of racial prejudice by the presence of large numbers of Chinese immigrants and American Indians who throughout the nineteenth-century bore the brunt of discrimination from the white population. As twentieth-century Seattle African Americans would soon discover, however, their growing numbers in the city would generate greater animosity toward their presence.[19]

But nineteenth-century Seattle was not without antiblack prejudice. Local white attitudes were a curious mixture of condescension and opprobrium. While Washington Territory never passed antiblack legislation, the early white settlers nonetheless sought to limit the black population. In 1865 Asa Mercer, already known for importing marriageable eastern women for Seattle's bachelors, asked the Territorial legislature to designate him Immigrant Agent to recruit settlers. Democratic legislators accused Mercer, a leading Republican, of using the designation as a subterfuge to recruit southern black freedmen into Seattle to support the GOP. Mercer, Arthur Denny, and other prominent Seattle Republicans were forced to disavow any such attempt and reiterate their belief in white supremacy. Fourteen years later, in 1879, when southern blacks began a mass exodus from Mississippi and Tennessee for Kansas, the *Daily Intelligencer* (forerunner of Seattle's largest newspaper, the *Post-Intelligencer*) discouraged their migration to the city. "There is room for only a limited number of colored people here," warned an editorial. "Overstep that limit and there comes a clash in which the colored man must suffer. The experience of the Chinese on this coast indicates that beyond question. . . . And so we fear it would be with the negro. The few that are here do vastly better than they would do if their number were increased a hundredfold."[20]

Much of the language of Seattle whites mirrored the rhetoric of white supremacy common throughout the nation. The Pacific Northwest was often described by land promoters and politicians as "the white man's country," and Seattle Republicans in the 1860s and 1870s reminded the local population that whatever "radical" proposals were made by national Republican leaders such as Massachusetts Senator Charles Sumner or Pennsylvania Representative Thaddeus Stevens to grant full civil and political rights to southern freedmen, the Washington Territory Republican Party did not advocate racial equality for blacks in the Pacific Northwest. In 1864, one year after emancipation became the policy of the Lincoln administration, the Olympia *Washington Standard*, a Republican newspaper in the Territorial capital, declared it would not endorse the views of Wendell Phillips, a leading abolitionist and equal rights advocate, any more than those of Clement Vallandigham, the Ohio politician who led northern supporters of the Confederacy. "Those who held to the tenets of Phillips, Garrison, John Brown & Co., we do not expect to agree with us," declared the editor. The *Standard* endorsed the views of the *San Francisco Journal*, which had earlier declared: "The old nigger-stealing Abolition idea is just as odious today as it was then, and if any man supposes . . . the idea is credible, he is very much in error." [21]

Despite such rhetoric, the historical record reveals few efforts to deny Seattle blacks civil rights, prevent their use of public accommodations, restrict them to certain sections of the city, or mete out disproportionate punishment through the criminal justice system. Occasionally local newspapers acknowledged black voting rights. In 1870 the Olympia *Commercial Age* declared that the Fifteenth Amendment did not affect Washington Territory because "the colored folks have been voters among us for some time." Moreover, most of Seattle's black population considered the city's treatment of African Americans far superior to race relations in the South and East. "The colored people of this country should make a bold strike for freedom," proclaimed newspaper editor Horace Cayton, Sr. "Here in the Northwest," he announced, "we are striking out in every direction. Negroes in this town have become small businessmen or skilled mechanics and live a good life. Their children are getting educations and will be able to stand up and compete with other men. Here the race is to the swiftest, and here the American dream is being won. . . . We are the new frontier and thousands of Negroes come to this part of the country and stand up like men and compete with their white brothers."[22]

Black euphoria over racial conditions prompted numerous unsuccessful attempts to organize wholesale migration to the Pacific Northwest. Declaring the position of blacks in the South untenable, Horace Cayton called on that region's African Americans to make a "bold strike for freedom" in the Pacific Northwest. The Washington State Afro-American League, a chapter of the largest black civil rights organization in the country, lent its voice throughout the 1890s to the call for African American settlement by providing information on employment opportunities and social conditions. Cayton's *Seattle Republican* endorsed black migration to the Pacific Northwest with a special caveat. By specifically advertising employment prospects for African American women in domestic service, the paper coupled the call for black settlers with the desire to redress the local gender imbalance. "Three hundred colored women," Cayton declared in 1900, "could find ready employment in Seattle and Tacoma tomorrow, were they here. . . . There are quite a number of colored men in this country who are living in single blessedness, who would willingly change their way of living, were there sufficient damsels of their own race to choose from."[23]

The various proposals for black immigration were largely unsuccessful. Far removed from the large concentrations of blacks in the South, Seattle was difficult and expensive to reach even after the Northern Pacific Railroad was completed in 1883. Moreover, although Seattle's economy expanded sharply after 1880, frequent depressions idled thousands of white workers. Its reputation for racial toleration for African Americans notwithstanding, few blacks were willing to migrate to a city where large numbers of white men were often unemployed.[24]

The paradox of racial tolerance and employment restriction is best seen by examining the job prospects of black settlers. Most nineteenth-century blacks were laborers, peddlers, bootblacks, maids, chimney sweeps, cleaning women, coachmen, janitors, porters, and valets. The concentration of African Americans in these low paying jobs reflected both discrimination and job stereotyping. African Americans entered the Seattle job market as menial laborers regardless of their prior skills or education because they usually encountered less resistance from white employers and coworkers. Most Seattle whites, however, ascribed black concentration in those categories to certain racial characteristics, including obsequiousness and servility, born of generations of enslavement and service to whites. That blacks and whites could have such disparate views on black employment indicates the wide chasm in racial perceptions even in liberal Seattle.[25]

Manuel Lopes and William Grose, the first blacks to arrive in Seattle, came as sailor and ship steward, respectively. Yet neither man pursued these occupations in the city, and few blacks would work on the fishing boats or in the numerous city sawmills, the largest employers until the 1880s. Seattle blacks were more likely to be barbers, cooks, or waiters, occupations Grose and Lopes held intermittently through their years in the city. Of the twenty King County blacks listed in the 1870 census, all were males and fourteen were barbers, cooks, and waiters. By 1880, half of the ten black adult males were in those categories while the others were shoemakers, farmers, and laborers.[26]

The rapid black population increase during the next decade reinforced the overwhelming concentration of African Americans in menial occupations. When the Rainier Grand Hotel opened in downtown Seattle in October 1889, for example, the management brought in a crew of forty black women and men from Chicago as waiters, chambermaids, laundry women, cooks, bellboys, and elevator operators. The Great Northern Railway employed blacks as porters and waiters in dining cars but rarely hired them on construction or maintenance crews.

Skilled blacks migrated to Seattle. Among the newcomers were boilermakers, butchers, carpenters, and machinists. Yet they rarely found work in their areas of training. Black workers blamed white union opposition for discrimination against them, and certainly evidence of such opposition was readily available. When James Blocker came to Seattle in 1878 to work as a butcher, the local union barred his membership and he took work as janitor. When a black man was hired in 1891 to mix mortar for construction of the Dexter Horton Building in downtown Seattle, white laborers struck the site until he was fired. The *Seattle Telegraph* in reporting the strike said the workers walked out because the laborer was nonunion, not because he was ''colored,'' but few black workers recognized the distinction in a city where most unions routinely denied blacks membership. Moreover, African American workers were mindful of the anti-Chinese agitation of 1885–86 and of the violence against black strikebreaking coal miners in the nearby Cascade mining towns of Roslyn, Franklin, and Newcastle between 1888 and 1891.[27]

The roots of both organized labor in Seattle and its exclusionary racial policies can be traced to the 1880s when the Knights of Labor attracted a huge following in the Pacific Northwest and became politically powerful in Seattle. Despite the national organization's progressive stance as an interracial union, the Seattle chapter, exploiting white workers' dissatisfaction with their wages and working conditions, and general community antipathy toward Asians, orchestrated the anti-Chinese riot of 1886, Seattle's first violent racial conflict. White working-class hostility toward nonwhite laborers continued into the twentieth century and was viewed by many as a reflection of commitment to (white) working-class solidarity. The *Seattle Union Record* asked in 1906: "Does a Chinaman do your washing? If so you are not carrying out the principles of unionism."[28]

The Western Central Labor Union, a federation of skilled craft locals, supplanted the Knights in the 1890s and in 1905 joined the American Federation of Labor as the Seattle Central Labor Council. The Council was firmly opposed to Asian membership, and many craft unions excluded blacks as well. It is tempting to dismiss the behavior of these organizations as simply reflecting the racism of the era. After all, many trade unionists fully accepted the tenets of Anglo-Saxon supremacy. Yet, in an era when employers routinely replaced groups of workers solely on the basis of race, ethnicity, and gender, it was hardly surprising that white workers, the largest segment of labor, erected racial barriers. As labor historian Robert Campbell reminds us in his study of the 1891 labor struggles in the Cascade coal mines, the striking Knights of Labor miners who fought black strikebreakers did not see themselves as "debating race relations" as much as they were defending their jobs and homes in a highly irregular industry. To them, the incoming African Americans "were not fellow workers but tools of corporations bent on lowering wages and eliminating unions."[29]

The policies of the White Cooks and Waiters' Union were typical of those of the fledgling craft locals in the city. As their name indicated, the union restricted membership on racial grounds throughout the 1890s. Their vulnerability in an occupation with significant numbers of nonwhite workers was exposed in 1891 when the union struck the steamer *City of Seattle* for higher pay. The four white cooks and fourteen white waiters were replaced by six Chinese and four black waiters. By 1900 the union had ended its all-white membership policy, but as late as 1901, when the Seattle Hotel hired two black bellboys, the six whites quit their jobs. "Regardless of how many colored men might join the waiter's union, if some of them should go to another place in the city outside of where they are regularly employed for work," declared Horace Cayton in a 1901 *Seattle Republican* editorial, "he [sic] would not get a situation long enough to earn a meal's victuals and that . . . on account of labor union . . . opposition to colored labor."[30]

A minority of Seattle unions opposed racially exclusionary policies and allowed black membership. The Seattle local of the Journeymen Stonecutters of America had open membership from the time of its organization in 1889. Ten black stonecutters joined the union, including Lloyd Ray and James S. Murray. Ray described a rare instance of interracial camaraderie among union members, who gathered regularly at a local saloon after work. The Journeyman Barber's Union, which established a Seattle chapter in 1890, included two black barbers, W. D. Highwarden and James Gayle, as early members, with the latter serving as secretary of the local.[31]

Organized labor was not solely responsible for the bleak black employment prospects. Nineteenth-century Seattle unions were in their formative stages, and nowhere did they have the kind of monopoly on hiring that would occur by World War I, when Seattle had became a "labor town." Working-class whites both inside and outside labor unions made stridently racial appeals particularly against Asian workers, and initiated strikes to back those appeals, but Seattle blacks were denied employment by a pervasive racism shared by employers as well as union and nonunion laborers.[32]

Indeed, historians who argue that white unions denied access to African American workers fail to understand the role of employers in the manipulation of racial tension to their benefit. Black workers in Seattle and elsewhere constituted, according to historian Carole Marks, part of a split labor market, a work force purposely introduced or recruited not simply as "cheap labor" but to replace other groups sympathetic to unionism. This strategy, already employed with Chinese workers in the 1870s and 1880s, would now be modified with African Americans as the "outside" group. In 1891, the Oregon Improvement Company, owner of the coal mines near Franklin and Newcastle, Washington, imported five hundred black strikebreakers. T. B. Corey, the superintendent of mines for the OIC, remarked that their introduction "made the issue one of race between the white and colored miners, and not one of wages or conditions of work between the coal companies and their employees." As the striking white miners vented their hostility on the blacks, their attacks on the OIC were less strident, leaving the coal operators in the enviable position of watching the black and white workers argue among themselves.[33]

Nineteenth-century black women faced an occupational spectrum far more limited than their male counterparts. It is here that the fallacy of blaming African American labor woes primarily on organized labor becomes apparent, for female workers were not organized in any industry. Black women could work as dressmakers, nurses, housemaids, cooks, or charwomen (cleaners), but little else was available to them. The 1891 Seattle Directory listed five black women as nurses, including Theresa Brown Dixon, the daughter of Robert Dixon. Alice Blocker, Victoria Susandt, and Sallie Day worked as dressmakers while Annie Jackson was employed as a music teacher. The experiences of "Auntie" Montgomery and Mattie Vinyerd Harris's mother were far more typical. Montgomery eked out a meager living alternately distributing samples of maple syrup at local drugstores and babysitting children. Mattie Vinyerd Harris recalled that her mother scrubbed floors at the Bon Marché, a large downtown department store, for virtually her entire adult life.[34]

Prostitution provided another means of livelihood, albeit a precarious one, for those with few other options. Prostitution was widespread in Seattle throughout its frontier period, and by 1889 descriptions of black prostitutes began to appear frequently in local newspaper accounts. By the 1890s the tideflats, Seattle's red-light district, had emerged along lower Jackson Street. Here in the saloons and brothels were women of almost every racial background. But black and Japanese prostitutes predominated among the small hovels or "cribs" along the "flats."[35]

Nineteenth-century black Seattleites established proportionately more businesses than the early twentieth-century black community. During the city's first three decades many African-Americans were self-employed in small businesses and trades because, with the exception of Yesler's mill, few businesses employed more than eight people. Virtually all black-owned businesses were dependent on a white clientele, yet their place in the overall commercial economy was almost as marginal as that of black wage earners, a fact reflected in the inability of any of these enterprises to grow large or achieve intergenerational success.

Most of Seattle's self-employed African Americans were barbers. Manuel Lopes, the city's first black resident, was also Seattle's first barber. By 1870 six of the city's thirteen African American residents listed barbering as their primary occupation. Indeed, a few black Seattleites earned a handsome living from the trade. Although he had been a resident of Seattle only nine years in 1900, John F.

Cragwell employed eleven barbers in his two downtown salons, making him the most successful African American entrepreneur in the city. Compared with other available occupations – porter, hotel waiter, personal servant – barbering held considerable prestige in the African American community.[36]

The black barbers who worked downtown and relied on white patronage usually barred African American customers from their shops. The fear that white customers would not frequent places that catered to an integrated clientele was succinctly expressed in 1874 by a black barber in Chattanooga, Tennessee. When local African Americans challenging his practice asked if their money was "not as good as a white man's," the barber responded: "Yes, just as good, but there is not enough of it."[37]

Such intraracial discrimination was particularly acute in Seattle in the 1880s and 1890s when barbers such as Cragwell opened elegant shops in downtown hotels and occasionally drew protests. Cayton wrote editorials condemning the practice and on one occasion physically confronted Cragwell. When Cayton attempted to get a shave in Cragwell's downtown salon and was refused, the barber had Cayton arrested and fined for disorderly conduct. In October 1895 a black coal miner from Franklin sued another Seattle barber who refused his patronage, contending that his civil rights had been violated. The barber responded that the plaintiff was denied service because of his unsavory reputation rather than his color, and the suit was dismissed.[38]

Restaurants were the second most common black-owned businesses and apparently welcomed all patrons. Matthias Monet opened the Seattle Restaurant and Coffee Saloon in 1864, and Our House Restaurant was opened by William Grose in 1876. Restaurant ownership increased dramatically in the 1880s and 1890s with the growing population. John Randolph and James Orr opened cafés in 1889 and 1890 respectively after working as waiters in white establishments. Thomas C. Collins and Allen Dean operated Collins and Dean's Restaurant in the 1890s, and two black women, Olivia Washington and Elizabeth Thorne, managed successful cafés on the eastern edge of the city during the last decade of the century.[39]

Monet's eight years in business illustrate the vicissitudes of entrepreneurial activity in nineteenth-century Seattle. An Oregon native, he arrived in 1864 and opened the Seattle Restaurant and Coffee Saloon across the street from the Yesler-Denny Company store in the heart of town. In 1865 he converted his restaurant into Connoisseur's Retreat, which he advertised in the *Weekly Intelligencer* as an "oyster saloon and chop house." Apparently encountering financial difficulty, he formed a partnership with William Hedges, a black barber, in which each partner would maintain his previous business while sharing the profits and risks of both. Two years later Monet, heavily in debt, sold out to Hedges for $250. By 1869 he was back in business, this time running the Railroad House, a restaurant and boarding house. The Railroad House proved far more successful than his earlier ventures: the 1870 census showed him as a boarding house owner whose real property was valued at $8,700 and personal property at $250. Although the economic depression of 1871 forced him to mortgage the business furniture, his business weathered the economic downturn. The last record of Monet, found in a city business directory published in December 1872, lists his Railroad House as one of only two hotels in the city.[40]

A number of small businesses emerged in the 1890s following the rapid increase in black population, but like their predecessors in the 1860s and 1870s, they depended on white patronage. Robert R. Brown and Edward Morrison had blacksmith shops, S. B. White ran a grocery store, and Irene Frances Woodson operated a cigar store in Pioneer Square, the original downtown business district. Cragwell's two barbershops in downtown hotels provided employment for nearly twenty black barbers, while Reverend Eugene Harris, pastor of the African Methodist Episcopal (AME) Church, ran a small stenography business to supplement his minister's salary. Robert and Anne Clark operated a dairy in the East Madison district and later a delivery service. The Clarks employed black men as teamsters and, after they expanded their business, provided a rare opportunity for black women to engage in office work. Lucille Irving, Lucretia Roy, and Elizabeth Anderson all maintained boarding houses.[41]

Some of the most successful black businesses emerged in the tideflats, the center of Seattle's demimonde. These brothels, gambling houses, and saloons employed numerous musicians, bouncers, maids, cooks, and janitors, and provided more jobs than the barbershops, restaurants, and other "respectable" establishments. Saloons owned by Denver Ed Smith, Richard Roman, and N. F. Butts ranked among the larger and more flourishing businesses in the tideflats and some of the more successful enterprises in black Seattle. Mary Thompson's Minnehaha Saloon, with its upstairs brothel, made her one of black Seattle's wealthiest citizens. By the time of her death in 1893, she had a fortune including real estate in Seattle and Butte, Montana, a horse and carriage, an extensive jewelry collection, and $20,000 in cash. But such prosperity was often precarious. Asian and black illicit operations, although ostensibly "protected" by corrupt police officers, were often raided and their owners arrested more frequently because of the underlying racial attitudes of the era.[42]

Nineteenth-century black Seattle had few professionals. There was no permanent physician before 1900. Indeed, Dr. Samuel Burdett, a veterinarian and Kentucky native, was Seattle's most prominent black professional. He joined the Union Army during the Civil War and was assigned to the all-black Ninth Cavalry between 1866 and his resignation in 1883. After moving to Seattle in 1891, he combined a lucrative practice with participation in local politics and several unsuccessful business ventures. Six attorneys practiced law in the city between 1889 and 1900 but, with the exception of John Edward Hawkins, all of them moved away by the first decade of the twentieth century. Robert O. Lee, who migrated to Seattle in 1889, became the first African American to practice law in Washington. He was soon joined by Conrad Rideout, a former Arkansas Democratic state legislator, who arrived in Seattle in 1891 and for the remainder of the decade maintained a small legal practice while organizing black Democrats and lobbying for political appointments. Hawkins, a Galesburg, Illinois, native, came to Seattle in 1890 and worked as a barber for five years while attending law school at night. When he was admitted to the King County Bar in 1895, he became the first locally trained black attorney. William McDonald Austin, a native of Barbados, was admitted to the University of Washington School of Law shortly after its founding in 1899, and three years later became the university's first black graduate, writing a thesis titled "The Civil Rights Act." But Austin immediately went to the Philippines to practice law.[43] Unlike most nineteenth-century African American communities, black Seattle had fewer ministers than lawyers. The small community supported only two churches, both established in the 1890s. Since the churches had a combined membership of seventy parishioners during the 1890s, ministers quickly moved in and out of the city, further reducing their influence.

The dearth of black professionals posed problems for the small African American community beyond the obviously limited services offered. Given their education and their economic and social standing, professionals usually served as community leaders and spokespersons. Their views on race relations were usually influential in the black community and occasionally in the white community as well. In Chicago, Cleveland, Milwaukee, and other northern communities, such professionals and their supporters frequently dominated civil rights organizations and were often the most outspoken opponents of racial discrimination. Black Seattle was forced to rely on a more eclectic group of spokespersons including newspaper editor Horace Cayton, barber and political activist John F. Cragwell, and Rainier Club waiter John Gayton to fill that role.[44]

The small numbers of African Americans in Seattle before 1880 and the absence of distinctive economic segregation precluded residential segregation based on race. But by the last decade of the century, blacks arriving in Seattle saw their housing choices become increasingly limited. As late as 1900 African Americans lived in all of the city's fourteen wards. But their concentration mainly in the first and ninth wards was similar to the racial clustering already common in northern cities as disparate as Milwaukee, Wisconsin, and Camden, New Jersey.[45]

To understand the changes occurring in the 1890s, it is best to examine the residential patterns of the earlier period. The pre-1890 residential integration, or to be more accurate, residential desegregation of Seattle, stemmed as much from what urban historian Kenneth Kusmer has described as structural forces – the type and location of housing available and the nature of the transportation system – as from racial toleration. Pre-1890 Seattle was a physically compact city whose buildings were confined to a narrow strip of land ringing the harbor at the foot of three imposing hills. The young city had not developed distinctive ethnic or economic neighborhoods. Because of its underdeveloped street car system, Seattle resembled pre–Civil War "walking cities" such as Boston and Baltimore where urban dwellers resided no more than two miles from work, a distance one could comfortably walk in thirty minutes. Roger Sale provides a fascinating glimpse of an 1880s ethnically and economically integrated neighborhood just south of the Central Business District: "the fishermen, sailors, and the apparently unemployed tended to live west of First Avenue, near the water. Nearer the heart of the city one found not just cooks, waiters, domestics, hotel managers, and janitors, but many others who obviously did not have to live there: doctors, lawyers, real estate and investment brokers, office managers, stenographers, and bookkeepers. . . . The alleys between the streets . . . were hives of activity then. In one stretch of alley between First and Second avenues were a print shop, a contractor's office, a painter's office, and a shoe outlet."[46]

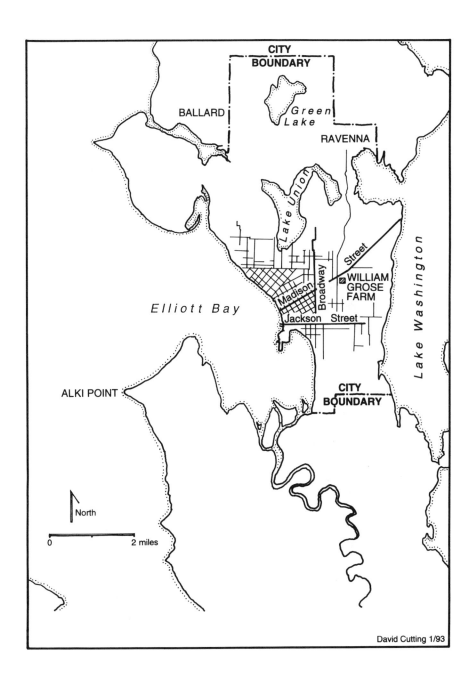

Map 2. Seattle in 1894

African American hotel bellboys, waiters, and porters lived on the premises of the Rainier and other large downtown hotels. Black railroad workers resided in inexpensive housing on lower Jackson Street near the railroad station. Personal servants of affluent whites lived in the homes where they worked, and African American businessmen lived on the second stories or in the rear of the buildings which housed their small shops or stores. Frequently these shopkeepers rented extra rooms to other blacks. Since these businesses were spread throughout the city, blacks lived in every section of Seattle. The Grose family, for example, resided in their hotel near the waterfront as did Robert Dixon, the hotel barber, and William Davis, the hotel cook. The parents of Mattie Vinyerd Harris, however, settled on Queen Anne Hill, north of downtown.[47]

Newcomers streaming daily into Seattle accounted for much of the city's spectacular growth from 3,533 in 1880 to 80,671 in 1900. But city officials also eagerly annexed surrounding suburbs as soon as public transportation became available. These annexations fueled a growing economic segregation; wealthy and middle-class Seattleites occupied the hills while the poor, of all races and ethnic groups, remained behind in the flatlands that hugged the harbor.

This emerging economic segregation fostered two distinct black residential concentrations: the Yesler-Jackson area, a working-class, transient neighborhood south of both downtown Seattle and the city's Chinatown; and the East Madison Street area, the hilly, heavily forested section on the northeastern edge of the city which soon became the home of Seattle's upwardly mobile African American population. Yesler-Jackson, initially an area of Victorian homes, had become by 1890 a neighborhood of "third class" hotels, lodging houses, saloons, and shops which catered to Seattle's sailors, loggers, and railroad workers. Single black males – railroad porters, cooks, and waiters – were attracted by the low rents and close proximity to the railroad station and downtown hotels. The opening in 1892 of the Sleeping Car Porters Club, an employment and recreation center for black railroad workers on lower Jackson Street, symbolized the emerging economic and racial character of the area.

In the same year, during one of its periodic campaigns to control vice, the Seattle City Council prohibited brothels north of Yesler and east of Fifth Avenue, thus confirming the "red-light" character of the neighborhood. Most of the city's bordellos relocated in Yesler-Jackson, joining those already operating, and creating a demimonde environment which attracted gamblers, swindlers, pickpockets, thieves, and

burglars. Drug addiction and alcohol abuse were common, and
homicide and suicide rates were by far the highest in the city.[48]

Yesler-Jackson was unhealthful as well as dangerous. The *Se*
Post-Intelligencer in 1900 graphically described pools of stagnant w.
that contributed to typhoid fever and malaria, the sidewalks litte
with "decaying fruit, refuse and garbage of all kinds, old cans ;
cast off clothing." Seattle's homeless, the "hollowed-eyed blanch
faced morphine fiends," to use the vivid language of the newspa
lived under railroad and street bridges.[49]

Middle-class blacks found homes in East Madison, on the cit
northeastern fringe, an area not unlike white streetcar suburbs su
as Rainier Heights or Madison Park. The core of the East Madis
neighborhood was owned by William Grose, who in 1882 purcha:
a twelve-acre farm from Henry Yesler. East Madison remained
underdeveloped, heavily wooded area just outside the city lim
until the Madison Street Cable Car line was extended east to La
Washington in 1889. With public transportation now available, t
area slowly attracted black professionals, business owners, and skill
artisans who purchased lots from Grose and, following his dea
in 1891, from his son, George. They constructed homes arou:
the farmhouse of Seattle's oldest black family. Elizabeth Oxendin
who arrived in Seattle in 1889, remembers the East Madison distri
in 1892 as an area of "unpaved streets" winding through "falle
trees, stumps and underbrush. There were no street lights. Whe
we went to church at night," she recalled, "we carried our la:
terns."[50] By 1900, East Madison had the largest concentration of blac
homeowners in the city and represented the aspirations of a nascer
African American middle class.

Yesler-Jackson and East Madison symbolized two distinct blac
Seattles, each generating an image held by most black resident
well into the twentieth century: Yesler-Jackson, the larger of the two
was impoverished and squalid, and yet risqué, while East Madiso:
was rapidly evolving into a bastion of middle-class decorum an
conformity. These two neighborhoods slowly expanded toward each
other, and by World War II would become, spatially at least, a singl
African American community: the Central District.

Before 1890 Seattle's African Americans took little action to
establish themselves as a self-defined black community, their numbers too small to sustain community institutions. But in the last
decade of the nineteenth century the nearly three hundred Afro-
Americans set out to create religious, political, cultural, and social

organizations that would provide psychological support in their new environment and link them with a national network of black cultural and political institutions.

Black newcomers from larger or more well-defined African American communities of the South and Midwest soon outnumbered the pre-1890 residents. They replicated churches, fraternal orders, and social clubs that symbolized "community" in their places of origin. While there is considerable evidence to suggest that Seattle's whites were quite willing to segregate themselves from Asians or African Americans, the desire to control their own institutions no doubt contributed to the drive by black Seattleites to create their own churches, fraternal orders, and social clubs.

Following the Civil War, black freedmen established, in the words of historian Armstead Robinson, a "panoply of voluntary self-help organizations, benevolent and mutual aid societies, lodges, literary associations."[51] Most southern-born Seattle blacks, growing to maturity in the racially charged atmosphere of the post-Reconstruction South when many of these organizations emerged, thus had little reason to doubt the efficacy of all-black associations. Furthermore, white Seattleites increasingly worked through their own social, civic, and cultural organizations which were usually based on ethnicity and religion as well as race. They found it desirable to interact with comparable Asian or black groups across racial lines. As the city grew and the new elites emerged, many of whom were themselves recent arrivals, they created a social and occupational hierarchy similar to their areas of origin. Thus the egalitarian frontier characterized by individual interaction across economic, social class, or racial lines was rapidly giving way to bureaucratic organizations which spoke for the group interests of capital and labor as well as various religious, ethnic, gender, and social constituencies. Pre-1890 Seattle had no segregationist ordinances, and individual contact across racial lines was frequent. But social, religious, and cultural segregation was so well established in the United States by the 1890s that few blacks, whites, or Asians challenged its development. Many twentieth-century Seattle African Americans would eventually question maintaining separate institutions, but nineteenth-century black Seattleites accepted and often welcomed them.[52]

The black church was the first community institution in the city. Before the 1890s influx of African Americans to Seattle, most blacks worshipped at white churches or held group services in homes. But with a growing population, black Seattleites felt they could support

a church. In 1886, Seaborn J. Collins organized the first meetings of the African Methodist Episcopal Church. Four years later the congregation, now led by Reverend L. S. Blakeney, purchased a lot with a small home on it, which Collins and other parishioners converted into a church. On August 13, 1891, Jones Street (now 14th Avenue) AME Church was incorporated. Reverend Blakeney, Collins, George H. Grose, and Alfred P. Freeman were among its founding members.[53]

Mount Zion Baptist Church was organized February 18, 1894, with eight founding members led by Reverend Hesekiah C. Rice, who had recently arrived in Seattle from Newcastle, Washington. Much of Mount Zion's congregation came from the predominantly white First Baptist Church. The members met in a rented hall on the University of Washington campus (still downtown at this time), until its first church building was constructed. Mount Zion struggled through the rest of the century with a small congregation and frequent changes in pastors.

The impetus for separate churches apparently came from blacks rather than any attempt at segregation by the established churches, for some black Seattleites, such as the Cayton family, continued to attend predominantly white churches. Blacks withdrew from the white churches for a number of reasons. Many African Americans were more comfortable with the emotional services of Jones Street AME and Mount Zion, both well known for hand clapping, fervent prayers, "fire and brimstone" sermons, and "old down home South" hymn singing. Moreover, church organizations also grew from close-knit circles of extended families and friends who coalesced around one or the other religious denomination. Much of the Jones Street Church congregation, for example, was related by blood and marriage. Yet Reverend Daniel G. Hill, in describing early twentieth-century black communities in Oregon in 1932, provided the most compelling reason for the importance of African American churches, particularly in isolated communities such as black Seattle in the 1890s. "The church is a social center, a club, a place of self-expression for the Negroes," he explained, "and they support it because it remains the one resort in the community where they may develop their latent powers without embarrassment or restraint."[54]

Seattle's two black churches in 1900 had a total of sixty members, 15 percent of the city's black population. Yet the size of these congregations could be misleading, since they formed the nucleus of the self-defined community and were part of a network of African

American churches in the Pacific Northwest which provided mutual support and encouragement. When the Puget Sound Conference of the AME Church was organized in 1891, it included congregations in Roslyn, Franklin, and Spokane, Washington, as well as in Portland and Salem, Oregon, and Victoria, Wellington, and Salt Springs, British Columbia. Later in the decade, AME churches in Idaho and Alaska joined the Conference. Mount Zion joined with Baptist churches in Tacoma, Newcastle, and Roslyn to form the Washington State Baptist Association in 1900.[55]

Jones Street AME and Mount Zion Baptist churches were the nexus of community social life. Church members often met new arrivals at the railroad station and invited them to services and to private homes for dinner. Much of the community entertainment and most of its fundraisers originated with the two churches. Holidays of particular relevance to the black population such as "Juneteenth" were celebrated with church services.* The churches educated the black community on public issues, and as Seattle historian Esther Hall Mumford has noted, "topics debated in Philadelphia, Chicago, or Memphis" were soon discussed in Seattle. When the national African Methodist Episcopal Church leadership, for example, divided on the issue of mass emigration back to Africa, the leading opponent, Bishop Richard Gaines, came to Seattle to explain his opposition while Reverend C. C. Halford, the Jones Street minister, defended Bishop Henry McNeal Turner, the leading proponent of emigration to Africa. Virtually all the black community protest or "indignation" meetings were held at Jones Street AME, and the Seattle branch of the Afro-American Council, the leading national civil rights organization of the era, was formed there in 1900.[56]

Seattle's two black churches sponsored a number of auxiliary groups which helped establish a sense of community. Mount Zion sponsored the Ladies Aid Society, which gave community fundraisers, and the Evergreen Literary Society, which presented lectures, plays, and concerts. Jones Street AME Church held an annual Educational Endowment Day to raise money for southern black colleges, and its Widow's Mite Missionary Society contributed to the support of local widows and orphans. In 1891 the church initiated

* The "Juneteenth" celebration dates to June 19, 1865, when General Gordon Granger, commander of Union forces in Texas, issued General Order No. 3, which ended slavery in the last state of the Confederacy occupied by federal troops. From that point Texas blacks, and soon other African Americans throughout the West, celebrated the anniversary of their emancipation on June 19, or "Juneteenth."

a black community-wide picnic which continued annually until the mid-1930s. The first all-day affair took adults and children to Lake Washington for a midday steamship excursion followed by an afternoon barbecue and band recital on Mercer Island and finally an evening variety show at a downtown Seattle hall.[57]

Some Seattle church members addressed the problem of the homeless, transient population along Jackson Street. In 1891, Mrs. Emma Ray organized fifteen female members of Jones Street AME Church into the Frances Ellen Harper branch of the Women's Christian Temperance Union. The group spent most of its time in the red-light district below Yesler and in the King County Jail working among the black and white poor. Its highly visible work with prostitutes, petty criminals, and drug addicts brought praise from local social reformers but angered Reverend J. Allen Viney, the Jones Street pastor, who felt the auxiliary's efforts were not proper "church work." Troubled that their work consumed funds needed to retire the church mortgage, the women resigned their WCTU membership as Jones Street AME withdrew its sponsorship. Emma Ray, however, joined the white WCTU chapter and continued her efforts in Yesler-Jackson.[58]

The schism that destroyed the Frances Ellen Harper WCTU reflected much deeper fissures in the small black community. The pioneers, a self-defined and increasingly self-contained group, viewed themselves as the only real community because of their permanence, their middle-class views and values, and their commitment to community-based organizations and institutions. The transients, the usually impoverished single men and women who resided in the tideflats or along lower Jackson Street, were often ignored by the middle-class community. Black Seattle, by narrowly defining community, acted much like its white and Asian counterparts. Yet just as all of black Seattle faced the paradox of racial toleration and limited opportunity, some Seattle blacks also generated their own paradox of community self-definition and exclusion.[59]

Fraternal lodges, after the churches, had the largest membership. Besides promoting fellowship they provided members with financial assistance, the guarantee of a decent burial, and some support for a deceased member's family. Most members belonged to the small black middle class, or aspired to such status, and saw membership in the lodges as indicating their social mobility. Such status was reflected in Elizabeth Oxendine's description of her parents' attire for the annual Masonic Ball: "Father bought mother a black silk dress for this occasion. Papa looked good in his regalia [and] the ladies were there in silk, satin, velvet."[60]

Three segregated chapters of national lodges were formed in Seattle between 1890 and 1892: the Knights of Pythias, the Masons, and the Odd Fellows. Although the Knights of Pythias preceded the Masons by one year, the latter was the largest of the orders. The Cornerstone Grand Lodge of the York Masons was founded in 1891 by William Grose, Dr. Samuel Burdett, and Conrad Rideout. When lodge members marched downtown in full regalia on March 1, 1892, in honor of the visit of the national grand master, Captain W. D. Matthews, they established an annual tradition that would continue until the 1940s. Wives, daughters, and other female relatives of the Masons formed the Queen of Sheba Court.[61]

By the last decade of the nineteenth century black Seattle had created other voluntary organizations which contributed to the sense of community. Political clubs such as the Frederick Douglass Republican Club and social groups such as the Queen City Club provided entertainment and diversion. Affiliations overlapped. Methodists and Baptists who seldom worshipped together on Sundays nevertheless met in the same hall Wednesday nights to discuss community issues. Such organizations served two purposes: they helped define the cultural and social boundaries of the community, and they afforded Seattle blacks a rare opportunity to control their own affairs and reaffirm their sense of self-worth in an era when African Americans were increasingly besieged by racial attacks.

Black Seattleites formed local chapters of two national civil rights organizations, the Afro-American League and its successor, the Afro-American Council. The local League chapter was formed in 1890, with Isaac W. Evans, Seattle's first black policeman, as its founding president. The Seattle chapter was inspired by the National Afro-American League, created five months earlier in Chicago to challenge racial discrimination nationwide, particularly the erosion of southern black rights. Contrasting deteriorating race relations in the South with the freedom of the Pacific Northwest, League members created a Bureau of Information to disseminate data on regional employment and business opportunities. Ostensibly nonpartisan, the League called on white Republicans and Democrats to recognize black voters with political appointments. In 1894 it raised relief funds for families of black miners killed in a coal mine explosion in nearby Franklin, and in the early 1890s sponsored "Juneteenth" or Emancipation Day celebrations.[62]

Political clashes ensured the demise of the Seattle Afro-American League. It proved an irresistible target for black politicians and their white sponsors who sought political endorsement. League president Gideon S. Bailey, a Canadian-born coal miner who resided in neighboring Newcastle, led fellow black Republican supporters in securing the seating of a League representative at the state Republican Convention in 1892. Two years later Thomas C. Collins and other black Democrats took control of a League meeting to obtain an endorsement of the Democratic slate of candidates. When the attempt failed, the remaining League members pledged to vote the Republican ticket and decided to adjourn for an "indefinite period." That rancorous meeting was the final gathering of the Seattle branch of the League.[63]

In 1899, Seattle attorney Conrad Rideout founded Local Council No. 2 of the National Council of Afro-Americans with thirty-five members. The Council's objectives were similar to those of the now defunct Afro-American League. It denounced southern lynching (and lobbied unsuccessfully for an antilynching bill in the state legislature), called on southern blacks to move to Washington, and drew up a memorial to Congress to proportionately reduce representation among those southern states disfranchising black voters. Despite its militant rhetoric, the Council operated in the shadow of Booker T. Washington and a much more conservative national political environment. Gideon Bailey, president in 1900, recognizing the disfranchisement of black voters in the South as a fait accompli, declared: "We are not opposed to the legitimate restriction of the suffrage, but we insist that restrictions shall apply alike to all citizens of all states." Bailey had offered a stronger resolution which stridently criticized disfranchisement and urged black southerners to migrate to Washington. He was opposed by the Council's vice-president, Daniel Webster Griffin, formerly of Franklin, Washington, and editor of the short-lived black newspaper, the *Seattle Bee*. Resigning himself to the new racial order in the South, Griffin concluded: "It is no use to keep looking back."[64]

Growing racism in Seattle forced the Council, unlike the League, to focus attention locally as well. At its founding meeting a committee was formed to request that local merchants hire blacks as clerks and janitors. Following a police crackdown of female pickpockets in the Yesler-Jackson neighborhood, which included a disproportionate number of African Americans, Police Chief William L. Meredith issued orders to arrest any "suspicious" black woman. Innocent women were arrested or subjected to police harassment, prompting a storm of protest in the black community. The Council, after a series of "indignation" meetings held at the Sleeping Car Porters Club on Jackson Street and at Jones Street AME Church, forced Police Chief Meredith to rescind his order.[65]

Its success in the police harassment case notwithstanding, the Afro-American Council was plagued by the partisan political rivalry that had caused the demise of its predecessor, the Afro-American League. Black Democrats and Republicans vied for endorsements and noisily quit the Council when they were unsuccessful. When Daniel Webster Griffin became the third Council president in the year of its founding, it was clear that the organization would not survive into 1901.

That the two nineteenth-century civil rights organizations fell victim to the maneuvering of black politicians and their sponsors is not surprising given the importance black Seattle ascribed to politics despite the apparently meager rewards. Yet their political status again illustrated the paradox of the city's racial order. Unlike southerners, black Seattleites fully exercised their franchise. Yet, with rare exception, black office seekers found it impossible to gain major elective or appointive office because of the small black population. Washington's U.S. Senator John L. Wilson succinctly explained the dilemma of black politicos in Seattle when he responded to a reporter's question concerning Horace Cayton's reward for supporting his candidacy. When the reporter asked, "What are you going to do for Cayton when this fight is over?" Jones responded: "Nothing. If I give him what he merits, the opposition will use it against us in the next fight. If I give him an insignificant place, the opposition will belittle me."[66]

African Americans spent considerable energy on political activities, even when they recognized the blatant disregard of black sensibilities by both Democrats and Republicans. When Cayton bitterly complained that the only reward Seattle black Republicans received for their fidelity to the 1894 city ticket was the position of "bull catcher"* at a salary of $60 per month, about half the amount paid the previous white appointee, he voiced the lament of Seattle's black voters throughout the decade.[67]

Yet African Americans eagerly sought elective office and political appointments. As Thomas C. Cox remarked in his study of black Topeka, "Public office confirmed civic responsibility and conferred status in black political and nonpolitical institutions. One became a decision maker rather than a mere petitioner." Seattle black leaders

---

* A dogcatcher.

believed that the success of "representative men," the term for the ambitious blacks of the day, would prove the capacity of blacks to participate as full-fledged citizens of their local and national communities. Moreover, those from the South well knew the importance of the vote and were determined to exercise the franchise precisely because it was denied to the vast majority of the nation's blacks.[68]

Between 1889 and 1900 a succession of political clubs sponsored by both major parties commanded the loyalty of nearly half the permanently resident African Americans in Seattle. These clubs unapologetically sought to influence the distribution of patronage jobs rather than to promote political reform or civil rights legislation. In October 1888, thirty-two men organized black Seattle's first political club, the Colored Harrison and Morton League, which supported the Republican Party nominees for president and vice-president. As was the prevailing custom, the "colored" club adopted the bylaws and principles of the Harrison and Morton Club, a white organization supporting the ticket. The colored club participated in parades and rallies during the remainder of the campaign and celebrated their candidates' victory the following month.

After the campaign, blacks pressed the Republican Party for some political appointment to reward their support. They advanced John N. Conna of Tacoma for assistant sergeant-at-arms of the 1889 Washington Territorial House of Representatives and James H. Orr of Seattle as messenger and postmaster of the Washington Senate. The appointments, they argued, would indicate GOP appreciation for both local and national black support for Republican candidates. GOP leaders selected Conna, who became the first black political appointee in the Territory's history. Orr, however, was rejected by the Senate and instead was unanimously elected porter of the Senate Chamber.

If black Republicans were disappointed in Orr's post, they did not repudiate the party, since two years later many of the Harrison Club members met at the King County GOP headquarters and formed the Young Men's Colored Republican Club. The new organization, which included I. Israel Walker, George Grose, and Reverend L. S. Blakeney, endorsed John F. Cragwell as their delegate to represent black voters at the upcoming King County Convention. Cragwell was subsequently appointed to the GOP county central committee and served as delegate to the state convention.

Although never elected to public office, Horace Cayton was the most influential black politician in nineteenth-century Seattle. His political influence rested not on votes he could deliver to white candidates but on his role as a partisan, crusading editor of a popular newspaper, the *Seattle Republican*. Cayton and Dr. Samuel Burdett, who briefly flirted with populism in the mid-1890s, were the two most prominent blacks affiliated with the state Republican Party. Cayton regularly announced his candidacy for various public and party posts but was successful only in 1896 when he was selected a Washington delegate to the Republican National Convention.

Cayton's political philosophy, shaped equally by his belief in the Pacific Northwest's egalitarian democracy and his firmly integrationist views, was best summarized by his statement on black political participation: "If a Negro feels he can hold his own among white campaigners and he wants to play the game, though without a Negro constituency, he should 'back his ears and pitch in.' If he gets knocked down, never admit it was on account of his color and never sulk in his tent."[69]

But black electoral success proved elusive, though African Americans occasionally convinced white voters to support them. In 1892, Seaborn J. Collins, one of the organizers of the Colored Harrison and Morton League, was nominated by the GOP as wreckmaster, the individual responsible for removing accumulated timber along the waterfront. He handily defeated John A. Coleman, the black Democratic candidate in the first city election that slated black candidates from opposing parties for the same political office. Collins became Seattle's first black elected official. His success would not be repeated until 1900, when Samuel Burdett was elected wreckmaster on the GOP ticket.

In an 1894 interview with a Spokane newspaper, Cayton facetiously claimed that of the 3,500 black voters in the state there were "only five pronounced Democrats and about ten Populists."[70] He described the political division as he might have wished it rather than as it existed, for a sizable group of local black political activists supported the Democrats despite the party's identification with slavery and southern black disfranchisement. Moreover, Seattle's white Democrats solicited black support despite the objections of their counterparts in rural areas of Washington. In 1889, local Democrats nominated John Randolph, a black man, as a King County delegate to the state convention in Ellensburg. While Randolph received the third highest number of votes in King County, rural Democrats adamantly protested his selection and Randolph was represented "by proxy."[71]

Conrad Rideout and John A. Coleman emerged as the leading spokesmen for Seattle's "Colored Democracy" in the 1890s. Rideout was an unabashed office seeker who campaigned for an appointment in the Grover Cleveland administration as a minister to Bolivia, and later as consul for the West Indian island of Antigua and at Cape Town, South Africa. Coleman claimed that the Democratic Party was the "natural" political home of Seattle blacks, since it represented the interests of workingmen. In 1892 Coleman, the first black Democrat nominated for office, was slated for the position of wreckmaster, which he lost to Seaborn Collins in the general election.

The Democrats offered no more than the Republicans in the way of meaningful appointments. Unclear about their options, Seattle's African American politicos vacillated between the major parties and occasionally flirted with the Populists, searching not so much for clear political principles as for the party that would offer more than the handful of menial jobs grudgingly provided for "loyal and faithful service."[72]

B lack Seattleites at the turn of the century were faced with a contradictory message of liberalism, paternalism, and race and class bias. Yet they established the foundations for many contemporary institutions and voluntary associations. Through their church, fraternal, and civil rights organizations, they consciously founded a community with links to other African Americans in the Pacific Northwest region and the nation. Moreover, despite poverty and prejudice, many of them created a satisfying life. "We Seattleites were sociable in those days," recalled Elizabeth Oxendine. "There was something going on all the time. Balls, barbecues, picnics, excursions. There was always some place to go. And, of course, weddings, births, and the passing away of some one of our group."[73]

Yet Seattle's African Americans could completely enjoy the "free air" of the city only if they could find suitable employment, a search that would prove frustratingly unsuccessful for many in the twentieth century. Moreover, the concept of community was narrowly defined. The group Elizabeth Oxendine described above comprised families tied together by marriage or church, club, and fraternal order membership. That sense of community did not extend to lower Jackson Street to include many – often jobless – black men and women. These people constituted a different community, one separated by class rather than racial boundaries. Much of the history of black Seattle until World War II would be marked by the uneasy interaction of these two distinct communities.

PART
TWO

The
Black Community
Emerges,
1900–1940

The fact that Negroes constitute about one per cent of the population here and that more of them work for a living than is true of the general population is significant. . . . The smaller number of persons in comparison to the total does not necessarily mean that the problems of the individual [worker] are fewer. The very smallness of the proportion may, in fact, make it more difficult for the worker to find his place. — Report of the Seattle Urban League, 1935

Chapter 2

Employment
and Economics,
1900–1940

"Race workers are the backbone of the Race," declared Milton
P. Webster, vice president of the Brotherhood of Sleeping Car
Porters, in a 1929 interview, "and upon their welfare . . . depends the
progress of all phases of our life, whether religious, social, fraternal,
civic, or commercial."[1] Webster's comments were particularly appropriate in Seattle, where the ebb and flow of employment opportunity
available to black workers affected virtually every aspect of community life. The fortunes of Seattle's black workers were inextricably
linked to the expansion of the city's economy, which underwent
cycles of boom and bust characteristic of capitalistic development
in a rapidly evolving western metropolis. Yet these workers also
confronted racial discrimination that relegated their participation to
the margins of the urban economy. Some signs of the marginalization
were evident in late nineteenth-century Seattle. But by the second
decade of the twentieth century the simultaneous growth and transformation of the urban economy would make that marginalization
apparent to the entire city.

Black women and men who migrated to Seattle during the first
decade of the twentieth century entered an urban economy undergoing the beginning of that transformation. Seattle's first economic
boom came with the completion of the transcontinental railroad in
1883, and was relatively short-lived, ending with the 1893 Depression

during which the city lost nearly half its residents. The second boom lasted through the end of World War I and ensured Seattle's preeminence as a major international trading center. That boom began with two related developments: the discovery of gold in Alaska's Klondike region in 1897, and Seattle's increasing dominance of trade with Asia. The gold rush generated both a population influx and considerable commerce as gold seekers passing through the city were supplied and outfitted in the numerous shops and stores created to accommodate the Klondike trade. Those fortunate enough to find gold cashed their diggings at the federal assay office established in Seattle in 1898 and usually spent most of their newfound wealth in the city. Although the rush itself was over by 1900, Seattle shippers and merchants continued to dominate the "Alaska trade," processing and shipping the territory's other major natural resources – lumber and salmon. By 1901, the Asian trade would become a major segment of the city's commerce when Japanese, German, and American shipping lines began regular service to China and Japan. That trade brought tea, silk, camphor, and soy oil from Asia in exchange for lumber, flour, cotton, machinery, and heavy hardware for the Asian market. The addition of other shipping lines and the growth of international commerce made Seattle the leading port on the Pacific Coast by 1916.[2]

Growing commerce and population stimulated Seattle's first significant manufacturing industry, shipbuilding, which evolved from the need to construct vessels for the Alaska gold rush. Robert and Peter Moran established shipyards in both Seattle and across the Puget Sound in neighboring Bremerton. (After making his fortune, Robert Moran often recalled having been "staked" by William Grose when he arrived penniless in Seattle.) The Moran Brothers constructed wooden vessels and in 1898 built the first steel and iron vessel, a torpedo boat, for the U.S. Navy during the Spanish-American War. Their federal contract signaled the beginning of the prominent influence of federal military spending on the city's economic fortunes. Although Moran Brothers was the largest firm, by 1900 a dozen shipyards would employ two thousand Seattle workers, making shipbuilding the city's largest industry.[3]

Shipbuilding stimulated related manufacturing, including boilermaking, toolmaking, sail production, and machinery work. Some workers were employed in processing lumber, milling flour, canning salmon and oysters, and making optical goods, plumbing and gasfittings, women's clothing, and bicycles. The manufacturing economy also supported a growing service sector including office man-

Unidentified black chauffeur driving Caroline McGilvra Burke, wife of Judge Thomas Burke, late 1800s. *Special Collections, University of Washington Libraries*

Crew of unidentified ship with black sailors, 1900. *Puget Sound Maritime Historical Society*

Two unidentified black women on a Seattle pier for a Sunday stroll.
Letcher Yarbrough Collection; reprinted from Seattle's Black Victorians
by Esther Mumford

AME church conference, ca. 1900. *Letcher Yarbrough Collection; reprinted from* Seattle's Black Victorians *by Esther Mumford*

Horace Cayton. *Special Collections,*
University of Washington Libraries

Integrated female shipyard crew, 1918. *National Archives*

Black railroad porters, 1934. *Pemco Webster & Stevens Collection, Museum of History and Industry*

CHARTER

National Colored Democratic Association

Know all men by these presents: That the
WASHINGTON STATE COLORED DEMOCRATIC CLUB, INC.

having met the requirements of the NATIONAL COLORED DEMOCRATIC ORGANI-
ZATION, incorporated in the year 1892, which is attested by a duly signed, sealed and
delivered instrument, is hereby created a unit of the national organization and authorized
to act in the work of building up membership, spreading the doctrines of the National
Democratic Party, and devoting itself to the advancement of the principles of social justice.

Be it understood also, that the WASHINGTON STATE COLORED DEMOCRATIC CLUB, INC.
has subscribed to the rules and regulations of the national body, membership in
which is composed of the duly elected officers of each local unit, and all other
citizens of good character, who may desire to qualify.

Be it also further understood, that except where authorized by the national body, each local unit shall be responsible FOR ITS OWN OBLIGATIONS
OF WHATEVER CHARACTER THEY MAY BE.

Witness our hands and seal _____this_____24th____ day of__Feb.____1940.

_____
President

_____
Secretary

Charter of the Colored Democratic Club, 1940. *Constance Thomas Collection*

WPA demonstration in downtown Seattle, July 15, 1937.
Seattle Post-Intelligencer Collection, Museum of History and Industry

Yesler Terrace, 1941. *Seattle Post-Intelligencer Collection, Museum of History and Industry*

Central District track and softball teams — primarily Asian Americans and blacks. *Seattle Post-Intelligencer Collection, Museum of History and Industry*

"STEVEDORE"

ALL SEATS RESERVED

40c

(Plus State Tax)

Reservations at

Seattle Repertory Playhouse
41st and University Way   MElrose 7700

COMMENTS

"A hell of a good show."
—Robert Benchley, **The New Yorker.**

"**Stevedore** deserves a distinguished run for it is a sound, mettlesome piece of dramatic writing. The characters are as real and rich as the earth."
—Brooks Atkinson, **New York Times.**

"Paul Peters and George Sklar write so theatrically and with such fascinating violence that I am lost in admiration of their showmanship."
—Percy Hammond, **New York Herald-Tribune.**

"If you relish finding out how long you can hold your breath **Stevedore** is the play. What raises it above ordinary melodrama is the sense of impending fate and the wonderfully human appeal of the characters."
—Eupemia Van Rensselaer Wyatt, **The Catholic World.**

"You have in **Stevedore** . . . a play which I believe to be a most important milestone in the history of the Negro on the American stage."
—Carl Van Vechten.

"**Stevedore** is the beginning of a new life in the theatre. It has revolutionized play-writing, play-going and play-producing."
—Erskine Caldwell.

2 6

NEGRO CAST AND CHORUS OF 75

Seattle Repertory Playhouse
41st and University Way   MElrose 7700

Flyer for Federal Theater Project/Negro Repertory Theater play, *Stevedore.*
Constance Thomas Collection

Scene from play, *In Abraham's Bosom*, 1933. In the center of the photograph (in suit) is Joseph S. Jackson. *Seattle Urban League Records, University of Washington Manuscripts Division*

Unidentified player, Ubangi Blackhawks, Seattle's black semi-professional team in the 1930s. *Albert J. Smith Collection*

Fans at Ubangi game. *Albert J. Smith Collection*

Albert J. Smith (right) and crewmate Lester Catlett on shore leave in Tokyo, 1936. The two were stewards on an American Mail Line steamship voyage from Seattle to the Far East. *Albert J. Smith Collection*

agers, physicians, attorneys, secretaries, cooks, janitors, hotel managers, waiters, stenographers, dressmakers, grocers, and boarding house operators. Most of these workers were newcomers, eager to achieve success in the bustling young city.[4]

A small, steady stream of African Americans migrated to Seattle during this period. The newcomers found jobs as railroad workers, as domestic servants for wealthy whites, and as construction laborers in the numerous building projects generated in this rapidly growing city. Between 1900 and 1910 black Seattle gained nearly 1,900 new residents. While the influx was hardly overwhelming in a city that grew by 156,000 during the decade, the rapid black population increase nevertheless initiated critical changes in Seattle race relations.

Like their predecessors in the late nineteenth century, these migrants took advantage of inexpensive railroad travel or worked their way to Seattle after successive stops in other cities.[5] William Moss, a North Carolina–born stone mason, arrived in 1904 as part of a construction gang recruited in his home state to build a Seattle brewery. Jamaica-born Edward Pitter came as a captain's steward on a passenger liner that docked in Seattle during the Alaska-Yukon-Pacific Exposition of 1909. Pitter liked the city, settled, and became a railroad porter. Margaret Cogwell arrived in 1910 from Newton, Kansas, on the advice of a friend who had migrated a decade earlier. Samuel and Maudie Warfield were part of a growing movement of Louisianians and Arkansans to Seattle. Richard Jenkins, originally from Texas, joined the all-black Twenty-fifth Infantry, served in the Philippines, and was transferred to Fort Lawton, on Seattle's outskirts, in 1902. He and his Filipina wife, Rufina, remained in the city after his retirement from the military and he became a longshoreman.[6] Thus Seattle's Filipino community traces its history to Rufina Clemente Jenkins, the first resident from the islands to settle in the city.

Many Seattle blacks viewed the years between the Spanish-American War and World War I as the premier period for employment. Joseph Sylvester Jackson, who became the first executive secretary of the Seattle Urban League upon its founding in 1930, offered this description of employment prospects during the interwar era: "Work at good wages was easily found in family service. Men found work as bellhops in hotels and apartments, as waiters and cooks in hotels and cafes, and as elevator operators in department stores and apartment houses. Women found employment as maids in hotels and as stock girls in department stores."[7]

Table 2
Growth of Seattle's Black Population, 1900-1940

Year	Black Population	Percentage Increase	Total Population	Black Percentage of Total Population
1900	406	42	80,671	0.5
1910	2,296	466	237,194	1.0
1920	2,894	26	315,312	0.9
1930	3,303	14	365,583	0.9
1940	3,789	15	368,302	1.0

Sources: U.S. Bureau of the Census, *Sixteenth Census of the U.S.,* 1940, *Population,* vol.1, Washington, table 2; *Negroes in the United States, 1920–1932,* table 11.

Census figures show that between 1900 and 1910 Seattle's black population, which jumped 466 percent from 406 to 2,296, grew more rapidly than during any previous decade. To be sure, virtually all jobs were in domestic service and related occupations which guaranteed long hours and low remuneration, but the steadily expanding local economy nevertheless meant that blacks could find work. (See Table 2.)

The Longshoremen's Strike of 1916, which idled more than 21,000 West Coast dockworkers, provided the first opportunity for black laborers to obtain work beyond "traditional" occupations. The International Longshoremen's Association (ILA) initiated the strike following the announcement of a pay reduction by the Waterfront Employers Association (WEA). When confronted with a work stoppage that threatened to close the Port of Seattle, the WEA brought in 1,400 nonunion dockworkers to break the strike, including Asians and 400 black longshoremen from New Orleans, St. Louis, and Kansas City. The black dockworkers were housed at a waterfront warehouse, fed at company expense, and protected from the strikers by armed guards who ringed the docks. James A. Roston, a local Seattle realtor and former lieutenant in the all-black Tenth U.S. Cavalry during the Spanish-American War, recruited many of these men for the WEA. Upon their arrival in Seattle they were organized into the Benevolent Protective Brotherhood headed by Roston.[8]

The 1916 strike was particularly bitter because of the racial conflict introduced by the arrival of the largest number of black strikebreakers in the city's history. Horace Cayton, Jr., the teenage son of the *Seattle Republican* editor, and one of the local blacks hired on the docks, vividly recalled the strike's racial overtones in his autobiography, *Long Old Road*. When Cayton and two other nonunion black workers attempted to get to the waterfront by trolley, the car they were riding was stopped by angry strikers, some of whom entered it looking for black strikebreakers. Cayton recounted the scene:

The three [strikers] went directly to the two Negroes [strikebreakers] sitting just in front of me. I realized that they were strikers and that we were in for trouble.

"Get up, you black son of a bitch! We'll teach you to break a strike and take the food out of our kids' mouths!" the biggest of them said to the Negro sitting on the aisle. "Didn't you hear me, nigger?"

Still the man didn't move. With that the striker swung his cargo hook and caught him in the neck just below the ear, pulling him to his feet like a half of beef. "We should burn you alive like they do down south!"

The pinioned man gave a muffled scream and tried to express his willingness to do anything, but because of the cargo hook he couldn't move his head. With an oath the striker pulled it out, and two of them held the man upright as he swayed desperately. The blood spurted out of the wound and formed a little rivulet down the man's collar. . . . Two of the strikers led the wounded man out of the car and the third turned to the second Negro.

"Will you come along or do you want us to hook you, too?"

The man stood up without speaking and was led out of the car.[9]

Confronted with such violence almost daily during the strike, black nonunion workers retaliated. In one instance a black strikebreaker shot and killed one of the strikers who taunted him. Mattie Vinyerd Harris recalled another occasion, the evening when the black dockworkers invaded the longshoremen's union hall during the labor conflict: "They went into the Longshoremen's Hall and they beat and cut and did everything that was possible. They gave as good as they got."[10]

The strike ended in April 1917, when the United States entered World War I and the federal government mandated the resumption of shipping. Despite the violence from both sides, the ILA, sensing the danger to its interests in racially exclusive unionism, quickly incorporated many of the black strikebreakers into its ranks. Yet once in the ILA, black longshoremen continued to face discrimination from other union members and employers. Frank Jenkins, one of the earliest Seattle blacks to join the newly integrated ILA, remembered conditions in 1917: "Blacks would sit on benches for up to two weeks in the union hall waiting for job assignments while whites went from one job to another." A fervent supporter of the ILA and later an officer in the Seattle local, Jenkins placed responsibility for the treatment on the Waterfront Employers Association, which in his view continued to exploit racial animosity among union members.[11]

Horace Cayton, Jr., however, held the ILA directly responsible for preferential assignments allocated to white longshoremen, many of whom, openly admitting their prejudice, refused to work in gangs that included blacks. Cayton, who said he was converted from strikebreaker to labor union supporter during the 1916 strike because of the influence of a white Industrial Workers of the World (IWW) organizer he knew only as "Red," nonetheless noted unfair treatment of black longshoremen after their acceptance into the union: "I did encourage Negroes to join the union, and others followed, so that within a short time we did have a black and white union, and a closed shop, and a union dispatching office. But it didn't stay that way for long. We noticed that the dispatchers were beginning to discriminate against Negro longshoremen on the pretext of union seniority. When work was slack, colored longshoremen were frozen out. Soon I lost my job and was then more convinced than ever that I'd been right: however desirable a mixed union was, you just couldn't trust any white man."[12]

The different conclusions reached by Jenkins and Cayton reflected the growing diversity of opinion in black Seattle about the merits of union membership, but also reflected the ability of employers and workers to pursue the same policy for entirely different reasons. Such discrimination proved a bitter reward for black dockworkers who had put aside their fears and reservations about joining the union that had so recently and fervently opposed their work on the waterfront. Ultimately many of them questioned their decision while other black dockworkers refused to join the ILA. Nonetheless, the integration of the longshoremen's union was the first step toward the integration of black workers into the core of Seattle's economy.

World War I provided a major, if temporary, boost to black Seattle. "There was plenty of work in Seattle once the war was in full swing," recounted Horace Cayton, Jr. "Good jobs for Negroes, in the shipyards and in many other places where we had not worked before. . . ."[13] Black women left their jobs as domestics to become metalworkers; black men who were mainly porters and waiters before

1917 now found employment in steel mills and post offices. Black men and women worked for the first time at Fort Lawton, the Puget Sound army installation established during the Spanish-American War.

But the shipyards offered the greatest opportunity. Lucrative federal contracts for shipbuilders such as Skinner and Eddy, by 1916 the largest shipyard in the city, and labor shortages prompted by large-scale enlistment of able-bodied white male workers, opened jobs for white women, Asians, and African Americans. Before the end of the war Seattle shipyards and allied industries employed nearly 35,000 workers and produced 26 percent of all ships built in the United States during the conflict. Antiwar Socialist Hulet Wells, who worked in the yards, described the managed disorder that was the huge Skinner and Eddy shipyard in 1918:

What a scene it was . . . a wilderness of strange machines, whirling belts and belching fires. Ten thousand men went through their motions wordlessly, for they had to shout to be heard above the din. . . . Boilers rang, planers screamed, long white-hot rods were smashed into bolt machines. Here was the angle bending floor where black men beat a tattoo with heavy sledges, and here a steam hammer thumped its measured blow.[14]

Edward Coleman's experience was typical of many Seattle blacks during World War I. He dropped out of high school when he turned eighteen to work in a foundry at the Navy Shipyard across Puget Sound in Bremerton. Employed as part of an integrated production crew, he made parts for submarines promised to the Russian navy. "My job," Coleman explained in an interview fifty-seven years later, "was to mix sand to make cones for them to make certain parts of machines. You'd have to make a cone and you'd pour the molting steel in."[15]

If World War I brought new opportunities to local African Americans, it did not prompt a wholesale migration to Seattle as occurred in northeastern and midwestern cities. During the entire second decade of the twentieth century, the city's black population grew by only 598 persons (Table 2). While the 26 percent growth over the decade appears statistically substantial, it should be viewed against an average of 195 percent for eastern and midwestern cities as 500,000 southern blacks began a sustained migration northward. The prospect of work in Chicago, Detroit, Cleveland, and other northern industrial cities proved far more appealing than moving to distant Seattle. Indeed, of

Table 3
Black Population Increases in Selected Cities, 1900–1920

City	Population, 1910	% Increase, 1900–1910	Population, 1920	% Increase, 1910–1920
Detroit	5,741	40	40,838	611
Cleveland	8,448	41	34,451	307
Chicago	44,103	46	109,458	148
Milwaukee	980	14	2,229	127
Los Angeles	7,599	256	15,579	105
Oakland	3,055	197	5,489	80
New York	91,709	51	152,467	66
Philadelphia	84,459	35	134,229	59
Minneapolis	2,592	67	3,927	52
Portland	1,045	34	1,556	49
Pittsburgh	25,623	26	37,725	47
San Francisco	1,642	− 1	2,414	47
SEATTLE	2,296	466	2,894	26
Denver	5,426	38	6,075	12

Sources: U.S. Bureau of the Census, *Negro Population, 1790–1915*, pp. 92ff; *Negroes in the United States, 1920–32*, pp. 55ff.

a number of northern and western cities only Denver had a smaller percentage increase than Seattle during the World War I decade (Table 3). Thus black Seattle's migration pattern differed from much of the rest of urban black America. The "great migration" of black newcomers into Seattle, like that of two other West Coast cities, Los Angeles and Oakland, occurred between 1900 and 1910 rather than 1910 and 1920.[16]

At the end of the war employers dismissed African Americans not only from war-related jobs but from menial and domestic service positions they had held before 1917. In the postwar recession the competition among blacks and between African Americans and Asians grew more intense. Moreover, the demands of returning war veterans partly accounted for the displacement, as did the cancellation of government contracts as the shipbuilding industry returned to prewar production levels. But Joseph S. Jackson suggests that changing employer attitudes and preferences during and after the war contributed to reduced employment opportunities for African American workers: "Negro workers lost many jobs held for years and were not replaced by other Negro workers. . . . It was easy to dismiss a staff of colored men elevator operators and replace them with white women." Sometimes an entire staff of black workers would be terminated because of the misconduct of one or two workers. "This occurred in connection with the loss of jobs at the Bon Marché [department store], the Bartell Drug Store chain, the Marlborough and Penbrook Hotel and others." Jackson's comments suggest an evolving gender as well as racial rivalry, pitting white women against black men.[17]

Black female workers were particularly vulnerable. The waitresses' union, according to Seattle historian Richard Berner, barred African American women from membership, making it difficult to obtain jobs in nonblack restaurants. Moreover, at a time when black women increasingly formed the majority of the servant class in the nation's largest cities, Seattle's black females faced competition from old rivals such as Japanese males and Swedish females, but also increasingly from Filipino men who began migrating to the city during the 1920s. These groups never completely replaced black women as domestic servants, but their willingness to take these jobs reminded local African Americans that in Seattle, unlike eastern cities, even menial positions could be contested.[18]

The loss of skilled jobs reverberated through the postwar black community. Black post office employees, for example, hired for the first time as clerks and mail carriers during the war, relinquished their jobs to returning white veterans. They, in turn, pushed out less well educated and less skilled blacks who had taken over jobs as elevator operators, doormen, waiters, and cooks.[19]

By 1920 it was clear that for Seattle blacks the period of job expansion was over. The region's surplus of white labor, the inclination of employment agencies to channel African Americans into domestic service rather than industrial work, continued union opposition, and southern migrants' poor education all combined to limit black occupational mobility.

But the declining employment prospects also reflected the postwar transformation of Seattle's economy. The myriad small industries that drove the economy from the 1880s through World War I gave way to larger but more slowly expanding meat packing, flour milling, lumber processing, and a fledgling industry centered around the Boeing Airplane Company, founded in 1916. Moreover, the loss of federal contracts after the war drove many small shipbuilders into bankruptcy and generated a restructuring among the surviving firms. By 1921, Seattle had become, according to labor historian Robert

Friedheim, an "industrial ghost town," as local business leaders struggled to convert to a peacetime economy. Correspondingly, the number of industrial workers dramatically declined during the years immediately following the war, from 40,000 in 1919 to 13,000 by 1921. Seattle would not exceed its 1918 employment peak until World War II.[20]

Unlike their counterparts in eastern cities, where the growth in manufacturing continued to generate unskilled and semiskilled entry-level factory jobs for African Americans until the end of the 1920s, Seattle's black workers remained concentrated in service occupations on the periphery of the local economy as railroad porters, hotel waiters, maids, and ship stewards. Even the longshore jobs which black strikebreakers forcibly opened in 1916 and which provided employment to about 200 black males during the war had declined to approximately 100 by 1920 out of a total of 15,000 longshoremen on the city's docks.[21]

Faced with the specter of declining postwar employment, black male workers eagerly sought the new opportunity presented to them as strikebreakers by the 1921 ship stewards' strike. These black strike-breakers and other African American males subsequently recruited would become the majority of ship stewards on Seattle-based passenger steamships operating from Alaska to San Diego. By 1925, for example, 500 black men, approximately 30 percent of Seattle's adult male black population, were stewards for the two major companies, Pacific Steamship and Alaska Steamship. [22]

In April 1921, the Seattle-based Shipowners and Operators Association announced a 15 percent wage reduction, precipitating a strike by the International Seamen's Union which included the all-white Marine Cooks and Stewards Association of the Pacific (MCSAP). The two Seattle shipping firms affected by the strike – the Alaska Steamship Company, which operated a fleet of passenger and freight steamers between Seattle and Alaskan ports, and the Pacific Steamship Company, whose Admiral Line ships sailed to both Alaskan and California ports – hired nonunion white women as waitresses and stewardesses.[23]

As the strike entered its third month, steamship company management grew increasingly dissatisfied with the female employees. James A. Roston, already known as a labor recruiter because of his role in the 1916 longshore strike, asked the firms to employ black men. Both companies agreed and began replacing the women with black stewards as each of their vessels returned to port that summer.

Roston's agreement with the shipping companies absorbed much of Seattle's small black male work force and soon he advertised in East Coast and California newspapers for experienced stewards. The 1921 waterfront strike generated for Seattle's black men the opportunity to work on "the boats" for the first time in two decades and provided a relatively well-paying alternative to work as restaurant waiters, railroad porters, and dining car attendants.

The strike was broken later that year, but blacks continued to find employment with the steamship companies through the mid-1930s, when the combined impact of the Depression and the growing popularity of rail and auto transportation reduced the appeal of regular ocean transit between West Coast ports. But at the height of the 1925 summer touring season, hundreds of African Americans found work on "the boats." Seventy-six stewards worked on the SS *H. F. Alexander*, the Pacific Steamship Company's largest and fastest ship, which accommodated 680 passengers and made the round-trip run from Seattle to Los Angeles in six days. The hiring of the stewards opened opportunities for other black employees, including singers, musicians, cooks, dishwashers, bellhops, and telephone operators.[24]

Roston organized the black stewards into the Colored Marine Employees Benevolent Association of the Pacific (CMEBA), a workingmen's group that vowed "to promote peaceful relations between employers and employees" and "to steer clear of labor or trade unions and their activities." The CMEBA withheld support from union organizing on the Seattle waterfront until 1934. Consequently, bitter hostility developed between the Marine Cooks and Stewards Union, whose members now competed for jobs with the CMEBA.[25]

Steamship employment proved a powerful attraction for many black Seattleites. The pay, averaging forty-five dollars per month, supplemented by tips, was considered substantial for the 1920s. However, work on "the boats" proved difficult and demanding. The frequent runs separated men from their families for months. Moreover, hotel waiters quickly found their shipboard assignments significantly different from their previous work.

Joseph Isom Staton, who was hired by the Pacific Steamship Company in 1925, described his work in an interview half a century later: "We had to get up at 5:00 in the morning and clean up, go down and have breakfast, get our tables ready and start serving around 7:30 . . . and after breakfast was served, why then we would clean up the dining salon and do other chores. . . . We would serve again at noon and the lunch would last a couple of hours, all depended on how many people were on the boat. . . . We had a chance to rest for a couple of hours in the afternoon, before time for dinner. Then we would go up one hour ahead of time and get the dining room ready to serve. Sometimes we wouldn't get away from the dining room until . . . midnight."[26] After dinner was served, Staton and the other stewards retired to the "glory-hole" – the bunks in the lowest section of the ship. Stewards such as Staton were also assigned an average of eight staterooms to service between breakfast and lunch. Beds were made, floors vacuumed, tubs and bowls scrubbed, walls and furniture dusted, and linen checked. Often after lunch the stewards donned overalls and painted unused staterooms and deck cabins.[27] Yet the work had intrinsic rewards. The steady wages provided many a family with resources to purchase homes in the city, giving black Seattleites in the 1920s one of the highest homeownership rates in the urban North. Work on the ships financed the college education of a small minority of Seattle blacks, and Horace Cayton, Jr., one of black Seattle's most prominent sons, recalled his stint on a passenger vessel as turning him from a desultory life.[28]

Black males not employed by the passenger liners had few options in the interwar years. Edward Coleman's occupational history from 1916 to the mid-1930s is suggestive of the range of jobs available. During the summer months of 1916 and 1917, Coleman worked in an Alaska cannery. When he turned eighteen he worked in a foundry at the Bremerton Navy Shipyard but was laid off in January 1920 as part of the postwar demobilization. He became a porter on the Northern Pacific Railroad, working the 2,300 mile Seattle-to-Chicago route, and then in 1922 hired on as a ship's steward on the *H. F. Alexander*. Coleman remained with the steamship line until 1929, when he was again laid off. His next job was as a steward in the men's locker room in the clubhouse at Broadmoor, an exclusive residential community in northeast Seattle. When his brother lost his job as a steamship steward in 1930, Coleman became the night janitor at Broadmoor to allow his unemployed sibling to take his former position. While holding the janitorial job, he worked as a substitute letter carrier for the post office between 1931 and 1935.[29]

If black men had the opportunity to move from the shipyards and foundries to the steamships after World War I, black women soon discovered that they had only one choice, a return to domestic service. Forty-three percent of Seattle's black women were in the work force in 1920 and 38 percent in 1930. The vast majority of these women were maids or laundry workers regardless of their education or prior work experience. Mattie Vinyerd Harris described her occupations in Seattle in the 1920s and 1930s: "I worked in the homes, I was a maid, a cook and finally did day work [housecleaning] which most [black] women did. That was the one thing open to you." Oklahoma-born Irene Grayson discussed her life as a maid from 1914, when she arrived in Seattle, until her retirement in the 1950s: "I worked seven years without a vacation [during the 1920s] and some weeks every Saturday and Sunday for $2.10 a day." Mary Ott Saunders began work as a fry cook in the Rose Garden Tea Room, a downtown restaurant, in 1926 and remained there for forty-two years until she retired at the age of seventy-eight. Prominent women shared these limited prospects. Susie Revels Cayton, wife of newspaper editor Horace Cayton and daughter of a former U.S. senator, was forced to seek employment as a "domestic" following the family's economic reversals in 1919, and her daughter, Madge, a University of Washington graduate with a degree in international business, was reduced to working as a waitress and cashier in various small black restaurants in the 1920s and 1930s.[30]

Black occupational mobility continued to be restricted due to educational limitations and employer discrimination even as whites and Asians expanded their range of opportunity. Seattle's economic base supported fewer industrial jobs in 1940 than in 1920, and thus many Seattleites experienced some downward mobility. Yet Asians and whites spread steadily across the occupational spectrum between 1910 and 1940 (see Table 4) while blacks remained concentrated in menial occupations. In 1910, 45 percent of black males were servants, waiters, and janitors; by 1940, 56 percent were in that category. Black women fared worse: in 1910, 84 percent were domestic or personal servants; by 1940, 84 percent were still in that category.[31]

This continuing concentration in personal service occupations prompted the *Northwest Enterprise*, Seattle's largest black newspaper, to bitterly declare in 1927: "In Seattle colored men should have jobs as streetcar motormen and conductors. [Black women] should have jobs as telephone operators and stenographers. . . . Black firemen can hold a hose and squirt water on a burning building just as well as white firemen. We want jobs, jobs, after that everything will come unto us."[32]

The Great Depression descended on black Seattle rather slowly. The 1930 census showed more blacks gainfully employed than whites. By the winter of 1932, however, the economic downturn

Table 4
Occupational Categories, 1910–1940

Percentage of Black Work Force in Various Occupational Categories

Category	1910 Men	1910 Women	1920 Men	1920 Women	1930 Men	1930 Women	1940 Men	1940 Women
Agriculture	1.4	–	1.6	0.2	0.4	0.4	–	–
Mineral Extraction	0.3	–	0.4	–	0.3	–	–	–
Manufacturing	13.5	9.5	25.3	6.2	19.5	4.9	18.1	4.5
Transportation	7.9	0.3	15.5	0.5	14.2	–	8.8	0.5
Trade	2.2	1.0	5.6	3.8	5.3	1.4	5.1	3.2
Public Ser.	24.9*	–	3.4	–	3.0	0.2	2.3	–
Professional Ser.	3.3	3.1	3.6	5.4	5.1	6.8	5.1	4.2
Clerical	1.4	2.2	1.9	4.5	1.2	3.3	4.3	3.8
Domestic Ser.	45.1	83.9	42.7	79.4	51.0	83.0	56.3	83.8

Percentage of Asian Work Force in Various Occupational Categories

Category	1910 Men	1910 Women	1920 Men	1920 Women	1930 Men	1930 Women	1940 Men	1940 Women
Agriculture	2.6	–	2.6	1.7	7.4	0.6	–	–
Mineral Extraction	0.1	–	0.1	–	0.2	–	–	–
Manufacturing	21.5	3.2	27.1	13.1	23.2	13.6	19.0	24.3
Transportation	11.9	–	7.8	0.3	6.5	0.1	3.3	0.8
Trade	12.9	2.7	21.3	17.9	20.8	22.2	25.4	13.7
Public Ser.	0.2	–	0.3	–	1.2	–	0.3	–
Professional Ser.	0.4	1.1	3.1	4.4	3.4	3.4	3.8	5.2
Clerical	1.6	1.6	4.0	3.1	3.6	7.9	15.1	26.8
Domestic Ser.	48.6	91.4	33.7	59.5	33.7	52.2	33.1	29.2

Percentage of White Work Force in Various Occupational Categories

Category	1910 Men	1910 Women	1920 Men	1920 Women	1930 Men	1930 Women	1940 Men	1940 Women
Agriculture	2.7	–	2.2	0.2	0.9	0.1	–	–
Mineral Extraction	1.1	–	0.7	–	1.6	–	–	–
Manufacturing	34.1	12.9	39.2	11.7	34.0	9.4	39.5	11.3
Transportation	12.3	4.5	13.1	4.8	12.4	2.9	3.5	0.1
Trade	24.6	12.4	20.1	14.7	23.9	15.2	16.7	6.8
Public Ser.	1.6	–	3.5	–	3.6	0.1	2.6	–
Professional Ser.	5.1	14.8	8.2	18.7	8.1	17.4	8.9	14.6
Clerical	11.1	30.1	8.5	29.6	10.4	30.4	22.4	40.9
Domestic Ser.	7.4	25.3	4.5	20.3	5.1	24.5	6.4	26.3

Sources: U.S. Bureau of the Census, *Thirteenth Census of the U.S.*, 1910, vol. 4, pp. 602–3; *Fourteenth Census of the U.S.*, 1920, vol. 4, *Occupations*, pp. 1232–33; *Fifteenth Census of the US.*, 1930, *Population*, vol. 4, pp. 1709–10; *Sixteenth Census of the U.S.*, 1940, vol. 3, *The Labor Force*, pt. 5, pp. 852–53.

* The large percentage reflects the number of black soldiers stationed at Fort Lawton in 1910.

had devastated the black community. Seattle African Americans relied principally on service occupations such as waiting tables on passenger ships, on trains, and in hotel dining rooms and restaurants. The impact was most dramatic among the largest group of black male workers in the city, those who worked "on the boats." During the winter of 1932 hundreds of black stewards lost their jobs when crew sizes were slashed by one-third. Those who remained saw their wages reduced from forty-five to thirty-six dollars a month. Fewer passengers sailed on the steamships and those remaining travelers reduced or eliminated their tips. The two major steamship companies abandoned their passenger business by the end of the decade. Railroads and local hotels followed suit and reduced their staffs, and private homes released black maids as well. A 1931 report from the newly formed Seattle Urban League to the national office estimated that relief cases for black families had quadrupled in one year, concluding that blacks had "supported themselves as long as they were able, using up their own resources as well as the resources of the relatives."[33]

Census figures for 1940, which show black Seattle with a 24 percent unemployment rate, second only to Milwaukee's 29 percent among major American cities, confirm the tremendous impact on the small community (Table 5). Samson Valley's comment about conditions in black Seattle during the Depression, however, suggests

Table 5
Unemployment Rates in Selected Cities, 1940

	White	Black	Asian
Milwaukee	11.8	29.7	16.1
SEATTLE	10.5	24.3	15.3
Minneapolis	11.6	23.1	12.6
Chicago	10.6	19.3	7.0
New York	15.0	19.1	11.6
Cleveland	12.1	18.4	10.4
Los Angeles	11.6	18.1	6.9
Detroit	10.1	16.9	8.5
San Francisco	10.1	15.5	12.9

Source: U.S. Bureau of the Census, Sixteenth Census of the U.S., 1940, vol. 3, The Labor Force, table 4.

that some African Americans, unlike working-class and middle-class whites, did not perceive a precipitous decline from prosperity in 1929 to poverty after 1930. "I remember one fellow asked me," recalled Valley in an interview four decades later, "'How you boys getting along in this Depression.' I said, 'well . . . we're doing better than we were during what you call prosperity. We've always been poor. Before you people got poor, you didn't know what poor was, so you let us suffer. We been used to it. . . . it's been Depression to us most of the time.'"[34]

Valley's assessment notwithstanding, the Depression took a toll on the already impoverished black community. Seattleite Sara Oliver Jackson remembered that during the early 1930s: "There wasn't any particular jobs you could get, although you knew you had to work. So, you got a domestic job and made $10.00 a month, 'cause that was what they were paying, a big 35 cents a day."[35]

As the local economy faltered, black Seattleites faced intensified competition from other groups. Positions as laborers, hotel waiters, and elevator operators became "white jobs" in a dynamic interplay of race and gender rivalry which pitted men and women against each other as well as blacks against whites. A major hotel dining room in 1931, for example, replaced black waiters with white waitresses. Occasionally Asians replaced both whites and blacks in some occupations, thus prompting greater anxiety among the small black work force.[36]

Many Seattle African Americans were persuaded that their particular economic fortunes turned at least as much on the attitudes and actions of exclusionary labor unions as on the vicissitudes of the national economy. For them, union discrimination seemed ubiquitous in the 1920s and continued unabated into the Depression. African American workers were, to be sure, excluded from hundreds of nonunion commercial enterprises in Seattle which collectively provided employment for 25 percent of the city's 1940 work force. Nonetheless, union exclusion from the shipyards, foundries, and machine shops palpably symbolized the relegation of black workers to Seattle's economic periphery. Such exclusionary practices prevented skilled blacks from applying their training and discouraged younger workers from acquiring comparable preparation for future employment. William Henry Lee, a skilled mechanic from Wenatchee, arrived in Seattle in 1925 only to be told he would not be allowed to join the Mechanics Union. "Why, a black had an awful time getting into a union," Lee recalled. "So I took up working on steamships as a room steward, then I became a pullman porter." When Samson Valley took a job as a meat inspector in 1917, blacks could not join the meat packing union. Valley remembers entering the plant and seeing all the packers drop their tools and proceed to walk off their jobs. He quickly revealed to the protesting workers that he was not a packer but an inspector hired by the federal government through a competitive exam. Satisfied with that explanation, the packers returned to work.[37]

The policies of the Marine Cooks and Stewards Association of the Pacific (MCSAP) suggest the range of devices employed in racial exclusion. Although African Americans had worked as stewards on Seattle-based steamships in the nineteenth century, no company had employed them in that capacity after the organization of the Marine Cooks and Stewards Union in 1901. When the union was founded, it had no official prohibition against black union membership and, according to one student of the period, had "one or two Negroes in the original membership." It was, however, adamantly anti-Asian and its first members declared their determination "to relieve ourselves of the degrading necessity of competition with an alien and inferior race. We have formed a union," they proclaimed, "for the purpose of replacing the Chinese and Japanese now on the [West] Coast by American citizens or those who are eligible for citizenship."[38] In a relatively short period the MCSAP through cooperation with the major shipping companies extended its prohibition to African Americans. Union regulations required blacks be employed by the steamship companies before joining MCSAP, yet the union threatened strikes if black workers were brought on the steamships. The consequence was the "unofficial" prohibition of blacks from the steamships before 1921.

Excluded from most jobs, blacks had little contact with much of the city's white work force, including, obviously, most union members. Such exclusion created a vicious cycle of mutual hostility and recrimination. White workers, claiming blacks were antiunion, adamantly refused to lower color bars, while black workers, and much of the African American community leadership, embraced strikebreaking to forcibly open restricted jobs.

But the entire blame for black occupational stagnation cannot be attributed to organized labor. Other forces, including poor education, the tendency of blacks to seek familiar kinds of employment, and their own deeply held antiunion views, made many African American workers "steer clear" of labor unions.

Ultimately employers must accept much of the responsibility, because their views on the necessity of controlling workers led them to manipulate racial, ethnic, and gender tensions for their benefit. In a regional practice dating back to the 1870s, employers readily eliminated employees who had union sentiments. The capricious replacement of white men with black men, or black men with white women, or all three groups with Asian workers during economic recessions or labor strikes suggests that racial and gender prejudices of employers could easily be jettisoned during labor-management confrontations.

Middle-class black leaders often assisted this process and through the 1920s used their considerable influence among working-class blacks to encourage antiunion sentiments and strikebreaking. With the encouragement of middle-class leaders such as Horace Cayton, Sr., for example, black workers became strikebreakers in the longshore strike in 1916 and the ship stewards' strike in 1921, generating employment at the expense of the bitter recriminations and intensified animosity such action provoked among white unionists.

Various reasons informed the sentiments and actions of black middle-class leaders. Some, such as labor recruiter James Roston, were not philosophically opposed to the open shop but simply exploited labor-management conflicts for personal interests or because they believed such opportunities were the best African American workers could expect as long as unions prohibited black membership. Other black leaders, such as Horace Cayton, Sr., identified with wealthy manufacturers or businessmen through political ties. Or occasionally the connection was through personal employment, as was true of John T. Gayton. These leaders were persuaded that the open shop was in the best interest of all workers, particularly African Americans. The antilabor views of the local black elite were buttressed by similar beliefs held by national black leaders, such as Tuskegee Institute founder Booker T. Washington and his successor Robert R. Moton, and the ambivalence of W. E. B. Du Bois and other progressive black leaders toward organized labor in this period.

But it would be naive to think that the strikebreaking actions of black workers stemmed solely from the advice of the black elite. Many working-class black Seattleites could relate experiences of indignities suffered at the hands of white unionists similar to those of Lee or Valley, to persuade their friends, relatives, and neighbors to oppose organized labor. Horace Cayton, Jr., who would, by the late 1930s, become one of the most prominent black intellectuals to embrace the emerging Congress of Industrial Organizations (CIO) unions, nevertheless expressed the sentiment of many pre-Depression black workers when he declared, "Negroes in Seattle had as much use for organized labor as organized labor had for them."[39]

Workers like Richard Jenkins and Sandy Moss who saw the futility of racial division in the ranks of labor nonetheless recognized their vulnerability as a tiny minority of workers fighting to gain entry into closed occupations. Moss, Jenkins, and other black workers resigned themselves to strikebreaking and the racial antipathy it generated even if it rendered more elusive the goal of interracial worker solidarity. Moss's response to labor union restrictions indicated the limited options available to black workers who supported, in principle, the goals of organized labor. Repeatedly denied union membership by the Carpenters and Electricians locals in the 1915–25 period, Moss nevertheless became a life member of the Amalgamated Transit Union Local 587, the streetcar operators and repairmen's union. Despite his affiliation he argued that minority groups benefited from strikebreaking because "usually when [a strike] was settled the contract [admitted] Negroes or minority groups to work on those jobs where they had never worked before."[40]

Just as Seattle African Americans were split between pro- and antiunion factions, organized labor was itself divided over black union membership. Thus black workers were likely to shift their views on the subject in response to labor's entreaties. James Roston, for example, known in labor circles as a notorious strikebreaker, nevertheless led a committee of black workers to the Seattle Central Labor Council in February 1919 to request that the color bar be removed from all unions affiliated with the SCLC. To his surprise, his proposal won endorsement. The *Seattle Union Record*, the voice of the Council, provided a synopsis of its decision when it reported that "by a practically unanimous vote [the Council] went on record as unqualifiedly for the equal rights of negroes with white men in organized labor." The implementation of the incorporation of black labor was "left to a committee . . . to be appointed later." But that committee could not overcome the hostility of the various locals affiliated with the Central Labor Council, and the exclusion policies remained intact.[41]

The Depression provided the first major opportunity for improving relations between progressive labor leaders and their counterparts among black workers both on the national level and in Seattle. The transition in Seattle dated back to the beginning of the century. By 1900 some locals, such as the Amalgamated Transit Union, Building

Laborer's Union, and Musicians Local 73, had broken ranks with the majority of locals and allowed black membership, creating a small but active core of prounion sentiment among Seattle's African Americans. The influence of the United Mine Workers (UMW) in nearby Newcastle and Franklin similarly played a role in the evolving black support for organized labor. Although black men entered the Cascade foothill coal mines as strikebreakers in 1891, by 1904 the UMW had successfully established an integrated local, District 10. Members who moved to Seattle brought with them strong prolabor views. Nor can the influence of the Industrial Workers of the World (IWW), particularly active in the Pacific Northwest in the first two decades of the twentieth century, be discounted. Although the IWW never dominated the labor movement, "Wobblies" offered a vision of a working class united across racial lines. The single largest demonstration of union integration came, however, in 1917 in the wake of the unsuccessful longshore strike, when the International Longshoremen's Association, recognizing the ability of the Waterfront Employers Association to exploit racial divisions among dockworkers, accepted black former strikebreakers into its ranks.[42]

By the early 1930s forces within and beyond Seattle were influencing the growth of interracial unionism. Calls for working-class unity emanated from the Communist Party, whose members used their positions within unions to promote integration. Similarly, the unions associated with the Council (later Congress) of Industrial Organizations (CIO) publicly espoused racially inclusive policies in sharp contrast to the older, more conservative craft unions affiliated with the American Federation of Labor. Australian-born Harry Bridges, who assumed leadership of the West Coast ILA locals, and who eventually led them out of the ILA to form the International Longshoremen's and Warehousemen's Union (ILWU) in 1937, was unequivocally supportive of integrated unions. Bridges's commitment to an egalitarian union was legendary. When confronted by a white longshore worker who wanted to know what was to be done about the "excessive number" of blacks on the San Francisco docks, he responded that if work ever slowed to the point that only two longshoremen were left with work, one should be black.[43]

The Maritime Strike of 1934, however, proved the major local catalyst for the most significant challenge of segregated locals during the interwar years. Encouraged by the National Industrial Recovery Act of 1933, which prohibited employers from interfering with employees' right to "organize and bargain collectively," various West Coast maritime labor unions seized this opportunity to organize the entire waterfront. The eighty-three day strike affected 1,500 longshoremen in Seattle alone, and eventually included nearly 2,000 sailors, deckhands, telegraphers, teamsters, cooks, and stewards, closing the entire Seattle waterfront for the first time in fifteen years. Black stewards, long considered adamantly antiunion, now walked picket lines and staffed temporary kitchens for white teamsters, sailors, and other fellow strikers.[44]

The younger black stewards in the Colored Marine Employees Benevolent Association, in particular, called for concerted action with other striking workers. Still angry over the reduction in pay two years earlier as well as the deteriorating working conditions, they saw the work stoppage, according to one of their spokesmen, as their opportunity "to get some of our work cut down as well as get more money."[45] Yet the evidence also suggests a growing class consciousness. CMEBA leaders including Fred Sexias in Seattle and Revels Cayton, the younger son of Horace Cayton, Sr., who now headed the San Francisco association office, urged their fellow workers to reject the antiunion stance of the older leadership and in 1933 openly called for cooperation with the MCSAP.

The Marine Cooks moderated their antiblack posture as well. E. F. Burke led a faction of the MCSAP which urged acceptance of the black stewards as union members. Burke and other union members were impressed by the solidarity of black and white striking longshoremen despite blatant attempts by the Waterfront Employers Association to use nonunion black dockworkers to break the strike and foment interracial animosity. MCSAP members watched approvingly as striking longshoremen now argued that those who "scabbed" should be encouraged to become union members rather than attacked for strikebreaking. Remembering the animosity generated by the 1916 strike and its aftermath, union dockworkers admitted that the ILA "had made mistakes in the past, but the union was going to try to correct those mistakes." Such calls for cooperation among previously bitter antagonists encouraged black and white stewards to reassess their own mutually exclusive organizations.

The Maritime Strike of 1934 created an all-union waterfront and ended the separation of MCSAP and CMEBA. Approximately three hundred CMEBA members joined the Marine Cooks and Stewards Association, with former CMEBA officials Fred Sexias and Revels Cayton becoming officers in the enlarged local. White and black workers who refused to affiliate with the new interracial union left the waterfront. After thirteen years of competition and infighting, the two labor groups formed a single union.[46]

The integration of the Marine Cooks and Stewards Association of the Pacific was a significant breakthrough for both black workers and organized labor, but it did not prefigure the general abolition of black exclusion policies by organized labor. As African American workers bitterly learned, other Seattle unions proved far less receptive to interracial working-class solidarity. The Sailors' Union of the Pacific, (SUP) for example, which also participated in the Maritime Strike of 1934, continued its policy of racial exclusion of Asians and blacks. The union had long opposed African Americans working as sailors and deckhands on Pacific Northwest vessels, but since shipowners did not recognize the SUP, black or Asian sailors occasionally were hired on ships operating from Seattle and other Northwest ports. The waterfront strike of 1934, however, allowed the SUP exclusive hiring through the Sailors' and Marine Firemen's Hall. After 1934, blacks and Asians were barred from entering the hall and thus prohibited from working as sailors.[47]

Away from the waterfront, racially exclusive unions continued to prevail. The opposition of the International Association of Machinists, for example, prevented blacks from working at Boeing. The building trades unions extended membership to fewer than a dozen black carpenters, plasterers, and painters and discriminated against them in the allocation of jobs. The powerful Teamsters Union, run by Dave Beck, had only four blacks in 1940 in a membership of eleven thousand. These three unions controlled nearly half the skilled and semiskilled jobs in the city and completely or virtually closed membership to blacks until the post–World War II period.[48]

With the exception of the Building Service Employees Union, which included porters, janitors, watchmen, and elevator operators; and the Cannery Workers Union, dominated by Filipinos, pre–World War II Seattle unions either overtly or covertly barred blacks from the "house of labor." By 1940 the nearly 75,000 union men in the city out of a male work force of 104,000 made Seattle one of the most unionized cities in the nation, "labor's mightiest fortress." Yet fewer than 400 of Seattle's 1,200 black workers were in the ranks of organized labor, and the vast majority were in the ILA and the Marine Cooks and Stewards Association.[49]

Seattle's black community in 1940 could point to few successes in its campaign to increase the range of its employment opportunities or to enter the labor movement. Community leaders simply could not persuade the city's most powerful unions to end exclusion. As urban historian Joe Trotter reminds us, this was not prompted simply by "irrational" racism but was based on the widely held belief that union and nonunion workers were in competition for better-paying jobs, scarce housing resources, and political influence.[50] Therefore, despite strident, sincere calls by IWW members, the Communists, and dissident labor leaders for working-class organizations that would ignore gender, race, and ethnicity, white union workers used exclusion practices to protect their "rights" to employment. Such practices, particularly when viewed in tandem with widespread residential and social segregation, seemed all the more appropriate.

The relationship between Seattle labor unions and black workers represented a paradox which lasted through the 1970s. (The campaigns to integrate the Aero Mechanics Union at Boeing in the early 1940s, and the building trades unions in the early 1970s, for example, recalled many of the same arguments concerning blacks and organized labor in Seattle in the 1920s.) Moreover, as Brotherhood of Sleeping Car Porters Vice-President Milton P. Webster declared, the progress of black workers affected the entire community. Their success determined the overall health, education, and well-being of black Seattle. Ironically, Seattle labor unions accounted, in no small measure, for the city's politically progressive image and its extensive social welfare programs which generated tangible benefits to its black citizens. Yet the general opposition of many of those unions to black membership foiled numerous attempts by African Americans to enter skilled occupations or establish a foothold in significant segments of the city's economy, prolonging their poverty as well as their antiunion stance and making them susceptible to strikebreaking and other antilabor activity.

The vast majority of black Seattleites between 1900 and 1940 were working-class people, but a small middle class of professionals and business owners (about 15 percent of the 1940 population) emerged to provide a variety of services to the community. This tradition of black entrepreneurial service was decades old by the 1920s. Many nineteenth-century Seattle blacks had been barbers, restaurateurs, boarding house owners, and shopkeepers, serving a predominately white male clientele. But as frontier town was replaced by rising metropolis, black businesses became increasingly bound to the evolving African American community, operating both literally and figuratively on the periphery of the city's economy. Consequently nineteenth-century notions of serving "all people," which typically meant a mainly white clientele, gave way to twentieth-century realities, which entailed serving black customers.

Spurred by racial pride and economic self-interest, black business-women and men extolled the virtues of an independent economy where African Americans could sell and service, if not produce, all they needed. Visions of a self-sufficient black metropolis emanated from local followers of Marcus Garvey and other economic nationalists, but the noticeable symbol of such self-sufficiency was Seattle's Nihonmachi (Japanese community) rather than distant black Chicago or Harlem. Black Seattleites were urged to support their businesses and, like the Japanese, build a proud community. Yet the small African American population, and ironically the success of Nihonmachi enterprises, doomed the development of an extensive black business community.

Seattle's early twentieth-century black businesses were a diverse, eclectic lot. Most were predictably barbershops, beauty parlors, pool halls, and grocery stores. But occasionally local entrepreneurs entered uncharted ground. Black Seattle in the interwar years could count among its enterprises the Anzier (later renamed Gala) Movie Theater, the 62-room Golden West Hotel, which touted itself as the finest "colored" hostel west of Chicago, and the Lincoln Discount Corporation, a local finance company which in 1931 was successful enough to absorb a white firm, the Central Washington Finance Holding Corporation of Wenatchee, Washington. Georgia N. Kelles, an Illinois native, arrived in Seattle in 1927 and soon established the Angelus Funeral Home, one of the city's most enduring businesses. Attucks Realty, owned by local dentist Dr. Felix B. Cooper, the North American Produce Company which sold fruits and vegetables, and the most ambitious enterprise in the community, N. J. Graffell's Liberian–West African Transportation and Trading Company founded in 1927, all suggest the range of black business possibilities.

The *Northwest Enterprise*, a newspaper founded in 1920 by William H. Wilson, was the most widely known Seattle black business, and arguably the most successful. Capitalizing on the isolation of small African American communities throughout the Pacific Northwest, Wilson expanded the *Enterprise* beyond black Seattle to a regional market, shrewdly utilizing a network of "correspondents" in outlying areas who reported local social affairs. The *Enterprise* had correspondents in such diverse cities as Billings, Montana, Pocatello,

Idaho, and Eugene, Oregon, and generated a regional circulation that by March 1927 reached 25,000.[51]

Wilson often chastised those contemporary business people who limited their clientele to African Americans. In a July 1927 editorial, the *Enterprise* declared, "Don't say you are a Negro merchant, don't run a Negro business. Be a merchant and run a business for the public – for all the people. We know of two black men who started a drug store with limited capital. Most of [their patronage] comes from people of other racial extractions. They are on the high road to riches because they had a vision that extends beyond color and race." In a 1928 editorial, he challenged blacks to risk competition in the general community: "Too many of us are obsessed with the idea that we must do business in the 'colored' section. Lack of capital might stop Negroes from opening a big bank or department store, but nothing but cowardice keeps him [*sic*] from going into smaller business in open competition with other racial groups downtown."[52]

But by the early 1930s, Wilson was more sympathetic to the "race business" concept. In November 1933 the *Enterprise* gave extensive coverage to a presentation by Urban League Executive Secretary Joseph S. Jackson titled "Black Money in a White City," in which he reported that local blacks spent $2 million in Seattle annually, most of which left their community because of the absence of black business. Reverend H. B. Ganntt, of the First AME Church, sounding a theme which would be increasingly supported by middle-class blacks the remainder of the decade, declared, "Negroes should support and patronize their professionals and businessmen, even at some sacrifice."[53]

Black Seattle, however, was not Chicago's South Side or New York's Harlem. Despite some modest successes, including notably the *Northwest Enterprise*, which was a regional rather than local business, Seattle's black firms could not exclusively rely on a community too small, too impoverished, too transient to provide much support. Moreover, Seattle's black businesses competed with white and Asian stores for the elusive African American customer in this tiny community. If white restaurants, hotels, and movie theaters shunned black patronage, there is little evidence that clothing stores, service stations, grocery stores, or other establishments rejected black dollars. And those blacks who believed their patronage was not welcomed by white establishments were eagerly courted by Asian entrepreneurs. Japanese grocers provided food and hotel owners offered rooms at affordable prices. Southside Japanese and Chinese restaurants welcomed working-class black customers when other establishments turned them away, and one café near the railroad depot developed a specialized menu of "soul food" to entice porters and ship stewards.[54]

Nowhere was the contrast between black Seattle and Japanese Seattle more apparent than in their business communities (see Table 6). Although Japanese Seattle in 1930 had a population of 8,400 compared with 3,300 in black Seattle, the 1930 census listed 402 Asian male (primarily Japanese) retail store owners in Seattle as opposed to 15 blacks, 150 male Asian hotel owners and managers (36 percent of the citywide total) compared with one African American, and 73 male Asian restaurant owners and only 6 black male owners.[55]

Occasionally Asian and black neighborhood stores vied directly for the support of black community residents in a contest that pitted ethnic loyalty against perceptions of superior service. Margaret Cogwell remembered that the Asian grocery store across the street from her own had far more black customers during World War I. Cogwell bitterly remarked, "The Negroes were always coming to the Japanese right across from me, and they'd go there and buy the same milk and bread . . . from the Japanese. Mine wasn't good enough even though it was delivered the same time and everything."[56] Eventually the Cogwell grocery closed and the family left Seattle in 1919. Cogwell's Japanese competitor had access to a regional distribution network that included Japanese wholesalers, other Japanese grocers, and neighboring Japanese farmers. Nonetheless, her loss was painful, particularly when it appeared that race "disloyalty" was partly responsible for the store's demise.

The palpable failure of African American businessmen and women as compared with their Japanese counterparts in Seattle is often explained solely by focusing on the initiative and frugality of the Japanese. While such attributes are undoubtedly critical in entrepreneurial success, it may be profitable to recall the particular difficulty African Americans had in developing their business expertise. Black Seattle's firms did not develop a rotating credit system to provide venture capital as did the Japanese, nor could such businessmen and women rely on a "captive market" generated by a large, residentially segregated African American population. And unlike the Japanese, blacks had long been immersed in American culture and thus had far fewer food or clothing requirements that necessitated specialized restaurants or stores.[57]

Despite often self-serving exhortations to "support the race" from

Table 6
Selected Occupational Statistics For Blacks and Asians in Seattle, 1930

Occupation	Blacks	Asians
Trade	*Males*	
Retail dealers	15	402
Salesmen	13	285
Hotel managers	1	150
Restaurant owners	6	73
Barbers	30	52
Clerks (except in stores)	11	99
Professions		
Lawyers	2	2
Musicians/Teachers of music	32	8
Physicians/Surgeons	2	9
Total male work force	1,405	4,875
Trade	*Females*	
Retail dealers	2	19
Saleswomen	0	82
Clerks in stores	3	27
Hairdressers	13	38
Waitresses	19	47
Hotel managers	1	19
Boardinghouse keepers	14	19
Professions		
Musicians/Teachers of music	10	3
Trained nurses	4	1
School teachers	1	11
Total female work force	487	685

Source: U.S. Bureau of the Census, *Fifteenth Census of the U.S.*, 1930, *Occupational Statistics, Population*, vol. 4, pp. 1709–10.

groups such as the Seattle Negro Business League and the Seattle Association of Professional Men, black Seattle never developed a major commercial community. Mindful of that fact, the *Enterprise* and community leaders by the mid-1930s shifted their emphasis from patronage of race enterprises to concentration on selective buying campaigns to force the hiring of more African American salespersons. Inspired by the success of "Jobs for Negroes" campaigns in New York, Chicago, and Los Angeles, the *Enterprise* laid the foundation for a local effort with editorials explaining the problem in Seattle. In July 1936 the paper revealed that Seattle blacks spent $500,000 a year on groceries while no black person was employed in a grocery store or supermarket in the city. "Any group of citizens," the *Enterprise* declared, "is entitled to a fair proportion of the jobs it creates by its buying power." A January 1938 editorial reported that Seattle's 1,323 black families spent $2,068,784 in 1937, equal to the expenditure of the city of Ellensburg. While carefully avoiding use of the word "boycott," the *Enterprise* urged Seattle's "consuming Negro population" to make their spendings "pay in jobs returned to the community." One week later in the strongest language yet employed it called on blacks: "Ascertain the policy of firms with whom you trade. Protest the policy of barring Negroes from the payroll. . . . Walk a block farther and spend with a CORRECT FIRM" (emphasis in the original).[58]

In December 1938 the *Enterprise* launched a drive for reciprocal purchasing where blacks would buy only from businesses that employed African Americans. One month later the paper claimed its first victory when McKales, Inc., a service station chain, agreed to hire Bruce Rowell as its first black employee. Rowell was scheduled to work at the Central District station at 17th and Madison. After the victory, a Job Campaign Committee was organized to provide permanent coordination of the selective buying campaign. The committee scored it first success in October 1939 when the management of Eba's, a regional department store chain with a store on 23rd Avenue, agreed to hire its first black salesperson.[59] While symbolically important, such victories were too scattered and infrequent to materially affect the economy of the black community. Thus in 1940, community leaders shifted their focus once again. This time the campaign was to integrate the Boeing work force. The opening of Boeing to African American workers, black activists presumed, would generate far greater long-term community benefits than the sporadic placement of African American workers in boycott-targeted commercial establishments.

Seattle's black businesses generated a fledgling African American bourgeoisie who, as self-professed guardians of the community's economic and cultural interests, advocated a concentrated campaign to develop the Central Area through self-help and racial solidarity, which they defined as support for "race business." The outline of this new entrepreneurial class could be seen in advertisements in newspapers such as *Cayton's Weekly*, the *Northwest Enterprise*, and the short-lived magazine, the *Progressive Westerner*, edited by Eleane

Dickson. The magazine was itself a product of the new assertiveness, as evidenced by its descriptive subtitle, "The Only Negro Magazine of the West."[60]

Representatives of this new middle class included apartment house owner Zacharias I. Woodson; William Chandler, founder of the Chandler Fuel Company; Russell Smith, owner of the Golden West Hotel; E. I. Robinson, a drug store owner; Harry Legg, a grocer and, prior to World War II, the only black member of the Seattle Chamber of Commerce; and N. J. Graffell, who owned a succession of businesses including the Liberian–West African Transportation and Trading Company. Georgia Kelles, owner of the Angelus Funeral Home, was one of the few successful businesswomen. Clarence B. Anderson, an attorney and real estate developer, and William H. Wilson, editor of the *Northwest Enterprise*, were the group's major spokesmen.[61]

In a community where the majority of people were unskilled laborers or domestic servants, this small middle class wielded disproportionate influence. It dominated the fraternal lodges, civil rights organizations, social service centers such as the Phyllis Wheatley YWCA, the Sojourner Truth Home, and most churches. The middle class controlled the local Republican organization and – until the 1930s – black politics in general. Black community views enunciated during this period to white Seattle almost always came from this socioeconomic group.

Despite the efforts of this bourgeoisie to promote greater community prosperity, black Seattle remained poor and marginal to the urban economy. Although black Seattle's employment difficulties and its underdeveloped economy appeared to many observers as separate problems, they stemmed from a common source, the exclusion of African Americans from the vital center of the local economy. The words of the first Urban League Annual Report in 1930 summarized the issue when it declared: "To the extent that the Negro is allowed to go forward in the industrial economy of our city . . . his home and family life will raise its level, his health will improve, his education will increase, delinquency will lessen, and he will find himself more and more in the heart of the civic life of our community."[62] After seven decades in Seattle the African American was still prevented from going "forward in the industrial economy of [the] city." And "his home and family life, his health and his education" were compromised accordingly. Cognizant of this bitter reality, Seattle's African American community threw a disproportionate amount of its meager resources into a valiant campaign for human dignity. If economic exclusion was at the heart of the black community's dilemma, and progress in this area appeared virtually impossible, then politics and civil rights would provide a way out.

Chapter 3

Housing,
Civil Rights,
and
Politics,
1900–1940

On a 1913 tour of western states, W. E. B. Du Bois, a founding member of the NAACP and editor of its publication, the *Crisis*, was enthralled with the beauty and civility of the Pacific Northwest. A sharp critic of the racial order and defender of black rights, he nevertheless wrote a paean to the region. "Here the fight against race prejudice has been persistent and triumphant. . . . Washington has over 6,000 Negroes and 2,500 live in Seattle. . . . Why [should] . . . 3,000 [people] in Seattle mean so much more to themselves and the world than 100,000 of the same people in parts of Alabama or Georgia. The answer is clear to the thoughtful. The colored folk . . . are educated; not college bred, but out of the shackles of dense ignorance; they have push, for their very coming so far westward proves it; and, above all, they are a part of the greater group and they know it. . . .Yet they have not forgotten their people. They want them to come and find freedom as they have."[1]

His view was shared by many of the nearly two thousand African American women and men who migrated to Seattle in the first decade of the twentieth century seeking economic opportunity and political freedom. They found a city freer than their former homes but nonetheless succumbing to a national upsurge in segregationist and discriminatory practices that began in the post-Reconstruction

South and reached its zenith in the urban North immediately after World War I. While Du Bois may have declared Seattle free of racial prejudice, its ugly specter loomed ominously over new arrivals and natives alike.

Segregation and discrimination were readily evident in the Pacific Northwest from 1900 through 1940 and indeed seemed to maintain an alarming consistency through periods of prosperity and depression. Examples abound. The city's major motion picture theaters such as the Strand and Palomar forced blacks into segregated balconies. Downtown department stores, such as MacDougall and Southwick, discouraged African American patronage. White (and occasionally Asian) restaurants and lunch counters turned away African American customers. George Schuyler, who later gained fame as a conservative black newspaper columnist for the *Pittsburgh Courier*, remembers the local manifestations of racism during his years as a soldier at Fort Lawton in World War I. He recalled that nightclub owners and employees charged black patrons excessively high prices for drinks or deliberately smashed their glasses after they were used. Even the prestigious Seattle Tennis Club in 1934 barred local tennis star Emmett McIver declaring the club to be "a social organization [that] does not admit colored persons."[2]

If black Seattle was spared the brutal face of the lynch mob or angry white rioters who burned African American homes with the slightest provocation, they were nevertheless subject throughout the first four decades of the twentieth century to what one local observer recalled as the "little nasties" — behavior and actions serving to remind African Americans of their inferiority in an overwhelmingly white city. In 1930 the Seattle NAACP filed a protest against a brand of peanuts marketed by a local firm, French Products, Inc., called "Three Lil' Niggers." The label showed three black children standing in a peanut shell. In the north end of Seattle along Bothell Way, a white family operated the Coon Chicken Inn, with an entryway dominated by a huge black face with pearly teeth. When in public school in the 1920s, Maxine Haynes remembers being called "nigger," "chocolate drop," and "coon." Her principal demanded that Haynes "be a lady" and not respond to such taunts. For the most part she complied but when the epithets escalated and she retaliated, the principal reprimanded her for breaking her "promise" rather than condemning the actions of the students who called her derogatory names. Years later Haynes painfully recalled that nothing was done to "make the other students understand that I was a human being and to do something about their behavior. I did not understand it at the time. I only knew that I was breaking my promise."[3]

Marguerite Johnson recalled a similar incident in a Seattle public school in the 1920s: "I had a school teacher named Miss Poucher, and how I hated that woman! . . . I had long hair, down to my shoulders then. My mother made braids. . . . I was running [at recess] and as I run past her she grabbed my hair, and said, 'Come back, little nigger.' . . . She admitted that the name 'nigger' had slipped out . . . .When I graduated from grade school, Miss Poucher had nerve enough to give me a gift and her picture! And I *still* hated that woman."[4]

When racial prejudice was coupled with sexual fears, the resultant actions often defied logic. In 1939, Irene Burns Miller, a Seattle social worker assigned to supervise the relocation of tenants from Yesler Hill rooming houses to make way for Yesler Terrace, the city's first federally funded public housing project, received two visitors she described as "society matrons" in her office to express their concern about the planned racial integration of the project. Although the women did not reside on Yesler Hill, they described their fear that incidents of rape would increase with the influx of black men into the area. In the midst of their discussion a mentally deranged derelict who frequented Miller's office in the Yesler Hill neighborhood interrupted the meeting with shouts, curses, and epithets directed at the women. As they regained their composure, they cited his intrusion as incontrovertible proof of the deficient character of black men. When told by Miller that the derelict was white, they refused to believe it and declared their intention to fight the project at the highest levels of city government.[5] Obviously their protests at that point could not have stopped the completion of the federal housing project, nor did it typify the response of all whites to African Americans in the city, but the episode reflected the extent to which racial fear could combine with the fear of crime to generate a deep, bitter, and at times irrational prejudice among some whites against African Americans.

More telling, however, was the uncertainty of racial etiquette in the city. Pre-1940 Seattle businesses seldom displayed "Whites Only" signs, but numerous observers recall incidents of particular establishments accepting their patronage if they were with white friends but refusing service when they appeared alone or with other African Americans.[6]

Black Seattleites responded in myriad ways to this treatment. Often they acquiesced, in the futile hope that the upsurge in hostility would give way to begrudging acceptance. As sociologist Robert

Colbert explained, "The lack of aggressiveness of the [Seattle] Negro was accepted as a fair price for the liberal civil rights." Thus some Seattle African Americans chose silence on certain civil rights issues, such as their access to public accommodations or their right to reside in any section of the city, in the hopes that others, such as voting rights, would be maintained.[7]

Other African Americans challenged the new racial order through organizations as diverse as the Universal Negro Improvement Association, the National Association for the Advancement of Colored People, and the Communist Party. Or, like Horace Cayton, Jr., who in 1924 staged a lone sit-in at the segregated Strand Movie Theater, they found individual ways of protesting.[8]

Housing segregation emerged after 1900 as the most comprehensive manifestation of this new racial order, affecting even the most wealthy Seattle blacks. As early as 1905 white homeowners attempted unsuccessfully to prevent attorney J. Edward Hawkins from moving into a home on Capitol Hill, the most prestigious neighborhood in the city. In April 1909 a white realtor went to court, charging that the Horace Cayton family, who had purchased their house on Capitol Hill in 1903, had caused real estate values to depreciate and asked that they be removed. The Caytons won their case. Yet five months later, declining family fortunes forced them to move. Other challenged black families were not as fortunate as the Caytons and Hawkinses. Later in 1909 a suit by the Hunter Tract Company, which developed the Mount Baker neighborhood, prevented a black family from moving into a home it had purchased in the area.[9]

Until 1900, African Americans were scattered through every section of Seattle, and their presence rarely sparked any alarm among their neighbors. But the housing market became racially segregated as the vast majority of Seattle's African Americans, including the 1,900 newcomers who swelled the black population between 1900 and 1910, concentrated in two neighborhoods, the Yesler-Jackson area near the waterfront and the East Madison neighborhood. These two communities slowly grew toward each other during the next three decades, creating a reversed L-shaped section stretching from the East Madison neighborhood south along 23rd Avenue, then turning sharply west in a corridor paralleling Yesler and Jackson Streets toward the waterfront. This enlarged section of east-central Seattle, from the edge of downtown east almost to Lake Washington, would, by World War II, be called the Central Area, or the Central

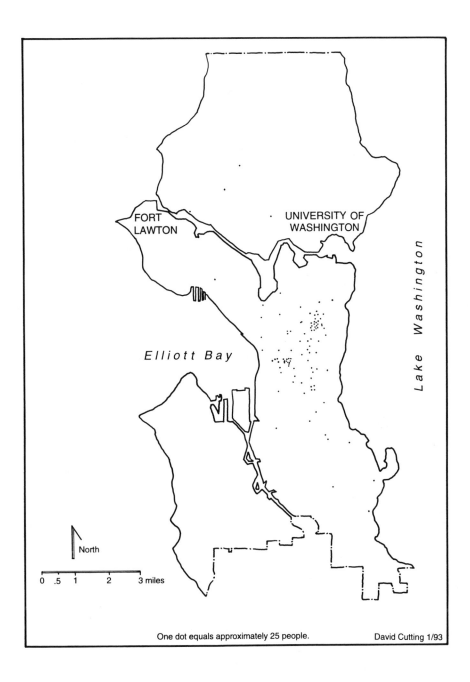

FORT
LAWTON

UNIVERSITY OF
WASHINGTON

Lake Washington

Elliott Bay

North

0   .5   1   2   3 miles

One dot equals approximately 25 people.

David Cutting 1/93

Map 3. Spatial concentration of Seattle's black population, 1920

District. White apartment owners refused to rent to African Americans outside the area, and restrictive covenants prevented blacks (as well as Asians and Jews) from becoming homeowners beyond this section. Typical of these covenants was the 1938 deed to a property on 23rd Avenue. It read:

This deed is given pursuant to the provisions of a contract dated June 1, 1938. . . . The purchaser must be of the white or Caucasian race and . . . the property is not to be sold, encumbered, conveyed, leased or rented to any person who is not of the white or Caucasian race. In the event of the violation of this covenant the title to the property shall revert to the [name deleted] Estate. This is also binding on the heirs, administration, successors and assigns of the purchaser.[10]

Elva Moore Nicholas recalled the difficulty blacks encountered in obtaining adequate housing in 1938: "We walked our heels off looking for 'For Rent' or 'For Sale' signs. You couldn't buy out of the central district. . . . An old lady . . . showed me a place where the paper was peeling off the wall. . . . It was old and dirty. . . . I said, 'This is not fit for a dog to live in.' She says . . . 'its good enough for niggers.' I said, 'Well, you keep it, it's yours.' We had no protection, and they could say anything they wanted to say, and you just had to take it or else."[11]

The case of Helen Walker, as described by Irene Burns Miller in her book *Profanity Hill*, was probably typical of the hundreds of small tragedies caused by housing segregation. The Walker family — husband, wife, and three small girls — had arrived in 1939 from Atlanta. Mr. Walker, an engineer, hoped to work at Boeing.[12] He was killed in an automobile accident and the family, bereft of funds, was forced to move to slum housing on Yesler Hill. In December 1940, Mrs. Walker and her three children were evicted from their apartment which was slated to be demolished to make way for Yesler Terrace. Walker attempted to find housing near the University of Washington, where she was pursuing an advanced degree in education. Miller and the Walker family set out to find an apartment three days before Christmas. Two apartment owners who had assured Miller on the phone of the availability of their units, nevertheless declared their buildings full when Miller and the Walker family arrived. When Miller asked one landlord if the refusal was based on color, he responded, "We have a real estate code (which prohibited rentals to non-whites), looks to me like you are trying to make trouble." Miller and the

Walker family proceeded to the next apartment where they were met by an Italian American who, when confronted with the Walker family, said to Miller, "You looka for place for yourself?" When she replied for the family, he said, "No renta niggers." Finally, a third landlord who was just mounting a vacancy sign said, "I've a hunch you'd make an excellent tenant, Mrs. Walker, but I've never rented to minorities and I'm afraid the neighbors might object." As they were about to drive off, the landlord came down the steps and said, "I'm going to follow my conscience. . . . After all, its Christmas." The Walker family moved into their new apartment the following day.[13]

Unfortunately, few Seattle landlords, homeowners, or realtors followed their consciences on housing discrimination. Residential segregation, enforced by restrictive covenants, had become so commonplace in Seattle by the late 1930s that a debate between city councilmen Hugh Delacy and Samuel Hume over the propriety of racially restrictive covenants in a new housing project prompted Hume to declare, "Oh, they don't hurt anybody. They only exclude Negroes and Orientals. They don't affect Jews at all."[14]

Pre-1940 Seattle black residents still debate the extent and intensity of residential segregation, with some emphatically arguing that determined African Americans, with white support, could move

Table 7
Black Homeownership Rates in Selected Cities, 1910–1940

| | Percentage | | |
	1910	1930	1940
Los Angeles	36.1	33.6	29.7
SEATTLE	27.0	38.8	29.2
Minneapolis	18.6	25.7	25.2
Detroit	17.2	15.0	17.1
Cleveland	10.9	8.3	10.5
San Francisco	16.3	13.6	9.2
Chicago	6.4	10.5	7.4
Milwaukee	5.1	5.5	5.6
New York	2.4	5.6	4.1

Sources: U.S. Bureau of the Census, *Fifteenth Census of the U.S.*, 1930, *Population*, vol. 2, *Families*, p. 156 and passim; *Sixteenth Census of the U.S.*, 1940, *Housing*, vol. 2, *General Characteristics*, pt. 2, p. 214 and passim. Figures for 1920 were unavailable.

anywhere in the city. But a clear pattern affecting the vast majority of blacks – those without white sponsors – had emerged by World War I. African Americans who had prior residence in some outlying areas might not be challenged but as housing developments became available, restrictive covenants rose with them to keep out "undesirables."

Residential segregation did not, however, transform the Central District into a teeming racial ghetto. Few all-black residential blocks and no exclusively African American neighborhoods existed in the area before 1940. Jackson Street, the city's oldest African American residential area, included a heterogeneous population that as late as 1935 was 68 percent Asian, 24 percent black, and 8 percent white. While many whites left the Central District as the minority population increased, a significant number remained for reasons that included the area's proximity to downtown and Lake Washington. The slow black population growth, averaging fewer than 500 new residents per decade between 1910 and 1940, allowed the city to escape the racial violence that frequently accompanied African American community expansion in other cities.[15]

African American homeownership rates in Seattle were relatively high compared with eastern cities. "Practically everyone owned their homes," recalled Edward Pitter. "They wasn't making no money but they owned homes and they were taking ten to fifteen years paying $15 per month." If Pitter's statement exaggerates the level of homeownership, it is nonetheless true that inexpensive land, lumber, and labor allowed a comparatively large number of Seattle blacks to acquire residences despite meager incomes and limited employment opportunities. In 1910, 27 percent of the city's blacks owned homes, and by 1930 it was nearly 39 percent (see Table 7). Although one-fourth of Seattle's blacks lost their homes during the Depression, a rate far in excess of most other black communities, African Americans still owned 29 percent of the housing they occupied in 1940, one of the highest rates in the urban North.[16]

Central District renters also fared well. Rents in the area were slightly below the city median, and rental housing units, with the exception of the Yesler-Jackson area, were slightly larger and in comparable condition to the average Seattle apartment. Before 1940 the quality and quantity of Central District housing was far superior to that of the larger black communities in the Northeast and Midwest.[17]

Discriminatory housing patterns upheld by restrictive covenants forced virtually all Asians, Indians, and about 65 percent of the Central

District's blacks to reside on the Southside (also known as lower Jackson Street), a quadrant south of downtown Seattle bounded by Yesler Hill, Beacon Hill, and an industrial and warehouse area adjacent to the harbor and Puget Sound. These groups shared the area with working-class and, to use a contemporary phase, "underclass" whites – transients, homeless women and men, prostitutes, pimps, and gamblers – all a stark reminder of an earlier era in the city's history when organized vice was a thriving and grudgingly accepted segment of the urban economy. The area's major thoroughfare, Jackson Street, became a metaphor for a particular lifestyle associated with its risqué street life.

Frequently Asians and blacks in the Jackson Street area were competitors for housing. Most of the city's black and Asian poor were found here, often in Chinese- or Japanese-owned rooming houses that charged what blacks felt were exorbitant rents. Asian landlords, however, claimed African Americans were unreliable tenants who frequently destroyed property and crowded far more people into the small rooms than was permissible.

The sections of the Central District that were overwhelmingly African American had few characteristics that would associate them with the teeming post–World War I ghettos of New York, Chicago, and Detroit. Both local residents and visitors repeatedly remarked on differences with the larger communities – the rate of homeownership, the availability of spacious accommodations at reasonable rents, the racial and ethnic diversity of the neighborhoods. But such differences were more apparent than real. Seattle blacks loathed restrictive covenants in the 1920s and 1930s as much as did their New York or Boston counterparts. Their hatred stemmed not from being crowded into crumbling tenements as in eastern cities, but because such devices were a palpable reminder of exclusion from the vast majority of the city's residential neighborhoods. These covenants would channel virtually all of the huge post-1940 influx of black newcomers into this four-square-mile area. Decades later in the 1950s when both black and white Seattle would "discover" the city's ghetto, few remembered that its boundaries were established by the racially based decisions of hundreds of individual homeowners during the first four decades of the twentieth century.

To defend their rights and interests, the early twentieth-century African American community created local branches of national organizations such as the National Association for the Advancement of

Colored People, Universal Negro Improvement Association, National Urban League, and National Negro Congress that utilized tactics developed in other cities. Furthermore, larger, more sophisticated, and more vocal black political clubs attempted to maximize their influence in the two major political parties.[18] Still, the small size of the black community prevented any wholesale duplication of political and protest strategies successful elsewhere. Lacking the numbers or resources to control a congressional or state legislative district, Seattle blacks engaged in a seemingly incongruous combination of race-conscious rhetoric and interracial coalition politics to promote and defend their interests. Black civil rights organizations formed temporary alliances with Asian groups such as the Filipino Community of Seattle, Inc. (a coalition of Filipino social and political clubs) and political organizations such as the Washington Commonwealth Federation (the left-liberal wing of the state Democratic Party).[19] These alliances became the hallmark of a very different type of urban politics from that practiced in much of black urban America at the time.

The Seattle branch of the National Association for the Advancement of Colored People (NAACP), the first of the national organizations established in the city, reflected both the prospects and problems of small city branches of national organizations. Letitia A. Graves, a beautician determined to protest President Woodrow Wilson's newly instituted policy of segregating black federal employees, founded the Seattle NAACP in 1913, only three years after the national association was created in New York.* The Seattle NAACP was one of the earliest branches formed west of the Mississippi River.[20]

With Graves as its first president and Horace Cayton as vice-president, the Seattle NAACP differed markedly from other chapters. Much of its initial leadership was female (eight of the twenty-two founders were women) and, in sharp contrast to the interracial character of virtually all the branches established at this time, it was exclusively black. The gender and racial composition of all branches was a major concern of the national office. When in 1914 the national office discovered that the Detroit chapter excluded women, officials quickly moved to revise the branch's bylaws. The Indianapolis branch, exclusively composed of black female schoolteachers, was directed to admit men. Convinced that the presence of whites was beneficial for fundraising, to counteract prevailing white southern attitudes on segregation, and to promote interracial understanding, the national

* See the Appendix for a list of the founding members of the Seattle NAACP.

office in 1913 advised the Seattle branch and other all-black branches to include white members. Although it is impossible to determine when the first whites joined the Seattle NAACP, they were clearly in evidence by 1919.[21] The Seattle chapter conformed to the standard for chapters of the period in one important respect, however. It was an overwhelmingly middle-class organization which represented many of the most successful African Americans then resident in the city. The founding members other than Graves and Cayton included the city's only black attorney, a newspaper editor, three ministers, a caterer, a merchant, a grocer, a clothing store proprietor, a dressmaker, a milliner, a chiropodist, a mover, and a barbershop owner. Five other founders, all women, were listed as property owners.[22]

Between 1914 and 1919 the Seattle NAACP staged protest marches, filed lawsuits, and sponsored celebrations of Emancipation Day and Lincoln's birthday. The young chapter also generated a controversy with the national office in 1915 when its members voted to ask Seattle Mayor George Fletcher Cotterill to establish an "all-colored" fire station over the fervent protests of Samuel DeBow, editor of the *Seattle Searchlight*. In response to the local chapter's request for advice from the national office on the matter, Joel A. Spingarn, chair of the NAACP board of directors, replied: "Our association can never approve of segregation. . . . we understand the attitude of the colored men who need these positions as firemen but this is a typical case where colored people should be willing to sacrifice their individual interests before the common cause."[23] The Seattle branch acceded to the directive.

In 1915 the NAACP took on theater owners who planned to show the controversial antiblack film, *Birth of a Nation*. After pursuing the advice of the national office, which suggested a letter-writing campaign by prominent local whites, Letitia Graves dejectedly wrote New York that she feared "nothing can be done to stop the showing of the film in Seattle." Nonetheless, the chapter persisted in its efforts to ban the film and when it played again in Seattle theaters in 1921, City Council President Robert B. Hesketh, aware of NAACP concerns and claiming the film tended to create dissension, ordered the chief of police to stop its showing.[24]

In 1921, the Seattle branch mobilized to fight an anti-inter-marriage bill under consideration by the state legislature. NAACP members O. H. Winston and James A. Roston went to Olympia to prevent its passage, but when they arrived they "found the matter being taken care of" by State Representative John H. Ryan, the sole black member of the lawmaking body and a Tacoma NAACP member. Ryan persuaded his colleagues to table the bill indefinitely. Through the rest of the decade the Seattle NAACP showed little activity. One rare exception occurred in 1927 when it organized relief for Mississippi River flood victims.[25]

By the early 1920s the Universal Negro Improvement Association emerged as a rival to the Seattle NAACP for the allegiance of the city's small black community. Marcus A. Garvey founded the UNIA in 1914 in Kingston, Jamaica, and two years later shifted its headquarters to Harlem. Appealing particularly to working-class blacks who grew increasingly skeptical of the NAACP's integrationist thrust, the UNIA promoted a vague but persuasive form of black nationalism based on support for African independence, worldwide black political unity, and local economic self-sufficiency. Such appeals proved exceedingly popular among persons of African ancestry on four continents. In 1919 Garvey spoke to an audience of two hundred at Seattle's Madison Street Theater. Soon after, Division 50 was formed with one hundred members including Edward A. Pitter, a West Indian immigrant, as its first president.[26]

Seattle's small black population and sense of isolation probably contributed to the UNIA's appeal. Juanita Warfield Proctor remembered vividly sixty-four years later how her parents, Samuel and Maudie Warfield, and other local UNIA members had established a sense of community among the Garveyites. On Sunday morning after Sunday School at First AME Church the Warfield children walked down 14th Avenue to the UNIA Hall where they would have meetings for the children: "Sometimes we kids wouldn't want to stay. 'Course we'd have to stay there until my parents came to the meeting. My mother used to fix a big dinner for us kids and bring it. They'd have their meetings about one or two o'clock."[27]

The local chapter was organized along gender lines with the men serving as members of the paramilitary African Legion and the women as Black Cross nurses. According to Proctor, about one hundred Black Cross nurses in the Seattle chapter learned first aid and, along with the men, marched in annual parades on Memorial Day and the Fourth of July. On those marches the women were dressed "in their beautiful white uniforms," recalled Proctor, "with the black cross up on the forehead and on the arm, and a red, black, and green sash. The men wore the red, black, and green sash too."[28]

Seattle's Garveyites were mainly working-class people, devout Sunday churchgoers who saw no contradiction between their religion and the objectives of the UNIA. "They were trying to teach us about Africa," recalled Proctor. "And they were working to . . . free . . . Liberia. I remember my mother and father talking about Marcus Garvey getting this ship to send Black people to Africa, the ones that wanted to go."[29]

Marguerite Johnson also recalled the Garvey era in Seattle: "My grandmother just adored Marcus Garvey. . . . Garvey's UNIA had a place down on 12th and Washington. There was a hall there and they had dances. Evelyn Bundy Taylor played down there. She had a little combo and we'd go down to dance once a week. . . . My grandmother wouldn't miss a lecture at the UNIA. . . . She donated money towards buying this big ship . . . and we were all going to go back to Africa. I don't remember what happened that we didn't go, [but] I do remember his visit here."[30]

Johnson's reference was to Garvey's second trip to Seattle in 1924, an event Juanita Proctor described: "We met him at the Union Station, [and] all the Black Cross nurses and the men were all there [in uniform to greet him]. . . . I was the little girl that they gave the flowers to give to him. I thought he was going to be a big tall man. He looked big in the pictures. When I went to give him the flowers, he was almost as short as I." Admittedly the focus of the UNIA in Seattle and throughout much of the black world was black political and economic empowerment, but to many Seattleites the most lasting contribution of the Garveyites was their promotion of racial pride. As Juanita Proctor explained: "My father used to always tell us we should be proud of Africa. . . . He used to say, 'Be proud of your race. . . .' We were never ashamed to be called Black. . . . That's why I'm not ashamed of people calling me Black, because my parents taught me differently."[31]

By 1924 Seattle had a second UNIA chapter, Division 97. Internal dissension and class differences probably prompted the second group, which included two lawyers, a real estate agent, and the owners of the city's only black trucking firm, but virtually no working-class Garveyites. Both divisions, true to the Garvey philosophy, called for racial, and in their case organizational, unity, accumulation of property, entrepreneurship, and other self-help measures. Division 50, for example, ran a taxi service for black Seattle. But Garvey's arrest and deportation for mail fraud depleted the enthusiasm and energy of local UNIA supporters and heightened black middle-class opposition to the Garveyites. In May 1927 the Seattle NAACP and prominent black citizens for the first time blocked the issuance of a parade permit for the Garveyites. Seattle's UNIA chapters, like most others throughout the world, could not sustain much activity after Garvey's imprisonment. By the end of 1927, both Seattle divisions were defunct.[32]

With the coming of the Great Depression, African American Seattle revived the NAACP and created other organizations reflecting the political spectrum from the conservative Seattle Urban League to the Communist-inspired League of Struggle for Negro Rights. Each group sought to respond to the economic crisis in black Seattle while promoting its own program of economic and political reform. The transformation of the NAACP began in 1928. On April 10, the national office declared the Seattle chapter dormant, allowing Lodie M. Biggs to reinitiate the branch. Biggs, a bacteriologist employed by the Crescent Biological Laboratory, and one of the few black professional women in Seattle, was joined by William H. Wilson, editor of the *Northwest Enterprise*, and attorney Clarence Anderson in providing the leadership for the now reactivated NAACP. Yet the new branch initially suffered the same problems as the first chapter – small membership and irregular participation. Its only significant first-year accomplishment came in April 1929, when the branch forced a public apology from the *Seattle Post-Intelligencer* for carrying a derogatory story on a community-sponsored health clinic.[33]

By the early years of the Depression, however, the NAACP, buoyed by a new core of activist members, emerged to play a crucial role in protecting what it defined as critical community interests. The Seattle branch blocked anti-intermarriage bills introduced in the state legislature in 1935 and 1937, and the following year led a successful campaign to indict three policemen in the Berry Lawson police brutality case. It also held monthly public forums in Central District black churches where the community could debate political and economic questions. Typical of such gatherings was the 1934 discussion at Grace Presbyterian Church on whether blacks should seek a forty-ninth state. Moreover, the Seattle NAACP took up dozens of individual cases of employment discrimination and racial harassment that in earlier decades would have gone unnoticed. Two such cases were a 1933 incident where Sam McCoy, a black longshoreman, was assaulted by a white streetcar driver when he requested a transfer, and a 1936 episode involving attorney Clarence Anderson, who was attacked with a billy club and ejected from a county office by an assistant tax collector, Edward S. Streeter. Apparently piqued by a remark Anderson made about his rights, Streeter angrily declared,

"This is a white man's office and a white man's country."[34] The Seattle NAACP gave maximum exposure to both incidents by well-publicized investigations.

Two disparate incidents in the 1930s – the John Scott rape case and the campaign against anti-intermarriage legislation – symbolized both the success and the limitations of the Seattle NAACP as a legal advocacy organization for the city's African Americans. In March 1935, eighteen-year-old John Scott of Duwamish, a suburb south of Seattle, was accused of raping a thirteen-year-old white girl. Scott was arrested by Renton police and was allegedly beaten by them and threatened with lynching until he confessed. Community wrath, however, was visited upon Scott's parents; their home of fourteen years was burned to the ground and they were forced to flee to Seattle.

The Seattle NAACP, initially sensing the similarities with the major interracial rape incident of the decade, the Scottsboro case in Alabama, raised a defense fund of $300 to support Scott but ultimately declined getting involved because, according to President William H. Wilson, "the case was not meritorious enough." The NAACP's abrupt reversal on the Scott case reflected the accused rapist's uncertain legal strategy. Scott at first confessed to the rape, then declared the confession coerced, and finally at the preliminary hearing, nearly one month after his arrest, reversed his plea a second time after confessing the crime to his lawyer. He was subsequently sentenced to five years in prison for the rape.[35]

If the Scott episode failed to become a Pacific Northwest Scottsboro case, the Seattle NAACP regained its stature by its successful campaign against the anti-intermarriage bill proposed in the state legislature in 1935. The NAACP led a broad-based political coalition in opposition to the racially provocative measure. While the bill would have affected few black residents in the state, many black Seattleites recognized its symbolic importance since such statutes were the cornerstone of the edifice of racially discriminatory legislation. Washington in the 1930s was one of only eight states that allowed interracial marriage and the only one in the Far West. The Seattle NAACP was determined to see the state maintain that distinction.

In February 1935, King County Representative Dorian Todd proposed House Bill 301, a prohibition on marriages of persons of Caucasian ancestry to "Negroes, Orientals, Malays and persons of Eastern European extraction." The measure, prompted by the request of a Filipino man and white woman to get a marriage license, persuaded King County Auditor Earl Miliken that permanent prohibitory legislation was needed. Miliken, who claimed to be acting at the request of parent-teacher and women's organizations, denied the license and contacted King County Prosecuting Attorney (later U.S. senator) Warren Magnuson, who in turn proposed the bill to Representative Todd.

Seattle blacks, in response, formed a Colored Citizens' Committee in Opposition to the Anti-Intermarriage Bill and chose veteran political leader Horace Cayton, Sr., and Prentice Frazier to go to Olympia to lobby against HB 301. Protest meetings were held at the Phyllis Wheatley YWCA and First AME Church, where the Citizens' Committee led a combined organizational effort by the South End Progressive Club, the League of Struggle for Negro Rights, the Filipino Community of Seattle, Inc., the Washington Commonwealth Federation, and the Communist Party. The Citizens' Committee, according to its chair, William H. Wilson, received thousands of protest letters and telegrams which were passed on to Olympia. The Committee claimed victory in March 1935, when HB 301 was killed by the State House of Representatives' Committee on Public Morals.[36]

By 1930 Seattle blacks had also formed a branch of the National League for Urban Conditions Among Negroes, generally known as the National Urban League. Founded in New York City in 1911, the National Urban League's primary objective was to secure employment for urban blacks and help rural migrants adjust to city life. Because of its focus on African American accommodation to social and economic conditions, the national organization functioned primarily as a social service agency rather than a civil rights advocacy group. But the National Urban League, whose founders included Booker T. Washington and wealthy whites such as railroad magnate William Baldwin and Sears, Roebuck President Julius Rosenwald, was created, in part, to counteract the influence of the more radical NAACP among both African Americans and sympathetic, philanthropically oriented white supporters.[37]

Seattle blacks, however, seemed unimpressed by the philosophical divisions between the two organizations. Lodie Biggs, who worked to revitalize the NAACP, was simultaneously laboring to create a local branch of the Urban League. In 1928 she formed the Seattle Urban League Committee, which addressed a number of pressing concerns in the black community including the need for a community center. By mid-January 1929, Biggs's committee included Clarence Anderson, Dr. Felix B. Cooper, Mrs. Alice Presto, Prentice Frazier, and Horace Cayton, Jr., all of whom were active in the revived NAACP.[38]

In January 1930, the Seattle League was granted a charter by the national organization and soon afterward Joseph Sylvester Jackson arrived from New York to assume the post of executive secretary. Operating with a "one-man professional staff and a small budget," Jackson nevertheless plunged the League into the social and economic problems facing black Seattle. In its first year the League sponsored community recreation and health programs such as Negro Health Week, the Vocational Opportunity program, and "inter-racial activities," essentially presentations to white and Asian groups about the League and black Seattle. In September 1931 the League organized a black branch of the Unemployed Citizens' League and two years later a secretarial school. The League's public forums announced job opportunities. Typical of such forums was the 1936 visit of Department of Interior official Dewey R. Jones, who described to a black Seattle audience job opportunities at the Grand Coulee Dam site in eastern Washington. One of the League's most important contributions was its systematic accumulation of statistics on the education, health, and employment of the black community.[39]

The Seattle Urban League, like the NAACP, was committed to improving the conditions of black life and fostering the full integration of African Americans into the general society. Such goals should have been mutually supportive, but in fact the Urban League had to grapple with the dilemma of whether badly needed facilities for the community could be provided without promoting the very segregation the organization opposed. The 1932 debate over the Seattle Urban League's sponsorship of a black baseball team highlights the dilemma and provides a fascinating glimpse into the approach of middle-class black activists toward this question.

On May 31, 1932, Frank G. Porter, chair of the League's Health and Recreation Committee, called an emergency meeting prompted by Lodie Biggs's threatened resignation from the League. Her action was brought on by the League's announcement that it would sponsor a black community baseball team, which she argued placed the organization in the untenable position of endorsing a segregated community activity. Eight persons attended the meeting: committee members Felix B. Cooper, Candace Black, and Ella Erickson, along with Biggs and Porter; William H. Wilson and Mrs. William McIver, Urban League board members, were also invited to the discussion, as was Executive Director Jackson. Lodie Biggs began the meeting by outlining her objections: "I think the Urban League should not approve of separate teams. . . . A Negro team would soon be known as that 'Nigger' team. . . . Separate teams mean the beginning of racial feeling. I do not approve and do not wish to be connected with an organization that would foster such a movement."

"Segregation is not involved," declared Wilson in his defense of the proposal. "If the teams are all colored, it is beneficial to the colored people. We have fine white members on the Board who have given of their time to map out a program . . . that would be of benefit to the colored group, not to benefit them, but to benefit us who need it."

Mrs. McIver agreed with Biggs's argument: "I would not like to be associated with an organization that practiced discrimination. . . . My children take advantage of the playfields and parks and I take an interest in their activities." Candace Black urged support for the proposed team; "There is no question of discrimination. The Urban League sponsored the Health program and the Vocational Opportunity program. . . . Rev. Harris' Church [First AME] sponsored competitive games and . . . the results have been far reaching."

"Sometimes we are so prone to feel the pressing heel of segregation that we overlook the actual facts in the case," mused Felix Cooper, trying to locate some middle ground. "There has been no effort by the parents to get the children to take part in the playfield activities. . . . No one is more careful in guarding against . . . segregation than I am. This is not a matter of segregation; it would not keep colored children from joining white groups if they wished to; it would only develop the competitive spirit and encourage the youth to take advantage of the recreational and health activities."

Wilson then directed questions at Biggs: "Can you draw the line between the Urban League sponsoring a health week program, a vocational opportunity program and an athletic program for the colored people?. . . . What is the difference in holding a picnic for colored people and holding separate athletic activities?"

"The Urban League," responded Biggs, "is to see to it that people take part in the facilities already existing – to find some way to encourage colored children to take part in the activities of the park."

Committee Chair Frank Porter, sensing Biggs's increasing isolation, tried to end the debate by calling on the committee to endorse the proposed team. He then added, "Since Miss Biggs is the main objector, I think her usefulness on this committee is over, and I am going to ask Miss Biggs to change to another committee."

"Just a minute, Mr. Porter, and I will save you that trouble. I will not work with a committee or a Board who would practice discrimination. I will – "

As Biggs was about to announce her departure from the committee and the organization she founded two years earlier, Executive Director Jackson, the only person in the meeting whose Urban League membership predated 1930, changed the direction of the debate by outlining the position he felt the national organization would take: "The Urban League exists for social service among Negroes. . . . If the fact is known that the Urban League has adopted such a program [segregated teams] a cry will go up from the community that the Urban League is sponsoring segregation."[40]

Deferring to Jackson's views because of his long association with the Urban League, Porter withdrew his request for Biggs's resignation and the committee agreed to refer the question to the national Urban League board of directors. One month later, after receiving a directive from National Urban League Executive Secretary T. Arnold Hill that segregated teams were against League policy, the full Urban League board voted against the proposal.[41]

Most pre–World War II Urban League chapters carefully avoided political or civil rights controversy, preferring to focus on employment referrals, interracial relations seminars, and statistical studies of African American communities. Jackson, however, frequently skirted the line between social welfare service and civil rights advocacy, and in the Berry Lawson police brutality case he breached it altogether.

In March 1938, Berry Lawson, a transient hotel waiter staying at the Mt. Fuji Hotel, was arrested for loitering in the hotel lobby when police officers found him asleep in a chair. An altercation ensued and Lawson was killed. The three officers who arrested Lawson – Patrick L. Whalen, Fred Paschall, and W. F. Stevenson – claimed the waiter resisted them and fell down the stairs, causing his death. Witnesses, however, said Lawson was pushed.[42]

When King County Coroner Otto Mittlestadt cleared the police officers of wrongdoing, he unintentionally ignited a firestorm of protest in Seattle's African American community. Jackson organized a committee of community representatives to hold protest meetings with Mayor-elect Arthur Langlie. The committee – composed of Republicans, Democrats, and Communists, men and women, working-class and middle-class residents – reflected rare unanimity in black Seattle. Meanwhile, as the black political clubs mounted pressure on County Prosecutor B. Gray Warner to bring charges against the officers, Jackson initiated his own investigation and found an eyewitness to the altercation, Travis Downs, a white hairdresser who had been "induced" to go to Portland following Lawson's death. Jackson persuaded Downs to return to Seattle to testify. These developments took place against the backdrop of a steady stream of articles and editorials in the *Northwest Enterprise* focusing on the Lawson case. One editorial called on Republicans to cross party lines to defeat Coroner Mittlestadt in the Democratic primary because of his "white wash" of the Lawson case.[43]

On June 10, 1938, the officers were convicted on manslaughter charges and sentenced to twenty years in prison. Following a series of legal and political maneuverings that temporarily resulted in their release, the Washington State Supreme Court in January 1939 upheld their convictions. "The officers used more force than was necessary," the Court declared, "in taking Lawson into custody." Four months later, however, Governor Clarence D. Martin granted a pardon to Stevenson and Paschall. Finally in December 1939, Governor Martin pardoned Whalen, who then took responsibility for the murder of Lawson.[44]

Pat Whalen and the other police officers involved did not, to be sure, serve much time in prison, but during an era when police often killed black citizens with scant public outcry, these men were stripped of their positions of authority by an angry and politically astute African American community. Black Seattle learned that despite its small numbers, timely concerted action coupled with the chastisement of certain public officials and cultivation of others could make law enforcement officials accountable for their actions against black people. That lesson would be well remembered by Seattle's postwar African American community.

The Seattle NAACP's success in the 1930s and the activist role of the Seattle Urban League were clearly spurred by more aggressive leadership provided by Biggs, Wilson, and Jackson, but they were also prompted by the rise of rival groups such as the Communists and their popular front allies, who like the UNIA in the 1920s battled for the allegiance of the black working class in Seattle. But if the UNIA based its appeal on black nationalism and economic self-sufficiency, the Communists in the 1930s offered the vision of a workers' utopia which would bring Seattle's African Americans both economic and racial equality.[45]

Numerous Communist and popular front organizations emerged during the Depression. Ranging from branches of national organizations, such as the League of Struggle for Negro Rights and the National Negro Congress, to distinctly local groups, such as the Provisional United Front Committee, all attempted to educate black workers on working-class solidarity, scientific socialism, and revolution. Local Communists made special appeals to blacks as the most oppressed element of the proletariat and received sympathy and some support in the Central District for their determined defense of the Scottsboro Boys and Angelo Herndon. Nationally prominent black Communists including Otto Hall and James W. Ford, the party's vice-presidential candidate in 1932, visited the city, encouraging African American workers to join their ranks and calling on progressive white workers to welcome them.

Some Seattle blacks responded. When a 1930 demonstration by one thousand unemployed workers on the steps of City Hall devolved into a confrontation with one hundred police officers, Hutchin R. Hutchins and Ernest Whitlow were two of the eleven party speakers arrested for inciting a riot. Soon afterward David Whitman, Bernard Williams, and Revels Cayton, the younger son of newspaper editor Horace Cayton, organized the League of Struggle for Negro Rights in 1930. By the mid-1930s other local blacks embraced the Communist movement, including Carl Brooks and Marshall Grey, who, after participating in various multiracial organizations, formed the Seattle chapter of the National Negro Congress in 1937.[46]

Of the small cadre of African American party activists in Seattle in the 1930s, Hutchin R. Hutchins was the ranking member. Hutchins was one of three party members, along with Lowell Wakefield and Alan Max, who arrived from New York and attempted to assume leadership of the state party. Of the three, Hutchins had the most extensive training in economics and party organization, having attended the Lenin School in Moscow. He was also considered by some local members as the most rigid and doctrinaire of the new leaders, insisting that Marxist teachings be accepted without question and warning that "party discipline" could be imposed on dissidents.[47]

If Hutchins was the outsider who arrived in the city to build the Communist Party, the majority of the party members were natives or longtime residents. The most surprising convert was Susie Revels Cayton. The daughter of Hiram Revels of Mississippi, the first black U.S. senator, and wife of Horace Cayton, Sr., who remained an active Republican until his death in 1940, she would seem an unlikely supporter of the cause of socialism, but Susie Cayton was an unusual woman. As Richard Hobbs, the family biographer, notes, Susie Cayton increasingly differed with her husband, in reaction to political events in Depression-era Seattle. If Horace Cayton looked longingly backward at the freedom of Seattle's frontier past, Susie's vision broadened as she looked forward to a more egalitarian future in an industrial democracy. She shared Revels's growing interest in socialism and became more politically radical and involved in community affairs. Although in her early sixties, Susie Cayton attended Scottsboro meetings in the community and became secretary of the Skid Road Unemployed Council. The grateful jobless men she assisted bestowed on her the title "Mother Cayton." Working with the unemployed she grew to believe that only radical political change could address the catastrophic Depression. Sometime in the mid-1930s she joined the Communist Party.[48]

In a letter to her daughter, Madge, Susie revealed both an active schedule and her ideological commitment to the cause of Marxism:

I will give you some idea of my activities and nothing but shortage of car fare ever keeps me from pursuing them. Monday night: P.W.U. Local, A.F. of L . . . meets in one of the Minor School portables (walking distance). Tuesday night: The Negro Workers Council, meets in a portable at the Horace Mann School. I'm Vice President and our President is out of the city at this time. Wednesday night: stay in and read late. Thursday: Party Unit always meets. (Some times walking distance, some times not.) Friday night: Stay home or visit in the neighborhood. Saturday: The Harriet Tubman Club meets. . . . Sunday night: The Worker's Forum, 94 Main Street. Besides, I try to attend the Legislative Council which meets every first and third Monday in the month, also the P.T.A. at Garfield, which meets every third Thursday in the month. Of course, there are mass meetings, dances and what not that come in at times. I'm having the time of my life and at the same time making some contribution to the working class I hope.[49]

Her work in the Communist Party brought Susie Cayton in close contact with leading black left intellectuals such as Langston Hughes and Paul Robeson, both of whom stayed at the Cayton home when they visited Seattle. Her introduction to Robeson was directly attributable to her growing local reputation in party circles. On one occasion Robeson arrived at the Cayton home unannounced to an astounded household and declared, "I'm Paul Robeson, and I'm on a concert tour here, and so many people have told me about you that I just wanted to come up and see you."[50]

If Susie Cayton came to Marxism via discussions with her son Revels, his conversion was probably more typical of the process in Depression-era Seattle and much of the country. By 1930, Revels

Cayton had already participated in left-sponsored organizations such as the League of Struggle for Negro Rights, but his formal conversion to communism came in 1931 while he was auditing classes at the University of Washington. Cayton met a friend who had earlier supplied him with pamphlets describing the plight of the Scottsboro Boys. The friend, Marian Tayback, a member of the Young Communist League, invited Cayton to meetings in the University District, where he found young, idealistic white college students: "I didn't learn anything about Communist theory. . . . All I knew was that I found a group that I fit into." They were "this little island of decent people . . . who had an ideological base not to be prejudiced."

As a member of a socially prominent black family, Revels Cayton quickly gained respect and recognition. To use Richard Hobbs's words, "they lionized him." In return, Cayton found an important personal mooring as he developed the intellectual and organizational skills that would mark much of his life as a labor union official and black political activist in Seattle, and later in San Francisco.[51]

Other members of prominent families were attracted to the Communist Party. Leonard T. Gayton, the son of community leader John T. Gayton, in 1969 described the Communists' appeal to young, idealistic middle-class Seattle blacks like himself: "I started reading newspapers like the *Pittsburgh Courier* that were brought out here by colored railroad hands. The papers told about . . . lynchings in the South and the race riot in Chicago, and I really got angry. I wondered how things like this could happen in America. When I was nineteen I started going to meetings of the Communist Party. I listened to all their speeches and read Marx and Engels and so forth."[52]

Much of the appeal of the Communists was predicated on one incontrovertible fact: at a time when segregation and discrimination seemed completely acceptable to most of white America, the Communists dared to form interracial "shock troops" to strike at the heart of the economics and "culture" of racial supremacy. Their slogan in support of the Scottsboro defendants, "They shall not die," soon became a rallying cry for non-Communists as well. Their special appeals to black workers were often inserted within the announcements of their meetings, which were liberally advertised in the *Northwest Enterprise* and other black media. Moreover, their willingness to chastise racist whites, even those they were attempting to organize, indicated a commitment to equality heretofore unknown among Seattle's predominantly white organizations. When in August

1932 the East Madison branch of the Unemployed Workers' Council expelled eleven white members who objected to African Americans serving as officers in the council, and to being "unduly familiar with white women," its action reflected radically different ideas about inter-racial contact. Such efforts were at least in part politically calculated to attract blacks to the party, but the sight of black and white workers jointly and openly challenging the police, insensitive politicians, bigoted employers, union leaders, or accommodationists in the black community proved a powerful message to all Seattleites concerned about racial justice but heretofore unwilling to act on their beliefs.

Leonard Gayton and Revels Cayton eventually grew disillusioned with communism (in contrast to Susie Revels Cayton, who died in 1943 still a proud party member), but in the 1930s their sense of outrage over economic and political conditions and their search for a just solution lured them and many other black Americans to Marxism.[53]

The vast majority of Seattle's black community, however, remained committed to the Republican and Democratic parties. That commitment was punctuated by occasionally strident criticism of their failure to pursue agendas of benefit to African Americans. Despite these grievances, only a minority of local blacks recognized options beyond the major parties. Black Seattle underwent a two-stage political transformation during the 1900–1940 era. The first occurred immediately after 1910, as permanent Republican and Democratic political clubs replaced fledgling organizations character-istic of nineteenth-century black Seattle. The focal point of the first transformation was the founding in 1915 of the King County Colored Republican Club (KCCRC) which brought together old leaders such as Horace Cayton, Sr., and newcomers such as Harry Legg, and dominated the political life of the black community through 1932. The KCCRC prided itself on its connections with the state's leading political figures. In September 1932, for example, it arranged the visit of Governor Roland H. Hartley to the First AME Church, apparently the first time a Washington governor had ever addressed a public gathering in the black community. Yet the KCCRC symbolized the limited vision of black political leaders in Seattle and the paradox of national black politics. Seattle's black GOP activists participated in party politics for the promise of tangible rewards – appointments to party or public office. They operated in a local environment with a small population and thus few votes with which to attract aspiring politicians. Moreover, they were aligned with a national party desirous of shedding its image as a political home for advocates of "social equality." Consequently, even if the KCCRC could claim important contacts with powerful political figures, few substantive political appointments were forthcoming. Legg, for example, became Washington's first black GOP committeeman in 1917, and Johnnie Green and Horace Cayton, Jr., were appointed deputy U.S. marshal and deputy county sheriff, respectively, in 1928. Yet most black Republicans were rewarded patronage jobs as janitors, elevator operators, or groundskeepers at state buildings. African American Republicans periodically protested these menial appointments but had few alternatives, as the state Democratic Party prior to 1930 expressed little interest in developing a black constituency.[54]

Although a number of African American women such as Candace Black and Blanche Smith participated in the predominantly male Republican and Democratic clubs, Seattle's females also created their own political organizations. The largest group was the nonpartisan Women's Political and Civic Alliance founded in 1916, with a membership of 200 by the end of its first year. By the mid-1920s the Black Republican Women's Club was formed and a Democratic counterpart existed in the Central District by 1933. These women's political organizations, in sharp contrast to the male clubs, seemed less concerned about political appointments and saw their role as providing a public forum for the discussion of issues affecting the local African American community and black America.[55]

The second, more significant political transition came in 1932, as the Democrats began to seriously challenge GOP hegemony in the Central District. Forty percent of the city's black voters cast Democratic ballots in the September primary election, surprising politicians in both parties. Their shifting allegiance reflected both national and local trends. President Franklin Roosevelt's New Deal programs promised needed jobs, public assistance, and political recognition. The 1932 primary vote was prompted partly by black anger with the Republican Party's handling of the Depression-dominated economy and local and state Democratic candidates' promises of more and better political appointments. Moreover, the Washington Commonwealth Federation, the left-liberal wing of the state Democratic Party that between 1936 and 1941 dominated the party organization, particularly encouraged black support.[56]

Black Democrats saw some improvement in the number and type of political appointments. Before 1932 virtually all GOP appointments (there were no Democratic appointments prior to that date) were for menial positions. Post-1932 Democratic appointments included

Candace Black as a county social worker and Mrs. L. B. Young, Judson Swancy, LeEtta King, and Marvin Gaston as state Relief Commission investigators. Nonetheless, since most Democratic appointees were – like their Republican counterparts – janitors, patronage promises still ran far ahead of performance.[57]

Yet the increased black participation in the Democratic primary and the growing list of Democratic voters among Central District African Americans signaled an unmistakable change in political allegiance. Some black Seattleites switched parties through a circuitous route. N. J. Graffell and Ira F. Norris, officers in the King County Colored Republican Club as late as 1932, were delegates to the Washington Commonwealth Federation state convention in Everett in 1936 where Norris was appointed a member of the Legislative Committee. By the end of the year, both men were active in one of the Seattle black Democratic clubs.[58] For other lifelong Republicans, the courage to vote the Democratic ticket was difficult to summon, as a 1932 exchange between Horace Cayton, Sr., and his son Revels attests.

"I came home . . . and found my father sitting on the front stoop of our house," recalled the younger Cayton. "'Hey, Dad, what's wrong?' I asked, seeing him looking thoughtfully at the ground. Looking up, he answered, 'I just voted for a Democrat, son.' 'Well, what's so bad about that, Roosevelt's gonna feed ya,' I snapped back. 'Yes, that's true,' he said, 'but the Republican Party *freed* me.'"[59]

Certainly there have been few eras in black Seattle's history when partisan politics was more lively, colorful, and chaotic than during the 1930s. The Central District produced four mostly male Democratic organizations as well as the Colored Women's Democratic Club. Rival clubs were denounced and meetings disrupted as each club vied to be the official representative of black Democrats in the city, which of course meant control of patronage. Black Democrats soon became known for rancorous meetings. During a February 1933 gathering of the Colored Citizens' Democratic Club, the president arrived intoxicated, prompting two other club members to "give him a drubbing" and the membership to ask for his resignation. In a lengthy guest editorial in the *Northwest Enterprise*, Andrew T. King, a black party activist, characterized the episode as "just one grand and glorious kaleidoscope of confusion or better still – just a plain mess."[60]

Chaotic meetings notwithstanding, black Democrats in the 1930s wielded growing influence in the Central District. But if defections to the Democratic Party virtually assured the extinction of GOP influence in the African American communities in New York, Chicago, and other eastern cities, a significant segment of Seattle's population remained loyal to the Republicans, assuring, at least in the 1930s and 1940s, vigorous two-party competition in the Central District. Working-class black Democrats gravitated toward Warren Magnuson (who recovered from his association with the anti-intermarriage bill effort by supporting black Democratic clubs) and other New Deal liberals. But Seattle Republican leaders, including most notably Mayor Arthur Langlie (later governor), retained the loyalty of virtually all the city's black business and voluntary organization by providing increasingly visible support for civil rights, fair employment, and other black community concerns.[61]

As black Seattle approached the 1940s, it clearly understood the advantages and limitations of being a small community in the Pacific Northwest. The wall of segregated housing appeared unbreachable in 1940, and African Americans were forced to regularly endure slights to their person and their race. But African Americans, armed with the ballot, skillfully maneuvered between the state Republican and Democratic parties, helped, of course, by the rise of radical political groups such as the Washington Commonwealth Federation and the Communist Party, which assiduously courted black support. Thus slowly through the 1930s at least, Seattle's African Americans generated influence beyond their small number at the polls.

More surprising was the ability of Seattle's African Americans at least by the 1930s to defend their rights under attack. In the Berry Lawson episode and the campaign against anti-intermarriage legislation, black Seattleites were able to prevent the erosion of their rights as citizens. As sociologist Robert Colbert asserted, black Seattleites pragmatically appraised their local political climate and gave ground on some rights to maintain others.[62] But Seattle's African Americans also looked longingly to the day when none of their rights need be sacrificed to maintain racial peace.

Chapter 4

Blacks
and Asians
in a
White City,
1870–1942

In 1909, against a backdrop of rising racial tension in the city, Seattle residents Powell and Katherine Barnett were refused service in a Japanese restaurant that had previously accepted black customers. Powell Barnett described the incident in an interview thirty years later: "We went into this place and were told that management had changed their policy and we couldn't be served because we were colored. I never went back." Edward Pitter, however, remembered an episode at another downtown Japanese restaurant in 1930 when a white patron entered and demanded, "Get these negroes out." The owner promptly responded, "These my people, you get out."[1] These contrasting accounts of Asian-black interaction reveal the complexity of understanding race relations where multiple racial groups occupy a single neighborhood.

Black urban histories have tended to focus on the dynamics of black-white interaction — a dichotomy reflected in census studies during the early decades of the twentieth century, which put nonwhites and blacks in one category. Such a designation may have been understandable in many southern and eastern cities, but was virtually meaningless in the West. Through World War II, African Americans rarely constituted the largest nonwhite population in western cities, but were part of a multiracial and multiethnic demographic pattern that included Asians, Chicanos, and Native Americans. Asians —

particularly the Japanese, Seattle's largest racial minority until World War II, the Chinese, and the Filipinos – competed with African Americans for employment and housing. Moreover, the virulent racism usually singularly directed against African Americans in eastern urban communities was diffused in the West among the four nonwhite groups.[2] All of Seattle's Asian groups were subjected to discrimination by white residents. The nineteenth-century Chinese engendered the greatest hostility, rationalized by claims of their alleged clannishness and their collective resistance to assimilation as well as their competition with white labor. The early twentieth-century Japanese and Filipinos were singled out for opprobrium for significantly different reasons. The Japanese were attacked because they competed successfully with white produce merchants and farmers. Filipinos were maligned for reasons similar to those ascribed to blacks: they were considered unmotivated, uneducated workers, given to sexual promiscuity and having pretensions to social equality with whites.[3]

Despite the rationalizations advanced to justify the ostracization of each group, all received strikingly similar treatment. When the personnel manager of Frederick and Nelson, one of Seattle's largest department stores, was forced to respond to public criticism of a discriminatory advertisement calling for "white only" temporary employees during the 1941 Christmas season, he replied tersely, "It just isn't in the picture to hire Japanese or Negroes."[4] Similar discriminatory patterns held in other areas. Public accommodations in the city either excluded both groups or made the rare patron particularly uncomfortable. Asians, like blacks, were barred from unions and thus saw their opportunities in manufacturing decline concomitantly with the rising political and economic influence of the city's white unions in the first decades of the twentieth century. And, like blacks, Asian American college graduates were denied employment commensurate with their education.[5]

Asian immigrants, however, were denied a prerogative that could not legally be withheld from African American immigrants: U.S. citizenship. The Naturalization Act of 1790 declared only white aliens eligible for naturalized citizenship. In 1870, naturalization eligibility was extended to foreign-born Africans but not to foreign-born Asians. Few Asian immigrants challenged the law until Takao Ozawa filed an application for U.S. citizenship in October 1914. Ozawa arrived in California in 1894 from Kanagawa Prefecture, Japan. After graduating from high school in Berkeley, California, and attending the University of California for three years, he worked in California and Hawaii until

Table 8
Population of Seattle by Race, 1900–1940

	1900	1910	1920	1930	1940
Black	406	2,296	2,894	3,303	3,789
Japanese	2,900	6,127	7,874	8,448	6,975
Chinese	438	924	1,351	1,347	1,781
Filipino	–	–	458	1,614	1,392
Native American	22	24	106	172	222
White	76,815	227,753	302,580	350,639	354,101
Other	–	70	49	60	42
Total	80,671	237,194	315,312	365,583	368,302

Source: U.S. Bureau of the Census, Twelfth Census of the U.S., 1900, vol. 1, Population, pt. 1, p. 645; Thirteenth Census of the U.S., 1910, vol. 1, Population, p. 226, vol. 3, p. 1007; Fourteenth Census of the U.S., 1920, vol. 3, pp. 1085, 1092; Fifteenth Census of the U.S., 1930, vol. 3, pt. 2, pp. 1209, 1231, 1256; Sixteenth Census of the U.S., 1940, Population, vol. 2, pt. 7, p. 401.

his fateful suit in 1914, which eventually reached the U.S. Supreme Court. "The petitioner," the Court conceded in its 1922 ruling in *Ozawa v. The United States*, "was well qualified by character and education for citizenship." But because the existing naturalization laws failed to include Asians, Ozawa was "outside the zone on the negative side."[6] Without the protection of citizenship, foreign-born Asians, as most of those residing in Seattle were before World War II, could not vote or own property. The property ban was particularly onerous, forcing Asian immigrants to resort, with the assistance of sympathetic non-Asians, to various creative subterfuges to maintain farms and businesses.

If Seattle's Asian Americans and African Americans recognized white fear and prejudice as the common source of their discrimination, each group responded in ways reflecting its particular culture, history, and perception of its destiny in America. Asians and blacks moved on vastly different trajectories that would end in diverse destinations. Sociologist Robert Blauner had European ethnics in mind when he made the observation that "all groups started at the bottom but the bottom has by no means been the same for all groups," but the statement aptly compared Seattle's Americans of Asian and African ancestry.[7]

Each community, moreover, had differing ideas of the appropriate response to discrimination. African Americans were concerned with economic opportunity *and* the end of formal discrimination – the "campaign for human dignity," to use the standard NAACP characterization during the interwar years. The Japanese and Chinese, while not unaware of discrimination and its impact on their economic progress, chose to wage their battle for human dignity within the confines of business success and academic achievement, and specifically avoided the confrontational tactics of African American civil rights organizations.

Asian immigration to Seattle in the nineteenth and early twentieth centuries was part of a larger process of global economic transformation generated by industrialization and colonialism. The Chinese and Filipinos responded to the growing control of their economies by Europeans and Americans. The Japanese eagerly embraced industrialization to avoid being victimized by colonial powers. Yet in all three societies, displaced agricultural laborers became candidates for emigration at the historical moment when the rapidly expanding Pacific Northwest regional economy offered numerous opportunities unavailable in Asia.[8]

Pacific Northwest capitalists eagerly sought Asian laborers because, as able-bodied young men without dependents, they could be subjected to onerous conditions including low wages, long hours, and poor housing. Moreover, their numbers could be regulated through immigration restrictions and deportation, which conveniently precluded their engaging in labor or political protests.[9]

Once in the Pacific Northwest, Asian newcomers followed a transient labor pattern established by nineteenth-century white loggers who seasonally moved in and out of Seattle. The particular employment demands of salmon canning, logging, vegetable and fruit farming, and other seasonal industries necessitated a highly mobile, tightly organized work force of bachelors. Dispatched by labor recruiters and contractors, these men worked away from the city, returning only when the canning or harvesting season ended.[10]

Yet the initial Asian immigrants differed from many of their European counterparts, as well as from the black migrants who moved to Seattle, in that they looked upon themselves as sojourners – temporary residents who planned eventually to return to their homelands. The sojourners' "center of gravity," according to historian Roger Daniels, was clearly fixed in Asia. Rose Hum Lee, in her sociological study of the Chinese immigrant community, described the sojourner's attitude as a "feeling of belongingness" to the Chinese village: "He spends a major portion of his lifetime striving in America for economic betterment and higher social status, but the full enjoyment and final achievement of his objective is to be in his place of origin." The sojourner, according to Lee, feels his cultural heritage is superior and resists assimilation.[11]

Sojourning partly explains the rapid success of the Japanese and Chinese in establishing a thriving commercial community in Seattle. Sojourning immigrants promoted thrift and hard work, not only as virtues but also because they wanted to amass capital as quickly as possible. Ethnically oriented service businesses, which could be rapidly liquidated, offered one opportunity for the sojourner to mesh his temporary and long-term economic objectives. Such ethnically based small businesses also encouraged group solidarity by molding social and business functions. Chinese and Japanese merchant associations, usually composed of immigrants from the same province or prefecture, established a collective fund (*hui* in Chinese and *tanomoshi* in Japanese) – in effect, a rotating credit system. Such funds, drawn from regular assessments of the members, were used to provide venture capital for newer businesses.[12]

The Chinese community in Seattle predates the African-American community by twenty years. Seattle's first Chinese resident was Chin Chun Hock, who arrived in 1860. He founded the Wa Chong Company, which manufactured cigars and clothing and sold Oriental goods, and also became Seattle's first Asian labor contractor, arranging employment for Chinese workers in logging camps, canneries, and eventually the railroads. Other Chinese men found employment as cooks and laundry workers, occupations disdainfully characterized by both the immigrants and the non-Chinese as "women's work" but nevertheless necessary in a frontier society with few women.[13]

Seattle's Chinatown had 250 male residents in 1876, a population periodically augmented by transient workers from throughout the Pacific Northwest. Chinese labor was crucial to the region's economic development and initially generated scant resentment. In 1868, for example, the Northern Pacific Railroad Company began recruiting workers from Hong Kong, transporting 450 to construct lines south of Portland. Four years later, 1,500 Chinese laborers were laying tracks throughout Oregon. The Oregon Railway and Navigation

Company eventually employed 5,000 Chinese and 1,500 whites in the construction of the line that linked its road with the Northern Pacific railroad at Wallula in eastern Washington Territory. "The work was so obviously needed," according to historian Robert E. Wynne, "[and] the lack of white labor so evident as to cause even the most ardent anti-Chinese to welcome their employment."[14]

Seattle's Chinatown evolved around the Wa Chong Company, located at the corner of Third and Washington. By 1877 three other Chinese merchants – Chin Gee-hee, Chen Cheong, and Eng Ah King – had opened shops, typically with second-story rooms rented to many of their ethnic kinsmen. These merchants served the diverse needs of the Chinese laborers migrating out to gold fields, logging camps, coal mines, hop fields, and railroad construction sites and returning periodically to obtain supplies or seek the next job.[15]

Seattle's Chinese subscribed to the sojourner ideal. These immigrants, primarily from Guangdong Province around Canton and Hong Kong, left behind family and security to pursue opportunity in Giu Gun San, literally "Old Mountain of Gold," as the United States was known among them, and envisioned an eventual return to China with their newly earned wealth. Most immigrants never reconciled themselves to their occupations as porters, laundrymen, cooks, and waiters in America. As Rose Hum Lee reminds us: "They conceived of those roles as temporary, even if they died before the preferred role – that of a retired 'Gold Mountain Guest' – was realized."[16]

By 1880, Seattle's Chinese constituted nearly 13 percent of the city's working males, a number large enough to generate calls for their forced removal. For the Chinaphobes the rallying cry "The Chinaman must go" succinctly encapsulated the necessary response to widespread fears of "barbaric Asiatic hordes" threatening to undermine occidental civilization. But the violence in Seattle, as elsewhere in the Pacific Northwest, must be seen in the larger context of regional economic depression, unemployment, and declining wages which escalated tensions between white workers fearful of displacement and capitalists who used Chinese labor to protect their economic interests.[17]

"The civilization of the Pacific Coast," a *Seattle Post-Intelligencer* editorial ominously declared in September 1885, "cannot exist half Caucasian and half Mongolian. The sooner the people of the United States realize this and take measures to make certain that the Caucasian civilization will prevail, the sooner discontent will be allayed and the [anti-Chinese] outbreaks will cease." The very day this editorial was published in Seattle's leading newspaper, a mob of whites invaded the quarters of Chinese coal miners in Newcastle, twenty miles southeast of Seattle, chased the miners away, and burned their property. Chinese residents were also driven out of Issaquah, Tacoma, Sumner, Black Diamond, Carbonado, and Snohomish – all in western Washington Territory.[18]

With the backdrop of escalating anti-Chinese violence, members of the Seattle Knights of Labor, unemployed workers, and Chinaphobes created the Puget Sound Anti-Chinese Congress on September 28, 1885. The Congress vowed to drive the Chinese out of the city unless they left voluntarily before November 1. Mindful of the Rock Springs, Wyoming Territory, massacre on September 2, where twenty-eight Chinese were killed, and similar if smaller outrages in Washington Territory towns, Seattle's Chinese merchants prepared to respond to the threatened assault on their community. Chin Chun Hock contacted Ou-yang Ming, then Chinese consul general at San Francisco, who in turn cabled Washington Territorial governor Watson Squire, demanding he take measures necessary for the protection of the Chinese. Chin also reached Cheng Tsao-ju, the Chinese ambassador in Washington, who extracted a promise of federal protection from L. Q. C. Lamar, U.S. secretary of the interior.[19]

Governor Squire requested that 350 federal troops be dispatched from Vancouver Barracks, 130 miles south of Seattle on the Columbia River, to maintain order in the city. Before they could arrive, however, anti-Chinese sentiment exploded into violence. On February 7, 1886, "committees" of white workingmen forced the 350 Seattle Chinese from their homes to the waterfront to board the steamship *Queen of the Pacific*. After 197 of them were forced to sail to San Francisco the next day, a mob confronted a hastily assembled contingent of deputies and militia led by King County Sheriff John H. McGraw, who were assigned to protect the remaining Chinese. When some workers tried to wrest guns away from the deputies, militiamen fired into the crowd. In the subsequent exchange, two militiamen and three rioters were seriously wounded. Taking advantage of the momentary confusion, Sheriff McGraw's men marched the remaining Chinese back to Chinatown to await the next steamer. Seven days later, 110 Chinese boarded the *George W. Elder* and the remaining 44 were sent to Port Townsend to board another waiting vessel. In one week virtually the entire Chinese population of Seattle was deported and the city's original Chinatown became history.[20]

The anti-Chinese riot illustrated that Seattle was not immune to western Sinophobia. But all the Chinese did not go. Some household servants and the merchants Chin Gee-hee, Eng Ah King, and Chen Cheong, who ostensibly remained behind to dispose of their property, became the nucleus of Seattle's second Chinatown. Despite the virtual universality of anti-Chinese public rhetoric among Seattle whites, these Asian workers continued to be, for many Seattle residents, the employees of choice. By 1890 the 359 Chinese in Seattle exceeded the number of their countrymen driven from the city four years earlier. As if a verification of their determination to remain, Chin Gee-hee, owner of the Quong Tuck Company, erected a brick building on the northeastern corner of Second and Main following the Seattle Fire of 1889, which became the nucleus of the second Chinatown.[21]

Chin and other merchants emerged from the anti-Chinese disturbances as powerful figures who exerted almost monopolistic economic control over the second Chinese community, destroying, as historian Patricia Limerick remarked, "any sentimental notion of solidarity among the oppressed." Their power stemmed from their position as labor agents for the railroads, canneries, and farms, exclusive importers and retailers of Chinese goods, and owners of the residential hotels utilized by their countrymen. Chin's rise to prominence reflected the development of a two-tiered class structure, with the merchants often amassing prodigious wealth while the vast majority of their ethnic kinsmen remained in poverty. Goon Dip, the former Chinese consul in Seattle, had created by 1910 a huge financial empire, including commercial real estate holdings in Seattle and Portland valued at $200,000 and part ownership of Alaska salmon canning factories. Chin Gee-hee was wealthy enough in 1905 to return to Guangdong Province to invest in and supervise the construction of the first railroad in China built without western assistance.[22]

Chinatown's merchant elite initiated and controlled the voluntary agencies such as the Chinese Benevolent Association, the governing body of Chinatown which selected official representatives of the community. The CBA maintained the Chinese school, policed the community, settled disputes, assisted new immigrants, and performed social welfare functions among the Chinese.[23]

A comparison of Chin Gee-hee with William Grose, Seattle's wealthiest black resident in the 1890s, is instructive. Like Grose, Chin was a community banker and his hotel, like Grose's Our House, was home to transient laborers. Moreover, Chin's position as community liaison with powerful white politicians was analogous to Grose's as the representative of black Seattle through the 1890s. But Chin's economic leverage in highly stratified Chinatown far surpassed Grose's influence among Seattle's blacks. Chin, who dispatched his countrymen in labor gangs, garnered leverage over both white employers and Chinese laborers while Grose never had the power to influence the employment of most of Seattle's black work force or to determine community leaders. Furthermore, Grose, although a successful hotel proprietor and restaurateur, had no commercial links with East Coast or African mercantile interests comparable to those of Chin with his kinsmen in China.[24]

If Seattle's nineteenth-century Chinatown did not disappear, immigration restrictions severely retarded its growth. After 1890, virtually all of Seattle's Chinese newcomers came from interior Chinatowns as far east as the Rocky Mountains and from a small

Table 9
Bachelor Societies in Seattle, 1900–1930

Males and Females 15 Years of Age or Older

	1900	1910	1920	1930
Japanese				
Men	2,886	4,988	3,932	3,047
Women	47	740	2,030	2,047
Chinese				
Men	399	789	1,041	773
Women	12	49	95	185
Filipino				
Men	—	—	—	1,529
Women	—	—	—	29
Black				
Men	186	1,256	1,492	1,560
Women	152	776	1,033	1,218
Citywide				
Men	43,477	113,337	133,208	149,058
Women	21,045	77,200	113,606	142,560

Source, U.S., Bureau of the Census, *Thirteenth Census of the U.S.*, 1910, *Population*, vol. 3, table 13, p. 994; *Fourteenth Census of the U.S.*, 1920, *Population*, vol. 3, table 8, p. 134; *Sixteenth Census of the U.S.*, 1940, *Population*, vol. 2, *Characteristics of the Population*, pt. 7, table A-36, p. 401.

stream of illegal immigrants smuggled across the Canadian border. Denied continuous regeneration by the Chinese Exclusion Act of 1882, Seattle's Chinatown was quickly surpassed by the spectacular growth of the Japanese and black communities, both of which by 1910 exceeded the city's Chinese population.[25]

Worse for Chinatown was its gender imbalance (Table 9). With 399 men and 12 women over the age of fifteen in 1900, Chinese Seattle epitomized the bachelor society. The Exclusion Act allowed merchants to bring their wives, or to send for potential marriage partners in China, a privilege denied Chinese male laborers. Prostitution flourished, although some evidence suggests that Chinese immigrants may have practiced polyandry.

Although sojourning ambitions predominated among the Chinese immigrants, the nineteenth-century restrictive immigration policies of the U.S. government played the greater role in generating this masculine gerontocracy. Moreover, the vast majority of Seattle Chinese in 1910 and 1920 – like the residents of Chinatown in the 1880s – were uneducated, unskilled laborers and house servants. This overwhelmingly male population effectively prevented the majority of Chinese from establishing families in the city. Virtually all of the new growth in Chinese Seattle through 1940 was the result of middle-aged men retiring to the city from the surrounding hinterland. The male population also affected the types of businesses created; the restaurants, retail shops, service enterprises, and other small businesses emblematic of Chinese communities in San Francisco and New York, or of the Japanese community in Seattle during the same era, would emerge only after World War II, when Chinese immigrant families arrived in the city.[26] Those Chinese who refused menial service and were without connections to prominent merchants turned to illegal or quasi-legal activity directed initially at Chinese laborers but eventually involving a citywide clientele. Chinese-owned pool halls, brothels, and gambling dens peppered the Jackson Street district, providing illicit but popular entertainment for Seattleites. Indeed Chinatown, long noted for flouting middle-class customs and mores, became a metaphor for Seattle's raciest street life during the interwar years.[27]

Few Chinese were prosperous enough to vacate Chinatown. Those who wanted to move faced the same restrictive covenants that prevented African American residential dispersal. Economically successful Chinese slowly moved "up hill" to First Hill and Beacon Hill in the 1930s. According to longtime Seattle resident Sam Wing, these neighborhoods were the only districts not covered by restrictive covenants. Furthermore, Chinatown was itself squeezed by the growth of other ethnic populations along Jackson Street. The Japanese in the 1890s, Filipinos in the 1920s, and African Americans throughout this period all took up residence, creating a rare Asian American and African American integration of social and cultural space where Chinese restaurants occupied commercial blocks with Japanese tailoring shops, Filipino dance halls, and black barbershops. Long before civic promoters dubbed the area the "International District" to enhance its image, Seattle's Chinatown had become one of the most cosmopolitan neighborhoods in the city. But for the city's 1,700 Chinese in 1940, the descendants of Seattle's first Asian immigrants, the integration of Chinatown reflected the relative powerlessness and dependency of an aging community increasingly reliant for its sustenance on marginal ethnically based businesses and illicit activity patronized primarily by non-Chinese.

Seattle's Japanese community began in the 1890s, formed by a second, larger wave of Asian immigrants to the Pacific Northwest. These new immigrants were generally farm boys, "younger sons with no prospect of inheriting land."[28] Like the Chinese who preceded them by two decades, the first arrivals intented to remain only a few years to accumulate sufficient capital to buy land in Japan. The prospect of higher wages in the Pacific Northwest was a powerful inducement to emigrate for those fearful of becoming part of Japan's impoverished urban proletariat. Japanese railway workers, for example, could make seven times their average salary in Japan, farmhands four times, and domestic servants nearly twenty-three times their wages at home.[29]

The first Japanese immigrants, the Issei, arrived in Seattle in 1883 as unskilled laborers. Their numbers grew slowly until 1886, when anti-Chinese agitation made them an acceptable alternative to the Chinese. The following year approximately two hundred Japanese men arrived from San Francisco to work in the canneries and logging camps in western Washington Territory. A few businessmen opened merchandise stores, restaurants, and lodging houses called "residential hotels" to serve and supply Japanese farmworkers, railroad crews, and sawmill employees throughout the Pacific Northwest.

Seattle's community of 125 Japanese in 1890 grew to 2,990 a decade later and constituted nearly 3 percent of the city's population. They formed a Nihonmachi ("Japantown"), essentially a cluster of hotels, rooming houses, saloons, and shops around Main and Jackson streets on the edge of Seattle's second Chinatown.[30] Unlike the Chinese community, however, whose growth was stymied by immigration restrictions, Seattle's Japanese population was directly augmented by immigrants from the homeland. Beginning with the *Nippon Yusen Kaisha* in 1896, Japanese passenger liners made regular voyages between Yokohama and Seattle. The transpacific voyage took approximately thirty days, and third-class passage between the two cities averaged $25, far less than railroad fares from Chicago or St. Louis or the passenger steamer fare of $250 from the East Coast to Seattle.[31]

The trickle of immigrant workers became a flood during the Alaska gold rush of 1897–99. Faced with a severe labor shortage following the gold discovery, the Great Northern Railway Company began actively recruiting Japanese in 1897. In 1899, Sometani Nariaki, the Japanese consul in Seattle, reported Pacific Northwest employment opportunities in a lengthy dispatch to Tokyo. The Northern Pacific and Great Northern railroads, Nariaki informed the Foreign Ministry, "welcomed Japanese workers with open arms," despite having to "offer higher wages than paid the Chinese." Employment prospects would remain high, he concluded, because each of these railroad companies still needed an additional 1,000 workers.[32]

The Issei accepted jobs held earlier by the Chinese but also pursued other kinds of employment, including commercial fishing and farming. Since most of these working-class males spoke no English, they, like the Chinese earlier, became part of a contract labor system with a Japanese boss conducting negotiations with white employers. Labor contractors who had direct access to their homeland until 1907 often recruited in Japan. Ototake Yamaoka, who represented the Seattle-based Toyo Boeki Kaisha (Oriental Trading Company) in Japan, persuaded hundreds of laborers from Shizuoka Prefecture to emigrate to America in the spring of 1900 to work for the Great Northern.[33] Initially the Japanese, like the Chinese, considered themselves sojourners in America, anxious to make money quickly and return to Japan. Yet as turn-of-the-century Seattle resident Banzo Okada remembered, such a return soon became impractical for most Japanese immigrants: "I planned to work three years in the states to save 500 yen and then go back to Japan. However . . . to save enough was out of the question." High expenses, often manipulated by labor contractors, left immigrants with little money. Faced with the prospect of returning to their native villages "in shame," they reconciled themselves to permanent residence in America.[34]

Between 1900 and 1907 a growing number of Japanese arrived in Seattle, prompting some earlier laborers to become entrepreneurs to meet the commercial needs of ethnic kin. Community leaders also recruited Japanese merchants both to provide additional services and to diversify the social class background of the heretofore lower-class immigrants. After the Gentlemen's Agreement of 1907–8 between the United States and Japan prohibited the entry of new contract workers, both middle- and working-class Japanese male immigrants began arranging marriages to "picture brides" in Japan, who subsequently arrived in Seattle. From 1909 to 1924, Japanese women entering Seattle each year outnumbered men until immigration was completely ended by the Immigration Act of 1924.

Seattle's 6,127 Japanese in 1910 were the fifth largest ethnic group in the city after Canadians, Swedes, Norwegians, and Germans. This population, unlike the Chinese or black communities, could support numerous community institutions. By 1916 ten churches, a variety of civic and social clubs, and five Japanese-language newspapers served Seattle's Nihonmachi and the population beyond the city. The largest newspaper, *Hokubei Jiji*, for example, had a circulation of 7,000 and was distributed throughout Washington. "Japanese Town in Seattle in those days was at the height of prosperity," remembers Miyoshi Yorita. "Main and Jackson Streets were occupied by Japanese restaurants and public baths. . . . Dance, [and] drama . . . were performed at Japanese Hall. . . . Well known singers like Tamaki Miura, Toshiko Sekiya and Yoshie Fujiwara came from Japan to perform. . . . So people could forget that they were living so far from home."[35]

Seattle's Japanese immigrants were more entrepreneurially oriented than the Chinese or blacks or, for that matter, other West Coast Japanese. The 1900 Nihonmachi included a hotel, a few barbershops, pool halls, restaurants, and cafés catering to the largely male unskilled laboring population. Sixteen years later a survey of community businesses revealed 3 banks, 95 hotels, 80 restaurants, 81 fruit and grocery stores, 29 laundries, 47 clothing stores, 10 jewelry stores, 3 movie theaters, 15 hospitals and clinics, and 7 drugstores. Lawyers, doctors, dentists, photographers, carpenters, plumbers, electricians, among other professionals and skilled craftsmen, advertised in the local Japanese newspapers. Significantly, a growing number of Japanese entrepreneurs had a predominantly white clientele. Nearly half of the restaurants were described as "western," meaning their patronage was largely non-Japanese.[36]

Would-be entrepreneurs received funds from the *tanomoshi*, particularly for large ventures such as residential hotels. Many laborers took advantage of the relatively high wages paid in the Pacific Northwest and simultaneously sacrificed all but necessities to save capital. One immigrant recalled his schedule at a Fourth Avenue café in 1900: "I worked every day from five in the morning until nine in the evening. On national holidays I went out and did day-work. For seven years I didn't have a single day off out of 365 days a year. I averaged about seventeen hours a day. Including tips, I made more than $3,000 a year, and I surprised even myself that I could work so hard."[37]

By 1920, Seattle's Nihonmachi, with 7,800 residents, was, after Los Angeles, the second largest Japanese community in North America. Augmented by another 2,700 in surrounding King County and 2,000 in neighboring Pierce County (Tacoma), the regional Japanese population numbered nearly 13,000. These populations had a symbiotic relationship in that Seattle's Japanese greengrocers were able to dominate the vegetable trade because of their links with nearby Japanese truck farmers, who controlled over 16,000 acres in western Washington. That relationship allowed an economic prosperity far greater than Seattle's black, Filipino, or Chinese communities could have achieved in this era.[38]

The weekly *Japanese American Courier*, Seattle's first English-language Japanese newspaper, was emblematic of the growing success and confidence of the community. Founded in 1928 by James Sakamoto, a Seattle-born former prizefighter who was now blind, the *Courier* quickly became the largest English-language Japanese newspaper in the United States. Sakamoto touted a philosophy of education, economic self-help, and nationalistic support of Japan. In that regard the *Courier* was not unlike other ethnic or immigrant newspapers. But like the *Northwest Enterprise*, it gave wide coverage to incidents of discrimination against the Japanese. The *Courier* often condemned race prejudice – if in milder language than employed by the *Enterprise* – and called for interracial understanding.[39]

The *Courier* was directed at the growing Nisei population – those Japanese, like Sakamoto, who were born in the United States. The Nisei were, he declared, American citizens with "inalienable rights to live the life of an American." Addressing those of his generation who seemed culturally adrift between the land of their birth and the homeland of their parents, Sakamoto urged complete, unequivocal identification with the United States. "It is high time," he declared, "to lower the anchor."[40] To that end, Sakamoto, fellow Seattle Nisei attorney Clarence Arai, and other second-generation West Coast Japanese community leaders founded the Japanese American Citizens League in 1930 to promote their rights as American citizens of Japanese ancestry. From its first convention in 1930, where eight charter affiliates met at the Seattle Japanese Chamber of Commerce Building, the JACL expanded between 1930 and 1940 to fifty chapters, with nearly six thousand members. Composed primarily of Nisei professionals and businessmen, its self-defined role was to educate the larger society about Japanese Americans while reminding the second generation of their commitment to American society.[41]

Sakamoto and other JACL leaders charted a course in contradistinction to the militancy of the Seattle NAACP and other black civil rights groups. "Agitation begets agitation," declared Sakamoto, "and this can never lead to the best results." While acknowledging the existence of discrimination in employment, Saburo Kido, another JACL founder writing in the *Nikkei Shimin* (*Japanese American Citizen*), urged the Nisei not to complain: "In technical or commercial vocations, we cannot afford to work with talents inferior to Americans. It is not enough even to be their equals; we must surpass them – by developing our powers to the point of genius if necessary. We believe that the complaints against race prejudice in the matter of vocational opportunities are not justified. They only show that something is lacking in the initiative or ability of the one who complains."[42] A 1928 incident involving alleged racial discrimination against a Japanese nursing student, Teru Uno, suggests the extent to which these attitudes were already accepted by segments of the community. The nurses training school associated with Providence Hospital refused to accept Uno into its program, prompting a strong rebuke by the *Courier* and some community leaders. Sensing that the incident would be an embarrassment to her family and the Japanese American community, Uno submitted an open letter to the *Courier* declaring that she "held no ill-feeling" toward the school for rejecting her application. Furthermore, she "deplored the agitation caused through her affair" and hoped that a "better understanding might result between the Japanese and American peoples and that it would continue."[43]

During the Depression decade, the Japanese population declined by 21 percent in Seattle, prompted partly by the delayed impact of immigration restriction and by the emigration of some Japanese Americans to other cities and occasionally to Japan in search of economic opportunity. Moreover, it curtailed the earlier spectacular growth of the Japanese business community. Nevertheless, in 1935 there were 183 hotels, 148 grocers (both figures higher than in 1916), 39 "American" restaurants, 24 Japanese restaurants, and 31 laundries. According to the 1930 census, 898 Japanese businesses in Seattle averaged $26,600 in annual income and employed 2,304 people, of whom 84 percent were Japanese and 38 percent were members of the proprietor's family.[44] Thus despite laws preventing the Issei from owning land and voting, and discriminatory practices excluding virtually all Japanese skilled and unskilled labor from most of the city's industrial occupations, and most college graduates from commercial enterprises outside the Nihonmachi, Seattle's Japanese community during the interwar years had established an enviable record of economic success.

The Filipinos, the third Asian group to settle in Seattle in significant numbers, began their immigration in the early years of the twentieth century. That immigration was both sudden and massive. Rufina Clemente Jenkins, the wife of a black Spanish-American War veteran who settled in Seattle in 1902, was the first person of Filipino ancestry to live in the city. Yet in 1910 only 17 Filipinos resided in the state and only 160 lived in the entire country. Twenty years later, 45,208 Filipinos lived in the United States, including 3,774 in Washington.[45]

Twentieth-century Filipinos were American nationals rather than foreigners, having come from a U.S. territory acquired from Spain in the Spanish-American War. That legal designation allowed them to travel on American passports and to enter the United States without restrictions. This proved particularly advantageous after the Immigration Act of 1924 closed Japanese immigration. Their legal status notwithstanding, Filipino immigrants soon faced the paradox long known to the Chinese and Japanese: American growers and canners might desire their labor, but American workers and nativists resented their presence.[46]

The Philippines in the late nineteenth century had not suffered the economic disruption that sent thousands of rural Chinese and Japanese workers abroad, but the colony's poverty and the prospect of significantly higher wages in the United States proved a strong inducement for many Filipinos by the 1920s. "The migrating Filipino," explained the *Manila Times* in a 1929 editorial, "sees no opportunity . . . in the Philippines. . . . Offer a job at 25 pesos a month, not a living wage in Manila, and you will get a thousand applicants. . . . Is it any wonder, then, that the lure of pay ten times as great in the United States draws the Filipino like a magnet?"[47]

Filipinos, as a "colonial people" exposed to American administrators, missionaries, and businessmen, and educated in the English language, felt an identification with United States culture unknown to Chinese and Japanese immigrants. Carlos Bulosan, the Filipino writer who arrived as an immigrant in Seattle in 1930, described the impact of the United States on his generation of Filipinos in his autobiography, *America Is in the Heart*: "the young men were stirring and rebelling against their heritage. Those who could no longer tolerate existing conditions adventured into the new land, for the opening of the United States to them was one of the gratifying provisions of the peace treaty that culminated the Spanish-American War."[48]

Many Filipino immigrants shared with earlier Asian newcomers the sojourning ideal. But they also soon realized the difficulty of returning home with American-earned wealth. Phenomenal wages by Philippine standards were quickly consumed by the high cost of living in the United States. Although they were understandably reluctant to return home impoverished, the agricultural migratory work they performed throughout the western United States often gave them little choice. Unlike the Chinese and Japanese, whose movements in and out of the United States depended on immigration control measures, the Filipinos could enter and exit the country at will until Congress passed restrictions in 1934 with the Tydings-McDuffie Act.[49]

Seattle by 1926 was the major center of the Filipino population in the Pacific Northwest and the dispatching point for hundreds of workers bound for Alaska canneries six hundred miles north. Workers traveled in steamship steerage to isolated canning sites in Valdez, Ketchikan, Juneau, and Sitka that would be their homes for two to four months. Before he became the owner and editor of the *Filipino Forum*, the monthly Seattle Filipino newspaper in the 1930s, Victorio A. Velasco was first a cannery worker. His curt 1924 diary entries for June 21 and 22 provide a revealing glimpse of migrant life in Alaska: "Worked in the ship unloading salmon cans, at $.75 an hour. It was my first time in America to work. Worked exactly ten hours. Donning the overall for the first time in my life, handling the wheelbarrow, and carrying salmon boxes, was a thrill and an unforgettable experience. . . . Was laughing at the easy job and easy money. $7.50 for working 10 hours. In the Philippines it takes a month for a policeman to earn that. Such is the better prospect of life in this beautiful country."[50]

Not all Filipinos recalled the cannery experience in such glowing terms. "You see, the conditions in Alaska at that time was so awful," explained Seattle resident Antonio Gallego Rodrigo. Cannery workers were "just like . . . slaves. They . . . get money from [the labor] contractor so they can go to Alaska to work. And then, when they come back, they are broke. They do the same things, year in and year out."[51]

By 1930, Seattle had the largest Filipino population in the United States. The rapid appearance of this community in Seattle's already multiethnic, multiracial Jackson Street district prompted the *Japanese American Courier* to declare that a "New Manila" had situated itself alongside "Chinatown" and "Little Tokio." The newspaper lauded the arrivals, claiming that since the exclusion acts had forced Chinese and Japanese merchants to look beyond their own racial groups for business, the Filipinos would make important new customers.[52]

Carlos Bulosan remembered well his June 1930 disembarkation from the steamer that brought him and hundreds of others to Seattle. The Filipino hotel and two restaurants in Chinatown and a second hotel on King Street, he recalled, were "the heart of Filipino life in Seattle." A few Seattle Filipinos opened barbershops, grocery stores, and cafés, but the largest and most impressive business was the Philippine and Eastern Trading Company, Inc., an importing firm that served an economic role similar to those of the Chinese and Japanese merchants twenty years earlier.[53]

Filipino businesses could not break the dominant hold of the older, better capitalized Japanese and Chinese businesses, and thus, like the African Americans, Filipinos did not develop a substantial commercial community. The paucity of Filipino merchants in Seattle stemmed from conditions both in the islands and in the city. Spanish colonial administrators who for four centuries controlled the islands were uninterested in developing a native capitalist class and instead allowed the Chinese to service the retail needs of the islands. Accustomed to the role of the Chinese as merchants, few Filipinos challenged their position in the United States. Nor did the Filipinos bring or establish any capital formation mechanisms such as the rotating credit system. Moreover, because they could speak English and had wider access to employment, they were not driven by economic necessity to create ethnic businesses as were the

Japanese and Chinese. But the timing of their migration just before the Great Depression was less than propitious, preventing many entrepreneurially oriented Filipinos from developing their interests.[54]

Although Filipino domestic servants, hotel cooks, and houseboys lived permanently in Seattle, the vast majority of immigrants, like Bulosan, became migrant laborers moving from hop fields to apple orchards to canneries, in a seasonal migratory pattern that took them from Alaska through the Pacific Northwest and into California. According to one estimate, Seattle's summer population of Filipinos in 1931 numbered a few hundred but by winter 3,500 had moved into the city's residential hotels, a population that exceeded the size of the permanent African American community resident in Seattle.[55]

The 1930 census showed 1,529 Filipinos and 29 Filipinas over the age of fifteen in Seattle. While Belen de Guzman Braganza might remember never having a problem getting dates as a University of Washington coed in the 1930s, the overwhelmingly male population generated intense sexual anxieties and resentment among some whites as young Filipinos with money, and no prospects of Filipina companionship, attracted adventurous teenage girls and lonely women as well as prostitutes. Seattle's Manila Dance Hall, where Filipino cannery workers and domestic servants vied for the attention of "brightly dressed white women," who "smoked marijuana in the back room" and then charged "ten cents a minute" for a dance, was a poignant reminder of the desperation of lonely men and disconsolate women attempting to survive in Depression-era Seattle.[56]

Such interracial liaisons generated growing concern among Asiaphobes. The 1935 campaign to ban intermarriage in Washington, so assiduously fought by black groups in Seattle, was prompted by the marriage license request of a white woman and a Filipino man. The major instances of anti-Filipino violence stemmed not from job competition and cultural challenge but from incidents involving Filipino men and white women. Thus with the exception of blacks, with whom they were often compared and occasionally mistaken, Filipinos generated the greatest amount of sexual jealousy and fear.[57]

The growing numbers of Filipinos sparked a nativist response similar to the earlier calls for Chinese and Japanese exclusion. Since the Immigration Act of 1924 did not apply to Filipinos, exclusionists ingeniously campaigned instead for independence for the Philippines, assuming that immigration restrictions would be easier to impose on another Asian country than on an American colony. In 1934 Congress passed the Tydings-McDuffie Act, establishing the Philippines as a commonwealth and providing independence in ten years. Under Tydings-McDuffie, Filipinos were reclassified as aliens and given a quota of fifty immigrants per year.[58]

But the Tydings-McDuffie Act came after Filipino immigration had already peaked. The spreading Depression, a rising number of anti-Filipino labor incidents, and the acrimonious public debate over Filipino immigration restrictions combined to discourage further immigration. Subsequently the number of newcomers fell in the 1930s as rapidly as it had risen a decade earlier. In 1929, 11,360 Filipinos entered the United States; by 1932 the number had dropped to 1,306. Seattle experienced a 14 percent decline in its Filipino population during the Depression decade as these men migrated to other West Coast cities or returned to the Philippines.[59] Although 1,400 Filipinos remained in Seattle in 1940, the development of a cohesive, institutionally based community would await the post–World War II migration.

By 1940 four distinct racial minorities had emerged in Seattle, each with their own aspirations and perceptions of their place in the urban milieu. Much has been written about each group's relationship with white society, but we have far less evidence about how they viewed or interacted with other nonwhites. Nineteenth-century black Seattleites, for example, said curiously little about Asians, perhaps because they were themselves new to the frontier city and thus uncertain of their place in the urban ethnic hierarchy. Horace Cayton, Sr., was an exception when in 1900 he announced his view of the region's well-known anti-Chinese sentiment. "The lands of this section are not being developed very rapidly by the Americans," Cayton explained, "and if the Chinamen will develop them, they are deserving of much personal praise instead of personal abuse and violent intimidations for so doing." But Dr. Samuel Burdett, a leading member of the black community, joined the avowedly anti-Asian American Protective Association and served as its president in 1895.[60] Although the sources are scant, surviving evidence for the period from 1900 through the Japanese evacuation of Seattle in the spring of 1942 suggests the range of interaction between these "peoples of color."

Early twentieth-century Asian and African Americans forged tentative links across a broad cultural divide. Throughout the 1920s and 1930s black, Asian, and white groups invited their counterparts to share aspects of their culture or discuss common problems. Typical of such gatherings was the May 1932 meeting of the Aeolian Society, a Japanese American club created to stimulate interest in classical music. The group invited Idel Vertner, secretary of the Phyllis Wheatley YWCA, to lecture on Negro spirituals and to give renditions of "Deep River" and "Go Down Moses." William H. Wilson's 1932 presentation to the University Interracial Society, which included white and Asian students and faculty, where he challenged his listeners to support intermarriage and full social equality for blacks, was another example of attempts at multiracial understanding. In 1941 at a meeting on interracial justice sponsored by the St. Francis House of Hospitality, a Catholic community center in the Jackson Street neighborhood, representatives of the Jewish, Japanese, and black communities spoke on the contributions of their groups to Seattle and America and reiterated their fidelity to the American political system. And interethnic athletic contests, such as the highly publicized 1928 meeting of the Japanese Girl's Club all-star basketball team with a comparable black all-star team, provided regularized contact in an informal setting.[61]

The Japanese evacuation from Seattle in 1942 tested the feelings and prejudices of all Seattleites. The *Northwest Enterprise* in 1941 became one of the few Seattle newspapers to oppose the evacuation of the Japanese from the West Coast. "Don't lose your head and commit crimes in the name of patriotism," warned the paper in a front-page editorial five days after the attack on Pearl Harbor. "As treacherous as was this unheralded attack on our country, it should bring no reprisals [on] innocent Japanese citizens on our shores. The same mob spirit which would single them out for slaughter or reprisal has trailed you through the forest to string you up at some crossroad. The Japanese [in the United States] are not responsible for this war. They certainly are good citizens. . . . Especially is it tragic that these native born should be singled out for abuse, insult and injury."[62]

The words of the *Northwest Enterprise* were matched by the actions of a few African Americans. Thomas Bodine, a Society of Friends interpreter who assisted in the government-mandated relocation of 1942, poignantly described an unidentified black man who drove a Japanese American family to the train that would take them to an Idaho internment camp. The man helped the family unload and then stood with them as they waited for the order to board their designated car. He said to the woman, "You know that if there's ever anything I can do for you whether it be something big or something small, I'm here to do it." He then turned to the husband and said, "Goodbye now and good luck." Finally he got on his knees and embraced, in turn, each of the three children.[63]

Other Seattle African Americans recalled the relocation and condemned the unfairness of the government's action. Gertrude Simons remembered what her Japanese friend and colleague said after the evacuation announcement: "Gertie . . . they're putting us into camps." "But you were born here," Simons responded, "you've always been here." "Well, they're sending us away . . . so I have some things I'm going to give you." And with that she left precious family heirlooms with Simons. "Oh that was a sad day," recalls Juanita Warfield Proctor. "They were really American people. They really shouldn't have been in the camp, because they were American-born Japanese."[64]

We know little of what Asians thought of African Americans, but some information is suggestive. While intent on establishing their colonial empire in Asia, Japanese nationalists portrayed themselves as defenders of "colored" peoples. In that regard, local Seattle Japanese expressed sympathy for the plight of Seattle's blacks. In a 1921 U.S. Naval Intelligence report of Japanese links to West Coast branches of the Universal Negro Improvement Association, one government informant recalled several Japanese delegates at a recent UNIA international convention in New York and described an unsuccessful attempt by Japanese nationalists and Garveyites in Seattle and other cities to create a "Colored Peoples' Union" inclusive of all "except the whites or Teutonic races."[65]

There is little evidence, however, of any organizational links between African American and Asian American groups after the decline of Seattle's UNIA branches in the late 1920s. James Sakamoto's *Japanese American Courier* occasionally denounced attempts to restrict interracial marriage, and his paper refrained from the negative stereotyping and derogatory cartooning often found in the major daily Seattle newspapers. Yet the *Courier* rarely commented on discrimination against blacks or other minorities. The one exception was the 1941 U.S. Supreme Court ruling that granted equal railroad accommodations for blacks in interstate travel, which the paper hailed as "a step toward racial toleration but only a step." Two weeks later, however, the *Courier* discredited a rumor that "Oriental trainees were to be segregated with Negroes in the training camps." Declaring its opposition to Japanese segregation while remaining silent on black exclusion, the *Courier* said, "Young Americans of Japanese ancestry are entitled to the same consideration as any other group."[66]

Did Asians discriminate against blacks? The evidence is mixed. Black Seattleites Gertrude Simons and Muriel Pollard remember the Chinese and Japanese restaurants as less discriminatory than white establishments. Gertrude Simons specifically described the welcome extended to black porters and ship stewards by Asian restaurateurs and landlords: "The one thing I can say for them . . . , the ones that had the hotels down around Jackson Street, you could always find a place to live." One Chinese restaurant near the railroad station, according to Muriel Pollard, served "soul food" to a mainly black clientele of railroad workers.[67] Yet Edward Pitter, a ship's steward in the 1930s, remembers the paradox of eating undisturbed in restaurants during his visits to China and Japan while being denied entry into Chinese American and Japanese American establishments in Seattle. No blacks would be served, according to Pitter, if whites were eating there. Perhaps Asians, mindful of their dependence on white patronage, chose, like nineteenth-century black Seattle barbers, to exclude African Americans because they feared unsettling white sensibilities on race. Occasionally, however, a rare restaurateur challenged that view.[68]

Fragmentary evidence from various sources suggests that Asian and African American residents of the lower Jackson Street area were tolerant, if uneasy, neighbors. Irene Burns Miller and Juanita Proctor described occasional interracial marriages between black men and Japanese women, although Proctor's account indicates that the Japanese community disowned the woman involved. But the daughter of a Japanese-language newspaperman, recalling the lower Jackson Street neighborhood of her childhood in the 1920s as one of "Negroes, Yugoslavians, and other Caucasians, as well as the Japanese," said: "We never did think about race. I guess Seattle was more or less a melting pot. We all got on well together."[69]

Asian-black rivalry was most pronounced in employment. When Bernard E. Squires, the new executive director of the Seattle Urban League, arrived in the city in 1939, he and his wife Melvina were shocked to find Japanese and Filipino redcaps at the train station and Japanese bellboys in their hotel, since these two occupations were usually identified with African Americans. Because Asians were excluded from industrial jobs, they competed with Seattle blacks for positions as hotel and railroad porters, janitors, houseboys, and

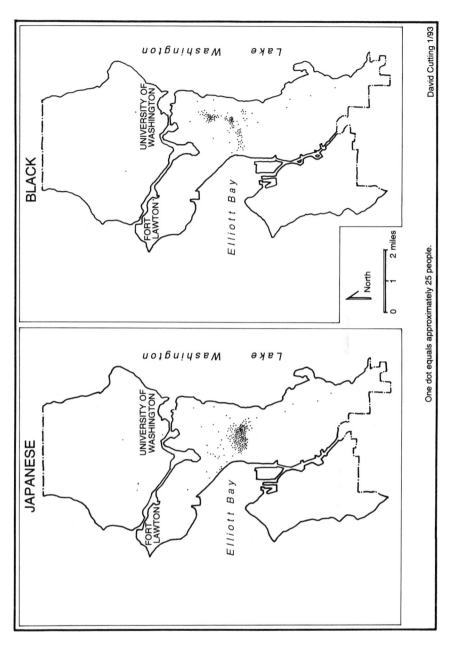

One dot equals approximately 25 people.

Map 4. Comparative Japanese and black population in Seattle, 1940

maids. But they had advantages over black migrants: they had arrived in Seattle in large numbers earlier than blacks, they relied on kin networks to obtain jobs, and Seattle's early twentieth-century whites were more familiar with Asians than with blacks as servants. Reflecting the insecurity inherent in racially divided labor markets, Depression-era black personal service workers complained about Japanese and Filipino competition. Yet the Japanese and Filipino waiters and bellboys were constantly reminded that they should accept prevailing wages and working conditions, since they could easily be replaced by African Americans. As one Japanese hotel waiter remarked in the 1930s, "I lived with the constant fear of blacks taking my job."[70]

Despite their employment rivalry, blacks and one Asian group, the Filipinos, recognized the importance of self-interested cooperation. In 1935 and 1937 the Filipino Community of Seattle, Inc., a coalition of clubs, lodges, and associations created to increase Filipino influence in the Democratic Party, worked with Seattle civil rights organizations, progressive labor unions, and the Washington Commonwealth Federation to successfully block the intermarriage ban introduced in the state legislature.[71]

Filipinos and blacks had particular reasons for cooperation. The ban had been prompted by the attempted marriage of a white woman and a Filipino man. But African Americans, knowing that the anti-intermarriage laws already on the books in most states served as the linchpin of antiblack legislation, were equally opposed to the measure. Moreover, blacks as citizens and Filipinos as nationals had expectations that America's egalitarian beliefs would inspire fair treatment. Carlos Bulosan's brother summed up that view of an inclusive multiracial democracy when he declared, "America is not one race or one class of men. We are all Americans . . . from the first Adams to the last Filipino, native born or alien, educated or illiterate — *We are America!*"[72]

Filipinos and blacks also found common ground in their exclusion from most labor unions. Filipinos were decidedly more pro-union than the Chinese and Japanese. Although some Japanese socialists resided in Seattle, most Japanese workers aspired to be employers and eschewed labor unions, while Filipino workers used collective action to protect their rights as laborers. When possible, they formed labor unions, including Local 7 of the Cannery Workers and Farm Laborers Union. Filipino unions were racially inclusive; they welcomed blacks.[73]

Despite sincere efforts by some Asians and African Americans to bridge the wide cultural chasm, vastly different group aspirations stemming from diverse cultural and historical experiences steered these groups along disparate trajectories. At the heart of these differences was the sojourning philosophy, which simultaneously promoted Asian economic success while reinforcing cultural alienation. Although all Asians initially adhered to the sojourner thesis, the Chinese most clearly embraced it. Chinese American leaders, almost always wealthy merchants, sought an accommodation with white Seattle and tried as much as possible to limit their interaction with non-Chinese to minimize friction and hostility. For the Chinese – an overwhelmingly male population engaged in menial, service-oriented activities outside the community or small businesses within Chinatown – confrontations were painfully absorbed to avoid placing their countrymen at risk. Vivid memories of the anti-Chinese violence of the 1880s no doubt encouraged their avoidance of occupations that would place them in competition with white labor. Moreover, protests against existing conditions were often ineffective since the Chinese were denied citizenship.

Although Japanese Seattle, like the Chinese community, initially saw itself as a sojourning population, the growing number of female émigrés after 1907 and the increasing realization that the return would be difficult discouraged notions of a reverse exodus. Unlike the Chinese or Filipinos, however, the Japanese were divided along generational lines: the Issei identified strongly with Japanese culture and hoped for an eventual return to Japan; the Nisei, in contrast, were far more assertive in demanding their rights in the United States than the Issei or the Chinese community.

But if Seattle's Nisei chafed under discrimination, their leaders had little tolerance for the protest strategy associated with the Seattle NAACP or Urban League. Striking a pose similar to Booker T. Washington's a generation earlier, James Sakamoto, editor of the *Japanese American Courier*, reflecting the thinking of younger community leadership, stressed accommodation to the racial status quo, educational advancement, and economic self-sufficiency. Although his newspaper highlighted particularly overt racist acts against the Japanese community, he seldom defended Issei rights as resident aliens, or challenged the federal government's discriminatory immigration policies and the nativist groups which called for continued Japanese exclusion and greater restrictions on those present in the United States. The Japanese, he said, should "stay within their own community, support small businesses within their area and emulate the patriotism of white America."[74]

Sakamoto and virtually all other Nihonmachi leaders agreed that education was the key to Nisei advancement. Education had long been extolled in the Japanese community – far more than in the Chinese, Filipino, and black communities – and its active promotion by both local leaders and Japanese diplomatic officials had considerable impact on educational achievement. Throughout the 1930s, Japanese Seattle proudly pointed to the unusually high number of Nisei valedictorians (in 1930 and 1937, Japanese students were three of the nine valedictorians for the city's nine high schools), salutatorians, and honor students among the city's high schools. To illustrate its collective appreciation and encourage younger students, the community staged special banquets to honor the achievers. In 1928 the *Japanese American Courier* proudly reported that the Japanese Students Club ranked sixth in scholastic average among the forty-five recognized student organizations at the University of Washington. Such encouragement had a salutary impact on Japanese college matriculation rates. In 1934 there were 88 Nisei students at the University of Washington, and by 1941 there were 458, compared with 35 Chinese students and 10 blacks. By the eve of World War II the Japanese and Jewish communities in Seattle were generally recognized as the most literate and educated of the immigrant communities in the city.[75]

Yet the spectacular Japanese success in education was not translated into commensurate employment opportunities outside the Nihonmachi. Nisei college graduates, like their Chinese, Filipino, or black counterparts, were forced to settle for low status jobs outside their community, work within family-owned businesses, or migrate from Seattle in search of opportunities. The larger, entrepreneurially oriented Japanese community, to be sure, could absorb far more college graduates than other nonwhite groups, and Japanese Americans could work as U.S. representatives for Japanese firms, but most people in the Nihonmachi knew the limits of employment opportunity in their community.[76]

Ironically the economic success of the Japanese seems to have precluded greater assertiveness in the face of discrimination. Japanese restaurants, laundries, and greengrocers dependent on white patronage were hardly willing to support highly publicized civil rights challenges that might alienate their clientele. Filipino and black workers, who by necessity sought employment outside their ethnic communities, felt compelled to challenge such acts to expand their employment opportunities. Of course, their challenges engendered corresponding hostility.

Filipinos were the group whose immigration pattern most resembled the sojourner model. Yet historical and cultural circumstances combined to encourage their assimilation. As American nationals they assumed the right to vote and to form unions to protect their interests as workers, and openly criticized those who would restrict their rights, including their choice of marriage partners. In asserting these rights, Filipinos generated considerable opposition from Asiaphobes. But their familiarity with American political principles and their awareness of the dire poverty of their homeland converged to create a radically different response to their new urban environment. Typical of that difference was their willingness to seek common cause with blacks and liberal whites on political and labor issues. Thus the most recent Asian arrivals (Filipinos) joined one of the oldest racial minorities in America (African Americans) to challenge the discrimination that limited their aspirations.

On the eve of World War II, Seattle's Japanese, Chinese, Filipino, and African American communities, while facing surprisingly similar racial restrictions, were nevertheless poised to move in different directions. Chinese Americans, whose homeland was a vital ally of the United States in the worldwide struggle against the Axis powers, would be the beneficiaries of the termination of exclusion policies. The Chinese were granted suffrage rights in 1943; and with the repeal of the "unequal treaties," the immigration of women and children slowly increased.

Seattle's Nihonmachi disappeared from 1942 to 1945 as its residents were taken to internment camps in the interior West. The wartime disruption of the community was followed, ironically, by a dramatic lowering of anti-Japanese enmity after World War II. Postwar Japanese American Seattle, far more middle class and well-educated than other nonwhites, was fortunately positioned to exploit liberalizing white attitudes. Indeed, internment camp Issei returnees found it difficult to recreate their community as the Nisei rapidly moved beyond the physical and psychological boundaries of Seattle's prewar Nihonmachi.[77]

Independence for the Philippines, delayed by World War II, came in 1946 and was accompanied by continued immigration restrictions. For the next two decades the annual quota was one hundred. Special exceptions that allowed immigration of Filipino "war brides" slowly moved the Seattle community to more balanced gender ratios; but immigrants, still heavily dependent on seasonal agricultural labor and work in the canneries, remained economically marginalized.[78]

Finally, African American Seattle would also undergo profound change. The huge World War II migration to the city, quadrupling the prewar population, made blacks indisputably the largest minority. They held this distinction until 1990, when Asians, augmented by continued Chinese immigration and rising numbers of Vietnamese refugees, again exceeded the city's African American population. But from 1945 to the 1970s the black migration spawned an extensive black ghetto which shared many of the characteristics of the rest of urban black America.

Chapter 5

The Forging of a Black Community Ethos, 1900–1940

Virtually all studies of black communities begin with the premise that the community was defined by denial and exclusion. Yet exclusion did not completely determine the nature of black Seattle or, for that matter, any African American urban community. Seattle's blacks forged a common ethos, a "guiding complex of beliefs," to borrow a phrase from urban historian Blaine A. Brownwell,[1] which reflected the psychological boundaries of community as much as restrictive covenants established the spatial boundaries. Most urban history case studies have focused on residential segregation, employment discrimination, and political impotence in determining the physical and psychological limits of the black community, providing an incomplete description of the essence of African American urban life. The community, according to this paradigm, was formed and maintained by denial and exclusion. While racial discrimination by both individuals and institutions is understandably critical in the fashioning of black life in urban America, it has not exclusively determined African American community development. That process was also forged by the manner in which black Seattleites, through their churches, fraternal orders, clubs, and sports activities, sought to retain and transform their rural values and sense of shared culture.

135

Thus it becomes necessary to examine institutional development, not out of any obligatory sense of explaining every facet of community life, but because these various organizations and institutions represented the nexus of community. As Sandra Schoenberg and Charles Bailey have written of African American St. Louis: "A community is the product of a combination of institutions, of residents who feel a sense of identification with a name and a set of boundaries, and of social networks which connect the people to the institutions." Without these social networks, and the concomitant racial consciousness such networks advanced, black Seattle would have been nothing more than aggregations of individuals seeking assimilation into the larger society.[2]

Seattle's blacks were bound together by an intricate web of mutually reinforcing kin, religious, fraternal, and social relationships. Those who might not belong to the same church nevertheless joined the same social club or fraternal order, met at picnics and dances or athletic events, participated in other community functions sponsored by the East Madison YMCA, or argued politics at the NAACP forum or political club meetings. Furthermore, in a community with relatively few newcomers between 1910 and 1940, numerous black Seattleites were invariably related by blood and marriage. Social pretensions were expressed and class distinctions evident, but with a 1940 population of 3,700 in a community where doctors and lawyers might share a church pew with unskilled or unemployed laborers or porters, class lines were understandably blurred.[3]

By the beginning of the twentieth century, an ethos of community was emerging in black Seattle. Sociologist Richard T. Schaefer defines culture as the sum of behaviors, values, and attitudes differentiating one group from another. Schaefer's definition seems particularly appropriate for Seattle's small black community, which assiduously molded its particular cultural values through thousands of mutually reinforcing interactions at home, in church, at the workplace, and on the streets of the Central District. Furthermore, Seattle's African Americans, most of whom were less than one generation removed from the rural South, were "poised between two worlds,"[4] to use Lawrence Levine's apt description, seeking a continuity between their rural folk heritage and the new, unfamiliar urban environment. To meet this challenge they created or reconstituted a host of institutions and organizations rooted in prior experience. The church, and its ancillary groups (the usher boards, youth choirs, women's auxiliaries), the fraternal orders, social service and recreational institutions such as the East Madison YMCA and the Sojourner Truth Home, all helped facilitate the transformation of a rural folk into an urban society.*

Black Seattle's community institutions kept alive and, in the process, helped define the African American heritage. Often the names of institutions or organizations – the Sojourner Truth Home, Phyllis Wheatley YWCA, Toussaint L'Overture Lodge of Prince Hall Masons – were conscious attempts to identify with that heritage. Through the 1920s and 1930s, "the Methodist Church has always kept up with Black history," recalled Sara Oliver Jackson. "I was so amazed that the young people [today] didn't know Black history. I realize now it's because I didn't take my children to the church. . . . Harriet Tubman, Sojourner Truth, we did all of these people. We had pageants . . . that portrayed *our* people."[5]

Unlike the city's other ethnic groups, Seattle's African Americans had no separate linguistic or territorial focus, yet as much as the Swedes or Japanese, they tried to conserve their cultural legacy by creating organizations reflecting the virtues and values, the modes of thought and action, crafted over generations by people with a profound understanding of their unique and troubled past. This is not to argue that blacks did not borrow from those around them. Nor did they accept in principle racial segregation or exclusion. But black Seattleites during the first four decades of the twentieth century were proud of the social and cultural sphere they created and willingly defended it.

That pride, however, was tempered by anxiety and ambivalence. Public apprehensions over southern dialects and boisterous speech, fundamentalist preaching styles, and the proliferation of jazz and blues nightclubs were not simply conflicts between old settlers and migrants, or clashes of bourgeois and working-class values. They also reflected the anguish of a people undergoing a transformation from the rural past to an urban present. The history of black Seattle, and numerous other African American urban communities, is rooted in this paradox of preservation and transformation.

Various religious, social, and fraternal institutions and organizations emerged after 1900 to give form to that community ethos, but the black church provided its foundation. "We always went to church. As far as Negro people are concerned, that is the nucleus of our

* See the Appendix for a list of black churches, fraternal orders, and social clubs in pre–World War II Seattle.

community anywhere you go," declared Sara Oliver Jackson. "The church was a very intricate part of your life," remembered Constance Thomas. "If you were a young black person [new] to the city, the first place you always would go would be the church. . . . That's how you met black people. Social events and musicals – all that was part of the church; the biggest barbecue of the year was held at Mt. Zion. We knew everyone through the church."[6]

By 1940 ten churches ministered to the spiritual needs of the community. The oldest ones, First African Methodist Episcopal, founded in 1886, and Mount Zion Baptist Church, formed in 1890, had the largest membership. First AME's 600 members in 1940, for example, represented nearly 15 percent of Seattle's black population. As early as 1920 these churches were complemented by religious bodies at opposite ends of the congregational and class spectrum. The Episcopalians had St. Philips Chapel and the Presbyterians had Grace Presbyterian Church, both noted for their "quiet, dignified" services. But there were also the exuberant, emotional fifty-member storefront churches such as the Full Gospel Pentecostal Mission, founded in 1929. By the 1930s "nontraditional" churches, such as Father Divine's Temple of Peace, had also emerged in the small black community.[7]

Virtually all the churches welcomed newcomers to the city, usually delegating members to meet arrivals at the train depot or the piers, and assisted them in locating housing or employment. More important, their services provided a familiar, comforting setting to recent migrants who otherwise found little to remind them of their former homes.

Seattle's churches also sponsored picnics, dances, athletic teams, and literary societies, group activities that formed the nexus of the community. First AME's annual picnics, beginning in 1891, were major community events through World War II. Many ostensibly secular organizations in black Seattle, including the Masonic lodges, political clubs, and social service centers such as the Sojourner Truth Home for single women, evolved from the local churches. The four largest churches – First AME, Mount Zion Baptist, Grace Presbyterian, and Ebeneezer AME Zion – opened their facilities for public forums and rallies. Interested parties debated repeal of the Volstead Act or learned of African or West Indian cultures and political struggles at First AME; heard W. E. B. Du Bois, Mary White Ovington, A. Philip Randolph, and Congressman Oscar DePriest address black Seattle from the pulpit of Mount Zion; or met at Ebeneezer AME Zion for protest meetings against union discrimination or police brutality and support rallies for the Scottsboro Boys or Ethiopia's resistance to Mussolini's invasion.[8]

Black fraternal orders had, after churches, the most broad-based membership in black Seattle. Although avowedly bourgeois in outlook, their ranks included individuals from virtually all of the economic, occupational, and denominational backgrounds. As Florette Henri remarked in her study of the post–World War I black migration to northern cities, fraternal lodges with their elaborate secret rituals, splendid regalia, and pompous titles were social clubs, nascent insurance companies, and burial societies. Seattle's fraternal orders provided financial assistance to sick members, trained new initiates in the tenets of ''good character,'' and prepared members for community leadership roles. They also provided low-interest loans to their members and financial assistance to widows (or widowers) and children of deceased members. They purchased property ostensibly for meeting and recreational purposes but also as a symbol of black financial success through cooperative endeavor.[9]

The first fraternal orders – the Knights of Pythias, the Masons, and the Odd Fellows – date back to the early 1890s; but by 1925 seven additional lodges, each with a women's auxiliary, were active in the city. And since these organizations were national in scope, reaching into virtually every black American community, their organizational structures, rituals, and public activities afforded familiar surroundings for lodge members new to the city, easing the transition from a rural to urban society.[10]

''Nothing,'' according to Lawrence Levine, ''could look more benign than the behavior of the black fraternal orders. When their role is finally studied with the care it demands, I suspect it will become evident that they played a subversive part.'' Seattle's African Americans did in fact join these organization because of their ''subversive part'' in undermining the negative stereotypes of themselves. In such orders, black folk could engage in activities that exuded pomp, pageantry, and power. Women and men who were denied notoriety and prestige outside the Central District could regally strut down 23rd Avenue, the main thoroughfare of the black community, during the annual Elks or Masonic parades. African Americans who had been told that they could not sustain viable organizations could proudly point to the Elks Home and Masonic Hall, two prominent Central District landmarks, as examples of voluntary, cooperative endeavor. Blacks could take center stage in their lodges, where they formulated the rules, voted, held office, administered budgets, and surrounded themselves with all the trappings of power.[11]

Black Seattle's social and cultural clubs also contributed to the definition of community. Many of these groups, such as the Bridge Club, were ephemeral gatherings of like-minded people pursuing recreational interests. But others were dedicated to community "uplift" and the preservation of the values and views which helped define black Seattle and set it apart from the rest of the city. "Uplift" was the term applied, recalled Horace Cayton, Jr., to any activity that would raise the general conditions and status of black people. The various "I will rise" societies in black Seattle, such as the Dorcus Charity Club founded by his mother, Susie Revels Cayton, were the organizational consequence of such efforts. Many of these clubs were educationally and culturally oriented, which meant, in the language of the time, "haute" culture — sponsoring literary societies and classical music appreciation societies.[12]

Black women like Cayton played a critical role in the various social clubs. Their male contemporaries who dismissed such organizations as "women's work" or "women's sphere" grossly underestimated the role of these societies in simultaneously preserving traditions and values while improving black life in the city. The work of the Dorcus Charity Club, founded in 1906, is one example. Eventually to become one of the longest-lived "uplift" organizations in black Seattle, the club was formed in response to an urgent request for assistance in placing abandoned twin baby girls in a private home. The black girls had rickets, thus no adoptive parents would take responsibility for them. Children's Home officials, unsure of what action to take, turned the girls over to the King County Hospital, which decided to send them to Medical Lake, an institution for the mentally ill. As a last resort, Medical Lake officials contacted Cayton and she and three other black women – Letitia A. Graves, Alice S. Presto, and Hester Ray – recognizing this as one of a number of such cases, organized the Dorcus Charity Club. The twins were placed in a foster home located by Cayton and three years later the club continued to provided their full support, "until a suitable home can be found for them."[13]

Not large enough to sponsor its own charity facility, as the Sojourner Truth Club would later do when it created the Sojourner Truth Home in 1919, the Dorcus Club paid the medical expenses of a destitute girl for the twenty months she remained in Children's Orthopedic Hospital and provided rent payments for indigent widows, collected and distributed Christmas toys to orphaned children, donated a bed to Orthopedic Hospital, and gave clothing to the Ryther Home for sick widows.[14]

As black Seattle's population grew, and during World War I became more prosperous, other female social clubs emerged. Although clubs such as the Lincoln Helping Hand Club with its twenty-four members and the Carter Industrial and Literary Club with twenty-six members in 1918 were small and therefore constantly seeking operating funds, they nevertheless pursued their work buoyed by the knowledge that they were part of the National Association of Colored Women, a network of voluntary groups across black America. The NACW was founded in Washington, D.C., in 1896, when two smaller federations merged. Less than twenty years after its founding it represented 50,000 women in twenty-eight federations and over 1,000 affiliated clubs throughout the nation including eight in Seattle.[15]

The NACW represented a departure from the established patterns of women's groups as auxiliaries of men's organizations. Mary Church Terrell, the first NACW president and one of black America's richest women, vowed that the organization would work with poor women, "the lowly, illiterate and even the vicious, to whom [we] are bound by ties of race and sex . . . to reclaim them." Coupled with help to the poor was the call for moral uplift, usually defined as moral training in the home combined with lessons on civic responsibility particularly for black children. "The Negro home," declared Josephine Bruce, another NACW founder, "is rapidly . . . becoming the center of social and intellectual life; it is building up strength and righteousness in its sons and daughters, and equipping them for the inevitable battle of life which grows out of the struggles for existence."[16]

The proposals of the NACW simply ratified the views to which Seattle black women such as Emma Ray and Susie Revels Cayton already subscribed. Ray's leadership of the Frances Ellen Harper WCTU in the 1890s in its work with Jackson Street prostitutes, and Cayton's highly attenuated sense of noblesse oblige conditioned by a childhood spent in the home of a U.S. senator and church bishop, did not require outside direction or motivation. But dozens of early twentieth-century black Seattle women engaged in the work of "uplift" were gratified by the knowledge that they were among African American women across the country who labored for self-improvement and support for others less fortunate.

The Phyllis Wheatley YWCA, which became one of the most enduring community institutions and the vital center of black Seattle social and cultural life, was, ironically, the consequence of the turn-of-the-century national campaign to impose racial segregation in the YWCA. Organized as a separate facility in 1919, it reflected the desire of the national body to encourage the "natural groupings of people along occupational, nationality and racial lines" and to follow the dictates of contemporary "American folkways" which mandated the separation of races. That policy had evolved from the first segregated YWCA established in New York in 1900, and by the time the Phyllis Wheatley Branch was created in 1919, such segregation was readily evident in most northern cities as well as throughout the South.[17] But the separate facility in Seattle also grew out of the activities of black clubwomen, who, while abhorring segregation in principle, nonetheless moved, in response to the pressing need for recreational facilities and temporary shelter for homeless black women, to create the Phyllis Wheatley YWCA.

The Sojourner Truth Home, in contrast, was an entirely black-initiated endeavor to meet the perceived social needs of the community. Sponsored by black clubwomen, the Home provided a facility for unwed mothers, single women, the destitute, and "friendless." It would be incorrect to place the burden of community and cultural preservation solely on the shoulders of these middle-class black women who presumed their views and values to be in the best interests of the entire black community or to argue that they alone were responsible for the self-help efforts so vital to black Seattle's survival. Nevertheless, their efforts reminded all of black Seattle of its particular interests, challenges, and aspirations.[18]

African American Seattle was concerned about preserving the links to its heritage, but it was equally attentive to its future and particularly the future of its children. Remembering the inferior education that was the lot of most southern black children, and stressing education and family cohesion as prerequisites for racial progress, black Seattleites ranked the education of their children a major priority. John T. Gayton's attitude was typical. "He believed," according to his son, John, Jr., "that education was the answer, and he wanted each of us to go to college and really make something of ourselves."[19]

John T. Gayton's sentiments about the importance of education were shared by many black Seattleites. In the spring of 1933 the Community Scholarship Fund was established to "stimulate cultural growth and level upward our economic status, by encouraging higher education and vocational guidance for the youth of the community." The fund offered two $100 scholarships to students of "promise and need." The first awards were presented to Winifred Ingram and Avis Dennis, who graduated from the University of Washington in 1937.[20]

Southern migrants to Seattle, like their counterparts throughout the urban North, immediately recognized greater educational opportunity in the city. Parents encouraged school attendance in the early grades and city school officials made no effort to segregate or isolate black pupils. Still, regular school attendance did not automatically translate into significant high school completion rates or college education. Blacks in 1940 completed 8.4 years of school, only slightly ahead of the immigrant rate but well below the city average of 10.8. Only 2.7 percent of the blacks completed college, while the city average was 8.3 percent (see Table 10). Conversely, 16 percent of the black population completed fewer than five years of schooling, far worse than the citywide average of 4.8 percent.[21]

The high percentage of African Americans completing fewer than five years of schooling obviously reflects the deficient education of many southern migrants, but the high rate of school attendance in the early grades compared with the small number of high school and college graduates is more problematic. Why were so many Central District children, given their parents' regard for formal training, apt to leave school before graduation? Some apparently dropped out to supplement parents' meager incomes, others to establish independent households. The Depression forced large numbers of African Americans – in fact, all groups – into the work force at a younger age. But perceived opportunity and pervasive discrimination induced many black teenagers into the labor force earlier than other groups. As Samuel S. Bowles has described, black students who left school may have been acting in an economically rational manner. They realized that additional education alone would not guarantee access to professional careers or more lucrative occupations; it would, in fact, interfere with wage earning during their younger, more productive years. According to Leonard T. Gayton, "There wasn't much money for college [during the Depression], and even if we had been able to graduate, what good would it have done?"[22]

Degrees from the best institutions were no guarantee of commensurate employment. Winifred Ingram and Avis Dennis, the first community scholarship recipients in 1933, are cases in point. Ingram, with a degree in sociology, took one of the few positions available

Table 10
Years of College Completed, Age 25 and Older, Seattle, 1940

	City Population			Black Population		
	Total	Male	Female	Total	Male	Female
Total population	249,522	125,563	125,959	2,738	1,643	1,140
Four or more years college	20,774	12,017	8,757	76	43	33
Percentage of total	8.3	9.5	6.9	2.7	2.6	2.8

Source: Juana Racquel Royster-Horn, "The Academic and Extracurricular Under-graduate Experiences of Three Black Women at the University of Washington, 1935 to 1941" (Ph.D. diss.: University of Washington, 1980), p. 133.

to a college-educated woman in the 1930s: she worked on the staff at the Phyllis Wheatley YWCA. Dennis, despite his engineering degree from the most prestigious university in the state, was nonetheless initially denied employment in the engineering section of the State Highway Department because of his race and was not hired permanently until 1945.[23]

Marjorie King, a 1937 University of Washington graduate, offered a slightly different explanation for the low number of Seattle blacks attending college, coupling gender with economics: "The men had to work. There was no such thing as someone sending them to school. They weren't considered for scholarships. They would take one or two courses and then they would leave." Her explanation is set against a skewed background of graduation rates. Of the forty-five black females and forty-four black males attending the University of Washington between 1935 and 1941, twelve females and one male received a bachelor's degree while one female and two males received a master's.[24] Even well-educated, solidly middle-class black parents were unable to pass their educational advantages on to their children. Madge Cayton, daughter of Seattle's most prominent black couple and granddaughter of a former U.S. senator, graduated from the University of Washington in 1925 with a baccalaureate degree in international business but could not find a job outside the black community unless she chose to "pass" for white. Refusing that option, she became a waitress and cashier in small restaurants in the black community before moving to Chicago in 1935 to become a social worker. Maxine Pollard, daughter of Dr. Charles Maxwell, black

Seattle's most prominent physician in the 1930s, chose not to enter college because she feared she could not get a position commensurate with her education: "I would have to go to the South. We didn't have any black teachers and only one black social worker when I graduated from high school, and no nurses that were known as black though there were some that passed." Pollard remained in Seattle and worked as a maid and stock clerk through World War II.[25]

Black Seattle was proud of the thoroughly integrated school system commonplace before 1940, a rare setting for most African American youth in the United States. Yet integration could also prove isolating and academically limiting for some black children. Seattle resident Sara Oliver Jackson remembers the schools as giving "very little push" to black youngsters: "The teachers we had didn't seem to give you much encouragement. The only encouragement you got was from being in church. . . . So I drifted along. I wasn't part of anything so nobody paid any attention to me. I could pass, I could do my work, but not up to any qualification at all, but I could get by. . . . You thought you were getting away with something, [but] you were doing exactly what the structure wanted you to do."[26]

Although the Japanese community in Seattle was about twice the size of the African American community in the 1930s, the number of Japanese students at the University of Washington averaged ten times the number of black students. Taking into consideration the black Seattle students who traveled to southern black colleges, it was nonetheless clear that Seattle's Japanese were far more likely to attend college. Yet Japanese college graduates faced the same discrimination that barred black graduates from virtually all positions commensurate with their education. A Nisei's lament in 1937 that while he "would much rather [be] a doctor or lawyer" he was forced to be a "professional carrot washer" expressed the profound sense of grievance of all nonwhites subject to restricted opportunities.[27] Yet Seattle's Nihonmachi had a much larger middle class supported by ethnically oriented businesses which could absorb far more college graduates than the black, Chinese, or Filipino communities could. Nisei graduates bitterly and correctly complained of their restricted opportunities. Nonetheless, the prospect of receiving employment in a predominately middle-class Japanese community, with a growing demand for the services of doctors, lawyers, and accountants, provided Japanese graduates with a significant advantage over a much more impoverished black Seattle. A comparison of the level of financial support for education is one example of the relative affluence of the two communities. While black Seattle was proud of its $100 scholarship given during the 1930s, Seattle's Nihonmachi as early as 1920 offered to contribute $10,000 toward the construction of a public school in its neighborhood.[28]

The sharply divergent rewards of education in a city where racial discrimination was widely and routinely practiced persuaded many black students against additional education. Such choices, no matter how rational in the context of the era, did not augur well for the future of black Seattle. The larger number of Japanese college graduates, while not substantially altering white attitudes in the 1920s and 1930s, positioned this Asian group to advance rapidly once barriers to employment were dismantled after World War II. The choices made by many Seattle African Americans in the 1930s ensured that they and their children would not be similarly positioned in the 1960s to take advantage of falling barriers.

There can be little doubt that the black family was undergoing modification at the beginning of the twentieth century, adopting a more flexible, extended family lifestyle to meet the challenges of urban life. Various historians have traced similar changes in the urban milieu to the oldest African American urban communities in the United States.[29] The 1910–40 period has often been described by urban historians and sociologists as the beginning of an era of family disintegration and social disorientation in the black urban North. Seattle's families, however, proved remarkably adaptive and capable of surviving the vicissitudes of urban life.

Seattle's black families were small. The median family size in 1930 of 2.13 children was far below both the native white median (2.79) and the foreign-born median (2.96). Moreover, 81 percent of Seattle's black households in 1930 had no children younger than ten.[30] Fewer dependents allowed for more economic maneuverability; during lean times, blacks could more readily absorb the loss or reduction of income or could migrate to other areas. But small families, particularly those without teenage children, could also prove a liability. As Olivier Zunz noted in his study of Detroit, immigrant families often pooled incomes of adult and teenage wage earners, a strategy that assisted those families during recessions, strikes, or plant closings and provided an economic boost during prosperity. Seattle's Asians, while generally excluded from industrial occupations, nevertheless incorporated their children into ethnic businesses to reduce labor costs and enhance family income. As recent arrivals with few working-age children, and with employment prospects confined to low paying, marginal jobs and virtually no self-employment prospects, black families could rarely rely on nonadult wage earners to supplement family income.[31]

The black community ethos was also fashioned by the way the city's African Americans entertained themselves. Although black Seattle numbered fewer than 4,000 people before World War II, its nightlife was remarkably vibrant. Edward Pitter described the scene in a 1973 interview: "We had dances all over town. . . . We had fully dressed dances, I mean fully dressed. Tails, I've got my old silk hat, it's up in the attic. I used to wear a silk hat and tails and I had a cape you throw back and monocle."[32]

Black nightclubs were the heart of the night-life scene, and most were located along Jackson Street in the red-light district, which extended from Yesler to Weller and from Fifth to Twelfth avenues. These clubs featured black entertainers and performers who attracted white patrons from throughout the city and region. As Robert Wright, the nephew of a leading black nightclub owner, recalled: "In 1935 and 1936 you could see as many white people on 12th and Jackson at midnight as you'd see on 3rd and Union in midday."[33]

E. Russell "Noodles" Smith, the owner of the Golden West Hotel, was the impresario of black nightlife. His establishments included the Golden West Club on Seventh Avenue, which during the 1920s developed a clientele of Pullman porters, steamship stewards, and travelers and was one of the city's "brightest spots." By the 1930s Smith owned three additional clubs: the Black and Tan Club, the Ubangi Club, with its distinctive African decor, and the New Harlem Club, appropriately enough "uptown," on the 1900 block of Fourth Avenue in Seattle's Central Business District. The New Harlem and the Black and Tan were large enough to accommodate full-size bands with lavish floor shows. Following a nationwide pattern, Duke Ellington, Count Basie, and Louie Armstrong, who played at predominately white establishments such as the Orpheum Theater, came to Smith's clubs afterward. Occasionally Smith brought talent directly to Seattle, such as the chorus line of six girls from Pittsburgh to perform before a mostly white audience at the Black and Tan Club.[34]

Noodles Smith lived the fast life in Depression-era Seattle. At a time when most blacks could hardly afford the cost of public transportation, Smith owned a Stutz Bearcat and a 1921 Packard, which he reputedly purchased from movie actress Mary Pickford in 1930. His only Seattle relative, nephew Robert Wright, had a car and chauffeur at his disposal. Surrounding himself with fast cars and fast women, Smith reveled in his role as club owner. "Whiskey is made to sell, not to drink," became his motto as he endeavored to entertain black, white, and Asian Seattle.[35]

Smith's success attracted rivals. John Henry "Doc" Hamilton, a native of West Point, Mississippi, arrived in Seattle in 1916 and held a succession of odd jobs before joining the army the following year. He spent two years in the service during World War I and returned to Seattle in 1919 and started a small nightclub. He owned a series of clubs and cabarets throughout the 1920s and 1930s, and the nightclub carrying his name was arguably the city's most famous cabaret in the mid-1930s. Fred Owen's Rocking Chair, Sherman Spates's Congo Club on Jackson Street, Dave Lee's Basin Street Club, the 300 Club, and the Mardi Gras all contributed to the nightlife of black Seattle. Often doubling as restaurants in the day and early evening hours, and promoting "Texas blues" and West Coast jazz on alternate nights, these clubs flouted law and custom by allowing gambling, after-hours drinking, and interracial mingling. They were the only places where well-to-do white businessmen and socialites met black and Asian laborers and maids as social equals. Seattle resident Marguerite Johnson recalled Seattle's interwar cabaret scene, contrasting it with post–World War II nightlife: "Men were men in those days; they didn't smoke dope. The music was going. They had live music. That's where I first remember [bandleader] Billy Daniels . . . twisting and turning and twisting. . . . And he was *terribly* good looking . . . and the women were just crazy about him. Women sat at the tables and drank their beer and whiskey, while the men sat at the bars. But the women didn't go to the bar, they just sat at the table."[36]

By the early 1920s, Seattle was "on the circuit" for numerous professional entertainers and athletes. Bandleaders Cab Calloway, Duke Ellington, and Lionel Hampton, who performed at downtown theaters or auditoriums, stayed at segregated hotels like the Golden West and performed at Southside nightclubs "after hours." Frank Fair's description of visiting celebrities at one hotel for one weekend in 1937 in his "Round the Town" column for the *Northwest Enterprise* suggests the extent to which Seattle had become integrated into the national black entertainment network: "The Golden West Hotel was the scene of much activity with Fletcher Henderson's band, the Harlem Globetrotters basketball team and Jessie Owens' outfit all stationed there while making their appearances in the Northwest.''[37]

Black nightclubs also provided employment for local entertainers, some of whom eventually became successful outside the Pacific Northwest. Despite the group's name, Cecil Finley and his Californians were a local band that worked most of the Southside clubs. Singers Stella Jackson and Frieda Jones, who became regular entertainers on the cruise ship *H. F. Alexander*, appeared at Doc Hamilton's and other clubs in the 1930s. Syvilla Fort, a jazz dancer who according to local lore ''got her start'' at the Mardi Gras, performed with Seattle's Negro Repertory Company and Katherine Dunham's dance troupe before opening a studio in New York, which provided training for dancer and choreographer Alvin Ailey and film actor Marlon Brando. Jimmy and Wayne Adams, two Seattle musicians, ventured the farthest from home in search of success when they played in Shanghai, China, nightclubs between 1935 and 1937 before returning to Seattle to organize a band at the Black and Tan Club.[38]

Leonard Gayton played with the Garfield Ramblers, a five-member jazz band formed at Garfield High School which featured Evelyn Bundy as its vocalist. The Ramblers developed a local following after stints at Doc Hamilton's and later at the Chinese Garden. Gayton in a 1976 interview recalled the possibilities for success and his own decision to leave the band: ''In the Roaring Twenties I had a hip flask and a supplier, and at night I played drums [with the Ramblers]. I made good money then, often as much as $30 in a single night, and I thought I would do this all my life. Pretty soon, though, the people I played with left town. . . . I thought of leaving with them, but I stayed home.'' Whether they stayed home like Leonard Gayton, or traveled to distant venues like Syvilla Fort and the Adams brothers, Seattle's black entertainers helped fashion the city's remarkably dynamic musical environment which later produced such legendary stars as Quincy Jones, Ray Charles, and Jimi Hendrix.[39]

Vaudeville, legitimate theater, and the concert stage provided alternatives to the jazz and blues scene and introduced whites and Asians to black theater. Dancers Dave and Tressie Stratton, and vaudevillian comedians George McClennon and Tabor and Green, played regularly at the Orpheum. In the 1920s and 1930s all-black troupes staged *Harlem Burlesque, Change Your Luck, Lennox Avenue Follies*, and Eubie Blake's *Shuffle Along, Jr.* at Seattle's Rex, Paramount, and Pantages theaters. Occasionally dramas such as Garland Anderson's three-act play *Appearances* were performed at the prestigious Metropolitan Theater. Roland Hayes, Paul Robeson, and Marian Anderson also gave frequent concerts in the city.[40]

Despite its minute population, black Seattle produced remarkably gifted local actresses and actors whose talents were showcased in the late 1930s through the Negro Repertory Company of the Seattle Federal Theater Project (FTP), one of numerous New Deal programs designed to reinvigorate the national economy during the Depression. The FTP was specifically designated to provide work for unemployed thespians while introducing live theater to segments of the American public previously ignored by the theatrical industry. The FTP was also committed to exploring via drama and comedy the diversity of the American population, according to historian Evamarii Alexandria Johnson. The theatrical "units" were encouraged to "explain the lives of the people in the social environment where the unit existed." Several ethnic units were established, including a Spanish-speaking unit in Florida and a Yiddish unit in New York. But the fourteen black groups formed in cities as disparate as New York, Raleigh, North Carolina, and Peoria, Illinois, attained the most notoriety of all the ethnic units. The Negro Repertory Company, one of five theater groups of the Seattle FTP during its three-year existence between 1936 and 1939, produced fifteen plays and its members collaborated on other Seattle productions. The Seattle NRC was third in the nation in the number of productions after New York and Boston.[41]

The stimulus for the Seattle NRC originated outside the black community. Florence Bean James and Burton James, two actors active in the New York theatrical community since 1916, moved to Seattle in 1928 and established the Seattle Repertory Playhouse near the University of Washington campus. Soon they began to follow the work of black amateur actors at First AME Church and in 1933 encouraged the most talented of the group to participate in a production of *In Abraham's Bosom* at the Seattle Repertory Playhouse. Joseph S. Jackson, executive secretary of the Seattle Urban League, was the leading actor in the production. The critical success of the play prompted the Jameses to submit a proposal in 1935 for a Negro unit of the newly created Federal Theater Project. The following January the Seattle NRC was created with seventy-three actors and singers.

The NRC's productions included classics such as Aristophanes' *Lysistrata* and Shakespeare's *The Taming of the Shrew* as well as political dramas like *It Can't Happen Here* by Sinclair Lewis and *Black Empire* by

Christine Ames and Clarke Palmer, which described the corruption of the Haitian government following that country's revolution. One production, *Natural Man*, a musical dramatization of the John Henry legend, was written by Seattle NRC member Theodore Brown. Some NRC plays such as *Stevedore*, which opened in 1936 with a cast of seventy-five black actors, challenged prevailing stereotypes and discrimination. It dramatized the campaign of white and black workers to organize a union, centering on the character of Lonnie Thompson, a black union organizer ostracized by white workers because of his race and criticized by black nonunion dockworkers as a "trouble maker and strike instigator." The play began with a white woman's false accusation of rape by a black man. Thompson, because "he refused to cooperate in his own degradation as one of the suspects," became the person accused. *Stevedore* concluded with black and white workers fighting side by side against company goons, and with Thompson dying during the confrontation. With its allusions to interracial rape and black-white labor rivalry, *Stevedore* was a provocative, socially conscious play which unquestionably met the FTP charter criteria of providing "free, adult, uncensored theater that was challenging, entertaining and experimental, and regionally inspired."[42] Although the setting was New Orleans, the play was particularly appropriate for Seattle, then in the throes of a longshore strike, and which had a long, tortuous history of black-white confrontation on the waterfront.

By June 1936, the novelty of black casts proved a constant draw and the NRC "was already being accepted as one of the moving forces in Seattle's cultural life" as reflected by the production of *Lysistrata*, performed by fifty black actors in the 1,400-seat Moore Theater. The Jameses decided to set the play in Ethiopia rather than Greece, against the backdrop of the Italian invasion which had begun one year earlier. Yet artistic and political sensibilities were not easily reconciled: the play was canceled after opening night. State WPA supervisor Don Abel ordered the production terminated and refunds given to 1,100 second-night ticket holders because his wife and secretary, who viewed it opening night, reported it "indecent and bawdy." The play's unabashedly anti-Fascist political message also doomed it as too politically controversial.[43]

Not every NRC production pushed predominately white Seattle audiences to the edge of social consciousness. Plays such as *Is Zat So* and *Swing, Gates, Swing*, while financially successful, nevertheless upheld the singing, dancing, "funnin'," and "jivin'" stereotype long identified with black Americans. For the most part, black performers and the African American community accepted these caricatures and no doubt obtained ironic satisfaction from playing theatrical roles Seattle whites naively assumed remained central to black life. The Jameses proved generally sensitive to local black actors' concerns about invidious caricatures of African American life. "Mrs. James tried not to affect us with White culture, but to let us bring out our Black culture," reported NRC actress Sara Oliver Jackson. "She was so surprised that here we had this Negro dialect in plays that we were supposed to do, but Seattle people didn't speak Negro dialect. These people didn't even understand the Negro dialect she was speaking! So she says, 'Well, just speak like yourself. Don't try any dialect. Speak the lines.'"[44]

One play, however, *Porgy and Bess*, proved so replete with offensive stereotypes that it sparked a rebellion by the NRC cast and protest by Seattle's black community. *Porgy* was the first play chosen by Florence and Burton James for the NRC but was never staged. The official reason given was the failure of the directors to secure the rights, but unofficially the play was sabotaged by members of the company and black community leaders. NRC actors, in fear of losing their jobs if outspoken, began a "whispering campaign" against the play because of its stereotypes. Meanwhile the Seattle Citizens Committee, a black civic group, and the King County Colored Progressive Democratic Club voiced their objections in a letter to George Hood, Washington State FTP administrator: "The play is something that really is not wanted in Seattle or any other place. It is too degrading. . . . Any play that is elevating to the race, we have no objections to . . . but there is nothing to be gained from [*Porgy*]. In *Porgy* the word 'nigger' is used consistently, and that is something that the general population [is] not going to tolerate. We do not need *Porgy*."[45]

Despite its short-lived history, the NRC had a profound impact on black Seattle. The *Northwest Enterprise*, although careful never to contradict the white press in its assessment of the content and quality of NRC productions, chronicled with obvious pride the activities and achievements of the theatrical company and its individual members. Moreover, the NRC provided badly needed employment. Sara Oliver Jackson, who became one of the leading NRC performers, recalled receiving $80 a month: "That was the most money that you could imagine! Believe it or not, $80 a month *was* a very good salary. You could rent a house and still have money left over to take care of other things." The NRC also opened cultural vistas for talented black amateur actors, playwrights, and choreographers. Syvilla Fort, for example, choreographed the 1936 production *Noah* while Shirley Lola Graham, who in 1951 married historian and political activist W. E. B. Du Bois, co-wrote a number of plays for the NRC during the 1930s. Joseph Isom Staton, a leading NRC actor, still remembered with obvious pride four decades later the telegram received from George Bernard Shaw congratulating the group on being the first black theatrical company to produce *Androcles and the Lion*.[46]

Negro Repertory Company members were neither hard core unemployed nor professional actors seeking theatrical work prior to their association with the NRC. They were churchgoing, working, and middle-class people who suddenly found themselves exposed to the professional theater as actors and stage crew. Perhaps as many as two hundred persons, five percent of black Seattle's 1940 population, worked on various NRC productions during its three-year history.[47]

A few fortunate members pursued their new career interests in the East or in Southern California. *Natural Man*, which played three performances at the Metropolitan Theater in downtown Seattle, attracted the attention of Rex Ingram, leading actor with the New York NRC unit, and in 1938 Theodore Brown moved east to New York to promote the play. Howard Biggs remained with the NRC as musical director until 1939, then went to New York to work with bandleader and playwright Noble Sissle. Syvilla Fort, a dancer with the NRC, eventually left Seattle for Chicago, where she worked in the Katherine Dunham dance company. Even for those who never left Seattle, the NRC provided the small black community with a link to the African American cultural activity in New York, Los Angeles, and Chicago.[48]

For white Seattleites who had scant contact with blacks, a Negro Repertory Company production provided an alternative to the stereotypes of African Americans as either uneducated menial servants or criminals. The most active unit of the Seattle Federal Theater Project, the NRC performed, usually for free, in institutions, parks, and hospitals in addition to its regular productions. Its members emerged as local celebrities beyond the Central District. The NRC became, according to its historian, "a tangible example of black achievement" and an informal theatrical ambassador of goodwill.[49]

Sports also helped define and distinguish black Seattle. Of course, the accomplishments of their athletic kinsmen had long been a source of pride and vicarious identification among most ethnic or racial groups in America. But black Seattle, viewing African American sports achievements as a refutation of racial supremacy arguments and as one of the few areas where black abilities were readily recognized, gave athletes and athletic activities central importance in their lives. Central District residents avidly followed the career of basketball star Charles Patterson when he played at Franklin High School and later became the first black athlete at the University of Oregon. Local boxers George "Gorilla" Jones and Henry Woods, and semiprofessional tennis player Emmett McIver, also thrilled residents with their athletic prowess and competitiveness. During the 1930s the Ubangi Blackhawks, a predominately black (it had two Japanese players on its twenty-player roster) semipro football team sponsored by nightclub owner "Noodles" Smith, were cheered by the community. In 1937 the Blackhawks, whose star players included Ernie Lewis, Sammy Bruce, George Height, and "Rhino" Nakamura, went undefeated in the Community League.[50]

Baseball, however, was the community passion. Businesses, churches, and fraternal orders sponsored teams that competed within and outside the Central District. But in 1929 the community coalesced behind the Seattle Royal Giants, its first semiprofessional baseball team made up primarily of local athletes. The Royal Giants "went on the road," playing white teams throughout the Pacific Northwest. Just before the game they would pass the hat among the predominately white fans who turned out to see their local team compete against these black Seattleites. Occasionally the proceeds amounted to only one or two dollars per player. Almost always the Royal Giants encountered discrimination. In The Dalles, Oregon, in 1938 they were refused accommodations until the county sheriff, who also served as the opposing team's manager, intervened and they were allowed to stay at the largest hotel in the city.[51]

But in Seattle the Giants were local heroes. During their first season they were undefeated until beaten in the citywide championship. Subsequent seasons were less illustrious, but for many local blacks the flair and enthusiasm exhibited by the Royal Giants epitomized the spirit of the black community.[52]

That black Seattle forged its cultural matrix in an admittedly benign racial environment generated considerable uncertainty among its residents as to their appropriate response to racial prejudice and discrimination. Certainly evidence of discrimination was so widespread that only the most naive or ill-informed could ignore it. But the harsh, caustic edge of race relations which found expression in both word and deed in the South and most eastern cities, and some neighboring

Pacific Northwest states, was noticeably absent in the Puget Sound region and subsequently generated a marked complacency among many Seattle African Americans. If a community rose with one voice to challenge the anti-interracial marriage bills or seek justice in the Berry Lawson case, it was equally clear that the same community residents seemed unwilling or unable to confront the myriad other restrictions. "Life was easy in Seattle," mused Sara Oliver Jackson. "You don't have that horrible struggle that you have in any other city. This is a mild climate; we don't have any cold, you can live a long time on very little. And because there weren't that many Blacks we didn't have that confrontation with the White folks that you have in the East or in the South. Now, there may be jobs you couldn't get, so you didn't go and ask for 'em. . . . There was a settled community here that had *not* really fought for change. I won't say that you accepted it, because I've talked with enough angry people to know it's not accepted, but they didn't do that much about it."[53] Although blacks were excluded from neighborhoods beyond the Central District, the area itself remained, according to Marguerite Johnson, an ethnic montage: "When I moved in this neighborhood . . . we had a lot of Jewish people, we had a Filipino family, we had a Chinese and a Japanese family, and we had Whites living here – we could go out and not even think of locking our doors or putting bars on the windows."[54]

Black Seattleites had long prided themselves on being in the most racially tolerant city on the Pacific Coast, and reassuringly cited the number of government jobs held by blacks in proportion to their population in the state as evidence of white liberalism and black progress. (This proportion of jobs was higher than the percentage of Negroes in the state in 1920.) By 1938 such notions of progress were largely a myth. Despite impressive job growth for the overall economy at the end of the Depression, particularly at Boeing, it was almost impossible for blacks to find employment at any level beyond menial service. The Seattle Urban League, usually working with well-trained black professionals, occasionally registered "gains" or token breakthroughs (e.g., the first Negro woman employed by the telephone company). Yet few blacks spoke out. One rare exception was Constance Pitter Thomas, daughter of Democratic Party activist Edward Pitter, and a University of Washington graduate in the late 1930s. Thomas urged the NAACP toward more militancy in its various battles to secure rights for minorities in Seattle and politely but repeatedly questioned the university's refusal to hire black faculty.[55]

Pioneer Seattle resident John Gayton attributed the complacency in the pre–World War II Seattle black community to the belief that, compared to the rest of the nation, Seattle's benign racial environment precluded activism: "A lot of these things could have been done more than twenty years ago . . . but nobody pushed for them. There was a chapter of the NAACP organized over twenty years ago but not many were interested in its work. . . . The colored people were more or less satisfied with things the way they were."[56]

Marjorie King, another Pitter daughter and University of Washington graduate, offered a slightly different opinion in 1978, ascribing the complacency to the realization of the daunting challenge of attacking discrimination in a city where paradoxically blacks were not subject to virulently racist acts and yet were impoverished by their economic marginality: "I guess you would say that Negroes were more passive than now, because we . . . came to realize what we were up against. We knew all along that you had to be twice as good to get half as much. This was something that you expected. Therefore do the best thing you can with it and just keep plodding along." Added her sister, Maxine Haynes: "Reading the literature about things happening in other parts of the country, like the *Chicago Defender* and the *Amsterdam News*, gave a sense that this is the way life is for black people in the United States; that you're going to be oppressed and you're going to have problems. We lived with that feeling. . . . We accepted second class citizenship, even though it wasn't as bad as in other parts of the country. I know lots of people who might disagree with me who have grown up here. But I think if we're very honest we did. . . . People boasted about how liberal Seattle was at that time; that it was a wonderful place to live, with no problems. But there were problems here, which people either did not perceive or did not want to admit."[57]

Whether black complacency stemmed from resignation in the face of racial bigotry or a genuine belief that conditions in the Pacific Northwest were significantly better than in the rest of the nation and thus racial agitation was superfluous, the small black community would soon be rudely confronted by the migration of thousands of blacks to Seattle, Tacoma, Bremerton, and other Puget Sound cities during World War II. The old rules of racial etiquette would never again hold sway, as black Seattle and the entire city would be permanently transformed by this influx and by what the national NAACP leadership called the "double victory campaign" – the international war against the Axis and the internal war against racial bigotry.

PART
THREE

Black
Seattle
in the
Modern Era,
1941–1970

We believe that Seattle is one of the few cities left in America which can solve its racial problem before it becomes unsolvable. The small Negro population, the current economic boom, the opportunity to do planned social engineering, and the remarkable talent in our city make this possible and feasible. We hope that the limitations of political and economic power by Negroes will not cause our community and its leaders to ignore us and reap the whirlwind of our discontent. — Reverend John H. Adams, Remarks before the Advisory Committee to the U.S. Civil Rights Commission Hearing, January 20, 1966

Chapter 6

The Transformation of the Central District, 1941–1960

Forty-five thousand African Americans migrated to the Pacific Northwest to work in World War II defense industries, radically transforming numerous small black communities in cities and permanently altering race relations throughout the region. Between 1940 and 1950, Seattle's black population grew 413 percent, from 3,789 to 15,666 (Table 11). The war-induced labor shortage coupled with President Franklin Roosevelt's Executive Order 8802, issued in June 1941, which prohibited employment discrimination in firms with government contracts, allowed significant numbers of blacks to move permanently into industrial work. The migration itself increased black political influence, strengthened civil rights organizations and black-related voluntary service organizations, and encouraged the enactment of antidiscrimination legislation in Washington for the first time since 1890. That migration, however, also increased racial tensions as the interaction of settlers and natives, white and black, came dangerously close to precipitating Seattle's first racial violence since the anti-Chinese riot of 1886. Severe wartime overcrowding was particularly acute in the black community and accelerated the physical deterioration in the Central District, by now the city's oldest residential area. And the arrival of mostly rural blacks from Louisiana, Arkansas, Texas, and Oklahoma generated the first significant intra-racial strife, as "old settlers" and migrants competed for leadership

Table 11

Growth of Seattle's Black Population, 1940–1960

Year	Black Population	Percentage Increase	Total Population	Black Percentage of Total Population
1940	3,789	15	368,302	1.0
1945 (est.)	10,000	164	480,000	2.7
1950	15,666	21	467,591	3.4
1960	26,901	72	557,087	4.8

Sources: U.S. Bureau of the Census, *Seventeenth Census of the U.S.*, 1950, vol. 2, *Characteristics of the Population*, pt. 47, Washington, Table 34; *Eighteenth Census of the U.S.*, 1960, vol. 1, *Characteristics of the Population*, pt. 49, Washington, table 21; Charles U. Smith, "Social Change in Certain Aspects of Adjustment of the Negro in Seattle, Washington" (Ph.D. diss., Washington State College, 1950), p. 79.

and influence in a greatly enlarged black community. The former group worried aloud about its declining social standing in this new racial environment, and the newcomers demanded the social freedom and political rights denied them in their former southern homes.

The African American migration to Seattle was part of a much larger regional transformation stimulated by the growth of World War II defense industries. The Second World War generated profound changes in economic and social conditions in the Pacific Northwest, prompting historian Carlos Schwantes to describe the years 1941–45 as the beginning of the modern era for the region.[1] The Puget Sound area soon became a major center for ship and aircraft construction, which in turn stimulated other sectors of the economy. The region's shipbuilding industry was revived in 1941 after its virtual collapse following World War I, as eighty-eight shipyards, twenty-nine in Seattle alone, furnished vessels for the Navy, Coast Guard, and Merchant Marine. Seattle's aircraft industry also came of age during World War II, although the process of growth and transformation had begun long before the Japanese attack on Pearl Harbor. The Boeing Airplane Company in September 1939 employed 4,000 workers making military planes for the Army Air Corps and some commercial aircraft such as the Clipper airships which crossed the Pacific. After fighting broke out in Europe, the British Royal Air Force purchased the company's B-17 Flying Fortress bombers for use against Nazi Germany. As orders came in, Boeing's work force grew accordingly to nearly 10,000 by June 1941, 20,000 in September, and 30,000 when the United States officially entered the war on December 8, 1941. In 1943, Boeing began production of the Super Fortress, a larger, longer-range B-29 bomber, from its facility in Renton, a Seattle suburb. Boeing workers soon produced one B-29 bomber every five days and one B-17 every twenty-four hours. By 1944, at the peak of wartime production, Boeing employed nearly 50,000 workers in the Seattle area and amassed total sales of more than $600 million annually, sharply contrasting with the $70 million value of all Seattle manufacturing in 1939.[2]

Although no other Seattle firm could rival Boeing in employment or production, other companies also experienced spectacular growth during World War II. Pacific Car and Foundry Company in Renton, which manufactured logging trucks before 1941, now produced Sherman tanks and employed nearly 4,000 workers in 1944. Shipyards in the Puget Sound area, including the Navy's facility at Bremerton and twenty-nine yards in Seattle, employed 150,000 workers by 1944. Seattle's wartime contracts, totaling $5.6 billion, ranked it among the nation's top three cities in per capita war orders.[3]

Greatly expanded wartime production quickly exhausted local labor pools, and in 1942 the War Manpower and Civil Service commissions began recruiting workers for plants in the Pacific Northwest. While recruitment took place throughout the country, most of the workers destined for West Coast production plants came from rural areas of Texas, Oklahoma, Louisiana, and Arkansas, an economically depressed region with surpluses of unskilled and semiskilled workers, including a large number of African Americans. By war's end, 45,000 black workers and their families had migrated to the Pacific Northwest.[4]

Although Seattle ultimately received the greatest number of newcomers in the region, its black population grew slowly at first, increasing from 3,789 to 7,000 between January 1940 and June 1944. In 1942 most black workers came to Seattle as shipyard employees, and by 1943 the National Youth Administration brought to the city the first group of blacks to work for Boeing, now the largest employer in the Pacific Northwest. By war's end 4,078 (7 percent) of the 60,328 shipyard workers and 1,233 (3 percent) of the 42,008 aircraft construction workers in Seattle were African Americans. Blacks also found work as nonmilitary government employees. Of

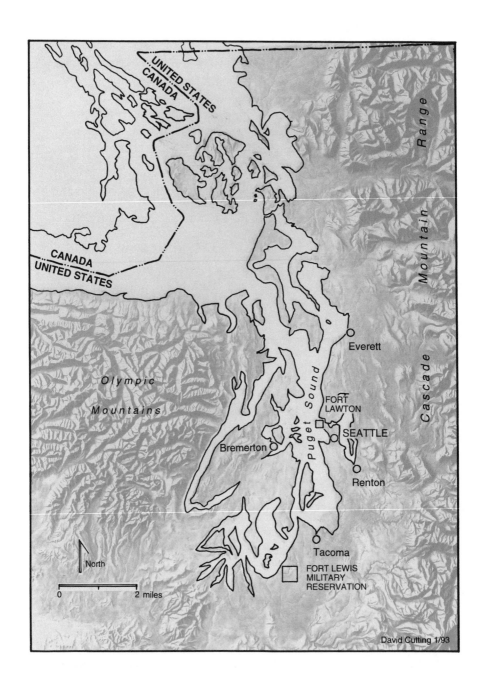

Map 5. World War II employment centers

18,862 nonmilitary federal employees in Seattle in 1945, 1,019 (5 percent) were black. Moreover, the 4,000 black soldiers and sailors stationed at Fort Lawton in Seattle and other military installations nearby contributed to the new employment diversity of the African American population. Wartime job demands had finally broken the seven-decade employment pattern of black workers as unskilled laborers and domestic servants.[5]

Despite the acute shortage of workers in Seattle's defense industries, some segments of organized labor opposed the hiring of African Americans. When President Roosevelt issued Executive Order 8802, the *Northwest Enterprise* noted that it "falls on deaf ears in the far northwest." The newspaper had valid reasons for its pessimism. Boeing had never hired blacks in any capacity. Moreover, that pattern seemed unlikely to change: in the ten weeks after the executive order became law, the company hired 1,000 new employees per week, but not one was black. In response, the black churches, fraternal organizations, and political and social clubs organized the Committee for the Defense of Negro Labor's Right to Work at Boeing Airplane Company.[6]

Some white Boeing workers were also attempting to integrate the company's work force. In 1940, Aero Mechanics Local 751 of the International Association of Machinists, the major union at Boeing, became the focal point of their efforts. In a contest unknown to most of Seattle's African American community leaders, or to the general public, advocates of equal employment opportunity at Boeing were soon embroiled in intraunion rivalry and forced to respond to charges of political disloyalty and communist subversion.

Local 751 was a young union, chartered only in 1935 with thirty-five founding members. Nevertheless, one year later it signed its first collective bargaining agreement with Boeing. Although essentially an industrial union, it was assigned by the American Federation of Labor to the International Association of Machinists, a craft union that had long denied membership to women and nonwhite males. The prohibition on membership was offensive to some Local 751 members, who worked to eliminate the clause from the IAM ritual and simultaneously to encourage Boeing to hire nonwhite workers. In 1940 those workers invited Bernard Squires, executive secretary of the Urban League, to address a 751 meeting. Union members at that meeting vowed to open their ranks to blacks and instructed President Barney Bader and Business Representative Hugo Lundquist to call for the removal of the membership ban at the International Convention in Cleveland in 1940.[7]

But internal union politics quickly ended the attempts at reform. In October 1940, C. A. Stone, editor of the union newspaper, the *Aero Mechanic*, released an unauthorized edition in which he "exposed Communists." Bader and Lundquist were among the accused. When a trial among Local 751 members exonerated the leadership, the IAM intervened, suspended the charter of the local, and called another trial in which fifty people including Bader and Lundquist were found "guilty of subversion," which in the terminology of the IAM meant they were advocates of communism. Bader, Lundquist, and most of the other members accused were expelled from the union.[8]

With the proponents of nonrestrictive membership removed from leadership in Local 751, the new union officers quickly rescinded the earlier decision to admit black workers. Nevertheless pressure from the federal Fair Employment Practices Committee, the intervention of William Green, president of the AFL, and the growing labor shortage forced Boeing and Local 751 to allow the first black production workers at the Seattle aircraft plant in the spring of 1942. Under the terms of the arrangement, nonwhite employees and white women, who had been allowed to work at the Boeing plant for the first time the previous summer, were required to purchase weekly temporary permits granting them permission to work at Boeing. Union leaders unequivocally voiced their displeasure with the "temporary" opening of jobs for black workers. "We rather resent that the war situation has been used to alter an old-established custom," declared James Duncan, IAM representative of Local 751, "and do not feel it will be helpful to war production."[9]

Boeing management and Local 751 were eventually reconciled to the permanent presence of African Americans in the work force. When Boeing began gradually integrating its work force in 1942, its first two African American employees were black women. Stenographer Florise Spearman was accepted as an office worker in January. Four months later, Dorothy West Williams, a sheet metal worker, became Boeing's first black production worker as well as the first black member of Local 751.[10] That the first African American employees at Boeing in white and blue collar positions were women reflected the expanding role of black female labor both in the overall World War II migration and in the industrial workplace. By July 1943, just eighteen months after Spearman was hired, African American women constituted 86 percent of the 329 black employees at Boeing. However, as Karen Tucker Anderson has shown, despite the obvious labor shortages, black women nationally continued to face gender and racial discrimination and thus remained an underutilized work force.[11] Boeing employed a wartime peak of 1,600 black workers, a presence large enough to persuade Local 751 leadership to again challenge the "whites only" provision in the membership ritual. Dick Powell, vice-president in 1945, led the local delegation, the largest at the International Convention in New York in 1945, where he introduced a resolution to remove the word "white" from the initiation ritual. Powell recalled that their aim was "to get rid of . . . a stigma on the IAM. In the 1945 convention we lost the fight to do this. We were outvoted. But it was the beginning of the end for discrimination." The succeeding convention removed the word "white" from the ritual. After a three-year campaign to obtain employment in the largest manufacturing facility in the Pacific Northwest, and another four years to get permanent union membership, the "battle for Boeing" was finally over.[12]

Once inside Seattle plants, black workers faced various forms of discrimination which heightened tension with white employees. Some discriminatory practices involved noneconomic issues, such as segregated lunchrooms and toilet facilities. In other instances, black workers were denied promotion or were laid off for protesting the union policy of deducting monthly dues from the wages of African American workers for membership in auxiliary locals while barring them from participation in regular union affairs. Occasionally a worker found herself challenging a discriminatory practice within a larger injustice. Ruby Black, for example, filed suit in Seattle Superior Court against Boeing and Local 751 asking for a restraint against the automatic deduction of $3.50 from the pay of black female employees for a work permit while white women, also denied regular union membership, were charged $1.50. Black noted in her suit that when she complained about the higher dues for black women, she was fired.[13]

African American workers at Pacific Car and Foundry in Renton also found that after initial employment barriers were removed they still faced opposition from various sources in management and labor. In May 1943 twenty-nine black employees, led by Marjorie Pitter, protested signs announcing the segregation of restrooms. Pitter explained the incident to a *Northwest Enterprise* reporter: "We protested to the superintendent of the foundry. He told us the signs were ordered by higher officials and would remain." Then Pitter said tersely, "We declined to work." The company vice-president, claiming the union asked for the signs, said, "It would be company policy for a few days." Union officials denied responsibility and the protesting workers eventually discovered a fellow employee, J. Columbo, had initiated the segregated restroom policy with the approval of a Captain Stretcher, the Thirteenth Naval District inspector responsible for oversight at the plant. Columbo said "he did not appreciate skilled negro workers . . . receiving higher wages than many whites"; and Captain Stretcher, who claimed credit for the segregated washrooms, declared that "if the black workers refused to accept the separate rooms they should resign immediately." Ultimately black workers won their protest and Stretcher was transferred to another naval district.[14]

Not every challenge by African American workers was successful. In 1944, white workers at Doran Brass Foundry demanded separate showers, prompting a protest by black employees. Some angry black workers then announced they would take their grievance to the War Labor Board, a threat met with a retort from the foreman that "two white workers were worth more than all the colored employees of the company." All the black workers then quit in protest, but Doran Brass refused to rescind its policy and the workers were not reinstated.[15]

In contrast to the treatment received at Boeing, Pacific Car and Foundry, and Doran Brass, Seattle's shipyards eagerly employed black workers. Unlike other West Coast cities, no major company dominated Seattle's shipbuilding industry. In addition to the Todd and Seattle-Tacoma shipbuilding companies, the largest in the region, the twenty-seven other shipyards in the Seattle area collectively employed about 60 percent of the shipyard workers. Furthermore, the powerful and racially exclusionist International Brotherhood of Boilermakers, which dominated shipyards in Portland, the San Francisco Bay area, and Los Angeles, had exclusive bargaining agreements only with Todd and Seattle-Tacoma Shipbuilding. Most of the smaller firms had contracts with the rival, racially integrated Industrial Union of Marine and Shipbuilding Workers of America. Consequently, Seattle's African American shipyard workers were not segregated into the auxiliary locals of the Boilermakers' union, nor were they denied promotion opportunities. Moreover, waterfront unions including the International Longshoremen's and Warehousemen's Union, the Marine Cooks and Stewards, and the Ship Scalers, all racially integrated, applied pressure to discourage the discriminatory practices of the Boilermakers' local. While there were sporadic complaints of discrimination in Seattle's shipyards, the systematic segregation of blacks that persisted throughout the war years in other West Coast ship construction facilities did not evolve in Seattle.[16]

Racial tension elsewhere in the city mounted, however, as growing numbers of black and white newcomers clashed both within and beyond the workplace. Such tensions were not unique to the city; in the summer of 1943 race riots broke out in Detroit and Harlem, and the primarily anti-Chicano Zoot Suit Riot erupted in Los Angeles. Against this backdrop of local and national racial tension, Seattle Police Chief Herbert D. Kimsey felt compelled to announce to the *Seattle Post-Intelligencer,* "We're preparing for anything that might result from a crowded, mixed and excited wartime population." Kimsey's concerns were well founded. In March 1944 a black woman was evicted from a city bus by the driver and arrested by four policemen who allegedly manhandled and cursed her. The *Northwest Enterprise* angrily denounced the police for using "Gestapo tactics," and speculated that the presence of black soldiers at the scene could have ignited a riot. Six months later a city bus driver advised some white persons about to board his bus that he had several black passengers, and suggested they wait for another bus. One of the black passengers accused him of trying to run a "Jim Crow" bus. The driver called the man a "black nigger" and was subsequently threatened with a knife.[17]

The violence that many feared that summer of 1944 finally erupted in August, not on Seattle city streets but at Fort Lawton. Black troops stationed there were subjected to humiliating treatment by the military and civilians. Their complaints included the Army's exclusive use of black soldiers to shovel snow in Seattle and their confinement to a single base tavern and PX while Italian prisoners of war were allowed outings to Mount Rainier and supervised visits to local bars that excluded black soldiers. Enraged by their treatment, the soldiers rioted at the fort, lynching private Guglielmo Olivotto, an Italian prisoner of war. In the mass court-martial that followed, thirty-six soldiers were brought to trial. Twenty-three were convicted on various charges, including murder and rioting, and sentenced to prison, while the remaining thirteen were acquitted.[18]

Concern about the possibility of racial violence prompted Seattle Mayor William F. Devin to form the Seattle Civic Unity Committee in February 1944. The mayor set the tone of urgency in a speech at the University of Washington in July, five months after the committee was founded and only weeks before the Fort Lawton riot: "The problem of racial tensions is one which is fraught with a great deal of dynamite. . . . it is going to affect us not only during the War, but also after the War, and it is our duty to face the problem together.

If we do not do that, we shall not exist very long as a civilized city or as a nation."[19]

Patterned after similar agencies in Detroit and New York – cities that had experienced race riots – the Civic Unity Committee was both an acknowledgment of racial tension and an attempt to combat it by gathering and disseminating information on interracial matters, encouraging programs to reduce tensions, and making recommendations to the mayor and other officials on policy regarding racial issues. Designed to be representative of diverse community views (with the notable exception of "leftist elements," who were purposely excluded), the committee was composed of a cross-section of citizens including a University of Washington educator, an industrialist, a Protestant clergyman, two women active in community work, two labor representatives (one AFL and the other CIO), one Chinese member, one Jewish member, and two black members – a minister (Reverend Fountain W. Penick) and a dentist (Dr. Felix B. Cooper).[20]

Seattle's growing black population faced increasing segregation and exclusion as "Whites Only" signs suddenly appeared in restaurants, theaters, motels, and recreational areas for the first time. Businesses and public accommodations that did not openly exclude blacks often discouraged patronage by providing poor service or by segregating them from whites. The *Northwest Enterprise* and the NAACP campaigned against such policies, with the latter filing successful suits against some of the worst offenders. Now, however, the NAACP was joined in the campaign for racial justice by old and new allies including the Christian Friends for Racial Equality, formed a year earlier by a local group of black and white clubwomen, the local Communist Party, and groups such as the University of Washington black students whose direct action demonstrations integrated the swimming pool at Colman Park in 1944.[21]

African American newcomers faced chronic wartime housing shortages which, although shared by the white and Asian populations, were exacerbated by residential discrimination. Unlike Los Angeles and San Francisco, where black residents quickly occupied housing vacated by the evacuated Japanese, Seattle African Americans found that the new white owners and managers of the former Japanese hotels and rooming houses barred black tenants. Reverend Fountain W. Penick, pastor of Mount Zion Baptist Church and NAACP president in 1942, reported that despite denials by owners that the evictions were not racially motivated, 90 percent of the tenants removed were black.[22]

By 1945, over 10,000 blacks occupied virtually the same buildings that had housed 3,700 five years earlier. Migrants crowded into established Jackson, Madison, and Cherry street sections or moved into newly created temporary housing projects such as Duwamish Bend Homes and Yesler Terrace. Because restrictive covenants confined African Americans to specific residential areas, newcomers soon found themselves doubling or even tripling up in houses that were already among the oldest in the city. One black defense worker attempting to purchase a home for his family in an all-white residential area was immediately confronted with various legal and extralegal maneuvers by neighborhood whites. Finally, a court ruled that the house violated Seattle's building code, and ordered the family to leave.[23]

Yet Seattle was the only city in the Pacific Northwest and one of the few major cities in the country that did not segregate blacks in its public housing projects. Jesse Epstein, director of the Seattle Housing Authority, instituted the unrestricted occupancy policy and easily integrated Yesler Terrace, Seattle's first public housing project when it opened in 1940. Located on Yesler Hill above the city's International District, the apartments, with their sweeping view of Seattle's harbor, were a vast improvement over the deteriorating Victorian homes and craftsman cottages that housed much of Seattle's Southside poor. During a Housing Authority staff meeting in 1940, Epstein reportedly declared, "We have an opportunity to prove that Negroes and whites can live side by side in harmony . . . but it's going to require skill and patience to make it work." Housing staffer Ray Adams commented that because of housing discrimination blacks had fewer options, and thus would concentrate in public housing, and asked Epstein: "Will you set up a quota to keep Yesler Terrace from becoming a ghetto?" "Let's avoid the ugly word 'quota,' Ray," Epstein replied, "but we must limit the number of Negroes if we are to achieve integration. Keep in mind that we are determined on that. Coloreds and whites will live side by side; this in itself is revolutionary. Tenant selection staff will need both patience and skill in dealing with this delicate problem." Epstein's approach to the problem of interracial adjustment included limiting black occupancy to 20 percent and quickly moving neighboring black and white tenants who clashed to other housing units in the project.[24]

Epstein's "social experiment" generated strident criticism and growing opposition from businessmen and residents when the Housing Authority built projects in the all-white areas of West Seattle,

Sand Point, Holly Park, and Rainier Vista. Those residents, already apprehensive over public housing for the white poor, including a disproportionate number of southern-born war workers, now feared an influx of southern black migrants into their neighborhoods. Conversely, some blacks were angry that the unofficial 20 percent quota to foster integrated public housing, as well as a 25 percent quota on welfare recipients, reduced their access to badly needed public housing for the sake of "social engineering." Despite such criticism the Housing Authority, unlike similar agencies in most American cities, refused to succumb to community demands for segregated public housing.[25]

Seattle's NAACP and Urban League grew rapidly during the war and became increasingly vocal against injustices toward African Americans. The NAACP increased from a prewar high of 85 members to 1,550 in 1945. Moreover, a new generation of leaders emerged, including E. June Smith and Philip Burton, local black attorneys who initiated suits against discriminatory practices and lobbied for stronger state civil rights laws, and Reverend Fred Shorter, a white minister who headed the chapter from 1943 to 1947. Seattle's NAACP sponsored chapters in Bremerton, Walla Walla, Vancouver, and the Tri-Cities of Richland, Kennewick, and Pasco – Washington communities that saw rapid increases in their black populations and a concomitant rise in racial tensions. Bremerton's black population increased from 77 in 1940 to 4,617 in 1945, a figure considerably higher than Seattle's entire 1940 black population. The 1944 meeting of Seattle NAACP officials with Governor Arthur Langlie, concerning the DuPont Company's decision to segregate buses transporting workers to the Hanford Engineer Works complex near the Tri-Cities, was typical of the organization's expanding regional responsibility in defending black rights.[26]

The Seattle Urban League doubled its membership and tripled its staff during the 1940s, benefiting from aggressive leadership by Bernard Squires, executive secretary from 1939 to 1943, and his successors, Dean Hart (1944–47) and Napoleon P. Dotson (1941–50). Under their leadership the League initiated or supported antidiscrimination suits and assisted lobbying efforts for a state fair employment practices act. Both the Urban League and the NAACP increasingly relied on the support of sympathetic white organizations, including the American Civil Liberties Union, the Jewish Anti-Defamation League, and a newly formed local civil rights group, the Christian Friends for Racial Equality (CFRE).[27]

The Christian Friends for Racial Equality was the largest local interracial civil rights organization formed in Seattle's history. Founded in 1943 by black and white clubwomen, it began examining cases involving public accommodations, housing discrimination, and police brutality. Members campaigned against numerous racially based practices including higher automobile insurance rates for nonwhite drivers, housing segregation at the University of Washington, and segregated cemeteries. By 1950, CFRE had two hundred members, an annual budget of $1,900, and an office in downtown Seattle. Among its other public activities it awarded an annual $300 scholarship to a minority student gifted in graphic arts and sponsored interracial meetings among the city's various religious denominations.[28]

The epitome of this aggressive new thrust in civil rights was the campaign to enact a state fair employment practices law. The first effort had been initiated both before World War II and outside the black community. In February 1939, Thirty-seventh District Representative Ernest Olsen had introduced a bill barring discrimination on the basis of race, creed, or color, patterned after a similar New York statute. But even the *Northwest Enterprise*, while expressing gratitude on behalf of black Seattle, was reluctantly forced to concede that the bill would not be reported out of committee because Olsen was associated with the "left wing" of the Democratic Party.[29]

Conditions had changed dramatically by 1944. Although blacks had made impressive gains in employment, they remained excluded from entire segments of the Seattle economy. Their more visible presence, and the accompanying tension, made the question of fair employment far more urgent. In 1944 the Seattle NAACP, the Urban League, the Brotherhood of Sleeping Car Porters, and the Negro Republican Club joined forces with the Seattle YWCA, the American Federation of Teachers, the Jewish Anti-Defamation League, and the International Longshoremen's and Warehousemen's Union to lobby in Olympia for a state fair employment practices law. Modeled after President Roosevelt's Executive Order 8802, the bill mandated a permanent state agency to prohibit racial discrimination in employment and to monitor compliance. Arguing that the bill was "communist-inspired," the Washington Federation of Labor opposed its passage. But proponents persisted, reintroducing the measure in 1947, garnering allies, or at least reducing opposition, along the way. The Fair Employment Practices Act, finally enacted by the state legislature in 1949, declared discrimination "a matter of state concern" and prohibited employment bias "because of race, creed, color or national origin." It also created the Washington State Board Against Discrimination (WSBAD) to encourage compliance.[30]

Although the NAACP, Urban League, and other civil rights and social service agencies were understandably focused on the general community reaction to the growing numbers of African American newcomers, black Seattle was itself bitterly divided. "Old settlers" who had arrived in the city before World War II expressed resentment against the defense workers. "I know I was quite ashamed of them," recalled LeEtta King. "They looked so bad. Women wearing . . . jeans. Dungarees weren't worn on the street by women, but these women would be wearing them . . . and their heads tied up with a handkerchief. . . . I just tried to not see them." "A lot of them were awfully aggressive," according to Elva Moore Nicholas. "They liked to fight. . . . They'd been pressured so much before they came up here, and then when they got here they didn't have that pressure, and a lot of them didn't know how to act. . . . Down there [they] had to step off the sidewalk and let the other fella pass by. They got up here, and they would push the other fella off!"[31]

Old settlers felt superior to the migrants in education and training, although many newcomers had more skills and a wider variety of prewar work experience than the Seattleites. Moreover, long-time Seattle black residents viewed the incoming migrants – with their "colloquial speech couched in Southern dialect" – as boisterous field hands who would upset the delicate racial balance in the city. "These people were pretty conspicuous," recalled Melvina Squires. "They were loud, and happy, and crude." Even the *Northwest Enterprise*, which stood to benefit financially from the migration and thus was understandably supportive, was forced to declare: "As long as one member of our race compels criticism from other races for being uncouth, ignorant and dirty, so does our entire race receive a full share of that criticism." Maxine Pollard's comments express the crux of this resentment: "There was discord because this had been such a small Black community and although we had our share of segregation we felt that we were better off if we were less visible. . . . the fewer of us the better off we were, and we felt that with more Black people there would be more problems. . . . We felt that Black people would come here and get arrested and be going to jail all the time and making a lot of noise and that we would all suffer." Some old settlers occasionally even solicited money for the return of the migrants to the South. Yet many of these newcomers would comprise part of the postwar leadership of black Seattle. Reverend Fountain Penick, for example, came to Seattle in 1942, and attorney Charles Stokes, who would eventually become Seattle's first black state legislator, arrived two years later.[32]

Not all Seattle blacks abhorred the newcomers. Samson Valley, who had come to the city just before World War I, declared: "They use to call them sharecroppers and they began to holler, 'they taking our positions' and I told them they could have mine cause I was glad to see them come in, so I treated them royally. I gave them every opportunity I could." Pre–World War II Seattle resident Armeta Hearst, when queried in a 1968 interview, described the myopia of many of her contemporaries: "We were talking about these 'sharecroppers,' we're all sharecroppers, we just got here first."[33]

Migrants harbored their own share of grievances against the old settlers. Pre–World War II residents were considered "snobbish" toward other blacks and yet too deferential to whites. Moreover, they resented old settler claims to status and community leadership simply because of pre-1940 residence. Numerous migrants believed that the earlier residents had not been aggressive in asserting their civil rights, and thus claims of "good race relations with whites" were vastly exaggerated. The newcomers were determined to take an active role in what they felt was increasingly becoming a national struggle for equality.[34]

Gradually the hostility between old settlers and migrants faded. In September 1943, community leaders created the Association for Tolerance, and one year later the black churches founded the Fellowship Committee "for the purpose of orienting the new residents into our way of life." The NAACP, Urban League, the *Northwest Enterprise*, and other organizations and institutions reminded both groups of their common interests. The *Enterprise* summarized the mood of self-interested cooperation when it declared in the caption to a now famous editorial cartoon: "Better try to lift them, you can go no higher than they." In the companion editorial the paper declared, "Let's all get acquainted with newly arrived people and . . . enlist them in our cause, invite them to attend our churches, organizations and homes – open the heart of our communities to them."[35]

The migration of the 1940s altered the racial configuration of Seattle, making blacks the largest nonwhite racial group for the first time in the city's history. Although they were initially evicted from Japanese-owned hotels in 1942, some African Americans by

1944 had moved into what had been Seattle's Nihonmachi. A few African Americans also took over many small Japanese American businesses. The Seattle *Northwest Enterprise* reported that the commercial properties of one black businessmen had increased 25 percent following the Japanese evacuation. But there is little evidence that African Americans desired to assume the economic role of the pre-1940 Japanese in Seattle's business community. In 1945 numerous evacuees returned to Seattle and reestablished their businesses. Those who did not return to the Pacific Northwest after the war were primarily from the rural areas of western Washington and Oregon where white prejudice and the fear of economic competition combined to discourage their reappearance. Their fears may have been exaggerated; despite the war with Japan, white prejudice in many areas of the Pacific Northwest was stronger against African Americans than against the Japanese Americans.[36]

One unfortunate corollary to the migration was the growing anti-Japanese prejudice by blacks just as white prejudice against the Nisei and Issei was subsiding. Many migrants, unfamiliar with the returning evacuees as neighbors and susceptible to the propaganda that regularly spewed forth during the war, became vehemently anti-Japanese. Wartime internee John Okada captured much of this feeling among the new African Americans who inhabited his former neighborhood, Jackson Street, when he returned from an Idaho camp, aptly terming it "persecution in the drawl of the persecuted."[37]

Despite this tension, the city's postwar Asian and African American communities attempted to establish their first institutional link through the Jackson Street Community Council. The JSCC was formed in 1946 ostensibly to support neighborhood businesses and voluntary social service agencies. Its accomplishments – getting traffic lights installed, supporting junior league baseball and basketball teams, and sponsoring girl and boy scout troops – were not particularly different from those of similar organizations throughout the city. Yet the JSCC became, however inadvertently, a model for interethnic cooperation. Its officers rotated among its Japanese, Filipino, Chinese, and African American members as did its Man of the Year selection. The JSCC's business and service directory reflected the long-standing integration of the shops and stores along lower Jackson Street. Moreover, in an early attempt at cultural pluralism and ethnic sensitivity, the Council in 1952 selected four queens – Foon Woo, Rosita DeLeon, Adelia Avery, and Sumi Mitsui – to represent the Chinese, Filipino, African, and Japanese American communities.

Avery was ultimately selected as Miss International Center, entitling her to represent the JSCC at all public functions.[38]

The migration of African Americans to Seattle continued into the postwar decade. Despite discrimination in employment and housing, the outlook for Seattle blacks in the early 1950s was so encouraging that the *Chicago Defender*, the nation's largest African American newspaper, urged in 1951 that blacks leave the Midwest and East for Seattle.[39] By 1946 the city's unemployment rate had dropped to half the prewar level, but more striking were the high wage rates. In 1948 the median income of white families in Seattle was $3,826, or 4 percent above the national norm. The median income of black families was $3,314, or 53 percent above that of blacks nationally. In fact, the median income of Seattle blacks averaged only 10 percent below that for white families nationally. Furthermore, most American cities experienced a postwar economic slump, but Seattle remained prosperous because Boeing continued to receive military contracts and saw a steady growth in commercial airline orders. Thus the city's African American population grew by 5,000 between 1945 and 1950 as defense industries continued to lure black workers.[40]

Wartime employment gains radically altered the types of jobs open to African Americans in the postwar period, accelerating the creation of a permanent industrial work force. At the close of the war, blacks continued to work at Boeing, in the shipyards, and at the Bremerton naval yard. The list of "firsts" grew in the 1940s when John E. Prim, a 1927 University of Washington Law School graduate and former NAACP president, became the first black deputy criminal prosecutor in 1943. The first black nurse was hired at Harborview Hospital the same year, and the Seattle Transit Company two years later hired Thomas J. Allen as the city's first black bus driver. (He was forced to quit four months later because of racial insults he received on the job.) In 1947 the Seattle public school system hired Thelma Dewitty and Marita Johnson as its first black instructors, followed by four other African American teachers and one Japanese American by the end of the decade.[41] Some African Americans moved into white collar positions in federal and state government, while others opened small businesses in Seattle's burgeoning Central District.

African Americans now regularly sought public office. In 1942, Reverend J. Richmond Harris, pastor of Grace Presbyterian Church, sought the Republican nomination for one of the two Thirty-seventh District legislative seats; this marked the first time a black candidate had run for office in Seattle since Revels Cayton was Communist Party candidate for City Council a decade earlier. In a primary election marked by a surprisingly low turnout Harris came in third, losing by twelve votes. When asked by a newspaper reporter, "To what do you attribute your defeat?" he replied, "I attribute my defeat to the fact that I did not get enough votes to win." Two years later Reverend Fountain Penick, former NAACP president and former pastor of Mount Zion Baptist Church, ran in the Republican primary for the same seat, and in January 1946, Reverend F. Benjamin Davis, the pastor of Mount Zion, entered the race for a City Council seat. With organized labor's endorsement, Davis garnered 27,000 votes, only 3,500 of which were black, in his losing bid for the post. Undaunted, he filed for the Thirty-seventh District seat in the Democratic primary against eight other candidates, including George Williams, another black Seattleite. Davis and Jack Steinberg won the primary but lost in the general election to Republicans. Finally in 1950, Republican attorney Charles Stokes was elected to the Thirty-seventh legislative seat, becoming the city's first African American representative in Olympia. Stokes, who had arrived in Seattle in 1944, quickly gained notoriety as an NAACP president and the organization's chief lobbyist for the Fair Employment Practice Act of 1949.[42]

But the growing black population seemed to strengthen the resolve of many white labor officials, employers, and residential associations to "keep the Negroes out." Despite significant wartime breakthroughs in the campaign against union exclusion, a number of Seattle labor organizations in the 1950s continued to bar black workers or utilized various subterfuges to limit their membership. The Boilermakers, some maritime unions, the building trades and construction unions, the Teamsters, and the railroad brotherhoods, for example, either disallowed black membership or limited it to a token number of workers. Thus segments of organized labor denied blacks access to numerous unionized jobs, despite the state FEP law and their own claims to the contrary. Those unions that accepted black workers nonetheless placed obstacles in the way of their obtaining promotions or rising in the ranks of the union hierarchy – practices which remained beyond the scope of state civil rights legislation.[43]

Steelworker Eugene Dennett has described how employment practices at the Bethlehem Steel Corporation in Seattle in the early 1950s reflected these obstacles. The plant instituted the practice of segregating ethnic groups into different departments several years before Bethlehem took over operations. The open hearth employees were Irish and Slavic. The pouring pit was Italian, the 16″ mill was Swede, and the 22″ mill was worked by white "Americans" – meaning whites born in the United States. African American workers were confined to the scrapyard and were responsible for mill cleanup. Such divisions were reinforced by the common use of terms such as "Mick," "Wop," "Dago," "Nigger," "Hunyak," and "Greaser" by both company officials and the workers themselves. Blacks, who bore the brunt of such discrimination, felt they could do little to address it since the Steelworkers' union leaders blamed the Corporation, which responded by declaring that union seniority rules and blacks' inability to perform more skilled tasks were the real sources of the inequality.[44]

Employment opportunities for Seattle blacks remained limited in large sectors of the city's economy not subject to union control. African Americans were almost completely excluded from the newer electronics and chemical industries which sprang up after World War II and in most of the manufacturing firms that employed fewer than two hundred people. That exclusion extended to rapidly growing service sectors such as retail sales, health care facilities, and banking.[45]

Police harassment and brutality continued to plague Seattle's blacks in the 1950s. Such conflict was hardly a new problem sparked by the World War II migration, or one specific to Seattle. As historian Joe Trotter remarked in his study of black Milwaukee, African Americans have historically been "both overpoliced and underprotected." Florence James, the director of the Seattle Repertory Playhouse, remembered the difficulty of obtaining cast members for the Negro Repertory Company in the 1930s because so many young black males were picked up "for investigation." And the Berry Lawson case in 1938 reminded black Seattleites of their precarious status when confronted with bigoted and violence-prone police officers.[46]

Police abuse of black Seattleites occurred frequently following the migration of the 1940s, although the proportion of those arrested who were black declined even as the number of harassment incidents increased. The legacy of police brutality in the rural South – a region where police power was blatantly used to maintain the political and economic dominance of whites – invariably meant black residents (most of whom were southern-born) frequently feared and mistrusted police officers. The problematic relationship between the police and black community stemmed from low levels of police pay, which often attracted poorly educated and bigoted men, and the strident opposition of many white policemen to hiring or promoting more than a token number of black officers. But police brutality also emerged from societal stereotyping of blacks, which was further exaggerated by the daily, usually acrimonious contact between officers and distrustful community residents.

In 1955, Mayor Allan Pomeroy appointed the Mayor's Advisory Committee on Police Practices to investigate charges of police brutality. The Committee, which police supporters hoped, and black community leaders feared, would exonerate the force, instead issued a harsh indictment of department practices in the Central District. The findings declared that the Seattle Police Department – like the Seattle white community – held essentially racist attitudes about black citizens, frequently stereotyping them as "criminal types." Some of the most common "facts" according to the report were that "All Negroes carry knives," "Any Negro driving a Cadillac is either a pimp or a dope-peddler," and "The bulk of the narcotic traffic in Seattle is among Negroes."[47]

The report prompted the mayor's office to initiate a program to improve police-black community relations. Representatives of the Seattle Police Department participated in intercultural workshops sponsored by the Seattle Public Schools, and several officers were assigned to race relations classes at Seattle University. The Department in 1956 sent an officer to the National Institute on Intergroup Relations sponsored by the National Conference of Christians and Jews, held at Michigan State University.[48] Despite these efforts, reports of police harassment and brutality continued – and still continue – partly because both the police and African Americans view the role of officers in the community as protecting the status quo, although they have radically different ideas about whether it should be protected.

Housing discrimination soon emerged as the most serious problem facing black Seattle. Many of the city's black homeowners and renters were encouraged, in theory, by the 1948 U.S. Supreme Court ruling in *Shelley v. Kramer*, outlawing restrictive covenants. Yet continued resistance by white homeowners and realtors prevented all but the most determined black Seattleites from leaving the Central District.[49]

The concentration of African Americans in substandard housing in the oldest sections of the Central District began, of course, long before World War II, but increased dramatically in the late 1940s and 1950s with the influx of black workers. In 1950, 69 percent of

Black World War II soldiers in Seattle shoveling snow, ca. 1944.
Seattle Post-Intelligencer Collection, Museum of History and Industry

Boeing bomber no. 5,000 rolling off the assembly line, ca. 1945.
Boeing Company Archives

Four workers, including one black man, as part of a construction crew for a Boeing bomber. *Boeing Company Archives*

Cartoon from the *Northwest Enterprise*, 1944

Aerial view of Seattle's Central District on a snowy day, November 1946.
Seattle Post-Intelligencer Collection, Museum of History and Industry

Multiracial officers of the Bailey-Gatzert PTA, no date but ca. 1947.
Seattle Post-Intelligencer Collection, Museum of History and Industry

Crowning of Miss International Center, 1952. *Albert J. Smith Collection*

Black teacher with integrated class, ca. 1950. *Seattle Urban League Records, University of Washington Manuscripts Division*

Dilapidated housing, Seattle, ca. 1951. *Seattle Urban League Records,*
University of Washington Manuscripts Division

First sit-in, Seattle City Hall, July 1, 1963. *Seattle Post-Intelligencer Collection, Museum of History and Industry*

Rev. John H. Adams, president of the Central Area Committee on Civil Rights, at the opening of a tenants' rights campaign, 1967. To his right is Rev. Mineo Katagiri. *Seattle Times*

Seattle freedom marchers, June 15, 1963. *Seattle Times*

Ten thousand people march to Seattle Center in a memorial for Dr. Martin Luther King, Jr., April 1968. *Seattle Times*

Stokely Carmichael at Garfield High School, 1967.
Seattle Times

Woman of the Black Panther Party addressing a downtown rally, 1969.
Museum of History and Industry

Black student ascends by rope to the office of Charles Odegaard, president of the University of Washington, May 20, 1968, during a Black Student Union sit-in. *Photo by Greg Gilbert, Seattle Times*

Seattle blacks lived within ten of the city's 118 census tracts in the Central District. By 1960, 78 percent lived in the same tracts even though the total black population had increased by 11,000 residents.[50]

Residential patterns were, in part, the result of economic conditions. Seattle's black neighborhoods were the oldest and usually the least expensive sections of the city, and often the only places impoverished African Americans could afford. But much of the residential segregation was also attributable to white hostility prompted by the fear of falling real estate values – a fear which often became a self-fulfilling prophesy. One West Seattle resident in 1951, distraught over the recent integration of his neighborhood, personally held Mayor William F. Devin responsible for the movement of a black family into a previously all-white public housing project. His handwritten letter to the mayor reflects his anger, frustration, and despair:

I'm in a terrible state of mind, brought about by your moving negroes in our district and across the street from our home. By your direct action you have taken unfair advantage of us. And we do not have the same peace of mind, freedom of thought or action as . . . a family living elsewhere in West Seattle. It is just as much your duty to protect my interests as anybody elses.

My wife and I have been trying to sell our house for several months now and have been subject to all kinds of humiliation. I was born and raised in this part of the country and have always tried to be fair with my fellow men. . . . I feel our city has done us a great moral injustice . . . and they can at least . . . help us get reestablished. We have just got to have a better understanding and try to help one another in times of stress.[51]

Restrictive covenants outlawed by *Shelley* were replaced by "voluntary agreements" between realtors and homeowners to refuse to sell or rent to African Americans, and in some neighborhoods pressure was exerted to remove blacks who had already purchased homes in white areas. One homeowner in 1950, when approached by a black GI and his wife who wanted to purchase his advertised home on 23rd Avenue, just north of a black neighborhood, declared, "There is not enough money in Seattle to make me sell to a Negro." When informed that racially restrictive covenants were declared illegal by the U.S. Supreme Court, he vowed to initiate legal action against the prospective buyers anyway.

Such resistance was often encouraged by federal officials, including the Seattle FHA housing appraiser who, in clear violation of agency regulations, told one white couple that the value of their residence had fallen by 10 percent when a black family moved next door. In 1948, the year of the Shelley decision, the Seattle Real Estate Board expelled one of its members who sold a home in an all-white area to an interracial couple. Article 34 of the National Real Estate Board's Code of Ethics mandated such expulsion; it read, "A realtor should never be instrumental in introducing into a neighborhood . . . members of any race or nationality or any individual whose presence will be clearly detrimental to property values in that neighborhood." The words "race and nationality" were removed from the code in 1950 but, as Seattle historian Howard Droker reminds us, "the intent and effect were no less discriminatory."[52]

In the mid-1950s the Madrona–Denny Blaine neighborhood on the edge of the Central District became the focus of resistance to black residential expansion. But the conflict engulfing this Lake Washington neighborhood also reflected deep generational divisions between white homeowners about the desirability of residential integration. The Madrona–Denny Blaine Neighborhood Association and its president, Leslie H. Dills, attempted to prevent "black infiltration" by frightening residents with the specter of lower property values and rising crime. A rival homeowners' group, the Central Seattle Community Association, challenged Dills's efforts by promoting residential integration. Armed with literature showing successful integration in other cities, CSCA members urged white homeowners to resist calls for exclusion and "panic selling" which came when a black family moved into a previously all-white neighborhood. During the next several months, homeowners debated whether residential integration caused falling property values, crime, and public school problems. While older homeowners were generally opposed to integration, younger residents saw the gradual movement of middle-class blacks into the area as an opportunity to create a permanently integrated neighborhood. Initially it appeared that the exclusionists had won the battle when association members voted down an amendment to the Madrona–Denny Blaine Community Association bylaws to admit nonwhites in February 1956.[53]

Four months later Dills attempted to buy out an African American family who had purchased a home in the area. He reportedly declared on the front lawn, "The neighbors won't stand for this," and then, directing his comments to the black woman standing in the doorway, "We want to buy you people out." Dills's action marked the beginning of the end for residential segregation in the area. Other neighborhood residents, shocked by his intimidation tactics, were encouraged by the Civic Unity Committee and the Central Seattle Community Association to quietly sell to black or Asian families, or, if their neighbors had sold, to resist the panic sales which inevitably depressed property values and disrupted neighborhoods. Yet the Madrona–Denny Blaine success proved an isolated victory, since none of the other predominately white residential associations elsewhere in the city followed this model in the 1950s.[54]

School segregation was a troubling outgrowth of the rising black population and its concentration in the Central District. The Enabling Act passed by the last Territorial Legislature in 1889 advanced, in unambiguous language, a commitment to open and equal schools: "It is the paramount duty of the state to make ample provision for the education of all children residing in its borders, without distinction or preference on account of race, color, caste or sex." Yet by the 1950s the inequality in school funding already evident in regional disparities between school districts became increasingly apparent in Seattle schools segregated, however inadvertently, by race. In 1950 none of Seattle's elementary and secondary schools were predominately black, but nine years later three schools were over 70 percent black and three others had black majorities (Table 12).[55]

The concentration of black children in certain schools did not automatically make the schools inferior, as some local advocates of school integration argued in the 1950s. But overcrowded facilities, the decline of parental involvement in school affairs, the insensitivity of many teachers and administrators to the special problems faced by black youth and particularly the southern-born children of the migrants, and inadequate or improper teaching techniques all combined to lower academic achievement. Unfortunately, few blacks, Asians, or whites who publicly lamented the "decline" of Harrison, Horace Mann, Leschi, or other Central District schools fully understood that the institutions mirrored rather than caused the poverty, violence, and alienation in the area. Nor did they realize that the growing segregation of these Central District elementary schools presaged the school integration crisis that would envelop the city for the next three decades.

Discrimination in employment and public accommodations was now a violation of state law – "a matter of state concern" to use the language of the Fair Employment Practice Act of 1949 – but

Table 12
School Segregation in Seattle, 1959

School	Percentage of School Population				
	Black	Japanese	Chinese	Other	White
Elementary Schools:					
Harrison	75.6	2.8	1.3	1.9	18.5
Horace Mann	79.3	5.6	3.0	4.4	7.7
T. T. Minor	72.8	7.4	2.7	3.2	13.8
Leschi	66.8	8.7	2.8	2.1	19.7
Madrona	62.9	4.5	1.2	1.9	29.5
Colman	59.8	8.5	4.9	6.5	20.3
Bailey Gatzert	37.3	24.0	13.3	7.1	18.3
Junior High Schools:					
Washington	48.2	21.2	5.6	4.1	21.0
Meany	27.5	3.3	0.7	0.6	67.9
High School:					
Garfield	33.9	10.7	4.8	2.6	48.1

Source: Howard Alan Droker, "The Seattle Civic Unity Committee and the Civil Rights Movement, 1944–1964" (Ph.D. diss., University of Washington, 1974), p. 74.

a curious confluence of cold war zealotry and bureaucratic inertia in the early 1950s undermined both the law and the effectiveness of its investigative body, the Washington State Board Against Discrimination (WSBAD). The 1950s Red Scare quickly and chillingly altered the political landscape. For most of the 1930s and 1940s black Seattle had been able to rely on the support of left politicians in its campaigns for racial justice. By the early 1950s such support was abruptly over as cold warriors now argued that advocates of civil rights and equal opportunity were often "un-American" – meaning Communist. Albert F. Canwell, a state legislator from Spokane, spoke for many Washingtonians when he declared in 1949: "If someone insists there is discrimination against Negroes in this country, or that there is inequality of wealth, there is every reason to believe that person is a Communist."[56]

The change was amazingly swift. As late as 1948, Seattle Congressman Hugh DeLacy ran for reelection using campaign literature featuring black political activist Paul Robeson. But in 1950, during the celebration of his election victory making him the first black state representative from Seattle, Charles Stokes declared: "In a lot of countries abroad, they say that some segments of our population are not getting the benefits of democracy: but I'm certain that's not so." One of Representative Stokes's first acts in the legislature was authorship of a resolution denouncing Robeson for declaring that African Americans would not fight in a war against the Soviet Union.[57]

The Washington State Board Against Discrimination, moreover, was never adequately funded. Andrew Brimmer, a graduate economics student at the University of Washington in 1951, who two decades later would be the first African American economist to become a member of the Federal Reserve Board, wrote as his master's thesis a study which examined WSBAD. Brimmer found the agency's December 1950 claim that discrimination in employment had been reduced since its appointment "thoroughly unwarranted." His thesis described the results of an opinion poll taken in May 1949, three months after passage of the FEP, which indicated that only 15 percent of the state's residents knew of the law. A similar poll taken in Seattle in the fall of 1949 showed only 37 percent of the residents were aware of it and WSBAD. Brimmer also compared funding for the New York commissioners assigned the same functions as WSBAD members. The New York commissioners each received $10,000 per year plus expenses as opposed to the WSBAD members' $20 for each day on duty plus expenses. WSBAD, Brimmer concluded, was administratively weak and grossly underfunded.[58]

Brimmer's assessment could be subject to criticism because of his inability to peruse WSBAD files and the youth of the agency itself. But such charges could not be leveled at Sidney Gerber, a WSBAD member who reached the same conclusion seven years later. Gerber, whom one historian of the period described as "a wealthy retired businessman with a flair for and dedication to the cause of minorities," was appointed chair of WSBAD in 1957 by incoming Governor Albert Rosellini. His notes described the state of affairs at WSBAD when he assumed the chair: "no funds in budget, no letterheads, mimeo paper, etc. But staff had state car, nice flowers, etc., [and] although the office partially closed [the executive director wants] to raise salaries." Seattle blacks were obviously not privy to such information, yet as early as 1950 there was growing skepticism, as indicated by Lenzie Shellman's letter to the *Northwest Enterprise* warning that WSBAD was "in grave danger of becoming an official agency to prevent anything really being done about discrimination."[59]

Some Seattle African Americans decided direct action was necessary to dramatize continuing discrimination. In 1950 the Citizen's

Committee for Fair Employment, a predominately white group headed by James McDaniel, a black political activist in the Washington Progressive Party, was organized to protest discriminatory hiring practices by Seattle's Safeway stores. The Committee waged a successful boycott despite well-publicized opposition from WSBAD and the Seattle Urban League. Later that year the Citizen's Committee led a successful boycott against Frederick and Nelson, a downtown Seattle department store.[60] In 1953 the Seattle branch of the National Negro Labor Council picketed Sears, Roebuck. The Seattle NNLC was led by Paul Bowen, a black labor official who at the time was a defendant in the Smith Act proceedings, a federal prosecution of prominent Seattle Communists and radicals in 1952. The NNLC's picketing resulted in the first black personnel being hired by Sears.[61]

Although black community leaders welcomed the employment breakthroughs in major retail businesses, not all of the local leadership was enthusiastic about the Citizen's Committee or the Negro Labor Council. NAACP and Urban League members who remained wedded to legislative and judicial strategies termed the use of picketing and boycotts "counterproductive." But much of the discussion of correct tactics masked philosophical difference between middle-class reformers and radical working-class activists as well as suspicions of the aims, motives, and sincerity of the white radicals, and of blacks such as Bowen and McDaniel who worked with them. That radical protest activity occurred against the backdrop of the McCarthy era no doubt prompted fears among NAACP and Urban League supporters that civil rights goals would become increasingly identified with "leftist" elements.[62]

Seattle ultimately proved to be the crucible for "black and red" coalition politics. The city's strong tradition of radicalism among segments of organized labor now came in confluence with growing black demands for social justice. The Seattle chapter of the Civil Rights Congress was an attempt to mesh the tradition and demands. The Civil Rights Congress was formed in 1946 from the union of three organizations: the National Negro Congress, the International Labor Defense, and the National Federation for Constitutional Liberties. It quickly emerged as an "activist" organization willing to use boycotts, pickets, and demonstrations to mobilize public opinion, adopting these methods at least a decade before such tactics were embraced by SNCC, CORE, and other primarily black civil rights organizations operating in the South. Civil Rights Congress activities included intervention in rape or murder cases involving black defendants and white victims, protests against segregated public and private housing, demonstrations to obtain employment opportunities for African Americans and other minority groups, and even projects as innocuous as promotion of Negro History Week in predominately white towns. The Congress did not concern itself exclusively with black rights, but the aspirations of African Americans were high enough on its agenda to attract the support of many blacks, and the attention of the FBI and other federal and governmental agencies who were convinced the organization was simply a "communist front."[63]

The Civil Rights Congress in Washington State proved to be one of the most active and successful in the country. By 1952 the CRC had 500 members in the state and held public meetings monthly in Seattle. The city's 350 members included 75 blacks. The Seattle CRC became involved in efforts to save the jobs of University of Washington teachers fired because of alleged Communist affiliations and supported striking woodworkers and metalworkers engaged in protracted work stoppages. The Congress brought Paul Robeson to the city in 1952, immediately generating controversy when city officials attempted to bar him from performing at the Civic Auditorium. Black and white Seattle ministers joined CRC-sponsored protests, and the King County Democratic Convention, which happened to meet during the controversy, went on record 731 to 1 in support of Robeson's right to sing at the auditorium.

Robeson did indeed sing at the auditorium and later performed before forty thousand people at the International Peace Arch on the U.S.–Canadian border at Blaine, about 120 miles north of Seattle. Yet the dramatic success of the Robeson concert could not overshadow the indictment of the "Seattle Six," prominent CRC leaders accused under the Smith Act of being members of the now outlawed Communist Party and agents of the Soviet Union. Included among the Seattle Six was Paul Bowen, the black labor leader and former congressional candidate on the Progressive Party ticket.[64] The various state and federal legal campaigns designed to break the American left ensured the demise of the black-progressive political alliance which had operated on the fringe and occasionally in the center of local black politics. Through the remainder of the 1950s and well into the next decade, conservative or moderate organizations – black Democratic and Republican politicians and the Seattle NAACP and Urban League – would set the political and civil rights agenda for the city without challenge from the left for the first time since the 1920s.

The postwar Seattle Urban League resumed its conciliatory approach in challenging racial discrimination. The League, which was reorganized and enlarged in 1946, negotiated with the management of individual companies, attempting to convince them of the desirability of hiring black and, in some instances, Asian workers. The League also conducted training programs for unemployed African Americans to provide them with the necessary skills and qualifications for available positions. Between 1950 and 1960 the League successfully placed Seattle blacks in local banks, breweries, and some large retail stores for the first time. It continued to handle complaints of job discrimination even though WSBAD was designated to investigate such cases. If the cases were minor, the Urban League approached the employer; in other instances it turned the cases over to WSBAD or enlisted the legal assistance of the NAACP.[65]

The Seattle NAACP, less conservative than the Urban League, frequently became involved in public accommodation discrimination cases and a growing number of prisoners' rights cases in the 1950s. The branch, headed by attorney Philip Burton, provided legal assistance and advice to smaller branches in other Washington cities. By the mid-1950s the Seattle branch had also assumed a number of "support" activities for national campaigns, such as the Montgomery bus boycott and the effort to convict those responsible for the lynching of fourteen-year-old Emmett Till in Mississippi in 1955.[66]

Correspondence between various voluntary organizations reveals the evolution of a civil rights "establishment" in Seattle by the mid-1950s. After the removal of the left as a serious force in local politics, this establishment included the NAACP, Urban League, and Anti-Defamation League as the "radical" organizations as opposed to the Seattle Civic Unity Committee and WSBAD as the "conservatives." To be sure, the NAACP, Urban League, and Anti-Defamation League were hardly organizations dedicated to sweeping change in race relations or politics, and they were critical enough of the conciliatory approach of the governmental agencies to resist any suggestion that they collectively dominated the civil rights issue. Nonetheless, the voluntary organizations and governmental agencies frequently exchanged information and expertise. Furthermore, African American or Jewish representatives on the governmental agencies usually also were members of civil rights organizations. Reverend Fountain Penick, for example, the first black member of WSBAD in 1949, and Reverend F. Benjamin Davis, who sat on the Civic Unity Committee, were former presidents of the NAACP. Indeed, black WSBAD members Ola Browning, Roberta Byrd, and Calvin Johnson – all appointed in the 1950s – were active in both the NAACP and the Urban League. These black leaders shared with white members of the government bodies a similar education, class background, and an abiding commitment to legislative and judicial redress of racial grievances and to the goal of complete integration. Moreover, despite often accurate criticism of the ineffectiveness of the governmental agencies, the NAACP, Urban League, and Anti-Defamation League knew that the existence of the governmental bodies, whatever their limitations, made easier the task of eradicating racial discrimination. But being part of the "establishment" would make the Urban League and the NAACP highly suspect in black Seattle when more militant leadership emerged in the Central District in the 1960s.[67]

Black Seattle grew by 164 percent during the war years and another 169 percent between 1945 and 1960, and in the process acquired a decidedly southern ambience with the arrival of thousands of rural blacks from Oklahoma, Texas, Arkansas, and Louisiana. With growth came new problems and challenges. Seattle's small black community was inundated with newcomers, placing a tremendous burden on its resources. Furthermore, many white residents and public officials who neither understood nor were prepared to cope with the growth, or the problems of migrant adjustment, resented the increased black presence – a resentment initially shared by some black residents. Newcomers and old settlers, however, after overcoming mutual suspicions, began an earnest campaign to force Seattle to live up to its reputation as the "most democratic city in America."[68]

The enlarged population eventually wielded more political and economic power, and a new generation of postmigration leadership emerged to unite the community and delineate programs to meet the needs of a burgeoning population. Although black unemployment in postwar Seattle remained significantly higher than white or Asian rates, the city's black population now had access to employment at Boeing, the region's largest employer, and was making significant inroads into the civil service and some private industry. Serious problems remained, including segregated private, rather than public, housing, and black exclusion from much of the rapidly growing "white collar economy" of commerce, banking, and finance as well as continued discrimination by segments of organized labor. And the growing school segregation in the Central District would soon capture the attention of black Seattle in the 1960s and eventually the whole city in the 1970s and 1980s.

Furthermore, some segments of local black leadership began to express concern about the changing tenor of race relations following World War II. "We have prided ourselves here in the Northwest," declared NAACP President Burton in a 1953 "Open Letter" to black community organizations, "with our relative lack of discriminatory behavior. Recent incidents however have shaken our confidence. There are strong indications that it is becoming more difficult for Negroes to receive equal justice."[69]

One problem increasingly apparent in the early 1950s would defy easy solution. Illegal drug use was growing rapidly among Central District youth. Drug use among urban African American adults was already commonplace in larger black communities and was not unknown in Seattle even in the late nineteenth century. But by the 1950s it was occurring with alarming frequency in black Seattle. Seattle in the late 1940s was "wide open," recalled legendary entertainer Ray Charles, who was introduced to the local drug scene in 1948, as an eighteen-year-old musician.[70] The drugs available to Seattle musicians included marijuana, cocaine, and heroin, according to Charles. Drugs such as heroin were growing in popularity among a larger stratum of black Seattle. The narcotics trade, coupled with rising crime and juvenile delinquency, would prove stubbornly resistant to the ameliorative panaceas proposed by the black civil rights organizations or social service agencies. *Northwest Enterprise* editor John L. Blount, in a 1951 front page editorial accompanying an article announcing the establishment of a Federal Narcotics Bureau office in Seattle, decried the growing drug trade. The "simple addict" was, in the editor's view, "an irresponsible criminal capable of almost any abnormal act, which he might not commit in saner moments." But Blount's main wrath was reserved for the "dope peddler" who preyed on teenagers and utilized "their schools as a convenient center of distribution." He recommended that "these human reptiles be treated as snakes – and exterminated whenever caught [since] the destruction of one such active peddler of narcotics would probably save one hundred or more worthwhile youth from eternal degradation." Blount's editorial concluded with a stern warning to Central District parents that "the menace is in Seattle as elsewhere – and probably close to your doors."[71]

The *Northwest Enterprise's* warnings on drug abuse, crime, and juvenile delinquency reflected the disintegration of the pre–World War II system of parental and community supervision subscribed to by many local black residents as a force of social control and internal discipline. Yet such control was far more difficult in a significantly larger black community with a disproportionate number of newcomers. The warnings also prefigured the concern in the 1960s and 1970s with the "deterioration" of the African American urban community prompted by the changing urban economy.

Yet few black Seattleites in the 1950s would have predicted that the drug problem highlighted in Blount's editorial, the evolution of de facto school segregation, or the residential isolation of black Seattle would prove particularly tenacious and intractable. Seattle's expanding economy, based in the early 1950s primarily on defense spending prompted by the cold war and particularly the fighting in Korea, seemed capable of absorbing black and white newcomers. Furthermore, economic growth generated a euphoria about local conditions which masked evolving problems. This euphoria about Seattle as the race relations "frontier," with its implicit suggestion that the city had managed to solve, or at least avoid, the problems of southern and eastern cities, found its way into articles written by local people and national observers. But the early 1960s would shatter long-held assumptions about both the Central District and the city, and black community residents – indeed all Seattleites – would soon realize that, in the matter of race, both the best and the worst were yet to come.[72]

Chapter 7

From "Freedom Now" to "Black Power," 1960–1970

The intensified migration of African Americans to Seattle continued unabated into the 1960s as the black population rose from 26,901 in 1960 to 37,868 a decade later (Table 13). That population, which for decades had hovered at one percent of the city's total, was almost 5 percent in 1960 and over 7 percent by 1970. But the growing visibility of black Seattle stemmed not simply from their larger numbers and concentration in the Central District, which by the 1960s had an overwhelming black majority. It was also the result of a remarkable civil rights campaign by community activists which although inspired by national goals and leadership nonetheless pursued a distinctly local agenda. Those activists would, in a single decade, mount the greatest challenge to Seattle's racial order in the city's century-long history. For many black Seattleites, "the Movement" was not simply a television or newspaper report of confrontations between demonstrators and police in Birmingham or Selma, Alabama, or agonizingly frustrating legislative debates in Congress. It was a direct action campaign to end job bias, housing discrimination, and de facto school segregation in Seattle as an integral part of the national effort to eradicate racism, empower African Americans, and achieve the full and final democratization of the United States.

The Seattle "Movement" was an entirely local effort mounted by African Americans and sympathetic whites and Asians. Like the

190

southern challenge, it had both striking victories and ignoble defeats. And the campaign, like the national effort, did not eliminate the basis for the poverty which disproportionately plagued the black community. Whether it succeeded in ending all the discrimination it challenged is still debatable. What is not debatable is the education it provided the city on the causes and consequences of racial inequality. By the end of the decade the entire city had wrestled with the questions of school desegregation, employment discrimination, and "open housing."[1]

Yet as important as this campaign was for both the city and the Central District, it also revealed the traumatic transformation of the political views and values of black Seattle which reflected and anticipated the changes occurring throughout black America in the 1960s. Integration, a term that symbolized the desire of African Americans to participate equally in every aspect of American society, was the watchword for most Seattle blacks at the beginning of the decade. By the end of the 1960s, however, a significant number of black Seattleites had turned away from that goal and sought instead to build a community within the Central District free of the economic and psychological control of white Seattle. For them the term "black power" signaled a radically different mood and future for race relations in the city and nation.[2]

David and Jean Garner, in October 1965, were typical of the ten thousand black migrants streaming into Seattle that decade. Having arrived eighteen months earlier from Louisiana, the Garners and their infant son, Xavier, lived on an all-black street in the Central District. The Garner residence was a one bedroom apartment rented for $50 per month. It was on an unpaved street, surrounded by ramshackle houses dating from the turn of the century. Cramped accommodations notwithstanding, the Garners, like many recent black migrants from the South, were optimistic about their future in the city. Seattle, they believed, offered far greater opportunity than the Louisiana town that was their former home. The Garners' optimism was hardly atypical. "African Americans who migrated west to improve their lot," declared Larry S. Richardson in his study of the Seattle civil rights movement, came to realize that Seattle was probably the "end of the line both socially and geographically. There was no better place to go."[3]

When he first arrived, twenty-five-year-old David Garner, a high school graduate, obtained a job unloading banana boats. He later

Table 13
Growth of Seattle's Black Population, 1950–1980

Year	Black Population	Percentage Increase	Total Population	Black Percentage of Total Population
1950	15,666	21	467,591	3.4
1960	26,901	72	557,087	4.8
1970	37,868	41	530,831	7.1
1980	46,755	23	493,820	9.4

Sources: U.S. Bureau of the Census, *1970 Census of Population*, vol. 1, *Characteristics of the Population*, pt. 49, Washington, table 27; *Eighteenth Census of the U.S.*, 1960, vol. 1, *Characteristics of the Population*, pt. 49, Washington, table 21; *1980 Census of Population*, vol. 1, *Characteristics of the Population*, pt. 49, Washington, table 15.

moved up to dishwasher, which paid $1.50 per hour. Despite his twenty job applications to places ranging from Boeing to a Central District service station near his home, Garner was finally hired at $1.92 per hour as a janitor at a downtown building. Reporting for work each day at 6:00 p.m., he never saw or was seen by the lawyers, businessmen, and secretaries who worked there. He was, according to Rillmond Schear, who profiled the Garner family in a 1965 *Seattle Magazine* article, "a phantom who comes and goes by night" and who "in an important sense . . . symbolizes the relationships between Seattle's Negro and white residents."[4]

For the Garners and countless other black Seattleites, the "invisibility" of the black community was a haunting reminder of the nearly century-old paradox of Seattle's reputation for liberalism. While both blacks and whites agreed that the racial climate was less hostile than in comparable cities, the African American community nonetheless faced what one longtime activist termed "a wall of vast indifference." "The deepest of our racial sins," declared Roger Sale in his interpretative history of Seattle, "is ignorance. In the south, where whites and blacks have lived, however badly, for generations, that ignorance turned out to be shallower than in many parts of the north; in Seattle the ignorance runs deep. People here were uninterested in the Chinese in the 1880s, in the Japanese in the 1940s, in the blacks in the 1960s."[5]

White Seattleites had a particular propensity for isolating themselves from any knowledge or concern about the local black population and its plight. Residents in Magnolia, Ballard, or West Seattle might acknowledge in principle the existence of some racial grievance by blacks, but most felt justified in ignoring the issue. "For them," according to Schear, "the Central District might just as well be a foreign country, which they occasionally pass through in their automobiles, peering with mild distaste at 'them' and their funny way of life."[6]

Thus Seattle's liberal image masked deeply held racial antipathies and anxieties. Although the city's black citizens had voting rights and access to public accommodations and never lived in fear of collective white violence, which so often undergirded race relations in southern communities,[7] racism nonetheless impacted the black community in many ways. Much of the poverty of the Central District rested on a foundation of job discrimination. Despite the 1949 state antidiscrimination law and a state agency, WSBAD, dedicated to monitoring bias in the job market, Seattle blacks, particularly the unskilled, made surprisingly little progress during the 1960s. That their employment stagnation coincided with the rapid growth of the Boeing Airplane Company, which generated the "biggest economic boom since the Alaska Gold Rush," was all the more frustrating (see Table 14). Between January 1965 and December 1967 more than 148,000 new jobs, many of them unskilled, were created in the Seattle-Everett metropolitan area. Yet that unprecedented boom did not absorb the estimated 3,000 unemployed in the Central District. In October 1967, black unemployment stood at 10 percent, triple the rate for the entire city and a full percentage point above the national black rate. Moreover, an ominous sign both locally and nationally appeared in a 1968 Urban League study of unemployed black males. Among those under twenty-four, the jobless rate had reached an all-time high of 25 percent.[8]

The persistent poverty stemming from unemployment and underemployment increasingly generated cleavages between working- and middle-class blacks. Kenneth Latcholia, the black executive director of the Jackson Street Community Council, expressed the fear of many social service agency representatives about the inability of existing agencies to address the needs of what would two decades later be described as "the underclass" when he declared in 1965, "These are people who are poorly educated, frustrated and unhappy. Somebody's got to get through to them because, right now, nobody is touching them."[9]

Table 14
Black Employment at Boeing, 1962–1970

Date	Number of Black Employees	Total Employment	Black Percentage of Employees
1962	1,978	106,483	1.8
1963	2,267	101,434	2.2
1964	2,153	91,204	2.3
1965	2,806	103,762	2.7
1966	4,876	136,918	3.5
1967	5,369	148,493	3.6
1968	4,698	148,672	3.1
1969	3,218	134,322	2.3
1970	1,533	107,962	1.4

Sources: John A. Priest, Chief, Equal Opportunity Corporate Urban Affairs, Boeing Aircraft Company, to Michael James, Black Oral History Project, Washington State University, Pullman, December 12, 1973; Boeing Company Records, Historical Archives, December 1990.

Much of Seattle's rapidly growing African American population was concentrated in areas of deteriorating housing. Seventy-five percent of the city's 26,901 black residents in 1960 lived in four Central District census tracts, and by 1965 eight out of ten black residents lived there – the highest percentage in the city's history. Seattle remained less segregated than most American cities in 1965, with a 79.7 rating compared with the national mean of 86.2 in the "segregation index" devised by social demographers Karl and Alma Taeuber. Nevertheless, the number of all-black blocks in the Central District, like the one where the Garner family resided, increased as African Americans filled multiple-residence structures that were either newly constructed apartment houses or, more likely, converted single family houses, many dating from the beginning of the century.[10]

If racially restrictive residential covenants no longer carried the force of law, then tradition, income, geography, changing land use patterns, and discrimination proved equally effective in limiting black residence to the Central District. To the west lay First Hill, originally a residential area but by the 1960s the center of a complex of hospitals and related medical facilities; to the north lay Capitol Hill, whose elegant homes were well beyond the price range of all but the most affluent Central District residents. To the east were the

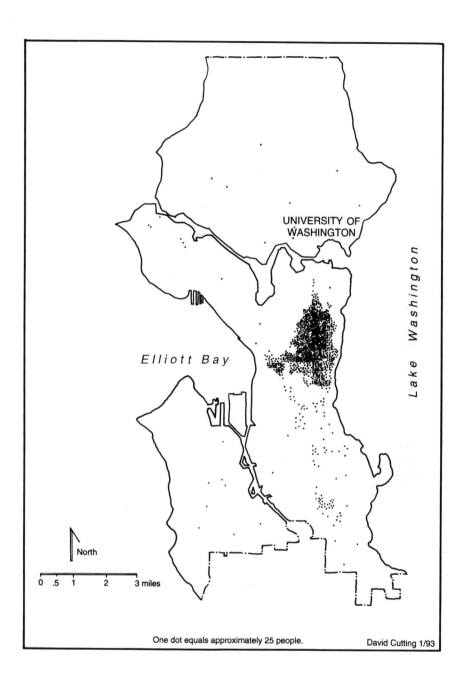

David Cutting 1/93

Map 6. Spatial concentration of Seattle's black population, 1960

ridges overlooking Lake Washington, which had long been settled by other members of the city's affluent elite. Only to the south, toward Rainier Valley and Beacon Hill, largely working-class districts, was there any possibility of expansion, and indeed this is the area that absorbed the growing population in the 1960s and 1970s. But ten years earlier, opposition to such expansion was so adamant that blacks discounted the possibility of moving there as much as they dismissed their wholesale migration to Capitol Hill.[11]

Some public officials recognized the potential danger of continued employment and housing discrimination. Carl B. Erickson, probation director of the Youth Service Center, concluded in 1961 that the Central District was the city's "trouble spot" in juvenile delinquency because the population had grown larger and more isolated: "If we don't develop housing opportunities in other parts of the city [for blacks], we will in time build a ghetto right in the center of our city." Erickson's comments were echoed two years later by Arthur Westberg, chair of the newly formed Seattle Human Rights Commission, who provided a sobering assessment challenging the widely held idea that Seattle had escaped the urban problems common among the nation's urban centers. The Central District, according to Westberg, had 5 percent of the city's population but it contained three thousand African American families in substandard housing. The area's school dropout rate was the highest in the city, and the district had five thousand single-parent families (25 percent of the citywide total). Over 40 percent of Seattle's welfare costs were incurred in the district.[12]

But Seattle was not, as Roger Sale reminds us, Detroit, Newark, or Watts. Because of its relatively small black population, the Central District had few blocks reflecting the physical deterioration so common in the racially exclusive slums of eastern cities, prompting most whites and some blacks to argue that "there was no racial problem" in the city, while ignoring the obvious signs of decay and discontent. Yet the small population guaranteed an equally small political base. Even though the African American population increased 72 percent between 1950 and 1960, as late as 1967 black Seattle had one state representative and no voice in the State Senate, the City Council, or School Board to advance its concerns.[13]

B lack Seattle was unquestionably affected by the massive southern civil disobedience campaigns in the early 1960s. The city's African Americans, including many with roots in the South, gave moral and financial support to the efforts of civil rights activists in that region and the national organizations sponsoring their activities.[14] Seattle blacks, however, increasingly came to recognize that the racism they encountered in the Pacific Northwest differed only in intensity. Indeed, local leaders eagerly challenged the problems facing black Seattle, naively believing that a brief but well-orchestrated campaign of civil disobedience would inform the white community of the plight of the city's African Americans and subsequently usher in a new era of racial understanding and economic opportunity. Such thinking was hardly unique to Seattle; national black leaders also assumed that eliminating job discrimination and, in the South, obtaining black voting rights, would generate a new egalitarian age in American race relations.

"Seattle is unique on the West Coast," remarked John Guernsey in his article on the local school segregation crisis for the *Portland Oregonian* in 1963, "in having a unified front pressing for city-wide racial reform."[15] He was referring to the newly created Central Area Civil Rights Committee (CACRC), which included the leaders of local racial amelioration groups ranging from CORE to the Urban League. This self-appointed leadership cadre reached a remarkable consensus on strategy and tactics which eluded their national counterparts throughout the 1960s. It provided a single voice on civil rights issues and, through 1968, determined the local civil rights agenda. Included in this group were Edwin Pratt, executive director of the 1,000-member Seattle Urban League. Holding his position from 1961 to his assassination in 1969 by unknown assailants, Pratt was considered the dean of the local civil rights establishment. But that establishment also included the ministers Mance Jackson of Cherry Hill Baptist Church, Samuel B. McKinney of Mount Zion Baptist Church, and John H. Adams of First AME Church. The 1,500-member NAACP was represented through the decade by attorneys and a physician. At the beginning of the 1960s, Charles V. Johnson, who by 1969 had become a municipal court judge, spoke for the NAACP in CACRC. E. June Smith, president of the branch in the mid-1960s (and the only female member of CACRC), and Andrew Young,* a former solicitor in the state attorney general's office, who assumed the presidency in 1967, continued that representation. Although an NAACP board member rather than an officer, Dr. Earl Miller was also a frequent spokesperson for CACRC. Walter Hundley and John Cornethan, presidents of the

---

* Seattle's Andrew Young was not related to Martin Luther King's lieutenant – with the same name – in the Southern Christian Leadership Conference.

local chapter of the Congress of Racial Equality (CORE), represented that organization in CACRC. With an interracial membership of 300, CORE provided the "shock troops" of the Seattle Movement. Two members of CACRC, McKinney and Adams, boasted personal ties with the foremost civil rights leader in the nation, Dr. Martin Luther King, Jr. McKinney attended Morehouse College with King, and Adams and King were fellow graduate students in the divinity school at Boston University.[16]

In a 1973 interview five years after he left Seattle, Adams recalled the early days of the civil rights movement. The impetus, he claimed, came from local issues – job discrimination, school segregation, housing bias – which mirrored national problems. But it was also sparked by "new militant personalities" – women and men such as Pratt, Smith, Jackson, and Adams himself who were prepared to use civil disobedience tactics already tested in Montgomery, Albany, Greensboro, and Atlanta to challenge the local racial order. "By 1963," declared Adams, "the Civil Rights Movement had finally leaped the Cascade Mountains."[17]

Seattle's civil rights leadership first confronted employment discrimination. The extent of the problem was revealed in October 1961, when WSBAD Executive Secretary Malcolm B. Higgins, at a luncheon of business representatives, depicted downtown Seattle as a place where "few, if any, negroes [were] employed in sales positions in major Seattle retail stores." He urged the business leaders to hire more blacks in "visible positions." Merchants attending the luncheon argued, however, that they wanted to hire black clerks, but feared incurring the public's wrath.[18]

Black Seattle responded to the downtown merchants with its first direct action campaign orchestrated primarily by the newly formed chapter of the Congress of Racial Equality. Seattleites created the chapter in 1961, electing Reginald Alleyne, Jr., as president. With its membership drawn mainly from college-age blacks and whites, CORE was originally intended to be a support group for the national organization's civil rights activities in the South. The Seattle chapter, however, after appraising local employment patterns, chose to launch its own campaign for black employment. Its tactics would alternate between negotiation with store managers and direct action boycotts with accompanying picketing of businesses.

In October 1961, CORE initiated the first of numerous "selective buying campaigns." Coordinated by Jean Adams and Walter Hundley, the campaign chose the Bon Marché department store as its first target but eventually included J. C. Penney, Nordstrom, Frederick and Nelson, A&P, Tradewell, and Washington Natural Gas among other firms by 1962. Picketing, the most widely used direct action, was conducted in front of these businesses, but CORE activists also engaged in controversial protest tactics which disrupted normal business operations. Such tactics included the "shoe-in," where demonstrators filled the shoe section of a department store and demanded to try on numerous pairs of shoes without purchasing any, and the "shop-in" at grocery stores, where they filled carts and went to the checkstands, waited for the costs to be tallied, and left the store without taking or paying for the items.[19]

The Seattle chapter's demonstrations generated the first boycott victories for CORE anywhere in the nation. By the end of 1962 the protests resulted in five positions at Safeway, and the following year twenty jobs at J. C. Penney and forty positions in other supermarkets. By January 1964 ten black workers had been placed at A&P, four at Wonder Bread, and twenty-eight at Frederick and Nelson. In the spring of 1964, Seattle CORE signed a landmark agreement with Nordstrom, one of Seattle's largest department stores, which instituted a broad-based "program of equal opportunity employment" for minority workers. Nordstrom promised to integrate its office staff as well as its branch stores and advertise itself as an Equal Opportunity Employer for minority workers. In announcing the accord, Elmer Nordstrom, company vice-president, pledged to CORE representative Tim Martin the "general integration of the Nordstrom working force through accelerated recruitment of minority employees, a training program for black salesmen, and seminars on civil rights issues."[20]

By the summer of 1964, however, it became apparent that CORE's approach to employment discrimination by targeting single stores or supermarket chains had not altered the job prospects for the majority of black workers. Thus the chapter launched the Drive for Equal Employment in Downtown Stores (DEEDS), which August Meier and Elliott Rudwick, historians of the national organization, characterized as one of the two "most ambitious employment projects undertaken by CORE chapters" anywhere in the United States.[21]

A downtown campaign, CORE leaders presumed, would focus the attention of the entire community on employment discrimination. Before initiating direct action, however, CORE formed a thirty-person research team comprising university social scientists as well as university and high school students and "housewives" who conducted surveys and interviews of downtown business owners and employees. After two months of research, the team issued a report on the scope of employment discrimination in downtown Seattle.[22]

The study found that only 2 percent of the 62,000 downtown employees were black and one-third of those were janitors. Of over 2,000 employees in sixty-five downtown restaurants there were no black managers, hostesses, cashiers, or waitresses, but 14 percent of the dishwashers were black as were all of the janitors. Ironically, retail stores with the largest number of African American customers also had the worst record of black hiring.[23]

Scrupulously careful to avoid the impression that white workers would be replaced, the researchers contended that 5,000 new hires would be made downtown in the next year and suggested that 1,200 of these be African American. "The proposals are . . . neither racial quotas nor rigid demands," the study solemnly announced. "They are negotiable suggestions put forward as first steps toward . . . full integration in the downtown work force and equal individual opportunity in downtown employment without regard to race."[24]

Federal governmental agencies located downtown were responsive to CORE's "suggestions" and Mayor J. Dorm Braman indicated a willingness to hire additional black city employees. However, most business leaders ignored the request, prompting CORE to respond with a downtown boycott on October 19, 1964. Striking the moralistic tone typical of pre-1965 civil rights activists convinced that their cause was righteous, and invoking the imagery of southern civil rights campaigns, CORE issued a call to battle: "An aroused community will now present its just grievances through the persuasion of popular protest, the strength of economic pressure, the force of an undeniable moral position, and the power of public opinion. We shall overcome!"[25]

The boycott lasted until January 1965 but produced no spectacular victory. Although some stores increased their hiring and promotion of black employees, the majority of businesses simply affirmed their belief in "equal opportunity" while making little apparent attempt to alter their policies. Moreover, the budget of Seattle CORE was exhausted by the downtown boycott and the simultaneous open housing campaign it mounted with other Seattle civil rights groups.[26]

While CORE's direct action protests did not generate employment for 1,200 black workers, the four years of protest demonstrations succeeded in making job bias a prominent citywide issue. Furthermore, CORE could, by the summer of 1964, remind downtown merchants that the recently passed Civil Rights Act of 1964 prohibited discrimination. Equally important, downtown store managers, after increasing their African American personnel, found that the argument that white customers would object to black sales personnel proved groundless.[27]

CORE's provocative, confrontational tactics lifted the veil of invisibility and ignorance concerning local job discrimination. By the summer of 1964, for example, civil rights leaders were regularly negotiating with city officials and leading businessmen about black employment opportunities. Both the city and the Chamber of Commerce initiated programs involving recruitment, training, and counseling to increase minority hiring. Though both plans were criticized by civil rights leaders as inadequate, they, along with the creation in the Central District of job training and placement facilities such as the Urban League–sponsored Job Opportunities Center and the Chamber of Commerce–sponsored Employment Opportunity Center, signaled, finally, a recognition of the problem of black employment.[28] Mayor Braman, for example, helped craft one of the nation's first affirmative action programs. When announcing the plan to increase minority city employees, he declared that the city would be ''very aggressive'' in seeking candidates for civil service jobs among blacks and other minorities, particularly for the police and fire departments, which at the time had seven and two blacks respectively.[29]

By the fall of 1965, CORE and other civil rights groups had embraced different issues. Nonetheless, as a growing number of African Americans appeared in downtown stores as sales personnel, and in its offices as secretaries, receptionists, and office managers, it was apparent that CORE's four-year effort had persuaded many employers to change their ''age-old'' practices. It would be naive, however, to assume that employment bias had been eliminated in the city. Toward the end of the decade, the employment question would be revisited by a new group of activists with decidedly different goals and philosophies.

Of the simultaneous campaigns waged by local civil rights groups in the 1960s, open housing was the most acrimonious and yet ultimately the most successful. The extent of the problem was metaphorically summarized by Gerald Hatcher, a black real estate agent: ''In an attempt to upgrade himself and his surroundings, the Negro in the Central Area finds himself moving from slightly better house to slightly better house until he has crisscrossed the narrow district with almost ludicrous redundancy – like a fly buzzing about in a closed jar."[30]

Although racially restrictive residential covenants were struck down by the U.S. Supreme Court in 1948, the widespread belief among white homeowners that black entry into a neighborhood ensured its demise as a desirable area forestalled any significant movement of blacks beyond the Central District. Moreover, realtors, who influenced the homebuying public, were often pressured to maintain existing racially based residential patterns. In January 1964, for example, a realtor in the Seattle suburb of Mercer Island who showed some houses to blacks was quickly told by her boss that she would be fired if she did so again.[31]

But open housing advocates were divided on how to achieve their goal. Many preferred a campaign of public education in conjunction with quiet attempts to locate "pioneer" black families in white neighborhoods.[32] Others argued that this voluntary approach represented tokenism which capitulated to the public's ignorance and prejudice. An open housing ordinance, they contended, would be the most effective means of integrating the neighborhoods because it would provide legal penalties for those who chose to discriminate. Toward the end of the decade a third view emerged that questioned residential desegregation in principle. Advocates of this view, influenced by the growing appeal of "black power," pronounced the entire open housing campaign as a misguided waste of black political capital at best, and at worst an insidious plan to destroy black Seattle.

The open housing campaign in Seattle began inconspicuously in the 1950s with the efforts of the NAACP, the Urban League, and the Jewish Anti-Defamation League (ADL) to assist blacks, Asians, and other persons of color who wanted housing outside the Central District. Typical of this voluntary approach was the Greater Seattle Housing Council formed in 1956 to encourage dialogue between proponents of open housing and the real estate industry. In the summer of 1962 the Fair Housing Listing Service was created by twenty-four organizations. It brought together African Americans willing to move out of the Central District and white homeowners amenable to selling to blacks, Asians, or Native Americans. The voluntary approach also benefitted from the efforts of Sidney Gerber, president of Harmony Homes, a nonprofit organization that constructed houses for African Americans in previously all-white housing tracts. By the time of his death in 1965, Gerber had built fifteen homes in various Seattle suburbs. Yet even this effort met with concerted opposition. The *Seattle Times* refused to run ads for Harmony Homes and only one real estate broker in the city listed Gerber's houses.[33]

The Fair Housing Listing Service and Harmony Homes were modest successes. But the voluntary approach was increasingly criticized by civil rights groups who wanted a citywide fair housing ordinance. CORE in particular called for direct action against the entire real estate industry. Influenced by this growing militancy, the Urban League and NAACP resigned from the Greater Seattle Housing Council in 1963, declaring its "program of gradualism. . . incompatible with the aims and aspirations of minority groups."[34]

Subsequently they joined other civil rights groups to campaign for a citywide fair housing ordinance. The ordinance's impetus can be traced to the state legislature's passage of the Omnibus Civil Rights Act of 1957, which made housing discrimination illegal. However, the law was successfully challenged two years later when King County Superior Court Judge James W. Hodson ruled against it in *O'Meara v. Washington State Board Against Discrimination*. He declared that while he was "fully cognizant of the evils which flow from discrimination because of race . . . the court rules for the right of the owner of private property to complete freedom of choice in selecting those with whom he will deal."[35] Both the Washington State Supreme Court and the U.S. Supreme Court upheld Hodson's ruling.

With the state law effectively emasculated, Seattle civil rights groups began their campaign to institute a citywide open housing ordinance. In 1962 those supporters were heartened to learn that Mayor Gordon Clinton's Citizen's Advisory Committee on Minority Housing recommended the ordinance. When the mayor and the City Council delayed action on the measure for nearly a year, Reverend Mance Jackson and Reverend Samuel McKinney on July 1, 1963, led a 400 person protest march from Mount Zion Baptist Church in the Central District to City Hall. Thirty-five young people from an interracial group called the Central District Youth Club left the march and staged Seattle's first sit-in, occupying the mayor's office for nearly twenty-four hours. Shortly afterward the City Council agreed to establish a Human Rights Commission and authorized it to draft an open housing ordinance. Fearing additional delay by City Hall, civil rights groups continued protest demonstrations, and on July 20, sit-ins involving nearly 300 people took place for the first time at City Council chambers. When a protestor tripped one of the councilmen, twenty-three demonstrators were arrested.[36]

The City Hall demonstrations, and the resultant public outcry, polarized the city along racial lines. Predictably the *Seattle Times*, the city's largest newspaper, declared that the demonstrations hurt the cause of open housing. However, Reverend Jackson spoke for the civil rights demonstrators, and reflected the growing impatience of African American Seattle, when he regretted the "violence" at the City Council chambers and defiantly declared: "A paternalistic concept of human relations in this country is all over. . . . We don't need to be taken care of. We want to be equal participants in our own problem-solving processes."[37]

Open housing demonstrations continued with a 1,000 person march on August 28 from First AME Church to the Federal Courthouse in downtown Seattle to coincide with the 250,000 person March on Washington in the nation's capital. Although U.S. Attorney Brock Adams welcomed the local demonstrators, "congratulating them on the peaceful exercise of their constitutional rights," Reverends Jackson, McKinney, and Adams, with Mayor Clinton looking on, denounced the City Council's failure to enact an open housing ordinance and vowed a continuation of the demonstrations. Those demonstrations extended into the fall of 1963. An October 20 protest march began at Mount Zion Baptist Church and concluded with a series of speeches at the Garfield High School playground where 1,200 people, about 25 percent of them white, braved a chilling rainstorm to call for open housing. Reverend McKinney, cognizant that an anticipated citywide referendum would likely reject open housing, declared "the white majority should not decide on my basic rights. . . . The question has already been settled in 1776."[38] Two days after the rally the City Council reluctantly enacted Seattle's first open housing ordinance after impassioned pleas from council supporters Wing Luke and A. Ludlow Kramer. The new law made discrimination in any kind of housing a misdemeanor punishable by a fine. Open housing opponents immediately instituted a successful petition campaign to place the measure on the ballot for the March 10, 1964, citywide election.

White homeowners feared the law would initiate declining property values. On the eve of the election, homeowner Philip Bailey wrote a guest editorial in the *Argus*, a weekly Seattle newspaper, voicing the fears of many opponents: "In America for the first time in history . . . almost every man can own his own home. It might be in a small subdivision or a pretentious house . . . but it is home, it is the owner's castle, safe and secure. . . . Suddenly these homeowners are asked to surrender part of this gain . . . for something called open housing. . . . For this surrender the voter gains nothing but the feeling that he may be helping the oppressed . . . negroes. . . . The homeowner today is not willing to weaken his right to privacy and freedom of choice."[39]

The open housing ordinance generated fears, rumors, and sporadic violence in white neighborhoods throughout the city and in suburbs beyond the scope of the law. Crosses burned in yards and incendiary devices thrown on porches attested to the anger of the most militant open housing opponents. In the suburb of Kent, for example, shotgun blasts were fired into the homes of two black families. One of the homes was owned by Reverend Luther Green, a twenty-one-year resident of Seattle who indicated that he had moved to Kent three months earlier "from [the] crowded Central District for more room to rear his children."[40]

The intensity of the opposition surprised and baffled civil rights leaders who resignedly coalesced behind the Citizens Committee for Open Housing which began a public relations campaign to educate Seattle's citizenry about the measure. Their efforts were palpably unsuccessful. Seattle voters rejected the ordinance 112,448 to 53,453. Moreover, in the simultaneous citywide elections for mayor, Dorm Braman, a leading opponent of open housing, handily defeated John Cherberg, the former University of Washington football coach, who supported it. One black leader bitterly declared: "If we got a majority to pass the law, we wouldn't have needed the law." Reverend John Adams was more explicit: "The Civil Rights battlefield is moving north and west, and Seattle may become a major battleground in the near future. I think we're in for a long hot summer."[41]

Taking up that theme, Seattle's civil rights leaders vowed to continue their campaign of civil disobedience for open housing. "We are not going to rest," declared E. June Smith, president of the NAACP, one month after the referendum, "until this city becomes in truth an All-American city." Black leaders promised "waves of picketing, phone-ins, sit-ins, buy-ins and even more types of civil disobedience."[42] Seattle CORE, however, was the only organization to initiate the threatened civil disobedience when it began a series of weekend sit-ins at the Green Lake and Lake City offices of Picture Floor Plans, the realty firm owned by the president of the Seattle Real Estate Board. These tactics prompted a court-ordered injunction which terminated the protests. Although CORE saw the injunction as a brief interlude in the struggle for open housing, it was, in fact, the last attempt to use direct action to generate desegregated housing in Seattle.[43]

Yet the citywide debate over the open housing ordinance persuaded a small but growing segment of white Seattle to reassess its opposition to residential desegregation. Following the referendum there was a noticeable increase in the activity of voluntary organizations such as the Fair Housing Listing Service. By 1965 the organization had "directly negotiated fifty-two sales with a dollar volume over $1,000,000" to black families in outlying Seattle neighborhoods and suburbs. Moreover, some white homeowners invited blacks to integrate their neighborhoods. In November 1963, Mrs. Felicita M. Schoenfield of Fir Meadows sent a letter to the Seattle Human Rights Commission announcing to realtors and Central District residents that "many here in the neighborhood would welcome them. . . . We would regard any new neighbors equally, with a little plus on the side of Justice for the deprived. In home, school, and church, we'll be friends."[44]

By the summer of 1965 even the staunchest proponents of the defeated open housing ordinance were slowly conceding that the voluntary approach allowed a growing number of blacks to purchase homes outside the District. Some Central District residents now feared that the most successful blacks would move elsewhere as housing outside the black community became available. Central District businessman and political activist Keve Bray suggested that the community would have little patience with "social climbers who were trying to get away from their people." Reverend McKinney, who just two years earlier was a forceful proponent of open housing, now declared, "I have little tolerance for the Negro who has received his education and acceptance and removes himself . . . from the problem."[45]

Despite such opposition, local civil rights groups intensified their efforts to encourage African Americans to vacate the district. In November 1967, Seattle became the second city in the nation (after Cleveland) to receive a $138,000 grant from the Ford Foundation for Operation Equity. Established the previous June, Operation Equity arranged, on average, ten sales per month to black families in white neighborhoods. The grant, announced in Seattle by Whitney Young, the executive director of the National Urban League, was designed to expand the program. Citing the acute housing segregation in the District, Young challenged Seattle to prove itself a "decent, democratic city" by accepting open housing.[46]

Seattle also initiated programs to improve housing in the Central District and undertook an ambitious program of rehabilitation designed to save nearly three hundred condemned houses in the area. That effort symbolized the nexus of a number of federal War on Poverty programs created to empower ghetto residents. The $110,000 development fund for the program came from antipoverty grants provided by the Seattle–King County Office of Economic Opportunity and private funds from the Olympia Diocese of the Episcopal Church. The rehabilitation work was performed by the "hard core" unemployed who were hired as on-the-job trainees with the Seattle Community Organization for Renewal Enterprises (SCORE), a division of the city's major antipoverty agency, the Central Area Motivation Program (CAMP). The initial training of these workers as carpenters, tile setters, and drywall installers came through the Central District's largest job training facility, the Seattle Opportunities Industrialization Center (SOIC). The program generated multiple advantages including vital job training, reduction of chronic unemployment, the rebuilding of deteriorated neighborhoods, and the continued development of single-family dwellings in the Central District rather than multiunit apartment complexes.[47]

Citizen involvement also helped prevent "neighborhood succession," a euphemism for the rapid transformation of predominately white neighborhoods on the edge of the ghetto into all-black areas. The best example of this involvement was the Leschi Improvement Council whose interracial membership included blacks such as Powell Barnett, an eighty-four-year-old community activist, Gene Warren, a jazz musician, and Leon Bridges, an architect, as well as whites such as James Sanders, another architect who was president of the organization, Roger Sale, a University of Washington English professor, and Sheila Bodemer, wife of a University of Washington Medical School professor. The neighborhood, one of the most racially and economically diverse in the city, included the "Gold Coast" of elegant homes and apartment houses along Lake Washington and, just a few blocks to the west, deteriorating housing typical of the expanding ghetto. Despite the differences in race and income, the residents made common cause in battling the blight and decay of their neighborhood of five thousand. Early in the 1960s, council members worked to allay fears of whites that African Americans would take over the community; later in the decade, they calmed the apprehensions of blacks that they would be edged out by high income whites returning to Leschi through gentrification.[48]

The dramatic decline in white opposition to residential segregation over the decade of the 1960s was best symbolized by the City Council's unanimous passage of an open housing measure in 1968, sponsored by its first black member, Sam Smith. The ease with which the ordinance was enacted reflected profound changes in local and national race relations. No doubt much of the council's attitude was predicated on keeping racial peace, for April 1968, the month the measure was adopted, was a time of uprisings in over one hundred cities in the wake of Martin Luther King's assassination. Many feared Seattle might also join the list, especially if a deeply divided City Council forced a second open housing referendum.[49] But the council also realized that extensive residential integration had occurred voluntarily since 1964.

In contrast to city officials, Governor Daniel J. Evans spoke out forcefully on the open housing issue. Evans, a liberal Republican, indicated the extent to which his dramatic meeting during the summer of 1967 with grassroots blacks in the Central District had shaped his thinking on open housing:

I think all citizens of this state must search their own background to recognize that people ought to be able to live where economics and where their desires would put them. Even though we obviously have no legislation that says today people can't move anywhere, there is no question in my mind that it is very difficult, if not impossible for some citizens of our central area to live where they might wish to live. This is an area where every citizen just joins in because legislation alone cannot solve the problem.[50]

Some Washington citizens did join in. Open housing advocates in Seattle suburbs began providing information on homes available in their areas. Typical of these voluntary groups were the Kirkland Fair Housing Organization in a northeast Seattle suburb and Operation Equity of the far south suburb of Federal Way. Consequently, by 1968, unlike the beginning of the decade, few Seattle suburbs were without some black families (see Table 15). The extent of that transformation became apparent one month after the City Council enacted the open housing measure. Thirty thousand King County residents – primarily white, non–Central District homeowners – signed petitions supporting open housing.[51]

The voluntary efforts of individuals such as Sidney Gerber, and organizations like Operation Equity, as well as the demands of

Table 15
Growth of Seattle's Black Suburbia, 1960–1990:
Black Population in Seattle and Its Suburbs

Year	Seattle-Everett SMSA	Seattle (City Only)	Suburbs	Percentage in Suburbs
1960	28,351	26,901	1,550	5
1970	41,609	37,868	3,741	9
1980	58,149	46,565	11,394	20
1990	81,056	51,948	29,108	36

Sources: *1960 Census of Population*, vol. 1, *Characteristics of the Population*, pt. 49, *Washington*, table 21; *1970 Census of Population*, vol. 1, *Characteristics of the Population*, pt. 49, Washington, table 23; *1980 Census of Population and Housing: Seattle-Everett, Wash. Standard Metropolitan Statistical Area*, Report 329, table P-3; *1990 Census of Population and Housing: Summary, Population and Housing Characteristics, Washington*, table 3.

CORE and other civil rights organizations engaged in direct action protests, had succeeded in persuading many whites of the desirability of residential integration. At a time when fears of "black power" and "white backlash" stalled resolution of the housing question in other areas of urban America, in Seattle, at least, significant progress was made. Few black or white Seattleites would recognize the magnitude of that progress until the next decade, when numerous black homeowners and renters moved southeast into Rainier Valley, and smaller numbers migrated east into Mercer Island and Bellevue, and north into Snohomish County. By 1980, for the first time in Seattle's history, the Central District would no longer be the home of the majority of black Seattleites.[52]

De facto school segregation was the most troubling outgrowth of the concentration of black Seattle in the Central District. In 1957 the Seattle School Board took its first census of enrollment by race and found that only 5 percent of its 91,782 students were black. That same census also showed black pupils heavily concentrated in certain schools. Nine elementary schools, eight of which were in the Central District, contained 81 percent of all elementary age black pupils. All-black schools in a city where African American residents had long prided themselves on their integrated educational setting were particularly frustrating to civil rights leaders, even if such schools were partly the result of continued black migration to the city. "We know the consequences when Negroes are forced to go to school together – in their penned up section of the city," asserted CORE Chairman Walter Hundley in 1965, "they learn to hate."[53]

Although it was relatively simple to assess the problem, the solution would be excruciatingly difficult. Seattle schools were not segregated by law, and no public official encouraged de facto segregation, as occurred in Chicago and other major northern cities.[54] The enemy in Seattle was indifference in the white population, born of its perception that there was no problem in the city. Thus civil rights leaders who complained about ghetto schools were often viewed as publicity seekers intent on blaming the entire community for the educational deficiencies of black children. Recalling the *Brown v. Board of Education* decision and the Seattle School Board's reaction, Mrs. Henry B. Owen, president in 1954, said, "Our feeling at the time was 'it was not our fault that the schools [in Seattle] were segregated.'"[55]

The segregation issue was further complicated by the quality of some Central District schools. One school board official remarked about the Central District's only high school: "There was [in the early 1960s] a type of euphoria that sort of centered around Garfield High School . . . what a great multi-racial educational institution it was. We weren't in too bad shape as long as we had more people in any given year who were Garfield graduates getting their Ph.D.'s than graduates of any other school." Such euphoria was sustained by statistics which showed 55 percent of the Garfield class of 1959 going to college. By race the figures were 66 percent of the 160 white graduates, 57 percent of the 71 Asian graduates, and 27 percent of the 124 black graduates.[56]

Pride in Garfield notwithstanding, the continuing growth of the black population of the Central District accelerated the concentration of blacks in the area's schools. In 1962, Garfield became the first predominately black high school in the state when school district census figures indicated it was 51.4 percent black. (See Table 16 for a comparison of black and Japanese enrollments in Seattle high schools.) The closest high school in percentage terms was Franklin, which was only 9.2 percent black, while six of the remaining nine high schools in Seattle had five or fewer black students.[57]

On August 28, 1963, the date of the March on Washington, Seattle became the first major city in the United States to undertake a districtwide school desegregation plan. The School Board

Table 16
Black and Japanese Pupils in Seattle Senior High School
Attendance Areas, December 1962

High School	Black Attendance	Japanese Attendance
Ballard	3	1
Cleveland	54	94
Franklin	157	87
Garfield	871	141
Ingraham	2	6
Lincoln	3	8
Queen Anne	5	11
Rainier Beach	13	14
Roosevelt	1	6
Sealth	50	3
West Seattle	1	1

Source: Calvin F. Schmid and Wayne McVey, Jr., *Growth and Distribution of Minority Races in Seattle, Washington* (Seattle: Seattle Public Schools, 1964), pp. 34, 42.

voted to initiate the Voluntary Racial Transfer Program (VRT) that would send an estimated 1,400 of the 7,000 black pupils in the city to various schools outside the Central District to arrest the growing racial isolation of black children in the public schools. Only 238 of the anticipated 1,400 black students participated in the transfer in 1963–64 along with seven white students, who, when apprised of Garfield's academic reputation, made "reverse" transfers.

Seattle's civil rights leaders, however, began working for rapid desegregation. In 1964, CACRC made Horace Mann school the center of a three-sided controversy between itself, the School Board, and grassroots community activists. The school, with a 97 percent black enrollment in 1964, was a sixty-two-year-old, two-story frame structure scheduled for eventual demolition. CACRC seized this opportunity to press for the immediate closure of Mann to encourage the dispersal of blacks into other schools. To provide additional pressure, CORE announced that the city faced the prospect of "peaceful, nonviolent direct action" if the board refused to move expeditiously to end de facto segregation. Neighborhood activist Isaiah Edwards and his supporters, however, citing the extreme overcrowding in Central

District schools, wanted a new facility to replace the building. The immediate education of "their children," he argued, took precedence over school integration. To show their support they presented a petition to the School Board signed by 447 Central District parents.[58]

The division of the community over the fate of Horace Mann school and desegregation in general highlighted the growing divergence among the city's blacks on the entire civil rights agenda, and anticipated the conflict between "integrationists" and "black power" advocates later in the decade — a conflict that would soon be replicated on the national level. The middle-class activists who dominated CACRC, and who were unalterably committed to integration, increasingly saw their position challenged by working-class black Seattleites. These blacks, although silent at the beginning of the decade because they, too, wanted improved educational opportunity for their children, began to express publicly their reservations about an integration effort which disproportionately burdened their children.

Integration advocates genuinely believed that any segregated school was a substandard one. Such leaders were well aware of the decades-old struggle in the South and in some northern cities to end both de facto and de jure segregation. Any public school enrollment pattern which even inadvertently appeared to support such segregation locally was immediately attacked. CACRC spokesman Dr. Earl Miller expressed as much when he declared, "One cannot have quality education when it is incomplete. Where whole vistas of human experience are absent, education is incomplete."[59]

Isaiah Edwards and his supporters, however, were equally sincere in their critique. In a guest editorial in *The Facts*, the local black newspaper, Edwards challenged CACRC's "integration at all costs" approach and its presumption to speak for the entire black community. Positioning his views as in the mainstream of Central District thinking on education and characterizing CACRC as a small minority, Edwards cited the failure of "responsible Negro citizens" to speak out against "irresponsible extremism on the part of individuals, and relatively small groups who appoint themselves as leaders and spokesmen for the Negroes of the Central Area."[60]

Edwards was joined in 1965 by Gertrude Dupree, another neighborhood organizer who attacked integration. "People who don't know the feelings of the Negro community," she declared, "are the ones who have been pushing for 'integration' of our children." She was particularly critical of CACRC member Reverend Samuel McKinney, who called for the closure of Horace Mann school, publicly asking why his two children were not relocated from mostly black Madrona "under the voluntary transfer program, if it were so important."[61]

Despite the attacks from neighborhood spokespersons, CACRC continued to support integration of Central District pupils into the other schools of the city, even if it required closing local schools. Moreover, for the first time, the civil rights leadership group called for mandatory busing of black children to distant neighborhoods. When the School Board appeared unreceptive to the latter demand, CACRC called for a school boycott to show black community displeasure over the slow pace of integration.[62]

The boycott took place on March 31 and April 1, 1966, and included nearly 4,000 students. An estimated 55 percent of the overall black enrollment in the school district participated, although in some elementary schools it exceeded 80 percent. Black students and sympathetic white and Asian students and teachers reported to various "Freedom" schools in the Central District. Five hundred children appeared at Reverend McKinney's Mount Zion Church and the overflow was accepted at nearby Temple De Hirsch. Integrated classes were held where students were taught black history, the meaning of the boycott, music and crafts, and Native American culture. To the surprise of its organizers, the boycott showed considerable white and Asian support for desegregation. Grace Katagiri, daughter of Reverend Mineo Katagiri, the only Japanese member of CACRC, and herself among the boycotters, said, "It was shocking to Roosevelt High School [teachers and administrators] when a lot of Roosevelt kids walked out in sympathy and attended the freedom schools." The freedom schools were a novel experiment where many white children attended schools with black children for the first time in their lives.[63]

Nonetheless, the boycott was the last example of African American political unity on the de facto segregation issue, as growing numbers of black parents came out against mandatory busing, the closing of Central District schools, and the disproportionate burden carried by black Seattle in the voluntary transfer program (over 500 black students were transferring out of the Central District while no more than 20 whites transferred in). That opposition would crystallize into two distinct factions: a group of conservative black parents allied with Gertrude Dupree, and a much larger group comprising primarily young radicals who identified with "black power." Dupree launched a well-publicized effort in the summer of 1966 to block the voluntary transfer program. Supported by the predominately white Save Our

Neighborhood Schools (SOS), she urged resistance to CACRC plans for integration. Central District support for Dupree and SOS soon waned, however, when it became apparent that the organization was primarily motivated by its fear of integration of white schools throughout Seattle.[64]

If Dupree could be quickly dismissed, much the same could not be said of the "black power" advocates who by 1967 had became a major force in the school controversy. While individuals such as Keve Bray and organizations such as the Nation of Islam provided critiques of the "integrationists" before 1966, the first major "black nationalist" alternative emerged in the spring of 1967 with the appearance of Stokely Carmichael at Garfield High School. After addressing an audience at the University of Washington, Carmichael made a rare visit to a high school campus, where 4,000 turned out for his speech. He chided the white press for distorting black power and said, "No one is talking about the blacks taking over the country, but about taking over our own communities." Carmichael attacked the integrationists for slowly destroying the black community: "What must be abolished is not the black community, but the dependent, colonial status forced upon it. . . . White people assume they can give freedom, but nobody gives freedom. They can only deny it. We are all born free. We are enslaved by institutionalized racism."[65]

Walter Hundley, acknowledging the speech as "a set-back for integrationists," provided a succinct assessment of the impact of Carmichael's visit and revealed his own frustration over CACRC's inability to maintain the loyalty of many young black Seattleites: "Kids get turned on with rhetoric. Stokely Carmichael was like one of those rock groups. . . . And there was no way we 'old heads' could tell them, 'Man, that's rhetoric!' Some of it was good . . . for a black person the kids respected to tell them that they are somebody, to stand up for themselves – this was good. . . . And I must admit that Carmichael got that portion of the message over much more strongly than our organizations had been able to do. . . . That's good. But the rest of it was [nonsense]. So the kids wandered around defiantly . . . instead of taking the whole message and working as hard on achievement."[66]

The first political repercussions of Carmichael's visit surfaced the following August when a new organization, the Central Area Committee for Peace and Improvement (CAPI), presented the School Board with a list of eight demands, including the dismissal of Garfield principal Frank Hanawalt, the introduction of minority history into the curriculum of every school in the city, and the hiring of additional black teachers and counselors.[67] Growing militancy was also evident among black students who organized a black power assembly at Garfield on December 15, 1967. Speakers included representatives from the University of Washington Black Student Union (BSU) and the newly formed Seattle Black Panther Party. Black administrator Roberta Byrd Barr, Carl Miller of the Student Nonviolent Coordinating Committee, and Bernie Yang of Students for a Democratic Society also spoke. Miller's speech reflected the sentiments of most of the participants when he declared Garfield "a slum school. . . . Quit kidding yourselves. They've been telling you Garfield's great. It isn't."[68]

Angry Central District parents turned their wrath on the civil rights establishment in a particularly acrimonious March 6, 1968, meeting at the East Madison YMCA which, according to many observers, marked the demise of CACRC as the leadership group for black Seattle. Organized ostensibly to rally support for integrated education, the meeting quickly became a referendum on CACRC and its vision of the future. Attendance was estimated at four hundred who represented the variety of views and voices in the Central District. Reverend John H. Adams opened the meeting by calling for support of integration and was immediately challenged by three dissident groups: the followers of Keve Bray, the Nation of Islam, and black university and high school students affiliated with the University of Washington BSU and the Black Panther Party. The integrationists were, according to one observer, "swept off the platform" and Adams soon left Seattle to assume pastoral duties at a Los Angeles church.[69]

Civil rights leaders saw the meeting as "a capitulation to hysteria," in the words of Walter Hundley, at that time director of Model Cities.[70] Yet others saw it as an assertion of working-class blacks in an area heretofore dominated by African American professionals. Future School Board member Alfred Cowles remarked, "The black professional leaders . . . said integration is going to be painful . . . so accept the pain that goes with it." Working class blacks replied, "We've been suffering pain already too long – let the other group suffer some pain."[71]

By 1969 the focus of the de facto segregation controversy had shifted from integration to decentralization and community control when the School Board created the sixteen-member Central Area School Council (CASC), an elective body which would assist the board in administering Central District schools. While this plan was not as sweeping as the most famous example of community control generated by the 1968 Ocean Hill–Brownsville school controversy in Brooklyn, New York, both the School Board and the black community increasingly saw community input through CASC into school curriculum, program structure, and administration as an effective alternative to desegregation. Community control offered a panacea to those who were frustrated with the inability of the larger Seattle community to come to terms with the question of race and education.[72]

The campaign for school desegregation had gone full circle between 1960 and 1970, with the goal of quality education for black public school pupils as elusive at the end of the decade as at its beginning. The initial effort to desegregate the schools, which seemed vitally important to the black community and which was ignored by much of white Seattle, had now become a struggle by black Central District residents to maintain their own schools in the face of proposed closures and dispersal of their children throughout the city. Whites who in 1961 had hardly known or cared about the educational deficiencies of the Central District, or de facto segregation, had been "educated" in the ongoing public discourse on black concerns. By 1970 virtually no white or Asian resident in Seattle, or its suburbs, could confess ignorance of the desegregation issue. Many had learned to be supportive of black claims for educational equity. Other groups such as Save Our Neighborhood Schools and its successor organization, Citizens Against Mandatory Bussing (CAMB), who, while expressing acceptance of integration "in principle," campaigned against measures that would accelerate that process. Indeed, by 1970 the School District's overall enrollment had declined by 10 percent but its white enrollment was 66,745, down by almost one-third from the 91,000 registered in 1960. Some of the decline obviously came from the city's decreasing and aging population, but much of it was prompted by a flight from the public schools in response to the debate over school segregation. White flight invariably meant that many of Seattle's black pupils were more isolated at the end of the decade than at the beginning. The 1,285 students at Garfield High School in 1970, for example, were 80 percent black, 15 percent white, 4 percent Asian, and 1 percent Native American. The de facto segregation controversy had divided whites and blacks but it also pitted blacks against blacks and whites against whites in the search for an honorable solution.[73]

The school campaign illustrated the developing intraracial cleavages in the Central District around the growing appeal of black power. Although few observers recognized it as such, black power reflected the deepening class divisions in African American Seattle and across the nation – accelerated, ironically, by the success of the civil rights movement. To well-educated middle-class African Americans, the Movement, with its emphasis on residential integration, access to prestigious universities, and the end of employment restrictions, particularly in white collar occupations, would demolish long-standing barriers to their full acceptance into American society. Working-class blacks, both those who held regular if poorly remunerated employment and those who constantly sought any work, suffered similar disabilities, but their difficulties were magnified by limited education and skills. For them, ending employment bias, whether it originated with employers or unions, and getting requisite job training to provide access to blue collar jobs so they could leave welfare or avoid its web, was far more important than access to suburban housing or busing children to achieve racial balance in the public schools.

When the Movement began in Seattle in the early 1960s, it appeared that the aspirations of both groups could be reconciled by a single leadership touting one set of tactics and goals. By the mid-1960s, as middle-class blacks achieved their particular goals, they lost interest in the Movement. Yet the poverty of those with meager education and skills persisted and intensified into the late 1960s, generating resentment not only against the white power structure but increasingly against middle-class blacks, who, with few notable exceptions, exhibited little interest in the plight of the black poor. Indeed after 1966, it seemed the only middle-class African American Seattleites who appeared concerned about the problems of the working and nonworking poor were those who staffed the various antipoverty agencies. For them, and the people for whom they spoke, "black power" seemed a viable alternative to "freedom now."

The immediate origins of the term "black power" and the aspirations it represented were traceable to Stokely Carmichael's speech in Mississippi in 1966, during the March against Fear.[74] That term and the growing militancy it reflected would be given urgency by major urban rebellions in Detroit and Newark in 1967, followed by even more uprisings in the aftermath of the 1968 assassination of Dr. Martin Luther King.

The premise of black power both in Seattle and nationally began with the idea that African Americans should define and control the major institutions in their community, whose economic and political resources should be mobilized for its development and eventual parity alongside other communities. Seattle's black power advocates specifically rejected those blacks "who now serve as spokesmen and leaders for the black community because whites feel at ease with them," declared Michael Ross, an investigator for the Legal Services Program and a future state representative. They wanted black leaders who could communicate "in the way and manner of the people who sit on ghetto porches and hang out on ghetto street corners." Ross called for black leaders who listed their occupations as carpenter, machinist, welfare recipient, or simply unemployed.[75]

Operating from the premise that deep-seated racism precluded any meaningful integration, black power advocates argued that their philosophy was the only option that would allow African American survival. "I am not a separatist but I am for independence of choice," declared Larry Gossett, leader of the Black Student Union at the University of Washington, "and the best choice that I feel black people can make is to continue to build a strong, creative and innovative black community." Roberta Byrd Barr, community relations coordinator for the Seattle Public Schools, reiterated that view: "Since we cannot, by stated common consent of the white majority, be the same as other Americans, we now use the symbol color 'black' to unite widely varying segments of our own people."[76]

Black power in Seattle, as nationally, had historic roots. The emergence of the Nation of Islam in the city in 1961 and the rise of political dissidents such as businessman-politician Keve Bray by 1964 suggest that some Seattle blacks were unwilling to accept integration as the paramount goal of the black community. They were joined after 1965 by Seattleites long associated with the local civil rights movement, such as Reverend Samuel McKinney and members of CORE, who also began to reassess the idea of a single integrationist objective.

The transformation of Seattle's CORE chapter symbolized the changing philosophies of both local and national black leadership. When founded in 1961, the interracial organization was "militantly integrationist" and was the principal exponent of the confrontational politics practiced by all of the local civil rights groups before 1965. Led successively by Reginald Alleyne, Walter Hundley, and John Cornethan, it continued its integrationist stance through mid-decade. By 1966, however, it was embroiled in internal controversy over its goals and direction. A November visit by Lincoln Lynch, the associate national director, prompted the schism. Lynch announced that the national organization was now on the "cutting edge" of the new militancy in black America and described his visit as part of a drive to "install that new militancy" in the Seattle chapter and "to clarify"

CORE's position on "black power, self-defense and the Vietnam War," a conflict he termed "immoral, unjust, and illegal."[77]

Lynch's visit was the opening salvo in a confrontation between the integrationists and their black power adversaries. By July 1967 the rift was public. During the national convention in Oakland, California, delegates voted to become a "mass-membership organization, to implement the concept of black power for black people," and to strike from its constitution the provision that made CORE a "multiracial" organization. John Cornethan, Seattle president, in defiance of the convention declared the Seattle chapter would remain integrated. Cornethan reported that the chapter had 116 whites and 68 blacks and that Seattle's four delegates to the convention, three of them white, opposed the constitutional revision regarding membership. He also categorically rejected the other national policies, including the development of a black political party and the assumption of ownership by blacks of businesses in their communities. Declaring that the Seattle chapter had ignored numerous portions of the national constitution for the past three years, Cornethan vowed that it would continue to seek integrated quality education, equal employment, and open housing. The black nationalist policies of the national office would, he concluded, be ignored.[78]

At the first postconvention meeting of the Seattle chapter it became evident that such a course would be impossible. Angry members, led by Frances White and Les McIntosh, publicly challenged Cornethan's leadership, forcing him to adjourn the meeting because it became "unruly." After Cornethan left, Ed Russell, the chapter's treasurer, reconvened the gathering with the remaining members, who then voted to hold a special membership meeting to discuss impeachment of Cornethan. Floyd McKissick, the national director, appointed a four-member interim governing committee for the chapter: Ira Oakes, Barbara Robertson, Bob Redwine, and Ed Russell. Russell was designated CORE's Seattle spokesman. McKissick intervened, he claimed, because Cornethan had "failed to implement national policies." The new governing committee vowed to bring the Seattle chapter's goals in line with the national organization, although it indicated it would continue to be an interracial body. But stringent conditions were set: whites who accepted black power had the primary role of working to remove prejudice against blacks in their own communities.[79]

If CORE was the first Seattle group to embrace black power, by 1968 numerous Central District organizations were calling for its adoption in various forms while competing for the allegiance of the Central District's working and nonworking poor. They included the Negro Voters League (NVL), formed in 1966 by Cliff Hooper, Ed Jones, Keve Bray, and 1950s activist Paul Bowen; the Student Nonviolent Coordinating Committee (SNCC), headed by Mattie Bundy and created in the wake of Stokely Carmichael's visit to Seattle in April 1967; the Forum Foundation, founded in 1968 and chaired by Pearl Fleming; the Seattle Central Area Registration Program (SCARP), headed by David Mills, and also started in 1968. The cultural and artistic manifestations of black power in Seattle evolved with the establishment of the Central Area School of the Performing Arts (CASPA) and Black Arts West, both founded in 1968.[80]

The Central Area Committee for Peace and Improvement (CAPI), headed by Les McIntosh, emerged as one of the leading black power groups. CAPI grew from a smaller ad hoc organization called We of the Grassroots, which gained notoriety in the summer of 1967 after a meeting with Governor Evans and a heated confrontation with Mayor Braman. The twelve-member Grassroots committee, led by antipoverty worker Infanta Spence and McIntosh, arranged a tour of the Central District for Governor Evans. Following the tour Evans agreed to establish a multiservice center in the district which would include health, employment, and public assistance offices. A similar meeting with Mayor Braman three days later, however, produced no agreement on issues such as the upgrading of the Garfield playground, a police review board, and the rerouting of the proposed Thomson Expressway to avoid dissecting the black community.[81]

The proliferation of black power groups prompted the creation of the United Black Front (UBF), which grew out of two days of meetings at the East Madison YMCA in September 1968. The UBF was a coalition of fifty organizations pledged to work for black political and economic empowerment, improved educational opportunity, and the elimination of white oppression. UBF leaders came almost exclusively from various antipoverty agencies, reflecting the importance of such federal programs in generating a new leadership cadre to challenge the integrationist-oriented CACRC in the Central District. UBF president David Mills, for example, was director of the Seattle Central Area Registration Program (SCARP), vice-president Michael Ross was a Model Cities staff member, secretary Gloria Henderson was a staffer with the Youth Opportunity Center, and sergeant-at-arms John Carson headed the Yesler-Atlantic Urban Renewal Project. Only treasurer Therusa Holly, who was listed as an educator, was not a poverty-program staffer. While such leadership was articulate and capable, it was often not indigenous to the Central District, and quickly moved on with the termination of many antipoverty programs in the early 1970s.[82]

The Seattle Black Panther Party, however, epitomized the new Central District militancy. Although the Panthers never had more than fifty members, they quickly became the most publicized and the most feared black group in the Central District. The Seattle Panthers were a contradictory collage of images. Formed in the spring of 1968 to "combat police harassment," they organized themselves into a paramilitary unit to monitor police activities in the Central District. They also ran candidates, E. J. Brisker and Curtis Harris, for the Thirty-seventh District legislative seats in the 1968 elections, "not to win but to educate the black community on their platform of full employment, decent housing, education for black people, military exemption for black males, and justice for all." Led by nineteen-year-old Aaron Dixon, whose official title was "Captain," the Panthers were the youngest members of the black power groups in the city. Most were in their teens and early twenties. Brisker, an Atlanta native and minister of education for the Panthers, was the oldest member at twenty-five. Simultaneously president of the University of Washington Black Student Union, he symbolized the link between the Panthers and the black university student activists.

Noted for their inflammatory Marxist-oriented rhetoric, provocative literature, and uniform of black leather jacket and beret, the Panthers in Seattle and elsewhere in the United States were quickly dismissed either as publicity-hungry opportunists or as dangerous criminals hiding behind the facade of political activism. Yet the range of their activities suggests that their concerns for the black community extended far beyond confrontation with the local police. Seattle's Panthers established a free medical clinic, prison visitation programs, a statewide sickle-cell anemia testing program, tutoring programs, and a free breakfast program for impoverished children. They were also credited with quelling random violence and attacks on police and property in the Central District in 1968 and 1969 and with participating in dialogue with Asian American business groups in the District through the Seattle chapter of the Japanese American Citizens League.[83]

The Panthers immediately became involved in several highly publicized incidents at local high schools and at the state capital. In March 1968, Panther leaders Aaron Dixon, Larry Gossett, and

Carl Miller were arrested following an African American student demonstration for black history courses and permission to wear the "natural" hair style at predominantly white Franklin High School. In September 1968, Dixon led fifteen armed Panthers to Rainier Beach High School to "get assurances their 'black brethren' would not be molested" following a series of interracial fights. When convinced of the safety of the students by Principal Donald Means, they left the school before police arrived. In February 1969, eight armed Panthers accompanied UBF members Dave Mills, Keve Bray, and Hank Roney, and Ron Carson of CORE, to the state capital at Olympia, where they presented a list of Central District grievances to the Senate Ways and Means Committee. Such bravado endeared them to many Central District youth, and their calls to remove the police from the community generated support from a segment of black Seattle which had long feared police brutality. But many whites and Asians were increasingly convinced that the Panthers were violence-prone thugs seeking to attack outsiders, rather than defenders of a besieged black community.[84]

The most notable achievements of the new militancy occurred not in the Central District but on the University of Washington campus. Although black students had attended the university since the 1890s, they constituted far less than the one percent that pre-1940 African Americans represented in the general population of Seattle. By 1967 some university faculty and administrators thought this 30,000-student institution with only 136 blacks, despite its location only a few blocks north of the Central District, should actively recruit African American students. This was the impetus for the Black Student Union, formed in January 1968 by the merger of the UW Student Afro-American Society and the UW chapter of SNCC. The BSU confronted deans and department heads, demanding that they both recruit additional students and accommodate their programs to the special needs of those already on campus. The conflict between widely accepted university practices and the perceived requirements of the black students generated the first serious confrontation on the campus, the Black Student Union sit-in during the spring of 1968.[85]

On Monday, May 20, 1968, at 4:30 p.m., forty Black Student Union protestors entered the building where the University of Washington Faculty Senate executives were meeting. After futile argument between university administrators and student demonstrators, University President Charles Odegaard and two other administrators retreated to the president's inner office where they were barricaded in by protestors. Despite the tense atmosphere, BSU representatives and university officials carried on negotiations by the telephones connecting the inner and outer offices and concluded an agreement which ended the sit-in by 8:30 p.m. The accord provided for a doubling of black enrollment at the university and allowed minority responsibility for recruitment of the new students. It also called for "adequate" financial support for minority students, a revision of admissions requirements, the recruitment of minority staff, faculty, and administrators, and, finally, a Black Studies Program.[86]

Many of the changes quickly became evident. President Odegaard announced that the number of black professors, already up to ten from one the previous year, would increase to fifteen with special recruiting efforts in Urban Planning, Medicine, Dentistry, and Engineering. The number of African American students grew from 150 in the fall of 1967 to 465 in the fall of 1968. The number of black university employees also increased from 327 in January 1968 to 493 in October. The interdisciplinary Black Studies major was initiated in the fall of 1968, with Professor James Goodman as the first chair. The most important signal of change came from President Odegaard himself, who, at a university memorial for Martin Luther King, spoke of the necessity of racism being "purged." Later, in a speech to students at Lander Hall, a recently integrated dormitory, he urged white students to make an extra effort to compensate for the past years of unequal treatment.[87]

The local civil rights movement brought into sharp relief the complex relationship between Seattle's Asian and African American communities. Since World War II the Asian population of the city, particularly the Japanese community, had experienced steady if not spectacular economic progress and far greater social integration than black Seattle. By the 1960s, if white Seattleites considered the "racial crisis" at all in their city, they almost exclusively focused on the black-white dichotomy. As one white homeowner opposed to open housing declared in 1964, "Well, Orientals are O.K. in some places, but no colored."[88]

Yet Asians, and particularly the business owners whose shops and restaurants still predominated along Jackson Street and in the International District, became concerned about the racial crisis initially out of self-interest. They feared that violent uprisings, like the Watts riot of August 1965 and numerous others during the subsequent summers, might eventually engulf their establishments. These business owners alternated between a strict "law and order" policy, popular with many of their white counterparts in the Seattle community, and a conciliatory approach which sought to understand the sources of black anger. Other Asians, particularly among the younger generation, seemed to genuinely identify with African American anger and aspiration, partly because they, not unlike middle-class white youth of the era, saw the demands of black Seattleites as growing out of legitimate grievances. But Asian identification with black issues also arose from the belief that despite the "success" of their groups, they were similarly marginalized and alienated in a society that refused to recognize racial diversity regardless of educational or economic success. For these Asian activists, the success of the civil rights campaign, and the attraction of black power (which for them became Asian power), represented the full and final conquest of anti-Asian bigotry.[89]

Although individual Asians such as City Council member Wing Luke (the first Asian elected official on the West Coast), Human Relations Executive Director Philip Hayasaka, Reverend Mineo Katagiri, the only Asian member of CARAC, and Victorio A. Velasco, a member of the Seattle Civic Unity Committee, were involved in civil rights activities in the early 1960s, the only institutional involvement of Seattle's Asian community emerged in 1964 when the Seattle chapter of the Japanese American Citizens League organized a Human Relations Committee. This committee proposed to "work towards the elimination of artificial barriers due to race, color, religion, or national origin, in all forms of community life."[90]

In the spring of 1965 the committee sponsored a series of community meetings on race relations addressed by University of Washington sociologists Frank Miyamoto and Donald Noel, Robert Bass, intergroup relations coordinator for the Seattle Public Schools, and Walter Hundley, director of CAMP. The JACL later sponsored smaller discussion groups called "confrontation" meetings involving Native American and African American participants. In composing his assessment of the meetings, Donald Kazama, Human Relations Committee chair, suggested that the gatherings helped the Nisei become known beyond their community and intimated that they also encouraged improved Nisei-Sansei communications.[91]

Yet black-Nisei tensions began to surface in Seattle. The JACL Human Relations Committee candidly admitted the apathy and occasional hostility it faced from many in the Japanese American community who felt that human rights had "no meaning personally to many Nisei." Japanese American concerns about juvenile delinquency, intermarriage, and interaction with their own children, the Sansei, were considered more pressing matters. Moreover, many Japanese Americans in 1964 were neutral, and a minority openly hostile, to the open housing ordinance campaign, despite their simultaneous appeals for black support to repeal the Anti-Alien Land Act. Three years later when the JACL executive board voted overwhelmingly to remain neutral on Referendum 35, a statewide antihousing discrimination ordinance, Philip Hayasaka felt compelled to criticize its action, declaring that "such a stand connoted opposition to open housing."[92]

The creation of the Central Seattle Community Council (CSCC) in February 1967 represented the strongest effort to arrest the growing rift between the Asian American and African American communities. The CSCC was formed by the merger of the Jackson Street Community Council and the Central Area Community Council. The twenty-one-year-old Jackson Street Community Council, though racially integrated, in fact represented the business and social agencies of the International Area, Seattle's Chinese-Japanese business and residential community just south of downtown. The Central Area Community Council was created in 1962 to represent neighborhood and voluntary service organizations in black Seattle. The new CSCC sponsored a number of ventures, including neighborhood crime prevention councils, day care centers, the Central Area Neighborhood Development Organization (CANDO), and a Civil Rights Coordinating Committee.[93] Moreover, it keep communications open between the Asian and black communities south of downtown which continued to occupy the same residential area. Yet events were conspiring to make communication far more difficult.

By 1968 the growing impatience of black Seattle with the slowly changing racial order contrasted sharply with the rising resentment of local whites over demands of the black power advocates. Many conservative Japanese American business owners, like their white counterparts, expressed scant sympathy for the grievances articulated by the young black leaders and were openly fearful of attacks on their stores and shops. Despite the growing chasm between the Japanese business community and the black power organizations, some JACL leaders remained committed to reconciliation and understanding between the two communities. It was this commitment that led to a remarkable two and a half hour meeting between the JACL and the Black Panther Party. The meeting, organized by Toru Sakahara, a Nisei attorney and past president of the Jackson Street Community

Council, occurred on August 6, 1968, at St. Peter's Episcopal Church, where Carl Miller represented the Panthers. Demands by Jackson Street storeowners for compensation for their riot-damaged businesses added extra drama to the gathering.[94]

Miller outlined the programs of the Black Panther Party and described its origin in the ongoing struggle against racial injustice, particularly by African Americans. But he also argued that "Indians, Mexican Americans, American Puerto Ricans, Oriental Americans, and all impoverished people, regardless of color, were oppressed." Miller offered an apology to the Asian and white small business owners "who were the victims of rocks, incendiaries, and other acts of vandalism" which he blamed on impulse, the exploitative policy of the storekeepers, and the lack of internal control in the black community. Miller then chided the Asians for their notable absence from the civil rights meetings, hearings, demonstrations, and rallies, and he particularly focused on their silence concerning police brutality. The Nisei business owners in attendance responded to his presentation with questions and countercharges. Some pointed to their participation in Model Cities activities and cited their personal interest in many of their African American customers. Although some Nisei explained why they had not been involved in the civil rights campaign that had engulfed the entire city for nearly a decade, their reasons were not reported in the meeting minutes.[95]

Despite the acrimonious debate, some JACL members such as meeting organizer Sakahara clearly believed the confrontation was helpful in making Seattle's Japanese American community aware of the racial crisis in the city. He suggested to the Nisei business owners, for example, that the black rage directed against them as "exploiters" reflected not anti-Asian bias so much as the culmination of feelings resulting from centuries of economic manipulation. But Sakahara also feared that Nisei quietude on the most troublesome social issues in the city might also generate black anger over the Asian community's betrayal not only of the ongoing civil rights struggle but of its own historic campaign against anti-Asian discrimination. "We are a minority, too," declared Sakahara, "and we must be involved in our way. We must not permit whites to use us as 'whipping boys.'" Moreover, Sakahara noted, the legitimate grievances of African Americans must not be sacrificed amid calls for control and order in black Seattle. In a poignant and prophetic statement on the importance of impartial justice, he declared, "The difference between the concept of *law and order* as distinguished from *law and justice* is not a semantic quibble.

Law can be enforced with understanding, sympathy and compassion without losing its efficacy. In our day, harsh and insensitive justice can only sow the seeds of disaster."[96]

If calls for black power and black self-determination frightened older, established Asian business owners, they served as a model and rallying point for many in the younger generation. Organizations such as the Asian Student Union at the University of Washington and individuals like Bernie Yang, of Students for a Democratic Society, and Jim Takisaki, a board member and negotiator for the predominately black Central Contractors Association, unabashedly supported the Black Panthers and student and community activism in all its myriad forms.[97]

By 1970, however, some young Seattle Asians were beginning to challenge black leadership's commitment to the campaign to eradicate racism and create an egalitarian, multiracial community in Seattle. Alan Sugiyama, in an editorial titled "Co-optation: A New Game?" catalogued the grievances Asians had developed against blacks during the civil rights era. Impoverished Asians who still comprised a large part of the Central District population received few services and were excluded from participation in Model Cities decision making, according to Sugiyama, by black administrators who argued that "Asians didn't deserve any funding because they played no part in getting the money." Asians who supported the Central Contractors Association efforts to generate more construction jobs for Central District residents received few of the new positions. And although Asian students supported the blacks at Seattle Central Community College who demonstrated in 1969 to get African American administrators, by 1971, Dr. William Moore, the new black president of the institution, refused, according to Sugiyama, to appoint an Asian administrator because "he would not allow Asians to come in through the back door."[98]

Sugiyama expressed openly what many in other nonwhite communities felt about the 1960s tendency to see both the local and national racial crisis expressly in black-white terms. And the charges leveled no doubt exacerbated the troubled black-Asian relationship in Seattle. Asian spokespersons such as Sugiyama, who admitted that blacks had been the "vanguard for change in this country, and for starting the movement for equality in our local communities,"[99] nonetheless reminded African American Seattle that not all Central District Asians had scored financial success or repudiated the black struggle.

Attempting to decipher intergroup dynamics through the prism of community organizations, and the opinions of the few individuals who left records, is admittedly problematic. Official groups tend to exaggerate their influence in the community, and representatives who purport to speak for entire groups or communities are often challenged. Yet the tentative attempts by the JACL and various Asian activists to reach out to black groups, from the Urban League and NAACP in the mid-1960s to the Black Panther Party and the Central Contractors Association in the later years of the decade, suggest that at least one Asian organization and several committed individual Asians sought to understand the vortex of racial conflict and change swirling around them.[100]

The campaigns against housing bias and de facto segregation produced deep fissures in Seattle's African American community. Yet the question of employment discrimination produced near unanimity. The struggle for jobs also highlighted the paradox of Seattle's past. Much of the city's putative reputation for liberalism stemmed from the decades-old power of organized labor in generating social conditions conducive to working-class well-being, including high wages, good working conditions, good housing, and a significant role in the governance of the city. Indeed Oregon Senator Richard L. Neuberger once described Seattle as "labor's mightiest fortress."[101] Yet labor unions, instinctively protective of their gains, used race as a line of division.

Black workers were particularly hurt by labor's exclusion. Decades of educational deficiencies, especially for southern-born blacks, and meager capital resources often compounded by discriminatory bank lending practices, which prevented blacks from becoming entrepreneurs, meant that skilled labor was often the only means of climbing out of poverty – a means frequently blocked by organized labor.[102] Although in the 1960s some powerful unions, such as the Teamsters, still discouraged African American membership, Seattle blacks chose to concentrate particularly on the building trades for both historic and contemporary reasons. Skilled southern black construction workers who migrated to Seattle found they could not pursue their crafts because they lacked union membership. Moreover, the highly visible major construction projects near or in the Central District, employing white workers who almost always lived outside the area, while unemployed but capable blacks were denied opportunity, underscored the consequences of racial exclusion. According to a Model Cities employment survey of the Central District in

1968, unemployment for black residents was 11.7 percent while that of whites in the city was 2.9 percent. That white construction workers made substantial wages, often in excess of $10 per hour, while denying union membership to impoverished blacks trapped in a pattern of welfare dependency and unemployment, generated anger and frustration far out of proportion to the actual job opportunities denied.[103]

The first salvo of the campaign to desegregate the construction unions came in 1965, and not surprisingly from CORE. When city officials announced the construction of a new federal office building in downtown Seattle, Walter Hundley of CORE wrote the General Services Administration about black participation in the project. "We insist that the contractors for this project," Hundley wrote, "be explicitly required to have Negro employees. . . . " Hundley believed these jobs more important to blacks than poverty funds, job training, and compensatory education since such employment would allow African American workers the opportunity "to become a part of our society and be integrated into normal community life."[104] The protest was registered, but no black workers were hired.

By 1968, as barriers to employment were falling throughout the city, the construction unions adamantly adhered to their discriminatory system apparently in defiance of city, state, and federal pressure to integrate their membership. Union leaders routinely refused to answer surveys on the racial composition of their membership or to participate in citywide forums designed to address employment discrimination. Their membership, they argued, was open to anyone. Black workers simply failed to meet their requirements. Their membership rolls suggested otherwise. The five major building trades unions in Seattle had a total membership of 14,850 in 1969, but only 29 workers were nonwhite (Table 17). Electricians, for example, had two nonwhite workers out of 2,700 members. Plumbers, with 2,600 members, had only one nonwhite in their ranks. The experience of Howard Lewis, a black welder with thirty years' experience, graphically illustrated the difficulties faced by African American workers in obtaining union membership. When Lewis, a permit workman (one obligated to pay union dues but prohibited from becoming a full union member), appeared before the Iron Workers examination board in 1966, one examiner told him, "There is no question about your welding. We know you are a damn good welder." Yet he was asked if he could tie knots and was advised that he could not become a member of the union unless he could do so. Lewis spent the next

Table 17
Membership by Race: Selected Seattle Building Trades Unions,
November 1969

Union	Total Membership	White	Nonwhite
Electrical Workers	2,700	2,698	2
Iron Workers	850	849	1
Operating Engineers	7,500	7,477	23
Plumbers	2,600	2,599	1
Sheet Metal Workers	1,200	1,198	2

Source: William A. Little, "Community Organization and Leadership: A Case Study of Minority Workers in Seattle" (Ph.D. diss., University of Washington, 1976), p. 75.

few weeks learning to tie various knots and then received another membership examination. After showing his knot-tying ability, he was asked to tie a knot he had never heard of. He angrily left the examination convinced he would never be allowed to join the Iron Workers Union.[105]

In 1969, Tyree Scott, a black Seattle contractor, emerged as the leader of the campaign to end black exclusion from the building trades. Scott joined the Central Contractors Association, a group of Seattle-area black construction workers. Concerned about the exclusion of black workers from the union and their own difficulty in obtaining construction contracts, they chose direct action protests to publicize their grievances.[106]

On August 28, 1969, the CCA led a demonstration which closed the swimming pool project at Garfield High School to protest the employment of an all-white construction crew. The following day Scott led 200 black workers and CCA supporters downtown to close the King County Courthouse construction site. From there they marched up First Hill to the Harborview Hospital construction site. CCA protests spread to sites at the University of Washington, where national television cameras recorded the overturning of bulldozers, and to the Seattle-Tacoma Airport, where demonstrators marched single file onto runways to prevent airplanes from landing.[107]

Less dramatic but ultimately more crucial in its campaign, the CCA brought suit against five Seattle unions: Iron Workers Local 86, Sheet Metal Workers Local 99, International Brotherhood of Electrical Workers Local 46, Plumbers and Pipefitters Local 32, and

Operating Engineers Local 502. The CCA soon found a powerful ally in December 1969, when the U.S. Department of Justice joined the case on behalf of the plaintiffs. Two months later Federal Judge William Lindberg found all the unions except IBEW Local 46 had violated Title VII of the Civil Rights Act of 1964.[108]

Taking into account what the court found to be pervasive discrimination "on a continuous basis," including the provision of false information to black workers about employment conditions, exaggerated estimates of training requirements for black apprentices, and aptitude tests imposing higher standards for blacks than whites, Judge Lindberg created the "Seattle Plan," which required the unions to end discrimination and also to take "affirmative action" to rectify past racially motivated exclusionary practices. Under the plan the federal court ordered the craft unions to open membership to African American workers and specifically decreed that they have a special apprenticeship program. It also altered the grounds of admission to the journeymen level and ordered the immediate admission of forty-five black journeymen.[109]

The campaign for opening the construction trade unions in 1969 was predicated on the same premise that had in the early 1960s stirred black Seattleites to protest against de facto school segregation and support open housing. Yet the strategy employed by the CCA also owed much to the black power period of the late 1960s when community empowerment supplanted integration as the goal of grassroots activists. As Tyree Scott asserted, "We don't just want the jobs . . . we want some control over them."[110]

The decade's last direct action campaign also reflected the ambiguous legacy of the Seattle civil rights movement. There were far more opportunities for black construction workers, and black contractors, in Seattle in 1980 than in 1970. Moreover, the public was educated on the extent and impact of racial discrimination in the construction industry. But the unions, despite the Seattle Plan, remained overwhelmingly white, and they continued to alternate between subterfuge and defiance, including public appeals to support them against "coercive" federal judicial power and "reverse discrimination." Moreover, the recession of the early 1970s reduced opportunities for all Seattle-area construction workers, intensifying the rivalry between black workers and the building trades unions.

The Seattle Plan's major legacy rests with the legal precedent it set in establishing affirmative action guidelines to redress structural and institutional inequality and in strengthening the Equal Opportunity

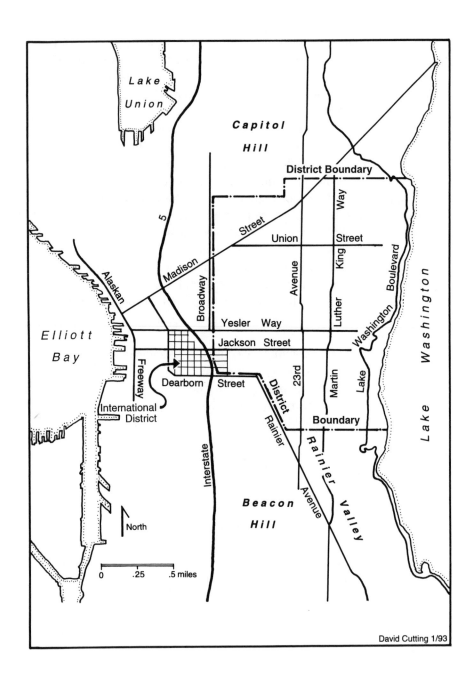

Map 7. Seattle's Central District, 1970

Commission by giving the federal agency the authority to sue in the courts on behalf of plaintiffs.[111] The Plan itself stemmed from the decision by a group of Seattle black workers to challenge job discrimination and of numerous community supporters of all racial backgrounds to help sustain that challenge, as well as the decision by a courageous federal judge and the Justice Department to support them.

The civil rights and political struggles of the 1960s highlighted the contradictions between the ideal and the reality of African American life in the Pacific Northwest. While racism certainly existed in Seattle before that period, the continued migration of blacks and the subsequent reaction of many whites to that migration shattered the illusions of many old settlers and newcomers that the region would readily accept and assimilate its new residents of color. This optimism initially permeated even the usually cautious civil rights organizations. These organizations, and blacks generally, began to make a more sober appraisal of their status and by the 1960s initiated a vigorous campaign to make the ideal a reality. They succeeded in eliminating some of the most egregious forms of discrimination in public accommodations and residential housing. They achieved far less success in generating employment opportunities, particularly for the most impoverished black Seattleites. Indeed, the problems of unemployment and, more important, underemployment – the inability of many local African Americans to obtain positions or income commensurate with their skills and education – proved as intractable at the end of the decade as at the beginning, and generated a host of ancillary symptoms including rising criminal activity, drug abuse, and single-parent homes headed by young, poorly educated women.[112]

Nonetheless, courageous Seattleites – primarily blacks but also some sympathetic Asians and whites – had, during the 1960s, demolished decades-old barriers to opportunity and equality throughout the city. But, as they would soon learn by the early 1970s, simply demolishing barriers would not ensure equality or opportunity. That challenge would await a future generation.

Conclusion

Black Seattle,
Past,
Present,
and
Future

This study of African American Seattle began as an intellectual exercise to situate one small black population's history in the national urban context of 1890 to 1940, the period when most modern black communities assumed their twentieth-century character. It was a search for unambiguous indications of similarities with the experience of the rest of urban African America, to ratify black Seattle's legitimate claim as an integral component of urban black life.

The similarities were not difficult to discover. A racially defined residential district emerged by 1910 which remained the home of the vast majority of the city's blacks until 1980. Seattle's African American workers experienced employment discrimination and its entire black population confronted the ubiquitous social segregation so common for the pre–World War II era. Black women and men responded to these challenges in a manner characteristic of most of their urban counterparts. They created branches of the Afro-American League, the NAACP, and the UNIA to defend their rights. They formed churches, fraternal orders, theatrical groups, and sports organizations to minister to their spiritual and secular needs as well as celebrate their history and heritage. Moreover, black Seattle's collective synergy forged a distinctive African American urban culture which, much like black urban populations elsewhere, provided a psychological haven from a hostile world.

Yet black Seattle prior to World War II was different. Many of the problems considered endemic to northern black communities during this era, while intermittently present, certainly did not dominate the Seattle scene as in other major cities. Much of what occurred – or did not occur – can be attributed to the small size of Seattle's African American population, which prior to World War II never exceeded 4,000 people or constituted more than one percent of the city's population. But the explanation lies beyond mere numbers. The nature of the local economy, in which the majority of blacks held domestic service rather than manufacturing jobs, the ability of local black residents to quickly absorb and assimilate newcomers, the presence of a significantly larger Asian population, and Seattle's ambiguous racial environment, rooted in its relatively recent frontier period, which denied blacks economic opportunities while allowing a select complement of civil rights, all contributed to a significantly different early history. This is not to argue that Seattle was unique, but it is to suggest that the Seattle experience – of a small, slowly growing black community in a major city, much like Minneapolis, San Francisco, and Denver – may be indicative of an urban black America heretofore neglected by historians. If anything, the extraordinary course of history of the 3,700 women and men of black Seattle on the eve of World War II persuasively illustrates the fallacy of the idea of a single African American urban experience.[1]

But as this study advanced to the Second World War, it became increasingly apparent that black Seattle would be permanently and profoundly transformed by the influx of newcomers arriving during and after that global conflict. By 1950 the African American population was 15,666, and in 1970 it stood at 37,868. Deteriorating buildings and rigidly segregated housing practices, crime, drugs, de facto school segregation, chronic intergenerational poverty, and welfare dependency all increasingly characterized the Pacific Northwest's largest African American community, and generated growing alienation, despair, and anger among black Seattleites.

Yet through the 1940s, 1950s, and 1960s, numerous Seattle African Americans remained optimistic that conditions in their city could be addressed. When Reverend John Adams, testifying before a U.S. Civil Rights Commission hearing in the city in 1966, declared, "Seattle is one of the few cities left in America which can solve its racial problem before it becomes unsolvable," he was speaking for many black, white, and Asian residents who still summoned the courage to believe in a peaceful racial future for the city and the nation.[2]

Moreover, his declaration implicitly recalled the prewar era when the sense of shared community mitigated the harsh realities of the urban environment, creating a place very much different from the image of black urban America.

The Central District is no longer the center of black Seattle. The 1960s prediction of demographers and community activists that Seattle would continue to attract newcomers who would propel the African American population above 100,000 by the mid-1970s was widely off the mark.[3] As of 1990 only 60,000 blacks lived in Seattle, comprising 10 percent of the population. Asians now constitute the fastest growing racial minority and, for the first time since 1940, the largest nonwhite group. Some Central District African Americans openly express their concern that they will be supplanted by upper income whites seeking inexpensive housing opportunities and convenient access to the downtown area, or recently arrived Southeast Asian "boat people," who flock to inexpensive inner city neighborhoods. Although black community reactions to these "invasions" have not taken on the intensity of the white resistance to residential integration in the pre-1970 era, it is strangely ironic to see those Central District residents, so very long excluded from other neighborhoods, now struggling to retain their own small homes and apartments.[4]

Nonetheless, black fears of displacement are more than a simple reaction to someone ethnically different moving onto their "turf." Even in the days of rampant segregation on the boundaries of the Central District, African Americans lived in enclaves, if not neighborhoods, which had sizable nonblack populations. The resentment toward upwardly mobile whites is grounded in apprehensions that the affluent newcomers will drive housing prices and rents beyond the affordability of most impoverished blacks. Concern about Asian immigrants, moreover, is based at least partly on the troubling prospect that one of Seattle's newest ethnic groups might be accepted into the social and economic mainstream more readily than one of its oldest. Thai, Cambodian, and Vietnamese cultural adjustment problems notwithstanding, blacks fear that the success of the new arrivals, much like the earlier educational and economic accomplishments of the Seattle residents of Chinese and Japanese ancestry, will be used to undermine public awareness of the continuing problem of racial discrimination and the subsequent necessity of compensatory programs in public schools and the workplace.[5]

Of the 46,565 blacks counted in all of Seattle in 1980 (Table 18), only 38 percent lived in the Central District. For the first time in the twentieth century the greater number of blacks resided outside the traditional core of black Seattle. Each of Seattle's 122 census tracts now shows some African American residents. This diffusion resulted from the citywide discourse on race, housing, and segregation which marked the open housing debates of the 1960s, as well as the growing body of federal, state, and local legislation which effectively outlawed housing discrimination based on race, sex, age, color, and religion. Yet the rapid spatial expansion of black Seattleites from their former Central District neighborhoods remained subject to the vagaries of race. Although African Americans reside in virtually every Seattle suburb, many of the blacks who exited the Central District moved southeast into the Rainier Valley. This migration, which began only in the late 1960s, has extended the visible black community to the southernmost city limits, as "valley" blacks now outnumber those in the Central District. Anyone familiar with the city's neighborhoods during the last three decades can only marvel at, or decry, the rapid expansion of the black residential area.[6]

If much of the rest of the United States is only now beginning to acknowledge and accept the growing racial and ethnic diversity of its population, Seattle can provide lessons for the entire nation. Seattle has always been a multiracial and multicultural city. However, the rapidly growing numbers of people of color as reflected in the 1990 census (Table 18) suggest that the dynamics of group interaction must, of necessity, change. While the Asian, Native American, Latino, and black populations constituted 25 percent of the population in 1990, the children in these categories were 40 percent. To argue that white Seattle must learn to accommodate this growing population is to reiterate much of the thesis of this study. But acceptance of multiethnicity also requires the various groups of color to begin to understand the complex nature of their own interaction – their commonality of interests as well as their competing interests. It is also to argue that they must begin to discern the historical dynamics of interaction among themselves as well as within the larger society, both on an organizational level and as individuals. The history of Seattle illustrates both what can be accomplished when the interaction proceeds and the disastrous consequences when it does not.[7]

For all that has changed over the past century in black Seattle, one feature remains as unmistakable as during the first years of

Table 18
Seattle Population Groups, 1980–1990

	1980		1990	
	Total	Percentage	Total	Percentage
Black	46,565	9.4	51,948	10.0
Asian/Pacific Islander	36,613	7.8	60,819	11.8
Latin/Chicano	12,646	2.5	18,349	3.5
Native American	5,628	1.4	7,326	1.4
White	392,766	80.0	388,858	75.0

Sources: U.S. Bureau of the Census, *1980 Census of Population*, vol. 1, *Characteristics of the Population*, chap. B, *General Population Characteristics*, pt. 49, Washington, table 15; *1990 Census of Population and Housing: Summary, Population and Housing Characteristics*, Washington, table 4.

the Yesler-Jackson and East Madison neighborhoods. Two African American economic and social classes co-exist in precarious balance. One is the middle class – socially conservative, staid, and increasingly successful and visible in the professions, in metropolitan area corporations, and at all levels of government. The other is a much larger impoverished population – derisively called "transients" in the late nineteenth century, "sharecroppers" during World War II, and now euphemistically the "underclass" by social scientists and social service agencies. For much of the past century these affluent and impoverished city dwellers inhabited the same spatial community (although now middle-class African Americans are as likely to live on Mercer Island or in Kirkland as in the East Madison area), but in many ways the two groups have always been worlds apart. Moreover, the division is, of late, exacerbated as the most affluent segment of the contemporary African American population now confronts dilemmas similar to those of the Nisei soon after World War II, with comparable consequences. Since their interests are no longer circumscribed by the overt racial segregation and discrimination that physically and psychologically linked them to the black community, middle-class black Seattleites do not provide the social cohesion, institutional support, economic resources, inspired leadership, or the vision of a united, communitywide struggle for social justice which characterized the Central District well into the 1960s.[8]

Yet the affluent and impoverished blacks of Seattle remain inextricably bound, not simply by skin color but by the many historical and cultural forces which continue to shape their lives in the city and in the United States. Indeed, when the *Northwest Enterprise* published its now famous editorial cartoon in 1944 showing middle-class black Seattleites looking on in horror at the sight of a desultory, inebriated migrant couple leaning against a lamppost, with the caption "Better try to lift them, you can go no higher than they," it reflected a past, present, and future reality for this African American community.[9] It also issued a challenge, which has yet to be effectively met. Those who have successfully negotiated the city's ambiguous economic and racial boundaries must offer guidance and assistance to those who could not. These groups are interdependent; between them lies the heart of the African American community.[10]

But the history of the largest black community in the Pacific Northwest also reminds us of the prospects and perils of racial liberalism. For most of the city's history, numerous black and white Seattleites were proud of their community's absence of racial animosity, of abrasive interracial encounters, and the threat of racial violence. Moreover, as a self-proclaimed politically progressive city, Seattle celebrated its image as a multicultural, multiracial democracy where opportunity was open to all. The reality for the entire century between 1870 and 1970 was vastly different for most of black Seattle. This is not to claim that sincere people, committed to racial equality and social justice for African Americans and for all Seattleites, failed to make significant contributions to the creation of an integrated community. Each era in the city's history reveals countless examples of individual courage from people of all racial, cultural, and economic backgrounds who struggled heroically to create a humane, inclusive city for all of its diverse citizens. Yet the forces arrayed against black aspirations were supported sometimes consciously, and often unwittingly, by the vast majority of Seattleites who chose to ignore the plight of the impoverished, the uneducated, the economically disadvantaged – particularly if they were of a different color.

Racial toleration is meaningless if people are excluded from the vital economic center and relegated to the margins of the urban economy. Seattle, whether in the 1870s or the 1960s, provided substantive evidence of the limits of a racial liberalism incompatible with economic inclusion.[11] Indeed Seattle's apparent success, and its underlying failure, in its race relations paradigm has been its meticulously crafted image which promoted the illusion of inclusion.

True societal integration – the creation of a single community that simultaneously reflects the diversity of its varied segments while recognizing the vital interdependence of all its citizens – must be constructed on a foundation of substantive economic integration. It is incumbent on all Seattleites who believe in a just and equitable society to ensure that unfair economic and social conditions that restrained black lives in the nineteenth and twentieth centuries do not prevail in the twenty-first century.

Appendix 1

Founding Members of the Seattle NAACP, October 23, 1913

Dr. E. A. Johnson	Presbyterian Minister
Rev. J. L. Williams	Methodist Minister
Horace R. Cayton	Apartment House Owner
Samuel H. Stone	Caterer
G. W. Jones	Merchant-Tailor
J. I. Reams	Clothing Store Proprietor
Miss Zoe Young	Milliner
Bonita Wright	Property Owner
Mrs. R. J. Allen	Property Owner
Andrew Black	Attorney
Mrs. S. H. Stone	Property Owner
Rev. W. D. Carter	Baptist Minister
Samuel P. DeBow	Editor, *Seattle Searchlight*
William Chandler	Mover (Moving Express Company)
Benjamin F. Tutt	Barber
Letitia Graves	Hairdresser
Alma Glass	Dressmaker
J. H. Graves	Chiropodist
Etta Hawkins	Property Owner
Beatrice Ball	Property Owner
G. W. Thompson	Grocer
L. Austin	(Occupation Not Listed)

Source: NAACP Branch Files, group I/box G, container 213, Manuscript Division, Library of Congress, Washington, D.C.

Appendix 2

Black Seattle: The Social Nexus

Churches (year of founding in parentheses)
St. Philips Episcopal Chapel
Grace Presbyterian Church (1912)
First AME Church (1886)
Mount Zion Baptist Church (1890)
Church of God in Christ (1927)
(Jackson Street)
Church of God in Christ (1927)
(Irving Street)
Pentecostal Assembly (1929)
Full Gospel Pentecostal Mission (1929)
Ebeneezer AME Zion Church (1933)
Father Divine's Temple of Peace (1934)

Religious Auxiliaries
Baptist Women's Missionary Circle
Women's Home and Foreign Mission Society
Baptist Literary Society

Social Clubs

Lone Star Art Club
Excelsior 500 Club
Industrial Art Club
ABC Club
Mystic Night Club
Lincoln Helping Hand Club
Golden Hour Club
Carter Charity
   and Benevolent Club
Artistic Twelve Club
Colored Women's Association
Golden Aid Club
Everready Social Club
South Side Social Club
London Bridge Club

Will Do Club
Sterling Relief Club
Semper Fidellis Club
Carter Industrial
   and Literary Club
Self-Improvement Club
Culture Club

Fraternal Orders

Male

Hercules Lodge No. 17, F&AM
Solomon Lodge, F&AM
Eureka Chapter No. 1,
  Royal Arch Masons
Harmony Lodge No. 2, F&AM
Toussaint L'Overture,
  Consistory 31
Henni Hassen Temple No. 64,
  Order of Mystic Shriners
Olympic Lodge No. 5,
  Knights of Pythias
Mt. Rainier Chapter No. 1, IOES
Puget Sound Lodge No. 109,
  IBPOE of Washington
Alpha Phi Alpha Fraternity

Female

Jephthah Chapter No. 9,
  Order of Eastern Star
Queen of Sheba Chapter No. 8,
  Order of Eastern Star
Star of Hope, Court of Calonthe, No. 448
Queen Esther Temple No. 7,
  UBF and SMT
Household of Ruth No. 2751,
  GUOOF
Hesperides Tabernacle No. 100,
  Knights and Daughters of Tabor
Evergreen Temple No. 157,
  IBPOE of Washington
Delta Sigma Theta Sorority

Meeting Halls

Alpha Tennis Club Hall
Chandler Hall
Masonic Hall

Veterans Organizations

United Spanish-American
  War Veterans

Athletic Clubs

Alpha Tennis and Outing Club
Puget Sound Athletic Club

Civic Betterment Clubs

Seattle Citizens Council
Women's Civic and
  Political Alliance
South End Civic Club
Young Men's Colored
  Progressive Clubs

Social Service Agencies

East Madison YMCA
Phyllis Wheatley YWCA
Sojourner Truth Home

Sources: *Club Journal of the Colored Women's Federation of Washington and Jurisdiction, 1917–1918*, issued at Spokane, Washington, June 25, 1919, in Nettie J. Asberry Papers, 1–1, Manuscript Division, University of Washington Libraries; various editions of the *Northwest Enterprise*, 1920–40; and Samuel P. DeBow and Edward A. Pitter, eds., *Who's Who in Religious, Fraternal, Social, Civic and Commercial Life on the Pacific Coast* (Seattle: Searchlight Publishing Company, 1927), pp. 14–45.

Appendix 3

Growth of Seattle's Black Population, 1860–1990

Year	Black Population	Percentage Increase	Total Population	Black % of Population
1860	1	–	182	–
1870	13	1,200	1,107	1.2
1880	19	46	3,533	0.5
1890	286	1,405	42,837	0.7
1900	406	42	80,671	0.5
1910	2,296	466	237,194	1.0
1920	2,894	26	315,312	0.9
1930	3,303	14	365,583	0.9
1940	3,789	15	368,302	1.0
1945 (est.)	10,000	164	480,000	2.7
1950	15,666	21	467,591	3.4
1960	26,901	72	557,087	4.8
1970	37,868	41	530,831	7.1
1980	46,565	23	493,820	9.4
1990	51,948	12	516,259	10.0

Sources: Clarence B. Bagley, *History of Seattle from the Earliest Settlement to the Present Time*, 3 vols. (Chicago: S.J. Clarke Publishing Company, 1916), 2:660–61; U.S. Bureau of the Census, *Negro Population: 1790–1915* (Washington, D.C.: Government Printing Office, 1918), table 12; and other census volumes listed in Tables 1, 2, 11, and 13.

Appendix 4

Seattle's Minority Population, 1900–1990

	Total	Black	Japanese	Chinese	Filipino	Native American
1900	80,671	406	2,990	438	—	22
1910	237,194	2,296	6,127	924	—	24
1920	315,312	2,894	7,874	1,351	458	106
1930	365,583	3,303	8,448	1,347	1,614	172
1940	368,382	3,789	6,975	1,781	1,392	222
1950	467,591	15,666	5,778	2,650	2,357	666
1960	557,087	26,901	9,351	4,076	3,755	1,729
1970	530,831	37,868	NA	NA	NA	NA
1980	493,820*	46,755	10,427	9,430	9,591	6,158
1990	516,259	51,948	NA	NA	NA	NA

*Includes other groups not listed above: Korean, 2,305; Vietnamese, 2,179; Asian Indian, 1,243; Samoan, 952; Hawaiian, 514; Guamanian, 127; Eskimo, 337; Aleut, 326; Other, 2,162; not determined, 5,249.

Sources: U.S. Bureau of the Census, *Thirteenth Census of the U.S.*, 1910, 1:226, 3:1007; *Fourteenth Census*, 1920, 3:1085, 1092; *Fifteenth Census*, 1930, 3 (pt. 2): 1231, 1256; *Sixteenth Census*, 1940, 2 (pt. 7): 401; Calvin Schmid, *Non-white Races: State of Washington* (Olympia, 1968), pp. 49–56; Seattle Chamber of Commerce, *Demographic Profiles: Seattle-King County*, November 1983; *1980 Census of Population and Housing: Seattle-Everett, Wash. Standard Metropolitan Statistical Area* (1983).

Notes

Introduction

1. See *Seattle Times*, November 8, 1989, pp. A1, A3, B3.

2. Du Bois's work stood alone until a series of sociological studies written principally by reformers emerged to explain the black urban condition. See, for example, Ray Stannard Baker's *Following the Color Line* (New York: Harper and Row, 1964; first published in 1908); Mary White Ovington's *Half a Man: The Status of the Negro in New York* (New York: Hill and Wang, 1969; first published in 1911); and John Daniels's *In Freedom's Birthplace: A History of the Boston Negro* (New York: Johnson Reprint, 1969; first published in 1914), all of which captured the sense of the small black communities before the World War I migration. For a discussion of these early works, see Florette Henri, *Black Migration, Movement North: The Road from Myth to Man* (Garden City: Doubleday, 1976), pp. 124–25, and Kenneth L. Kusmer, "The Structure of Black Urban History: Retrospect and Prospect," in Darlene Clark Hine, ed., *The State of Afro–American History* (Baton Rouge: Louisiana State University Press, 1986), pp. 91–94.

3. See, for example, Abraham Epstein, *The Negro Migrant in Pittsburgh* (New York: Arno Press, 1969; first published in 1918); Herbert J. Seligmann, *The Negro Faces America* (New York: Harper and Row, 1969; first published in 1920); Emmett J. Scott, *Negro Migration during the War* (New York: Arno Press, 1969; first published in 1920); Louise V. Kennedy, *The Negro Peasant Turns Cityward: Effects of Recent Migrations to Northern Centers* (New York: Columbia University Press, 1930); and Clyde V. Kiser, *Sea Island to City: A Study of St. Helena Islanders in Harlem and Other Urban Centers* (New York: Atheneum, 1969; first published in 1931). James Weldon Johnson's *Black Manhattan* (New York: Atheneum, 1968; first published in 1930) attempted to capture the evolving worldview of urban blacks. However, St. Clair Drake and Horace Cayton's *Black Metropolis* (New York: Harcourt, Brace, 1945), an examination of Chicago's South Side, returned to the familiar ground of a black community in profound disarray, traumatized by economic and political forces the newcomers neither anticipated nor understood.

4. The two most influential 1960s studies were Gilbert Osofsky's *Harlem: The Making of a Ghetto, 1890–1930* (New York: Harper and Row, 2d ed., 1971; first published in 1966) and Allan H. Spear's *Black Chicago: The Making of a Negro Ghetto, 1890–1920* (Chicago: University of Chicago Press, 1967). By the 1970s and 1980s a number of influential studies emerged, including Kenneth L. Kusmer, *A Ghetto Takes Shape: Black Cleveland, 1870–1930* (Urbana: University of Illinois Press, 1976); David Levine, *Internal Combustion: The Races in Detroit, 1915–1926* (Westport, Conn.: Greenwood Press, 1976); Thomas Philpott's *The Slum and the Ghetto: Neighborhood Deterioration and Middle-Class Reform, Chicago 1880–1930* (New York: Oxford University Press,

1978); Douglas Daniels, *Pioneer Urbanites: A Social and Cultural History of Black San Francisco* (Philadelphia: Temple University Press, 1980); James Borchert, *Alley Life in Washington: Family, Community, Religion and Folklife in the City, 1850–1970* (Urbana: University of Illinois Press, 1980); Joe W. Trotter, *Black Milwaukee: The Making of an Industrial Proletariat, 1915–45* (Urbana: University of Illinois Press, 1985); Peter Gottlieb, *Making Their Own Way: Southern Blacks' Migration to Pittsburgh, 1916–30* (Urbana: University of Illinois Press, 1987); and James R. Grossman, *The Land of Hope: Chicago, Black Southerners and the Great Migration* (Urbana: University of Illinois Press, 1989). Ironically, the first important monograph of this decade has been a study of a southern city affected by the black migration, Earl Lewis's *In Their Own Interests: Race, Class, and Power in Twentieth-Century Norfolk, Virginia* (Berkeley: University of California Press, 1991). For a comprehensive review of the literature on black urban history, consult Joe William Trotter, Jr., "Black Migration in Historical Perspective: A Review of the Literature," in Trotter, ed., *The Great Migration in Historical Perspective: New Dimensions of Race, Class, and Gender* (Bloomington: Indiana University Press, 1991), pp. 1–21.

5. See Lawrence B. de Graaf, "The City of Black Angels: Emergence of the Los Angeles Ghetto, 1890–1930," *Pacific Historical Review* 39:3 (August 1970): 323–52, and Daniels, *Pioneer Urbanites*.

6. Blaine A. Brownwell, *The Urban Ethos in the South, 1920–1930* (Baton Rouge: Louisiana State University Press, 1975), p. xvi.

7. John Blassingame was one of the first urban historians to call for an examination of black aspirations, ideals, and institutions as a more rewarding way of reconstructing the significance of African American urban life. See his "Before the Ghetto: The Making of the Black Community in Savannah, Georgia, 1865–1880," *Journal of Social History* 6:4 (Summer 1973): 484–85. For a background discussion of the cultural ethos, see Quintard Taylor, "The Question of Culture: Black Life and the Transformation of Black Urban America, Seattle's Central District, 1900–1940," in *Essays in History: The Journal of the Historical Society of the University of Lagos, Nigeria* 6:4 (December 1989): 13–20.

8. Recent studies of black communities in Chicago and Pittsburgh emphasize the strong ties between northern urbanites and their rural homes – ties that were reinforced by the frequent movement between the regions. Such a migratory pattern was probably common in other border cities such as St. Louis and Cincinnati but was far more difficult to maintain in Seattle. For an analysis of this migration and its impact on black urban community life, see Gottlieb, *Making Their Own Way*, pp. 28–33.

9. See Quintard Taylor, "Black Urban Development – Another View: Seattle's Central District, 1910–1940," *Pacific Historical Review* 58:4 (November 1989): 429–48.

10. For a discussion of the "proletarianization" of the African American work force in one midwestern city see Trotter, *Black Milwaukee*, pp. 39–40, 275–77.

11. Few of the works on black history study the period after 1930. For two rare exceptions, see Dennis R. Dickerson's *Out of the Crucible:*

Black Steelworkers in Western Pennsylvania, 1875–1980 (Albany: State University of New York Press, 1986), a study of the metropolitan Pittsburgh area, and James Borchert's *Alley Life in Washington*, which describes events through the 1960s.

12. See Lewis, *In Their Own Interests*, pp. 167–98, for a discussion of the impact of World War II migration on another African American community.

13. Richard White, "Race Relations in the American West," *American Quarterly* 38:3 (1986): 397. See also Albert Broussard's *Black San Francisco: The Struggle for Racial Equality in the West, 1900–1954* (Lawrence: University Press of Kansas, 1993).

14. Quoted in Larry S. Richardson, "Civil Rights in Seattle: A Rhetorical Analysis of a Social Movement" (Ph.D. diss., Washington State University, 1975), p. 32.

1. Origins and Foundations, 1860–1899

1. U.S. Bureau of the Census, *Eleventh Census of the United States*, 1890, *Population*, part 2 (Washington, D.C.: Government Printing Office, 1897), pp. 620–21; *Twelfth Census of the United States*, 1900, *Occupations* (Washington, D.C.: Government Printing Office, 1904), pp. 408–10; Joanne Wagner Bleeg, "Black People in the Territory of Washington, 1860–1880" (M.A. thesis, University of Washington, 1970), pp. 57–70.

2. Quintard Taylor, "The Emergence of Black Communities in the Pacific Northwest, 1865–1910," *Journal of Negro History* 64:4 (Fall 1979): 342–51. For accounts of anti-Asian violence, see Jules Alexander Karlin, "The Anti-Chinese Outbreaks in Seattle, 1885–1886," *Pacific Northwest Quarterly* 39:1 (April 1948): 103–30; Clayton D. Laurie, "'The Chinese Must Go': The United States Army and the Anti-Chinese Riots in Washington Territory, 1885–1886," *Pacific Northwest Quarterly* 81:1 (January 1990): 22–29; and Roger Sale, *Seattle, Past to Present* (Seattle, University of Washington Press, 1976), pp. 37–49.

3. The Harris quotation can be found in Esther Hall Mumford, *Seattle's Black Victorians, 1852–1901* (Seattle: Ananse Press, 1980), p. 39. Many nineteenth-century northern African American communities faced a similar dilemma. For an overview of the connection between the poverty of these communities and their political vulnerability, see David A. Gerber, "A Politics of Limited Options: Northern Black Politics and the Problem of Change and Continuity in Race Relations Historiography," *Journal of Social History* 14:2 (Winter 1980): 236, 241.

4. Janice L. Reiff, "Urbanization and the Social Structure: Seattle, Washington, 1852–1910" (Ph.D. diss., University of Washington, 1981), pp. 11–14; Sale, *Seattle*, pp. 7–8.

5. *Puget Sound Directory, 1872*, quoted in Reiff, "Urbanization and the Social Structure," p. 35.

6. Norbert MacDonald, "Population Growth and Change in Seattle and Vancouver, 1880–1960," *Pacific Historical Review* 39:3 (August 1970): 299; C. William Thorndale, "Washington's Green River Coal Company: 1880–1930"

(M.A. thesis, University of Washington, 1965), pp. 7–10. See also Reiff, "Urbanization and the Social Structure," pp. 35–36.

7. Lopes was not listed in the 1857 Seattle census, but he is included in Clarence Bagley's listing of the 182 inhabitants of Seattle in 1860. See Clarence B. Bagley's *History of Seattle from the Earliest Settlement to the Present Time*, 3 vols. (Chicago: S. J. Clarke Publishing Company, 1916), 2:660–61. See also Bleeg, "Black People in the Territory of Washington," p. 59; Mumford, *Seattle's Black Victorians*, pp. 12, 23, 66. For an account of Grose's role in founding the East Madison black community, see William Dixon, "Unpublished Memoirs," William H. Dixon Collection, University of Washington Libraries (hereafter cited as Dixon Collection); Samuel P. DeBow and Edward A. Pitter, eds., *Who's Who in Religious, Fraternal, Social, Civic and Commercial Life on the Pacific Coast* (Seattle: Searchlight Publishing Company, 1927), p. 31; and Calvin Schmid, *Social Trends in Seattle* (Seattle: University of Washington Press, 1944), pp. 137–41.

8. See Mumford, *Seattle's Black Victorians*, pp. 68–70. Douglas Daniels provides a similar discussion of early black San Francisco settlers in *Pioneer Urbanites: A Social and Cultural History of Black San Francisco* (Philadelphia: Temple University Press, 1980), pp. 59–62.

9. Bagley listed 182 inhabitants in Seattle in 1860: 123 men, 25 women, and 34 children. The overwhelmingly male character of the town was also confirmed by the 1870 census. See Bagley, *History of Seattle*, 2:660–61. According to Janice Reiff, only 65 of the town's 1,107 residents in 1870 had lived in Seattle throughout the previous decade. Of the 3,533 Seattleites in 1880, only 336, or 10 percent, were long-term residents. This pattern continued into the first decade of the twentieth century, when 22.3 percent of Seattle's males over eighteen who lived in Seattle in 1900 remained there in 1910. See Reiff, "Urbanization and the Social Structure," pp. 109, 130: See also U.S. Bureau of the Census, *Compendium of the Ninth Census* (Washington, D.C.: Government Printing Office, 1872), p. 590; Mumford, *Seattle's Black Victorians*, p. 67.

10. Reiff, "Urbanization and the Social Structure," pp. 4–5, 138.

11. See Richard C. Berner, *Seattle, 1900–1920: From Boomtown, Urban Turbulence, to Restoration* (Seattle: Charles Press, 1991), p. 8. See also MacDonald, "Population Growth and Change in Seattle and Vancouver," p. 304; Sale, *Seattle*, pp. 50–55.

12. See "Account of Mother Wright" and "Memories," by Elizabeth Grose (Oxendine) in Dixon Collection, and Richard Stanley Hobbs, "The Cayton Legacy: Two Generations of a Black Family, 1859–1976" (Ph.D. diss., University of Washington, 1989), pp. 35, 54. For a discussion of the origins of the Seattle population, see Berner, *Seattle, 1900–1920*, pp. 60–76.

13. Hobbs, "The Cayton Legacy," pp. 3, 13, 36, 54, 61. See also Quintard Taylor, "A History of Blacks in the Pacific Northwest: 1788–1970" (Ph.D. diss., University of Minnesota, 1977), pp. 172–73.

14. Patrick Douglas, "The Family of Two Revolutions: The Gaytons," *Seattle Magazine* 6:58 (January 1969), pp. 22–23, and Mumford, *Seattle's Black Victorians*, pp. 12, 186.

15. See Emma J. Ray, *Twice Sold, Twice Ransomed: The Autobiography of*

Mr. and Mrs. L. P. Ray (Freeport, N.Y.: Books for Libraries Press, 1971; first published in 1926), pp. 37, 40, 56; Taylor, "A History of Blacks in the Pacific Northwest," pp. 172–73; and Mumford, *Seattle's Black Victorians*, pp. 12, 46.

16. See Arnold H. Taylor, *Travail and Triumph: Black Life and Culture in the South since the Civil War* (Westport, Conn.: Greenwood Press, 1976), pp. 23–30; Jacqueline Jones, *Labor of Love, Labor of Sorrow: Black Women, Work, and the Family from Slavery to the Present* (New York: Basic Books, 1985), pp. 52–78; Joel Williamson, *The Crucible of Race: Black-White Relations in the American South since Emancipation* (New York: Oxford University Press, 1984), pp. 111–19, 130–39. Williamson's study posits that the antiblack violence in thought and action which was so identified with the restoration of white conservative governments in the ex-Confederate states in the mid-1870s foreshadowed the far more turbulent 1885–1915 era, during which growing numbers of southern African Americans arrived in Seattle.

17. See Elizabeth (Mrs. Brittain) Oxendine, "Memories," in Dixon Collection; Mumford, *Seattle's Black Victorians*, pp. 14–15, 85–86.

18. Walker and Lee are quoted in Mumford, *Seattle's Black Victorians*, p. 14. For the full text of the Public Accommodations Act see *General Statutes and Codes of the State of Washington*, vol. 1, General Statutes, p. 1016. Background discussion of black civil rights in the region can be found in a variety of sources including Franz M. Schneider, "The 'Black Laws' of Oregon" (M.A. thesis, University of Santa Clara, 1970), pp. 3–15; J. W. Smurr, "Jim Crow Out West" in J. W. Smurr and H. Ross Toole, eds., *Historical Essays on Montana and the Northwest* (Helena: Western Press, 1957), pp. 149–203; and Quintard Taylor, "Slaves and Free Men: Blacks in the Oregon Country, 1840–1860," *Oregon Historical Quarterly* 83:2 (Summer 1982): 153–58. Other northern states, notably Ohio, New York, and Massachusetts, enacted similar public accommodation laws in the 1880s, but Washington was unique among the states of the Far West in creating such comprehensive civil rights legislation. See Lawrence Grossman, *The Democratic Party and the Negro: Northern and National Politics, 1868–1892* (Urbana: University of Illinois Press, 1976), pp. 75–95. Washington women voted until 1887, when the Territorial Supreme Court overturned the Territorial Legislature's suffrage code. See T. A. Larson, "The Woman Suffrage Movement in Washington," *Pacific Northwest Quarterly* 67:2 (April 1976): 52–55; and Murray Morgan, *Skid Road: An Informal Portrait of Seattle* (Seattle: University of Washington Press, 1982; first published in 1951), p. 78. See also Elizabeth McLagen, *A Peculiar Paradise: A History of Blacks in Oregon, 1788–1940* (Portland: Georgian Press, 1980), pp. 163–64, and Taylor, "The Emergence of Black Communities in the Pacific Northwest," pp. 347, 350. Voting rights for blacks in all western territories were guaranteed by the Territorial Suffrage Act of 1867. For a background discussion of the act and western white attitudes toward blacks during Reconstruction, see Eugene H. Berwanger, *The West and Reconstruction* (Urbana: University of Illinois Press, 1981), chapter 5.

19. See Karlin, "The Anti-Chinese Outbreaks," pp. 104–5, and Roger Daniels, *Asian America: Chinese and Japanese in the United States since 1850* (Seattle: University of Washington Press, 1988), pp. 36–66.

20. *Seattle Daily Intelligencer*, May 28, 1879, p. 2. For a background on

the 1870s migration of blacks to Kansas, see Nell Irvin Painter, *Exodusters: Black Migration to Kansas after Reconstruction* (Lawrence: University Press of Kansas, 1986; first published in 1977), pp. 184–201, and Robert G. Athearn, *In Search of Canaan: Black Migration to Kansas, 1879–80* (Lawrence: Regents Press of Kansas, 1978), chapter 5.

21. (Olympia) *Washington Standard*, February 20, 1864, p. 2. Robert W. Johannsen described the Pacific Northwest Republican press in 1860 as adamantly opposed to black emancipation and argued that the party had no more violent and unprincipled enemies than the abolitionists. See Johannsen, *Frontier Politics on the Eve of the Civil War* (Seattle: University of Washington Press, 1955), p. 203.

22. (Olympia) *Commercial Age*, March 26, 1870, p. 2. See also Horace Cayton, Jr., *Long Old Road: An Autobiography* (Seattle: University of Washington Press, 1970), pp. 18–20.

23. *Seattle Republican*, June 15, 1900, p. 1.

24. Seattle's Chinese had already felt the wrath of unemployed white male workers when virtually the entire Asian community was expelled from the city and surrounding communities in 1885 and 1886. See Karlin, ''The Anti-Chinese Outbreaks,'' pp. 103ff., and James A. Halseth and Bruce A. Glasrud, ''Anti-Chinese Movements in Washington, 1885–1886: A Reconsideration,'' in Halseth and Glasrud, eds., *The Northwest Mosaic: Minority Conflicts in Pacific Northwest History* (Boulder: Pruett, 1977), p. 117. See also the interview with Mattie Vinyerd Harris, by Esther Hall Mumford, Oral/Aural History Collection, Washington State Archives, Olympia, Washington, transcript, p. 30. Mumford and her associates conducted over fifty interviews in the mid-1970s as part of the Black History Project sponsored by the Washington State Division of Archives. Tape transcripts are housed at the Washington State Archives in Olympia. Those interviews are hereafter cited as OAHC.

25. See U.S. Bureau of the Census, *Twelfth Census, 1900, Occupations* (Washington). According to David Nicandri, other racial and ethnic groups predominated in various trades and professions and consequently generated similar stereotypes. Washingtonians of British ancestry were often found in skilled positions as machinists, steamfitters, boilermakers, and white collar workers. Germans were often the watchmakers and cabinetmakers, and Asians were heavily concentrated in fish and meat wholesaling and fruit canning. Thus developed stereotypes of the British ''manager'' or ''foreman,'' the German ''craftsman,'' and the Asian ''petty tradesman.'' Of all the major ethnic groups only Italian Americans approximated blacks in overconcentration as peddlers and porters. But because Italian men were far better represented in the petty bourgeoisie as restaurant and saloon keepers, retail and wholesale merchants, bakers, boot and shoe repairers, and tailors, they could more easily overcome the image of menial laborer. The evidence suggests that black workers were unable to transcend the weight of stereotype established early in Seattle, and indeed throughout the nation, and this burden would hamper them well into the twentieth century. See David L. Nicandri, ''Washington's Ethnic Workingmen in 1900: A Comparative View,'' unpublished paper delivered at the Pacific

Northwest History Conference, Portland, Oregon, April 7, 1979, in North-west Collection, University of Washington Library. Joe Trotter and Peter Gottlieb have traced similar racial stereotyping in Milwaukee and Pitts-burgh, cities with vastly different economies. In these cities the stereotyping of blacks' capacity to handle hot, dirty, heavy manual labor encouraged their entry into the lowest ranks of the steel industry. See Trotter, *Black Milwaukee: The Making of an Industrial Proletariat, 1915–45* (Urbana: University of Illinois Press, 1985), pp. 54–55; Gottlieb, *Making Their Own Way: Southern Black's Migration to Pittsburgh, 1916–30* (Urbana: University of Illinois Press, 1987), pp. 99–100.

26. Bleeg, "Black People in the Territory of Washington," pp. 59–60, 64.

27. See Alan A. Hynding, "The Coal Miners of Washington Territory: Labor Troubles in 1888–1889," *Arizona and the West* 12:3 (Autumn 1970): 221–36; Robert A. Campbell, "Blacks and the Coal Mines of Western Washington, 1888–1896," *Pacific Northwest Quarterly* 73:4 (October 1982): 146–55; and Mark Stern, "Black Strikebreakers in the Coal Fields: King County, Washington – 1891," *Journal of Ethnic Studies* 5 (Fall 1977): 60–70.

28. *Seattle Union Record*, January 20, 1906, p. 1. For a discussion of the convergence of labor solidarity and race solidarity in the Pacific Northwest see Carlos A. Schwantes, "Protest in a Promised Land: Unemployment, Disinheritance, and the Origin of Labor Militancy in the Pacific Northwest, 1885–1886," *Western Historical Quarterly* 13:4 (October 1982): 379–80; and W. Thomas White, "Race, Ethnicity, and Gender in the Railroad Work Force: The Case of the Far Northwest, 1883–1918," *Western Historical Quarterly* 16:3 (July 1985): 266–68.

29. See Campbell, "Blacks and the Coal Mines of Western Washington," p. 155; Karlin, "The Anti-Chinese Outbreaks," pp. 103–30; Robert Bedford Pitts, "Organized Labor and the Negro in Seattle" (M.A. thesis, University of Washington, 1941), pp. 10–14; and Carlos Schwantes, *Radical Heritage: Labor, Socialism, and Reform in Washington and British Columbia, 1885–1917* (Seattle: University of Washington Press, 1979), pp 134–40, 157. For a fascinating discussion of the employment of black, female, Japanese, and East European workers by the Northern Pacific Railroad as a model of intergroup manipulation, see White, "Race, Ethnicity, and Gender in the Railroad Work Force," pp. 265–84.

30. Mumford, *Seattle's Black Victorians*, pp. 46–47.

31. Ibid., p. 45. Carole Marks has suggested that the inclusion of some African Americans in nineteenth-century labor unions reflected the con-cern of those organizations for general reform embracing comprehensive, utopian solutions. Since such solutions were inclusive of all workers, their interracial composition seemed appropriate. But as a more conservative trade union movement evolved, concerned with making unions "practical" rather than utopian, the membership drew racial boundaries. In Seattle, at least, that distinction is not clearly apparent. The "utopian" Knights of Labor and its successor, the "conservative" Western Central Labor Union, were both adamantly anti-Asian, and if their actions in Franklin and Newcastle are indicative, antiblack as well. See Carole Marks, "Split Labor Markets and Black-White Relations, 1865–1920," *Phylon* 42:4 (December 1981):

303; Campbell, "Blacks and the Coal Mines of Western Washington," pp. 150–51, 153.

32. See Schwantes, *Radical Heritage*, pp. 22–30; Robert L. Friedheim, *The Seattle General Strike* (Seattle: University of Washington Press, 1964), pp. 24–25; and Bruce Nelson, *Workers on the Waterfront: Seamen, Longshoremen, and Unionism in the 1930s* (Urbana: University of Illinois Press, 1988), pp. 48–49.

33. See Marks, "Split Labor Markets and Black-White Relations," p. 294; Campbell, "Blacks and the Coal Mines of Western Washington," p. 153.

34. Harris interview, p. 5, OAHC, and Mumford, *Seattle's Black Victorians*, pp. 129–31.

35. Mumford, *Seattle's Black Victorians*, pp. 200–201. See also Robert A. Wilson and Bill Hosokawa, *East to America: A History of the Japanese in the United States* (New York: Quill, 1982), pp. 33–34, and Kazuo Ito, *Issei: A History of Japanese Immigrants in North America* (Seattle: Japanese Community Service, 1973), pp. 765–71, for a comparative discussion of Japanese prostitutes in Seattle. Two studies of prostitution in the nineteenth-century West examine the particular role of African American women in the profession: Anne M. Butler, *Daughters of Joy, Sisters of Misery: Prostitutes in the American West, 1865–90* (Urbana: University of Illinois Press, 1985), pp. 4–16, and Paula Petrik, *No Step Backward: Women and Family on the Rocky Mountain Mining Frontier, Helena, Montana, 1865–1900* (Helena: Montana Historical Society Press, 1987), pp. 26, 48–49.

36. Mumford, *Seattle's Black Victorians*, p. 94. See also David M. Katzman, *Before the Ghetto: Black Detroit in the Nineteenth Century* (Urbana: University of Illinois Press, 1973), pp. 115–17; Kenneth Kusmer, *A Ghetto Takes Shape: Black Cleveland, 1870–1930* (Urbana: University of Illinois Press, 1976), pp. 75–76; Trotter, *Black Milwaukee*, p. 99; and Darrel E. Bigham, *We Ask Only a Fair Trial: A History of the Black Community of Evansville, Indiana* (Bloomington: Indiana University Press, 1987), pp. 61–62, 65, for discussions of the role of black barbers in other nineteenth-century African American communities.

37. Quoted in Howard N. Rabinowitz, "From Exclusion to Segregation: Southern Race Relations, 1865–1890," *Journal of American History* 63:2 (September 1976): 347.

38. *Seattle Post-Intelligencer*, January 10, 1895, p. 8. See also Mumford, *Seattle's Black Victorians*, pp. 82–84.

39. Mumford, *Seattle's Black Victorians*, p. 78.

40. Bleeg, "Black People in the Territory of Washington," p. 59, and Mumford, *Seattle's Black Victorians*, pp. 68–69.

41. Mumford, *Seattle's Black Victorians*, pp. 95–100.

42. Ibid., pp. 94, 200. Berner, *Seattle, 1900–1920*, p. 62. See also Butler, *Daughters of Joy, Sisters of Misery*, pp. 4–16, and Petrik, *No Step Backward*, pp. 48–49. William L. Lang provides a fascinating discussion of the role of African Americans in prostitution in another Northwest city during the same period: "Tempest on Clore Street: Race and Politics in Helena, Montana, 1906," *Scratchgravel Hills* 3 (Summer 1980): 9–14.

43. Mumford, *Seattle's Black Victorians*, pp. 97, 101.

44. See Allan H. Spear, *Black Chicago: The Making of a Negro Ghetto, 1890–1920* (Chicago: University of Chicago Press, 1967), pp. 51–65; Kusmer, *A Ghetto Takes Shape*, pp. 25–31; and Trotter, *Black Milwaukee*, pp. 25–27.

45. Spencer Crew, Lee Williams, and Joe W. Trotter found similar patterns of racial clustering in Camden, New Jersey, Toledo, Ohio, and Milwaukee, Wisconsin, respectively: Crew, "Black Life in Secondary Cities: A Comparative Analysis of the Black Communities of Camden and Elizabeth, New Jersey, 1860–1920" (Ph.D. diss., Rutgers University, 1979), pp. 86–87; Williams, "Concentrated Residences: The Case of Black Toledo, 1890–1930," *Phylon* 43:2 (June 1982): 168–69; and Trotter, *Black Milwaukee*, pp. 21–24.

46. Sale, *Seattle*, p. 55. For a discussion of structural forces and their impact on residential segregation, see Kenneth Kusmer, "Black Urban History in the U.S.: Retrospect and Prospect," *Trends in History* 3:1 (Fall 1982): 80–81. For a discussion of the concept of "walking cities," see Raymond A. Mohl, *The New City: Urban America in the Industrial Age, 1860–1920* (Arlington Heights, Ill.: Harlan Davidson, Inc., 1985), pp. 28–29, and Maury Klein and Harvey A. Kantor, *Prisoners of Progress: American Industrial Cities, 1850–1920* (New York: Macmillan, 1976), pp. 96–97.

47. Mumford, *Seattle's Black Victorians*, pp. 108–9, 116.

48. *Seattle Post-Intelligencer*, June 10, 1900, p. 10. See also Ray, *Twice Sold, Twice Ransomed*, pp. 76–78; Reiff, "Urbanization and the Social Structure," p. 119; and Sale, *Seattle*, p. 57. Kusmer, *A Ghetto Takes Shape*, pp. 48–49, discusses the frequent tendency of vice districts to be located in or on the periphery of black residential areas.

49. *Seattle Post Intelligencer*, June 10, 1900, p. 10.

50. Elizabeth (Lizzie) Oxendine to William Dixon, November 1, 1936, Dixon Collection. See also *Seattle Post-Intelligencer*, July 27, 1898, p. 5, and Schmid, *Social Trends in Seattle*, pp. 137–40.

51. Quoted in Armstead L. Robinson, "The Difference Freedom Made: The Emancipation of Afro-Americans," in Darlene Clark Hine, ed., *The State of Afro-American History: Past, Present, and Future* (Baton Rouge: Louisiana State University Press, 1986), p. 64.

52. For a discussion of similar developments in southern cities in the latter third of the nineteenth-century, see Rabinowitz, "From Exclusion to Segregation," pp. 347–48. On the rise of all-black churches in the post–Civil War South, consult Taylor, *Travail and Triumph*, pp. 142–44. Janice L. Reiff provides examples of Norwegian and Swedish ethnic women's clubs and organizations, while Karen Blair describes the role of native-born middle-class white women in creating specialized voluntary organizations. See Reiff, "Scandinavian Women in Seattle, 1888–1900: Domestication and Americanization," in Karen J. Blair, ed., *Women in Pacific Northwest History: An Anthology* (Seattle: University of Washington Press, 1988), pp. 171–73, and Blair's *The Clubwoman as Feminist: True Womanhood Redefined, 1868–1914* (New York: Holmes and Meier, 1980), pp. 39–56.

53. Mumford, *Seattle's Black Victorians*, p. 148.

54. Ibid., p. 162. See also Daniel G. Hill, "The Negro in Oregon: A Survey" (M.A. thesis, University of Oregon, 1932), p. 63. For a discussion of the secession of black parishioners from predominately white congregations in the

post-Civil War South, see Katherine L. Dvorak, *An African-American Exodus: The Segregation of the Southern Churches* (Brooklyn, N.Y.: Carlson, 1991), pp. 69–114; Robert L. Hall, "Tallahassee's Black Churches, 1865–1885," *Florida Historical Quarterly* 58:2 (October 1979): 192–95; and Taylor, *Travail and Triumph*, pp. 142–44.

55. In 1901 the *Seattle Republican* (June 21, p. 4) reported fifty-three members for Jones Street AME and fifteen for the Baptist Church. See also Taylor, "The Emergence of Black Communities in the Pacific Northwest," p. 342.

56. Mumford, *Seattle's Black Victorians*, pp. 147, 154–55.

57. Ibid., pp. 154, 161.

58. Ray, *Twice Sold, Twice Ransomed*, pp. 75–79, 103.

59. See, for example, Reiff, "Urbanization and Social Change," pp. 119, 137–38; Sale, *Seattle*, pp. 56–57, 80.

60. Elizabeth Oxendine, "Memories," in Dixon Collection. See also William A. Muraskin, *Middle Class Blacks in a White Society: Prince Hall Freemasonry in America* (Berkeley: University of California Press, 1975), pp. 3–42, and Loretta J. Williams, *Black Freemasonry and Middle-Class Realities* (Columbia: University of Missouri Press, 1980), pp. 103–34, for a background on the role of fraternal orders in middle-class African America.

61. See Reiff, "Urbanization and the Social Structure," p. 133; Mumford, *Seattle's Black Victorians*, 168–69.

62. Mumford, *Seattle's Black Victorians*, pp. 171–72.

63. Ibid., pp. 172–73.

64. *Seattle Post-Intelligencer*, February 18, 1899, p. 6. See also Mumford, *Seattle's Black Victorians*, pp. 177–78.

65. Ibid., p. 175.

66. Quoted in Arna Bontemps and Jack Conroy, *Anyplace But Here* (New York: Hill and Wang, 1966), p. 263. See also Hobbs, "The Cayton Legacy," p. 110.

67. *Seattle Republican*, August 13, 1894, p. 4. Cayton's complaints were echoed by black political leaders from Massachusetts to Illinois. See Gerber, "A Politics of Limited Options," p. 241.

68. Thomas Cox, *Blacks in Topeka, Kansas, 1865–1915: A Social History* (Baton Rouge: Louisiana State University Press, 1982), p. 122. See also Spear, *Black Chicago*, pp. 51, 54; Kusmer, *A Ghetto Takes Shape*, pp. 113–21.

69. Quoted in Bontemps and Conroy, *Anyplace But Here*, p. 262. See also Hobbs, "The Cayton Legacy," pp. 79–81.

70. (Spokane) *Spokesman Review*, September 21, 1894, p. 4.

71. See *Seattle Post-Intelligencer*, September 5, 1889, p. 2; Mumford, *Seattle's Black Victorians*, p. 190.

72. John A. Coleman, one of the founders of the Black Democratic Club, had been a Republican before arriving in Seattle. By 1894 he rejoined the GOP and secured the party's nomination for wreckmaster. N. F. Butts was expelled from the Republican Party in 1890 only to join the Democrats and be expelled by them in 1892. Attorney Allen A. Garner and Thomas C. Collins, brother of Seaborn Collins, left the Republicans for the Democrats only to return in 1894, while Gideon Bailey and Reverend Eugene Harris,

two of the most respected members of the Seattle community and heretofore lifelong Republicans, joined the Democrats in 1900. See Mumford, *Seattle's Black Victorians*, pp. 190–94.

73. Elizabeth Oxendine to William Dixon, Dixon Collection.

2. Employment and Economics, 1900–1940

1. Quoted in the *Chicago Defender*, December 21, 1929, p. 2.

2. Richard C. Berner, *Seattle, 1900–1920: From Boomtown, Urban Turbulence, to Restoration* (Seattle: Charles Press, 1991), pp. 9–10, 21–29, 33, 38. See also Earl Pomeroy, *The Pacific Slope: A History of California, Oregon, Washington, Idaho, Utah, and Nevada* (Lincoln: University of Nebraska Press, 1991), pp. 147–48. Urban historian Carl Abbott recognizes the role of the "Alaska" trade and the development of the rich agricultural hinterland of the interior Pacific Northwest as crucial in the ascendancy of Seattle over its chief regional rival, Portland. But he also suggests that Seattle's success derived equally from astute local responses to the changing scale of commercial activity and the changing range of opportunities in the national and international economies. In short, Seattle's entrepreneurial and expansive local elites seemed determined that their city would garner a growing share of Pacific Rim trade, and promoted the development of commercial networks to ensure their city's competitive advantage in an increasingly global economy. See Carl Abbott, "Regional City and Network City: Portland and Seattle in the Twentieth Century," *Western Historical Quarterly* 23:3 (August 1992): 293–319.

3. Clarence B. Bagley, *History of Seattle from the Earliest Settlement to the Present Time*, 3 vols. (Chicago: S. J. Clarke Publishing Company, 1916), 2:605–9.

4. Berner, *Seattle, 1900–1920*, pp. 26–28. See also Bagley, *History of Seattle*, 2:597–635; Roger Sale, *Seattle, Past to Present* (Seattle: University of Washington Press, 1976), pp. 50–53.

5. See Douglas Henry Daniels, *Pioneer Urbanites: A Social and Cultural History of Black San Francisco* (Philadelphia: Temple University Press, 1980), pp. 59–63, for a discussion of the travelcraft skills of blacks. See also Richard Hobbs, ed., *The Autobiography of Horace Cayton, Sr.* (Manama, Bahrain: Delmon Press, 1987), pp. 39–40, and Emory Tolbert, *The UNIA and Black Los Angeles* (Los Angeles: University of California Press, 1980), p. 31, for ways black porters helped and guided black residents across the nation.

6. Sandy Moss interview, Seattle, December 21, 1972, transcript, p. 1; Edward Pitter, Seattle, November 19, 1973, transcript, p. 1; Margaret Cogwell, Seattle, September 4, 1973, transcript, p. 1. These three interviews are part of the Black Oral History Research Project conducted under my direction in the early 1970s. Fifty interviews of black pioneers and their descendants in Washington, Oregon, Idaho, and Montana, were conducted by me and my associates between 1972 and 1975. The tapes and transcripts are housed at Holland Library, Washington State University, Pullman. These and other interviews in the collection are hereafter cited as Black Oral History Interviews, BOHI. Juanita Warfield Proctor interview, Seattle, September 22,

1976, transcript p. 1, and Albert Joseph Smith interview, September 23, 1976, transcript, p. 5, are part of the Oral/Aural History Collection, Washington State Archives, Olympia. They are cited as OAHC; Frank Jenkins interview, Seattle, June 6, 1972, Frank Jenkins Papers, University of Washington Libraries (hereafter cited as Jenkins Papers).

7. Joseph Sylvester Jackson, "The Colored Marine Employees Benevolent Association of the Pacific, 1921–1934, or Implications of Vertical Mobility for Negro Stewards in Seattle" (M.A. thesis, University of Washington, 1939), pp. 13–14.

8. See Robert Bedford Pitts, "Organized Labor and the Negro in Seattle" (M.A. thesis, University of Washington, 1941), pp. 39–40. See also Lester Rubin, *The Negro in the Longshore Industry* (Philadelphia: University of Pennsylvania Press, 1974), pp. 136–38, for a history of the Longshoremen's union in Seattle and other West Coast ports. Rubin inaccurately asserts that blacks did not work on Seattle docks before 1920. For information on Royston consult the *Seattle Searchlight*, August 19, 1916, p. 1. According to Richard Berner, tension between the ILA and black strikebreakers was already heightened because African American workers were employed as sailors by the Puget Sound Navigation Company during a strike by the Puget Sound Steamshipmen's Union just before the longshore walkout. See Berner, *Seattle, 1900–1920*, p. 214.

9. Horace Cayton, Jr., *Long Old Road: An Autobiography* (Seattle: University of Washington Press, 1970), pp. 112–13. Despite his experience with angry white striking dockworkers, Cayton became one of the nation's leading advocates for the unionization of black labor. See Cayton, *Black Workers and the New Unions* (Chapel Hill: University of North Carolina Press, 1939), p. 425.

10. Mattie Vinyerd Harris interview, OAHC, p. 40. See also Berner, *Seattle, 1900–1920*, pp. 214–15.

11. Frank Jenkins interview, by Richard Berner, Seattle, June 6, 1972, Jenkins Papers.

12. Cayton, *Long Old Road*, pp. 115, 118 (quotation).

13. Ibid., p. 99.

14. Hulet Wells quoted in Berner, *Seattle, 1900–1920*, p. 273.

15. Interview, Edward Coleman, Seattle, transcript, p. 13.

16. See Florette Henri, *Black Migration, Movement North: The Road from Myth to Man* (Garden City: Doubleday, 1976), pp. 68–72; and Peter Gottlieb, "Rethinking the Great Migration: A Perspective from Pittsburgh," and Darlene Clark Hine, "Black Migration to the Urban Midwest: The Gender Dimension, 1915–1945," in Joe William Trotter, Jr., ed., *The Great Migration in Historical Perspective: New Dimensions of Race, Class, and Gender* (Bloomington: Indiana University Press, 1991), pp. 68–82, 127–46, respectively.

17. Jackson, "The Colored Marine Employees Benevolent Association," p. 14. The pitting of Asian male workers against white females was also common, as indicated by the Butler Hotel's replacement of white waitresses with Japanese men in 1915. See Berner, *Seattle, 1900–1920*, p. 172. Moreover, there were nineteenth-century precedents for the manipulation of female and male workers against each other. See W. Thomas White, "Race, Ethnicity, and Gender in the Railroad Work Force: The Case of the

Far Northwest, 1883–1918," *Western Historical Quarterly* 16:3 (July 1985): 280–81. For a fascinating background discussion of the debate over married women in the Seattle workplace, see Maurine Weiner Greenwald, "Working-Class Feminism and the Family Wage Ideal: The Seattle Debate on Married Women's Right to Work, 1914–1920," *Journal of American History* 76:1 (June 1989): 118–49.

18. Berner, *Seattle, 1900–1920*, p. 75. For a discussion of similar national trends in black female labor, see Jacqueline Jones, *Labor of Love, Labor of Sorrow: Black Women, Work, and the Family from Slavery to the Present* (New York: Basic Books, 1985), pp. 167–68; David M. Katzman, *Seven Days a Week: Women and Domestic Service in Industrializing America* (New York: Oxford University Press, 1978), pp 76–79; and Mary Romero, *Maid in the U.S.A.* (New York: Routlege, 1992), pp. 60–64.

19. Jackson, "The Colored Marine Employees Benevolent Association," pp. 15–17.

20. Robert L. Friedheim, *The Seattle General Strike* (Seattle: University of Washington Press, 1964), p. 162.

21. See Pitts, "Organized Labor and the Negro," p. 42; Cayton, *Long Old Road*, p. 118.

22. Pitts, "Organized Labor and the Negro," p. 31.

23. Ibid., pp. 18–21.

24. See Jackson, "The Colored Marine Employees Benevolent Association," pp. 21, 25–26, and Marylou McMahon Haughland, "A History of the Alaska Steamship Company" (M.A. thesis, University of Washington, 1968), p. 25.

25. Roston was secretary of the CMEBA until his death in 1924. See Jackson, "The Colored Marine Employees Benevolent Association," p. 31. See also "Objects [*sic*] of the Colored Marine Employees Benevolent Association of the Pacific," quoted on the same page, and Roston Papers, box 1–1; Pitts, "Organized Labor and the Negro," pp. 20–21.

26. Joseph Isom Staton interview, OAHC, transcript, p. 4.

27. See Jackson, "The Colored Marine Employees Benevolent Association," pp. 27–29, 56. Jackson worked on a steamship one summer to gather information for his thesis on the CMEBA.

28. Cayton, *Long Old Road*, pp. 125–26.

29. Coleman interview, pp. 35–42.

30. Irene Grayson interview, OAHC, p. 10; Mattie Vinyerd Harris interview, OAHC, p. 19; Mary Ott Saunders interview, OAHC, p. 12. See also U.S. Bureau of the Census, *Fourteenth Census of the U.S.*, 1920, vol. 4, *Occupations*, pp. 1232–33; *Fifteenth Census of the U.S.*, 1930, *Population*, vol. 4, pp. 1709–10; and Richard Stanley Hobbs, "The Cayton Legacy: Two Generations of a Black Family, 1859–1976" (Ph.D. diss., University of Washington, 1989), pp. 214, 234. See also Jones, *Labor of Love, Labor of Sorrow*, pp. 167–168; Katzman, *Seven Days a Week*, pp. 76–79; Romero, *Maid in the U.S.A.*, pp. 78–79.

31. Analysis of occupational census data over three decades, 1910 to 1940, generates challenge and frustration. Occupational categories were gradually increased and refined to provide more precise data. Unfortunately,

this meant that some occupations appearing in one category in 1910 or 1920 were listed in different categories in 1940. Nevertheless, for comparative purposes I have collapsed three 1940 categories, Craftsmen, Foremen, and Kindred Workers; Operatives and Kindred Workers; and Laborers, under the Manufacturing and Skilled Trades rubric, as it most closely approximates the 1910 and 1920 Census Bureau scheme of classification. *Thirteenth Census of the U.S., 1910*, vol. 4, pp. 602–3; *Fourteenth Census of the U.S., 1920*, vol. 4, *Occupations*, pp. 1232–33; *Fifteenth Census of the U.S., 1930, Population*, vol. 4, pp. 1709–10; *Sixteenth Census of the U.S., 1940*, vol. 3, *The Labor Force*, pt. 5, pp. 852–53.

32. *Northwest Enterprise*, July 21, 1927, p. 4.

33. National Urban League, "Unemployment Status of Negroes" (New York: National Urban League, December, 1931), pp. 44–45. See also Seattle Urban League, "What to Tell Them" (Seattle: Seattle Urban League, 1935), p. 3. See also Jackson, "The Colored Marine Employees Benevolent Association," pp. 55–56.

34. Samson C. Valley interview, OAHC, p. 15.

35. Sara Oliver Jackson interview, OAHC, p. 2.

36. National Urban League, "Unemployment Status of Negroes," p. 44.

37. William Henry Lee interview, OAHC, p. 5. Despite being rebuffed by the Mechanics Union, Lee supported A. Philip Randolph in his effort to form the Brotherhood of Sleeping Car Porters. For an account of Valley's encounter with the Butchers' Union, see Samson Valley interview, OAHC, p. 4.

38. "History of the Marine Cooks and Stewards Union," quoted in Bruce Nelson, *Workers on the Waterfront: Seamen, Longshoremen, and Unionism in the 1930s* (Urbana: University of Illinois Press, 1988), p. 48.

39. Cayton, *Long Old Road*, p. 42.

40. Sandy Moss interview, OAHC, pp. 17, 23.

41. *Seattle Union Record*, February 27, 1919, p. 1. See also Berner, *Seattle, 1900–1920*, p. 298.

42. The organization of the integrated UMW local in the Cascade Coal Mining District coincided with the 1904 national convention which unanimously recommended to the American Federation of Labor convention that all of its affiliates be asked to end racial discrimination. The UMW delegates also voted in favor of universal suffrage, without regard to race. See Maier B. Fox, *United We Stand: The United Mine Workers of America, 1890–1990* (Washington, D.C.: United Mine Workers, 1991), pp. 68, 111. Howard Kimeldorf views much of the radicalism of the Pacific Coast ILA and subsequent ILWU, which resulted in their accepting blacks as full members decades before other unions, as stemming from the influence of IWW members among the Pacific Northwest longshoremen. For a discussion of the IWW's role, see Kimeldorf, *Reds or Rackets? The Making of Radical and Conservative Unions on the Waterfront* (Berkeley: University of California Press, 1988), pp. 22–27.

43. Quoted in Kimeldorf, *Reds or Rackets?* p. 148. See also p. 4, and William H. Harris, *The Harder We Run: Black Workers since the Civil War* (New York: Oxford University Press, 1982), p. 19, and Nelson, *Workers on the Waterfront*, p. 84.

44. See various issues of the *Seattle Post-Intelligencer*, June 1–30, 1934; Ford Bellson, "Labor Gains on the Coast: A Report on the Integration of Negro Workers into the Maritime Unions of the Pacific Coast States," *Opportunity: Journal of Negro Life* 17:5 (May 1939): 142–43, and Haugland, "A History of the Alaska Steamship Company," pp. 31–33. For background on the strike, see Charles P. Larrowe, *Harry Bridges: The Rise and Fall of Radical Labor in the United States* (Westport, Conn.: Lawrence Hill and Company, 1972), pp. 32–61, and Nelson, *Workers on the Waterfront*, pp. 127–55.

45. Jackson, "The Colored Marine Employees Benevolent Association," pp. 53–56.

46. For a discussion of the merging of the two unions, see Bellson, "Labor Gains on the Coast," pp. 142–43, and Pitts, "Organized Labor and the Negro," pp. 27–30.

47. Nelson, *Workers on the Waterfront*, pp. 49, 246.

48. Pitts, "Organized Labor and the Negro," p. 18.

49. The description of Seattle as "labor's mightiest fortress" is attributed to Oregon Senator Richard L. Neuberger and is quoted in David Brewster, "Solidarity Forever! Black Demands for Construction Jobs Have Revived Labor's Old Fighting Spirit – Not on Behalf of All Workers, But *White* Workers," *Seattle Magazine* 6:69 (December 1969): 34. See also Sandy Moss interview, BOHI, pp. 15–17; U.S. Census, 1940, *The Labor Force*; Pitts, "Organized Labor and the Negro," p. 18.

50. See Joe W. Trotter, *Black Milwaukee: The Making of an Industrial Proletariat, 1915–45* (Urbana: University of Illinois Press, 1985), p. 3.

51. See *Northwest Enterprise*, March 25, 1927, p. 2, and Quintard Taylor, "A History of Blacks in the Pacific Northwest, 1788–1970" (Ph.D. diss., University of Minnesota, 1977), pp. 179–80.

52. *Northwest Enterprise*, editorials, July 1, 1927, and October 4, 1928.

53. Ibid., November 30, 1933, p. 1.

54. See Muriel Pollard interview in Esther Hall Mumford, *Seven Stars and Orion: Reflections of the Past* (Seattle: Ananse Press, 1986), p. 65.

55. U.S. Bureau of the Census, *Fifteenth Census of the United States*, 1930, *Occupational Statistics, Population*, vol. 4 (Washington, D.C.: Government Printing Office, 1933), pp. 1709–11.

56. Margaret Cogwell interview, BOHI, p. 2.

57. See Pollard interview in Mumford, *Seven Stars and Orion*, p. 65.

58. *Northwest Enterprise*, editorials, July 31, 1936, and January 7 and 14, 1938.

59. Ibid., January 27, 1939, p. 1, and October 13, 1939, p. 1.

60. For examples of this view see *Northwest Enterprise*, editorials, July 31, 1936, and January 14, 1938; Spear, *Black Chicago*, pp. 71–75, 111–12; Kusmer, *A Ghetto Takes Shape*, pp. 243–46. See also *Progressive Westerner* 1:5 (March 1915), copy in Samuel DeBow Papers, microfilm reel, University of Washington Libraries.

61. T. Arnold Hill to Georgia N. Kelles, August 2, 1929, National Urban League Records, Manuscript Division, Library of Congress, Washington, D.C., series 4, box 36; *Cayton's Weekly*, August 25, 1917, pp. 4–5, 11–12; *Northwest Enterprise*, October 4, 1928, p. 3, and editorial, June 6, 1929, p. 7.

62. Seattle Urban League, Annual Report, 1930, quoted in "The Silver Scoreboard," the 1955 Annual Report of the Seattle Urban League, p. 4.

3. Housing, Civil Rights, and Politics, 1900–1940

1. W. E. B. Du Bois, "The Great Northwest," *Crisis* 6 (September 1913): 237–40.

2. Quoted in the *Northwest Enterprise*, June 15, 1934, p. 4. See Marguerite Johnson interview in Esther Hall Mumford, *Seven Stars and Orion: Reflections of the Past* (Seattle: Ananse Press, 1986), p. 34; George S. Schuyler, "Black Warriors," *American Mercury* 21 (November 1930): 293–94; Horace R. Cayton, Jr., *Long Old Road: An Autobiography* (Seattle: University of Washington Press, 1970), p. 22. See also Quintard Taylor, "The Emergence of Black Communities in the Pacific Northwest, 1865–1910," *Journal of Negro History* 64:4 (Fall 1979): 343, 349–50. Ronald Coleman and Joe W. Trotter have found similar patterns in Salt Lake City and Milwaukee. Trotter argues that by 1900 the nation increasingly adopted the racial outlook of the South. See Ronald Coleman, "Among the Saints and the Gentiles: Blacks in Utah, 1850–1910" (paper presented at the Blacks in the American West Symposium, University of California, Davis, 1983), p. 30, and Joe W. Trotter, *Black Milwaukee: The Making of an Industrial Proletariat, 1915–45* (Urbana: University of Illinois Press, 1985), p. 25.

3. See *Northwest Enterprise*, December 11, 1930, p. 1; Richard Berner to Quintard Taylor, July 25, 1990; and Juana Racquel Royster-Horn, "The Academic and Extracurricular Undergraduate Experiences of Three Black Women at the University of Washington, 1935 to 1941" (Ph.D. diss., University of Washington, 1980), pp. 94–95.

4. Mumford, *Seven Stars and Orion*, pp. 34–35.

5. Irene Burns Miller, *Profanity Hill* (Everett, Wash.: The Working Press, 1979), pp. 99–102.

6. See, for example, Revels Cayton's account of the capriciousness of restaurant discrimination in Richard Stanley Hobbs, "The Cayton Legacy: Two Generations of a Black Family, 1859–1976" (Ph.D. diss., University of Washington, 1989), p. 203.

7. Robert E. Colbert, "The Attitude of Older Negro Residents toward Recent Negro Migrants in the Pacific Northwest," *Journal of Negro Education* 15:4 (Fall 1946): 697.

8. See Cayton, *Long Old Road*, pp. 35–36.

9. *Seattle Republican*, April 9, 1909, p. 4, and November 12, 1909, p. 1; Esther Hall Mumford, "Seattle's Black Victorians – Revising a City's History," *Portage* 2:1 (Fall/Winter 1980–81): 16–17.

10. Quoted in a memorandum from Irene B. Miller to George H. Revelle, Jr., May 5, 1950, in the Seattle Civic Unity Committee Records, University of Washington Libraries (hereafter cited as CUC Records).

11. Quoted from Elva Moore Nicholas interview, in Mumford, *Seven Stars and Orion*, p. 25.

12. Despite his qualifications, Walker was mistaken about the prospects

of his employment at Boeing. No African Americans were hired at the company before 1942.

13. Miller, *Profanity Hill*, pp. 50–51, 125–27.

14. While most covenants in neighborhoods surrounding the Central District were directed at blacks, the Broadmoor area northeast of Madison Street barred Asians and Jews as well. See N. P. Dotson, Jr., "Seattle Urban League Pilot Study of the Seattle Negro Community," unpublished paper, 1948, Urban League Records, University of Washington Libraries (hereafter cited as Seattle Urban League Records). For a detailed analysis of the role of restrictive covenants on the West's largest black community, see Lawrence B. de Graaf, "The City of Black Angels: Emergence of the Los Angeles Ghetto, 1890–1930," *Pacific Historical Review* 39:4 (August 1970): 336–38, 346–49.

15. A 1930 Seattle Urban League study estimated that 45 percent of the East Madison neighborhood was black, the remainder white. See Dotson, "Seattle Urban League Pilot Study," p. 4; interview, Fred P. Woodson, 1968, transcript in Fred P. Woodson Papers, University of Washington Libraries, and Calvin F. Schmid, *Social Trends in Seattle* (Seattle: University of Washington Press, 1944), p. 140. For a discussion of violence directed against black residential expansion, see William Tuttle, Jr., *Race Riot: Chicago in the Red Summer of 1919* (New York: Atheneum, 1970); David Allan Levine, *Internal Combustion: The Races in Detroit, 1915–1926* (Westport, Conn.: Greenwood Press, 1976), pp. 153–65; Thomas Lee Philpott, *The Slum and the Ghetto: Neighborhood Deterioration and Middle Class Reform, Chicago, 1880–1930* (New York: Oxford University Press, 1978), pp. 162–81; and Olivier Zunz, *The Changing Face of Inequality: Urbanization, Industrial Development, and Immigrants in Detroit, 1880–1920* (Chicago: University of Chicago Press, 1982), p. 374.

16. Edward Pitter interview by Quintard Taylor, November 19, 1973, transcript, p. 10. The Pitter interview and all others that were part of the Black Oral History Research Project are hereafter cited as BOHI. See also *Fifteenth Census of the U.S.*, 1930, *Population*, vol. 4, *Families*, pp. 66, 1402; *Sixteenth Census of the U.S.*, 1940, *Housing*, vol. 2, pt. 5, p. 731.

17. *Fifteenth Census of the U.S.*, vol. 4, p. 61; *Sixteenth Census of the U.S.*, vol. 2, p. 731; U.S. Bureau of the Census, *Negroes in the United States, 1920–1932* (Washington, D.C.: Government Printing Office, 1935), pp. 278–79.

18. For a discussion of this changing ideology at the national level, see William Toll, *The Resurgence of Race: Black Social Theory from Reconstruction to the Pan-African Conferences* (Philadelphia: Temple University Press, 1979), pp. 213–20.

19. See Fred Cordova, *Filipinos: Forgotten Asian Americans* (Dubuque: Kendall-Hunt, 1983), p. 177, on the Filipino Community of Seattle, Inc.; Murray Morgan, *Skid Road: An Informal Portrait of Seattle* (Seattle: University of Washington Press, 1982), pp. 238–39; and Albert A. Acena, "The Washington Commonwealth Federation: Reform Politics and the Popular Front" (Ph.D. diss., University of Washington, 1975), p. 21 and passim, on the Federation's role in state politics in the 1930s.

20. "Report of the Seattle NAACP, February 10, 1914, NAACP Branch Files, group I/box G, container 213, Manuscript Division, Library of Congress, Washington, D.C. (hereafter cited as NAACP Files, Library of Congress).

21. See NAACP Files, Library of Congress, and Charles Flint Kellogg, *NAACP: A History of the National Association for the Advancement of Colored People, Vol. I, 1909–1920* (Baltimore: Johns Hopkins Press, 1967), pp. 118, 129–30.

22. NAACP Files, Library of Congress.

23. J. A. Spingarn to Letitia Graves, January 28, 1915, NAACP Files, Library of Congress.

24. Graves to May Childs Neary, Secretary, NAACP, June 12, 1915, NAACP Files, Library of Congress. See also Robert B. Hesketh to Samuel DeBow, July 8, 1921, in Samuel DeBow Papers, University of Washington Libraries. One of the most fascinating pieces of correspondence came to the Seattle branch in 1920 after Mrs. Saul H. Hall, now local secretary, wrote to Mary White Ovington, chair of the Association board of directors, requesting information on the Universal Negro Improvement Association and its proposed convention in New York. James Weldon Johnson, responding for Ovington, wrote that the NAACP had no official connection with the UNIA and that neither the Association nor its branches would send official representatives. "On the other hand," commented Johnson, "we have no word to utter against any honest effort at united action and as individuals our members have naturally every right to take part as they see fit." Soon the national NAACP would have numerous words to utter on Marcus Garvey and the UNIA as the two organizations became bitter rivals for the allegiance of black America in the 1920s. See Johnson to Hall, July 14, 1920, NAACP Files, Library of Congress.

25. See *Northwest Enterprise*, May 13, 1927, p. 8. On the 1921 anti-interracial marriage campaign, see "Bulletin of Mrs. Saul Hall to House Bill #36," March 14, 1921, NAACP Files, Library of Congress.

26. For a discussion and assessment of the UNIA and its impact on black communities in the United States and also Latin America and Africa, see Tony Martin, *Race First: The Ideological and Organizational Struggles of Marcus Garvey and the Universal Negro Improvement Association* (Westport, Conn.: Greenwood Press, 1976); Judith Stein, *The World of Marcus Garvey* (Baton Rouge: Louisiana State University Press, 1986); and Emory J. Tolbert, *The UNIA and Black Los Angeles* (Los Angeles: University of California Press, 1980).

27. Juanita Warfield Proctor interview in Mumford, *Seven Stars and Orion*, pp. 43–44.

28. Ibid., p. 44.

29. Ibid.

30. Marguerite Johnson interview, ibid., p. 36.

31. Juanita Proctor interview, ibid., pp. 44–45.

32. *The Messenger*, May 22, 1922, p. 425; *The Negro World*, September 15, 1923, p. 7, and March 28, 1925, p. 8. Leonard Gayton interview, OAHC, p. 45. See also Robert A. Hill, ed., *The Marcus Garvey and Universal Negro Improvement Association Papers*, vol. 2 (Berkeley: University of California Press, 1983), pp. 262–64, 534.

33. The news article was titled "Pickaninnies to Have Own Clinic." See

Seattle Post-Intelligencer, April 11, 1929, p. 6. The reorganization of the Seattle NAACP was described in Report of the Seattle NAACP, April 1929, NAACP Files, Library of Congress.

34. *Northwest Enterprise,* August 10, 1933, p. 4, and October 23, 1936, p. 2.

35. Marshall Gray, "Report on the Renton Rape," NAACP Files, Library of Congress; *Northwest Enterprise,* April 2, 1935, p. 1, and April 25, 1935, p. 4.

36. *Northwest Enterprise,* February 7, 1935, p. 4, February 14, 1935, pp. 1, 4, and March 14, 1935, p. 4. Seattle NAACP Report for the Year 1935, in NAACP Papers, Library of Congress. See also the *Japanese American Courier,* February 9, 1935, pp. 1–2, and the *Voice of Action,* February 15, 1935, p. 1. A second anti-interracial marriage bill was introduced in the 1937 legislative session by King County State Senator Earl Maxwell. Again, after spirited protest meetings, this time at Mount Zion Baptist Church, the NAACP led a multiracial coalition of seventy-five whites, blacks, and Filipinos to Olympia and persuaded Senator Maxwell to withdraw his measure. *Northwest Enterprise,* February 26, 1937, p. 1, and March 5, 1937, p. 1.

37. See Nancy J. Weiss, *The National Urban League, 1910–1940* (New York: Oxford University Press, 1974), pp. 71–79; John H. Franklin and Alfred A. Moss, Jr., *From Slavery to Freedom: A History of Negro Americans* (New York: McGraw-Hill, 1988), pp. 289–90.

38. Lodie Biggs to T. Arnold Hill, April 26, 1929, in National Urban League Records, Industrial Relations Affiliates File (Seattle, 1926–39), series 4, box 36, Manuscript Division, Library of Congress (hereafter cited as National Urban League Records). Biggs's rationale for the creation of the Seattle Urban League is advanced in an article she wrote for the *Northwest Enterprise,* January 3, 1929, p. 4, and January 10, p. 4.

39. The Seattle Urban League Annual Report for 1930 and for 1931, and the circa 1935 pamphlet "What to Tell Them," which was directed at Seattle's youth, are three examples of the numerous reports and studies of black Seattle. See, typically, the Seattle Urban League Annual Report for 1931, National Urban League Records, Library of Congress. See also the *Northwest Enterprise,* July 6, 1933, p. 4, and March 6, 1936, p. 2.

40. Minutes of the Health and Recreation Committee Meeting, Seattle Urban League, May 31, 1932, National Urban League Records, Library of Congress.

41. Ibid. See also T. Arnold Hill to Joseph S. Jackson, June 9, 1932, National Urban League Records, Library of Congress.

42. See *Northwest Enterprise,* April 1, 1938, p. 1, and April 8, 1938, p. 1.

43. Ibid., April 8, 1938, p. 1; April 22, 1938, p. 1; and April 29, 1938, pp. 1–2.

44. Ibid., June 10, 1938, p. 1; January 6, 1939, p. 1; and December 22, 1939, p. 1. The same week officers Paschall and Stevenson were pardoned, John A. Follings, another black Seattleite who was allegedly beaten by Paschall and Pat Whalen at the downtown police station in 1937, received a $15,000 false arrest judgment. See *Northwest Enterprise,* April 7, 1939, p. 1.

45. Numerous studies have emerged recently to assess the role of the Communist Party in local black activism during the 1930s. Among the

most important are Mark Naison, *Communists in Harlem during the Depression* (Urbana: University of Illinois Press, 1983), and Robin D. G. Kelly, *Hammer and Hoe: Alabama Communists during the Great Depression* (Chapel Hill: University of North Carolina Press, 1990).

46. *Northwest Enterprise*, January 10, 1929, p. 4; February 27, 1930, p. 1; April 16, 1931, p. 8; October 29, 1931, p. 8; and December 24, 1937, p. 1.

47. Hutchins was described unflatteringly by Eugene V. Dennett, a Seattle party member from the 1920s to the 1940s, who frequently clashed with the new leadership in general and Hutchins in particular after 1930. See Dennett, *Agitprop: The Life of an American Working-Class Radical: The Autobiography of Eugene V. Dennett* (Albany: State University of New York Press, 1990), pp. 35, 47.

48. Hobbs, "The Cayton Legacy," pp. 250–51.

49. Susie Revels Cayton to Madge Cayton, n.d., quoted in Hobbs, "The Cayton Legacy," p. 311.

50. Ibid., p. 251.

51. Ibid., pp. 237–238.

52. Quoted in Patrick Douglas, "The Family of Two Revolutions: The Gaytons," p. 24.

53. For a discussion of the appeal of communism to New York blacks and an analysis of interracial socialist culture that emerged along with left-wing politics, see Naison, *Communists in Harlem during the Depression,* pp. 33–34, 47–48.

54. On the visit of Governor Hartley to First AME Church, see the *Northwest Enterprise*, September 1, 1932, p. 8.

55. See *Club Journal of the Colored Women's Federation of Washington and Jurisdiction, 1917–1918,* issued at Spokane, Washington, June 25, 1919; in Nettie J. Asbury Papers, University of Washington Libraries.

56. See *Northwest Enterprise*, February 27, 1930, p. 4; October 1, 1931, p. 8; September 15, 1932, p. 6; April 13, 1933, p. 4; April 20, 1933, p. 1 (editorial), p. 4; January 10, 1936, p. 1; December 24, 1937, p. 1. See also Morgan, *Skid Road*, pp. 238–39, and Acena, "The Washington Commonwealth Federation," p. 21.

57. *Northwest Enterprise,* February 23, 1933, p. 6.

58. Ibid., March 27, 1936, p. 6, and April 10, p. 4.

59. Quoted in Hobbs, "The Cayton Legacy," p. 237.

60. *Northwest Enterprise,* November 4, 1935, p. 1; see also February 23, 1933, p. 6.

61. Powell Barnett Papers, University of Washington Libraries; *Northwest Enterprise,* September 16, 1932, p. 6, and April 3, 1936, p. 6; Acena, "The Washington Commonwealth Federation," pp. 154, 452. Samuel Smith, the first black city councilman in 1967, who nonetheless was active in local politics as early as the 1940s, remembers the influence of the "few professionals" in the GOP as opposed to working-class blacks who were mostly Democrats. See interview with Sam Smith, November 20, 1973, BOHI, p. 4. For an interesting comparison of this political transformation with another small northern community – Providence, Rhode Island – see Norma LaSalle Daoust, "Building the Democratic Party: Black Voting in Providence in the

1930s," *Rhode Island History* 44:3 (August 1895): 81–88. See also John M. Allswang, *A House for All Peoples: Ethnic Politics in Chicago, 1890–1936* (Lexington: University of Kentucky Press, 1971), pp. 206–12, for a discussion of both the local and national implications of shifting black voter allegiance.

62. See Colbert, "The Attitude of Older Negro Residents toward Recent Negro Migrants," p. 697.

4. Blacks and Asians in a White City, 1870–1942

1. See Powell R. Barnett, "Work in the Democratic Party," in Powell Barnett Papers, University of Washington Libraries, and Edward Pitter interview, Seattle, November 19, 1973, p. 14. The Pitter interview and all other interviews that were part of the Black Oral History Research Project are hereafter cited as BOHI.

2. A survey of the literature suggests that few studies moved beyond the black-white dichotomy in exploring themes of African American community development. See, for example, Allan H. Spear, *Black Chicago: The Making of a Negro Ghetto, 1890–1920* (Chicago: University of Chicago Press, 1967); Kenneth L. Kusmer, *A Ghetto Takes Shape: Black Cleveland, 1870–1930* (Urbana: University of Illinois Press, 1976); and Gilbert Osofsky, *Harlem: The Making of a Ghetto, 1890–1930* (New York: Harper and Row, 1971), all major studies which defined the field of urban history but which excluded comparisons of blacks with other nonwhite groups. For a discussion of antiblack violence, see Richard Maxwell Brown, *Strain of Violence: Historical Studies of American Violence and Vigilantism* (New York: Oxford University Press, 1977), pp. 205–18. For a provocative discussion of the complexity of race in the multiracial West, see Patricia Nelson Limerick, *The Legacy of Conquest: The Unbroken Past of the American West* (New York: Norton, 1987), pp. 260–61.

3. See Roger Daniels, *Asian America: Chinese and Japanese in the United States since 1850* (Seattle: University of Washington Press, 1988), pp. 75–77, 134–41, and Bruno Lasker, *Filipino Immigration to the Continental United States and Hawaii* (Chicago: University of Chicago Press, 1931), p. 11.

4. *Northwest Enterprise*, December 12, 1941, p. 1.

5. Typical of union discrimination in Seattle was the Central Labor Council's displacement in 1916 of all Asian porters in saloons, cafés, and restaurants for "American citizens" who were quickly organized into a local of the Hotel and Restaurant Employees Union. See Richard C. Berner, *Seattle, 1900–1920: From Boomtown, Urban Turbulence, to Restoration* (Seattle: Charles Press, 1991), p. 212. For a general discussion of anti-Asian discrimination, consult Kazuo Ito, *Issei: A History of Japanese Immigrants in North America* (Seattle: Japanese Community Service, 1973), pp. 95–99; Art Chin, *Golden Tassels: A History of the Chinese in Washington, 1857–1977* (Seattle: Art Chin, 1977), pp. 100–101; and Daniels, *Asian America*, p. 162.

6. The Ozawa decision is reprinted in Eliot G. Mears, *Resident Orientals on the American Pacific Coast: Their Legal and Economic Status* (New York: Institute of Pacific Relations, 1927), pp. 507–14. See also Yuji Ichioka, *Issei: The World of the First Generation of Japanese Immigrants, 1885–1924* (New York: The Free

Press, 1988), pp. 219–26, and Sucheng Chan, *Asian Americans: An Interpretive History* (Boston: Twayne, 1991), p. 47.

7. Robert Blauner, *Racial Oppression in America* (New York: Harper and Row, 1972), p. 63.

8. See Lucie Cheng and Edna Bonacich, *Labor Immigration under Capitalism: Asian Workers in the United States before World War II* (Berkeley: University of California Press, 1984), pp. 11–12, 27–29. For a description of those opportunities, see Yuzo Murayama, "The Economic History of Japanese Immigration to the Pacific Northwest, 1890–1920" (Ph.D. diss., University of Washington, 1982), pp. 118–20, 151–53, 239.

9. Murayama, "The Economic History of Japanese Immigration," pp. 32–33.

10. Robert A. Wilson and Bill Hosokawa, *East to America: A History of the Japanese in the United States* (New York: Quill, 1982), pp. 68–69.

11. Rose Hum Lee, *The Chinese in the United States of America* (Hong Kong: Hong Kong University Press, 1960), pp. 69–71. Historians of Japanese and Filipino immigration to America also subscribe to the sojourner thesis. See H. Brett Melendy, "Filipinos in the United States," in Norris Hundley, Jr., ed., *The Asian American: The Historical Experience* (Santa Barbara: Clio Press, 1976), p. 117; Evelyn Nakano Glenn, *Issei, Nisei, War Bride: Three Generations of Japanese American Women in Domestic Service* (Philadelphia: Temple University Press, 1986), p. 50; Ito, *Issei*, pp. 16–17, 30–33; Daniels, *Asian America*, p. 99; and Murayama, "The Economic History of Japanese Immigration to the Pacific Northwest," p. 145.

12. Yuzo Murayama provides an excellent description of the *tanomoshi* in his dissertation, "The Economic History of Japanese Immigration to the Pacific Northwest," pp. 106–7. See also Edna Bonacich and John Modell, *The Economic Basis of Ethnic Solidarity: Small Business in the Japanese American Community* (Berkeley: University of California Press, 1980), pp. 22, 30; and Ivan H. Light, *Ethnic Enterprise in America: Business and Welfare among Chinese, Japanese, and Blacks* (Berkeley: University of California Press, 1972), pp. 22–30.

13. Doug and Art Chin, *Up Hill: The Settlement and Diffusion of the Chinese in Seattle, Washington* (Seattle: Doug and Art Chin, 1973), pp. 10–11.

14. Robert E. Wynne, *Reaction to the Chinese in the Pacific Northwest and British Columbia, 1859–1910* (New York: Arno Press, 1978), p. 84. See also Shih-shan Henry Tsai, *The Chinese Experience in America* (Bloomington: Indiana University Press, 1986), p. 18; and Doug and Art Chin, *Up Hill*, pp. 3–4, 11.

15. Chin, *Up Hill*, p. 5.

16. See Lee, *The Chinese in the United States of America*, p. 81. The sojourner thesis is the subject of spirited debate among historians of Chinese America at least in part because its implicit assumption of unassimilability and cultural arrogance was the central argument of nineteenth-century Chinese exclusionists. For examples of the various arguments, see Gunther Barth, *Bitter Strength: A History of the Chinese in the United States, 1850–1870* (Cambridge: Harvard University Press, 1964), p. 1; Anthony B. Chan, "The Myth of the Chinese Sojourner in Canada," in K. V. Ujimoto and

G. Hirabayashi, eds., *Visible Minorities and Multiculturalism: Asians in Canada* (Toronto: Butterworths, 1980), p. 34; Yuen-fong Woon, "The Voluntary Sojourner among the Overseas Chinese: Myth or Reality?" *Pacific Affairs* 56:4 (Winter 1983–84): 673–90; Stanford Lyman, "The Chinese Diaspora in America," in Chinese Historical Society of America, *The Life, Influence and Role of the Chinese in the United States, 1776–1960* (San Francisco: Chinese Historical Society of America, 1975), p. 28; and Daniels, *Asian America*, p. 16.

17. See James A. Halseth and Bruce A. Glasrud, "Anti-Chinese Movements in Washington, 1885–1886: A Reconsideration," in Halseth and Glasrud, eds., *The Northwest Mosaic: Minority Conflicts in Pacific Northwest History* (Boulder: Pruett, 1977), p. 117. The earliest anti-Chinese riot occurred in Los Angeles in 1871. Twenty-one Chinese were shot, hanged, or burned alive by white mobs, which, as Roger Daniels has noted, must have included a sizable number of the town's 5,700 residents. The Los Angeles riot was the first of thirty-one confrontations in California during the 1870s which resulted in the destruction of Chinese stores and expulsion of Chinese residents. There were also anti-Chinese riots in Denver in 1880, where a Chinese laundryman was beaten to death, and Rock Springs, Wyoming, in September 1885, where 28 Chinese miners were ruthlessly shot, according to one eyewitness, while "they were fleeing like a herd of hunted antelopes," by 150 men who invaded the Chinese quarter. See Elmer C. Sandmeyer, *The Anti-Chinese Movement in California* (Urbana: University of Illinois Press, 1973), pp. 48, 97–98; Paul Crane and Alfred Larson, "The Chinese Massacre," *Annals of Wyoming* 12:1 (January 1940): 47–55; and Daniels, *Asian America*, pp. 59–63.

18. *Seattle Post-Intelligencer*, September 11, 1885, p. 2; Chin, *Up Hill*, pp. 13, 15.

19. See Jules Alexander Karlin, "The Anti-Chinese Outbreaks in Seattle, 1885–1886," *Pacific Northwest Quarterly* 39:1 (April 1948): 108; Shih-shan Henry Tsai, *China and the Overseas Chinese in the United States, 1868–1911* (Fayetteville: University of Arkansas Press, 1983), p. 78; Daniels, *Asian America*, p. 62.

20. See Clayton D. Laurie, "'The Chinese Must Go': The United States Army and the Anti-Chinese Riots in Washington Territory, 1885–1886," *Pacific Northwest Quarterly* 81:1 (January 1990): 25–27; Karlin, "The Anti-Chinese Outbreaks in Seattle," pp. 120–24. See Chin, *Up Hill*, pp. 15–16, and Janice L. Reiff, "Urbanization of the Social Structure: Seattle, Washington, 1852–1910" (Ph.D. diss., University of Washington, 1981), pp. 59–61. Doug and Art Chin report that some of the federal troops ostensibly sent to protect the Chinese and maintain law and order used the occasion to visit Chinatown on November 9 to collect a "special tax" for each resident. Their extortion efforts netted approximately $150. See Chin, *Up Hill*, p. 15.

21. Chin, *Up Hill*, pp. 17–19. See also Art Chin, *Golden Tassels*, p. 60.

22. Willard G. Jue, "Chin Gee-Hee, Chinese Pioneer Entrepreneur in Seattle and Toishan," *Annals of the Chinese Historical Society of the Pacific Northwest* 1:1 (1983): 31–38, and Chin, *Up Hill*, p. 26–28. See also Limerick, *The Legacy of Conquest*, p. 268.

23. Chin, *Up Hill*, p. 29. For a discussion of the role of associations in Chinese American urban communities, see Stanford Lyman, *Chinese Americans* (New York: Random House, 1974), p. 28.

24. Jue, "Chin Gee-Hee," pp. 31 and 36, and Taylor, "A History of Blacks in the Pacific Northwest," p. 131. Lucie Cheng and Edna Bonacich provide an interesting discussion of the power of the Asian labor contractor in *Labor Immigration under Capitalism*, p. 34.

25. For a discussion of the smuggling of illegal Chinese immigrants, see Hyung-chan Kim and Richard W. Markov, "The Chinese Exclusion Laws and Smuggling Chinese into Whatcom County, Washington, 1890–1900," in *Annals of the Chinese Historical Society of the Pacific Northwest* 1:1 (1983): 16–27.

26. Lucie Cheng, "Free, Indentured, Enslaved: Chinese Prostitutes in Nineteenth Century America," in Cheng and Bonacich, *Labor Immigration under Capitalism*, p. 411; Chin, *Up Hill*, p. 42.

27. See, for example, Berner, *Seattle, 1900–1920*, p. 66. For a background on the relationship of Chinatowns to vice districts, see Ivan Light, "The Ethnic Vice Industry, 1880–1944," *American Sociological Review* 42 (1977): 464–79, and Light, "From Vice District to Tourist Attraction: The Moral Career of American Chinatowns, 1880–1940," *Pacific Historical Review* 43:3 (August 1974): 367–94.

28. Wilson and Hosokawa, *East to America*, p. 44.

29. Yasuo Wakatsuki, "Japanese Emigration to the United States, 1866–1924: A Monograph," *Perspectives in American History* 12 (1979): 399–400, 411; John Modell, "Tradition and Opportunity: The Japanese Immigrant in America," *Pacific Historical Review* 40:2 (May 1971): 164–65.

30. See Murayama, "The Economic History of Japanese Immigration to the Pacific Northwest," pp. 118–22, 140–41, 156–76; Calvin F. Schmid and Wayne McVey, Jr., *Growth and Distribution of Minority Races in Seattle, Washington* (Seattle: Seattle Public Schools, 1964), p. 15. See also S. Frank Miyamoto, "An Immigrant Community in America," in Hilary Conroy and T. Scott Miyakawa, eds., *East Across the Pacific: Historical and Sociological Studies of Japanese Immigration and Assimilation* (Santa Barbara: Clio Press, 1972), pp. 210, and Chin, *Up Hill*, pp. 34–35.

31. Wakatsuki, "Japanese Emigration to the United States, 1866–1924," p. 479; Ito, *Issei*, p. 14. See also Reiff, "Urbanization and the Social Structure," p. 117.

32. Dispatch Official, No. 4; Seattle, April 18, 1899, from Eleve-Consul Sometani Nariaki of the Seattle Branch of the Consulate of Japan in Tacoma to Vice-Foreign Affairs Minister Tsuzuki Kaoru. Quoted in Wilson and Hosokawa, *East to America*, pp. 116–17. For a discussion of the growing symbiotic relationship between Japanese immigrant workers, Japanese labor contractors, and Pacific Northwest railroads, see Murayama, "The Economic History of Japanese Immigration to the Pacific Northwest," pp. 156–215.

33. Yamaoka was the most colorful of the various labor recruiters. A former political activist in the People's Rights Movement, Yamaoka was jailed in 1886 for plotting to assassinate Meiji government leaders. Released from prison in 1897, he immediately emigrated to Seattle and became a labor agent for Toyo Boeki Kaisha. Two years later he returned to Japan to recruit

laborers in Shizuoka Prefecture. When Japanese government restrictions prevented him from reaching his recruitment goals, Yamaoka resorted to illegal means, including falsifying and forging government documents. The company claimed it obtained nearly 3,000 laborers through these methods. See Ichioka, *Issei*, pp. 61–64. See also Murayama, "The Economic History of Japanese Immigration to the Pacific Northwest, 1890–1920," pp. 156–62.

34. Ito, *Issei*, p. 30. See also Modell, "Tradition and Opportunity," p. 166, and Wilson and Hosokawa, *East to America*, p. 44.

35. Kazuo Ito suggests that the large number of newspapers and magazines was due in part to the concentration in the city of political dissidents who fled Meiji Japan. These men and women were by the standards of the time well educated and often college graduates, but as their Socialist views were anathema in Japan they relocated in Seattle and continued political agitation. Ito, *Issei*, pp. 729–30, 801.

36. See Miyamoto, "An Immigrant Community in America," p. 222; Glenn, *Issei, Nisei, War Bride*, pp. 78–79; Ito, *Issei*, p. 800.

37. Quoted in Ito, *Issei*, pp. 540–41. See also Murayama, "The Economic History of Japanese Immigration to the Pacific Northwest," pp. 244–46, 253. Not all Japanese laborers were disposed to earnest sacrifice to accumulate savings. Ito also reports of many Issei workers whose earnings were regularly consumed by gambling and prostitutes. See *Issei*, pp. 402–5, 752.

38. See Daniels, *Asian America*, p. 134.

39. See, for example, the coverage of the exclusion of a Japanese girl from a YWCA swimming pool in 1929, the opposition to the anti-interracial marriage bill, and the editorial "On Segregation" detailing the paper's opposition to segregated army training camps for Japanese American soldiers. The *Japanese American Courier*, March 24, 1929, p. 1, and editorial, p. 3; May 17, 1941, p. 2. See also Mayumi Tsutakawa, "The Political Conservatism of James Sakamoto's *Japanese American Courier*" (M.A. thesis, University of Washington, 1976), pp. 11, 66, 70.

40. *Japanese American Courier*, August 31, 1929, p. 3. See also Paul R. Spickard, "The Nisei Assume Power: The Japanese Citizens League, 1941–1942," *Pacific Historical Review* 52:2 (May 1983): 148–51, for a discussion of the cultural clash between the Issei and Nisei and the latter's determination to be accepted as patriotic Americans.

41. For an account of the founding convention in Seattle, see Bill Hosokawa, *JACL in Quest of Justice* (New York: Morrow, 1982), pp. 36–47. Spickard offers a more critical view of the JACL and its self-defined role in the Nihonmachi. See Spickard, "The Nisei Assume Power," pp. 153–55.

42. *Nikkei Shimin (Japanese American Citizen)*, July 15, 1930, quoted in Ronald Takaki, *Strangers from a Different Shore: A History of Asian Americans* (Boston: Little, Brown, 1989), p. 223. The belief in Japanese intellectual superiority in America was long held in the Japanese community. A Seattle Japanese American newspaper, commenting on the disproportionately large number of Nisei high school valedictorians and salutatorians in 1937, declared that the second generation seemed to be "by heredity, of a superior quality. . . . This is equivalent to saying the Japanese people are of a superior

biological quality; but the way in which they have surpassed the white students in all fields of high schools and university, and shown their superiority almost makes them out to be of an entirely different class." Cited in S. Frank Miyamoto, *Social Solidarity among the Japanese in Seattle* (Seattle: University of Washington Press, 1984; first published in 1939), p. 56. See also Hosokawa, *JACL*, pp. 33–47.

43. *Japanese American Courier*, September 1, 1928, p. 3.

44. Miyamoto, *Social Solidarity*, p. 18. My cursory examination of representative businesses advertised in the *Japanese American Courier* on January 3, 1931, reveals the following: Togo Investment-Real Estate; Sara Shina-Noodles; Gosho Drug Company; Jackson Pool Parlor; New Jackson Meat Market; Ariizuma Drug Company; J. Suzoki, physician; Dr. James Unosawa, general surgery, gynecology, genital and rectal diseases (his residence is listed as the Japanese-owned Atlas Hotel); Japanese-American Electric Company; Tanaka Dressmaking School; Asahi Garage; George Y. Nishimura, salmon packers; New Richmond tailors; Tokyo Cafe; H. I Saik, contractors for fish packers; Japanese Photography Association (five studios listed); Kondo Jewelry Company; Sumitomo Bank.

45. Calvin F. Schmid, Charles E. Nobbe, and Arlene E. Mitchell, *Non-White Races: State of Washington* (Olympia: Washington State Planning and Community Affairs Agency, 1968), p. 10.

46. Takaki, *Strangers from a Different Shore*, p. 315.

47. *Manila Times*, November 26, 1929. Quoted in Honorante Mariano, "The Filipino Immigrants in the United States" (M.A. thesis, University of Oregon, 1933), p. 15.

48. Carlos Bulosan, *America Is in the Heart: A Personal History* (Seattle: University of Washington Press, 1973; first published in 1943), p. 5.

49. Prior to Tydings-McDuffie, the number of Filipinos leaving the United States from 1920 to 1934 ranged from 16 to 50 percent of the entering immigrants, inducing J. C. Dionisio, a Filipino official studying the migratory pattern of his countrymen between the United States and the Philippines during the 1930s, to aptly describe the migrants as "birds of passage." See J. C. Dionisio to Manuel Quezon [president of the Philippines], March 7, 1944, Manuel L. Quezon Papers, quoted in Melendy, "Filipinos in the United States," p. 108.

50. Diary, Victorio A. Velasco Papers, University of Washington Libraries.

51. Quoted in Fred Cordova, *Filipinos: Forgotten Asian Americans* (Dubuque: Kendall-Hunt, 1983), p. 65.

52. *Japanese American Courier*, March 22, 1930, p. 1. See also Schmid and McVey, *Growth and Distribution of Minority Races in Seattle*, p. 21.

53. Bulosan, *American Is in the Heart*, p. 99. See also Cordova, *Filipinos: Forgotten Asian Americans*, pp. 106–11.

54. Takaki, *Strangers from a Different Shore*, pp. 336–37.

55. Lasker, *Filipino Immigration*, p. 21.

56. Bulosan, *America Is in the Heart*, pp. 104–5. See also Cordova, *Filipinos: Forgotten Asian Americans*, p. 124.

57. The incidents of violence against Filipinos were a confrontation at Sunnyside, Washington, in 1928, in which all the local Filipino laborers

were deported from the city, and the Watsonville, California, riot in 1929, in which hundreds of white men attacked a Filipino dance hall, precipitating four days of assaults in which one Filipino was killed and hundreds were beaten. See Mariano, "The Filipino Immigrants in the United States," p. 62; Bulosan, *America Is in the Heart*, p. 105. See also Lasker, *Filipino Immigration*, pp. 10, 14–15, and Takaki, *Strangers from a Different Shore*, pp. 326–31, for a discussion of the sexual fears generated by Filipino males who associated with white women. For examples of Filipinos being confused with blacks see Takaki, pp. 324, 343.

58. Sonia E. Wallovits, "The Filipinos in California" (M.A. thesis, University of Southern California, 1966), pp. 3–9, and Harry H. L. Kitano and Roger Daniels, *Asian-Americans: Emerging Minorities* (Englewood Cliffs: Prentice-Hall, 1988), p. 11. See also Takaki, *Strangers from a Different Shore*, pp. 331–32.

59. The migratory pattern of Carlos Bulosan is not atypical. Bulosan traveled from Seattle south to San Diego and as far east as Chicago in his first four years in the United States seeking gainful employment. Despite his wide-ranging sojourn, Bulosan invariably met other Filipinos, occasionally including some former residents of his village. See Bulosan, *America Is in the Heart*, pp. 168–75, and Melendy, "Filipinos in the United States," pp. 108–9.

60. See *Seattle Republican*, March 30, 1900, p. 2, and Esther Hall Mumford, *Seattle's Black Victorians, 1852–1901* (Seattle: Ananse Press, 1980), p. 178.

61. See *Japanese American Courier*, April 7, 1928, p. 2; May 21, 1932, p. 4; May 10, 1941, p. 2; and the *Northwest Enterprise*, November 24, 1932, p. 6. For a discussion of organized sports in the Japanese and black communities, see Miyamoto, "An Immigrant Community in America," p. 257, and Chapter 5 in this volume.

62. *Northwest Enterprise*, December 12, 1941, p. 1.

63. Letter of Thomas Bodine, May 11, 1942, Conrad-Duveneck Collection, Hoover Institution Archives, Palo Alto, California. Quoted in Roger Daniels, *Concentration Camps, North America: Japanese in the United States and Canada during World War II* (Malabar, Fla.: Krieger, 1981), pp. 87–88.

64. Gertrude Simons interview with Esther Hall Mumford, June 10, 1975, Washington State Oral/Aural History Collection, Olympia, transcript, pp. 16–17; hereafter cited as OAHC. See also Esther Hall Mumford, *Seven Stars and Orion: Reflections of the Past* (Seattle: Ananse Press, 1986), p. 49.

65. See J. J. Hannigan, Commandant, Twelfth Naval District, to the Director, Office of Naval Intelligence, December 3, 1921, "Subject: Weekly Report of Japanese Activities, Universal Negro Improvement Association," in Robert A. Hill, ed., *The Marcus Garvey and Universal Negro Improvement Association Papers*, vol. 4 (Berkeley: University of California Press, 1985), pp. 233–37.

66. *Japanese American Courier*, May 17, 1941, p. 2.

67. See Leonard Gayton interview, OAHC, p. 34; Mumford, *Seven Stars and Orion*, pp. 65, 98.

68. Edward Pitter interview, BOHI, pp. 13–14.

69. Irene Burns Miller, *Profanity Hill* (Everett, Wash.: The Working Press, 1979), p. 19, and Mumford, *Seven Stars and Orion*, p. 49. Audrie Girdner

and Anne Loftis, *The Great Betrayal: The Evacuation of the Japanese-Americans during World War II* (New York: Macmillan, 1969), pp. 76–77.

70. In 1930, Asian male house servants outnumbered blacks 848 to 159 and had an edge of 65 to 21 as store porters. See Howard Droker, "Seattle Race Relations during the Second World War," *Pacific Northwest Quarterly* 67:4 (October 1976): 163; Lawrence B. de Graaf, "Race, Sex, and Region: Black Women in the American West, 1850–1920," *Pacific Historical Review* 49:2 (May 1980): 298; *Fifteenth Census of the U.S.*, 1930, vol. 4, pp. 1709–10, and *Sixteenth Census of the U.S.*, 1940, vol. 3, pp. 852–53. See also Lasker, *Filipino Immigration*, p. 45, on black complaints about Filipino competition in the hotels, clubs, and restaurants.

71. See *Northwest Enterprise*, February 7, 1935, p. 3; Cordova, *Filipinos: Forgotten Asian Americans*, p. 177: Albert A. Acena, "The Washington Commonwealth Federation: Reform Politics and the Popular Front" (Ph.D. diss., University of Washington, 1975), p. 154.

72. See Bulosan, *America Is in the Heart*, p. 189.

73. See Robert Bedford Pitts, "Organized Labor and the Negro in Seattle" (M.A. thesis, University of Washington, 1941), pp. 86–88; Cordova, *Filipinos: Forgotten Asian Americans*, pp. 73–80; and Daniels, *Asian America*, pp. 113–14, 158–59, 182.

74. Tsutakawa, "The Political Conservatism of James Sakamoto's *Japanese American Courier*," pp. 66, 70. See also Spickard, "The Nisei Assume Power," pp. 154–56, 163–64.

75. Tsutakawa, "Political Conservatism," p. 11. See also Miyamoto, *Social Solidarity among the Japanese in Seattle*, pp. 108–10, and Robert W. O'Brien, *The College Nisei* (New York: Arno Press, 1978), p. 136.

76. Monica Sone described how upon attempting to enroll in Washington Vocational Institute she was forced to get a guarantee of employment from some firm in the Japanese community before she could be accepted. The school argued that since it would be unfortunate to train her and other Nisei girls who would then be denied employment in the city's thousands of business houses, it was far better for her to have a guarantee of employment before she was accepted. See Monica Sone, *Nisei Daughter* (Seattle: University of Washington Press, 1979; first published in 1953), pp. 133–35.

77. See Tolbert Hall Kennedy, "Racial Survey of the Intermountain Northwest," *Research Studies of the State College of Washington* 14:3 (September 1946): 237–42.

78. Melendy, "Filipinos in the United States," pp. 103, 126–28; Cordova, *Filipinos: Forgotten Asian Americans*, p. 224.

5. The Forging of a Black Community Ethos, 1900–1940

1. Blaine A. Brownwell, *The Urban Ethos in the South, 1920–1930* (Baton Rouge: Louisiana State University Press, 1975), p. xvi.

2. See Sandra Schoenberg and Charles Bailey, "The Symbolic Meaning of an Elite Black Community: The Ville in St. Louis," *Missouri Historical Society Bulletin* 33:2 (January 1977): 99. See also Quintard Taylor, "Black Urban

Development – Another View: Seattle's Central District, 1910–1940," *Pacific Historical Review* 58:4 (November 1989): 431.

3. For a discussion of interaction within the small black community, see Marguerite Johnson interview in Esther Hall Mumford, ed., *Seven Stars and Orion: Reflections of the Past* (Seattle: Ananse Press, 1986), p. 33. See also Juana Racquel Royster-Horn, "The Academic and Extracurricular Undergraduate Experiences of Three Black Women at the University of Washington, 1935 to 1941" (Ph.D. diss., University of Washington, 1980), pp. 63–65.

4. Lawrence E. Levine, *Black Culture and Black Consciousness: Afro-American Folk Thought from Slavery to Freedom* (New York: Oxford University Press, 1977), p. 138. See also Richard T. Schaefer, *Sociology* (New York: McGraw-Hill, 1989), pp. 63–82.

5. Sara Oliver Jackson interview in Mumford, *Seven Stars and Orion*, p. 70.

6. Jackson is quoted in *Seven Stars and Orion*, p. 70. The Thomas quote appears in Royster-Horn, "The Academic and Extracurricular Undergraduate Experiences of Three Black Women," p. 64.

7. Accounts of the various activities of these churches can be found in virtually every issue of the *Northwest Enterprise* for the 1920s and 1930s. See also Samuel P. DeBow and Edward A. Pitter, eds., *Who's Who in Religious, Fraternal, Social, Civic and Commercial Life on the Pacific Coast* (Seattle: Searchlight Publishing Company, 1927), pp. 50–71.

8. Accounts of these activities pepper the pages of the *Northwest Enterprise* from 1921 to 1940. For representative examples, see February 3, 1928, p. 8; September 29, 1932, p. 6; and April 20, 1933, p. 4.

9. See Florette Henri, *Black Migration, Movement North, 1900–1920: The Road from Myth to Man* (Garden City: Doubleday, 1976), pp. 116–17. See also DeBow and Pitter, *Who's Who*, pp. 10–11; William A. Muraskin, *Middle Class Blacks in a White Society: Prince Hall Freemasonry in America* (Berkeley: University of California Press, 1975), p. 27; Julius Nimmons, "Social Reform and Moral Uplift in the Black Community, 1890–1910: Social Settlements, Temperance, and Social Purity" (Ph.D. diss., Howard University, 1981), pp. 59–60; and George C. Wright, *Life Behind a Veil: Blacks in Louisville, Kentucky, 1865–1930* (Baton Rouge: Louisiana State University Press, 1985), p. 132.

10. Sandy Moss interview with Quintard Taylor, December 21, 1972, transcript, p. 2. The Moss interview and all other interviews that were part of the Black Oral History Research Project are hereafter cited as BOHI. See also DeBow and Pitter, *Who's Who*, p. 10 and passim. See also William H. Grimshaw, *Official History of Freemasonry among the Colored People in North America* (New York: Negro Universities Press, 1903), pp. 296–97.

11. Levine, *Black Culture and Black Consciousness*, p. 268.

12. Horace R. Cayton, Jr., *Long Old Road: An Autobiography* (Seattle: University of Washington Press, 1970), pp. 6–7. For a description of black social clubs across the nation, see Willi Coleman, "Keeping the Faith and Disturbing the Peace, Black Women: From Anti-Slavery to Women's Suffrage" (Ph.D. diss., University of California, Irvine, 1982), pp. 70–77, 83–85; and Nimmons, "Social Reform and Moral Uplift in the Black Community," pp. 77–82. See Karen J. Blair, *The Clubwoman as Feminist: True Womanhood*

Redefined, 1868–1914 (New York: Holmes and Meier, 1980), pp. 39–56, for a description of the role of native-born middle-class white women in creating comparable organizations.

13. *Seattle Republican,* "Northwest Negro Prosperity Number," 15:11 (June 1909): 21.

14. Ibid., pp. 21, 23.

15. See *Club Journal of the Colored Women's Federation of Washington and Jurisdiction, 1917–1918,* issued at Spokane, Washington, June 25, 1919, in Nettie J. Asbury Papers, University of Washington Libraries; Elizabeth Lindsay Davis, *Lifting as They Climb: The History of the National Association of Colored Women* (Washington, D.C.: National Association of Colored Women, 1933), pp. 399–400; Paula Giddings, *When and Where I Enter: The Impact of Black Women on Race and Sex in America* (New York: Morrow, 1984), pp. 93, 95. See also Cynthia Neverdon-Morton, *Afro-American Women of the South and the Advancement of the Race, 1895–1925* (Knoxville: University of Tennessee Press, 1989), pp. 2–9. Karen J. Blair describes a parallel movement toward social activism among middle-class white clubwomen during the same era. See Blair, *The Clubwoman as Feminist,* pp. 118–19.

16. Giddings, *When and Where I Enter,* pp. 95–100.

17. Quoted in Dorothy Salem, *To Better Our World: Black Women and Organized Reform, 1890–1920,* which is volume 14 of Darlene Clark Hine, ed., *Black Women in United States History* (New York: Carlson, 1990), p. 48. For a discussion of the growing segregation of YMCAs and YWCAs, see Henri, *Black Migration,* pp. 114–15.

18. Pollard interview, Mumford, *Seven Stars and Orion,* p. 60.

19. Patrick Douglas, "The Family of Two Revolutions: The Gaytons," *Seattle Magazine* 6:58 (January 1969): 24.

20. *Northwest Enterprise,* June 2, 1939, p. 1. See also Royster-Horn, "The Academic and Extracurricular Undergraduate Experiences of Three Black Women," p. 120.

21. See Timothy L. Smith, "Black and Foreign Whites: Varying Responses to Educational Opportunity in America, 1880–1950," *Perspectives in American History* 6 (1972): 311–12, 329. See also *Thirteenth Census of the U.S., 1910,* vol. 3, p. 1004; *Sixteenth Census of the U.S., 1940,* vol. 2, pt. 7, pp. 402–3; and Richard Berner, *Seattle, 1900–1920: From Boomtown, Urban Turbulence, to Restoration* (Seattle: Charles Press, 1991), p. 81.

22. Quoted in Douglas, "The Family of Two Revolutions: The Gaytons," p. 24. See also Samuel S. Bowles, "Toward Equality of Educational Opportunity," *Harvard Educational Review* 38:1 (Winter 1968): 89–99; and Smith, "Black and Foreign Whites," p. 332 and passim.

23. *Northwest Enterprise,* July 16, 1937, p. 4, and August 4, 1938, pp. 1–2. Despite his early exclusion from the Highway Department, Dennis remained with the state agency for three decades. During that time he headed the design team for the elevated roadway on the Evergreen Point floating bridge, and designed the welded plate girders for the Columbia River Bridge at Biggs Rapids in eastern Washington and the welded steel girders for the approaches of the Hood Canal Bridge. See Esther Hall Mumford, "Washington's African American Communities," in Sid White and S. E. Solberg, eds., *Peoples of*

Washington: Perspectives on Cultural Diversity (Pullman: Washington State University Press, 1989), p. 97.

24. Royster-Horn, "The Academic and Extracurricular Undergraduate Experiences of Three Black Women," p. 135.

25. Hobbs, "The Cayton Legacy," pp. 214, 274; Mumford, *Seven Stars and Orion*, pp. 63–65.

26. Jackson interview, Mumford, *Seven Stars and Orion*, pp. 68–69.

27. Roger Daniels, *Asian America: Chinese and Japanese in the United States since 1850* (Seattle: University of Washington Press, 1988), p. 178.

28. See S. Frank Miyamoto, "An Immigrant Community in America," in Hilary Conroy and T. Scott Miyakawa, eds., *East Across the Pacific: Historical and Sociological Studies of Japanese Immigration and Assimilation* (Santa Barbara: Clio Press, 1972), pp. 234–35; and Daniels, *Asian America*, pp. 162, 174, 178.

29. See Gary B. Nash, *Forging Freedom: The Formation of Philadelphia's Black Community, 1720–1840* (Cambridge: Harvard University Press, 1988), pp. 76–77, 161–63; Jacqueline Jones, *Labor of Love, Labor of Sorrow: Black Women, Work, and the Family from Slavery to the Present* (New York: Basic Books, 1985), pp. 112–14, 123–27; Theodore Hershberg and others, *Philadelphia: Work, Space, Family and Group Experience in the Nineteenth Century, Essays Toward an Interdisciplinary History of the City* (New York: Oxford University Press, 1981), pp. 438–46; Herbert Gutman, *The Black Family in Slavery and Freedom, 1750–1925* (New York: Pantheon, 1976), pp. 444–60; and James Borchert, *Alley Life in Washington: Family, Community, Religion, and Folklife in the City, 1850–1970* (Urbana: University of Illinois Press, 1980), pp. 57–66.

30. *Fifteenth Census of the U.S.*, 1930, vol. 2, *Families*, pp. 59, 64, 1403. As Lawrence B. de Graaf has shown, small families were common in the Pacific West. See de Graaf, "Race, Sex, and Region," pp. 288–89.

31. See Olivier Zunz, *The Changing Face of Inequality: Urbanization, Industrial Development, and Immigrants in Detroit, 1880–1920* (Chicago: University of Chicago Press, 1982), p. 378; John Modell, Frank Furstenberg, and Theodore Hershberg, "Social Change and Transitions to Adulthood in Historical Perspective," *Journal of Family History* 1:1 (Autumn 1976): 29; John Bodnar, Michael Weber, and Roger Simon, "Migration, Kinship, and Urban Adjustment: Blacks and Poles in Pittsburgh, 1900–1930," *Journal of American History* 66:3 (December 1979): 560 and passim. For a discussion of Asian child workers and family income, see Edna Bonacich and John Modell, *The Economic Basis of Ethnic Solidarity: Small Business in the Japanese American Community* (Berkeley: University of California Press, 1980), pp. 188–95.

32. Edward Pitter interview, BOHI, tape B, p. 3.

33. Robert Wright interview, OAHC, p. 1.

34. Ibid., pp. 13–16.

35. Ibid., pp. 23–24, 32.

36. Marguerite Johnson interview quoted in Mumford, *Seven Stars and Orion*, p. 36. See also the *Northwest Enterprise*, September 11, 1942, p. 1, for a synopsis of Hamilton's career in Seattle. See also Carver Gayton interview, August 7, 1973, BOHI, pp. 7–8, for a discussion of the popularity of "Texas blues" into the 1950s.

37. See Frank Fair, "Round the Town," *Northwest Enterprise,* December 17, 1937, p. 4.

38. Robert Wright interview, OAHC, p. 38. Esther Hall Mumford, "Washington's African American Communities," p. 105.

39. Quoted in Douglas "The Family of Two Revolutions: The Gaytons," p. 24. See also Leonard C. Gayton interview, OAHC, pp. 24, 27; Sandy Moss interview, BOHI, p. 14; and the *Northwest Enterprise* editorial, "Seattle Celebrity Minded," May 28, 1937, on the influence of nationally famous entertainers of the local African American community. Carver Gayton remembered the various social activities of the East Madison YMCA as affording a venue for both Quincy Jones and Ray Charles. See Carver Gayton interview, BOHI, p. 3. Although eighteen-year-old Ray Charles arrived in Seattle a full decade after the period under discussion, he nonetheless recalled in his autobiography a similarly vibrant local music scene in which he began a long association with local Seattle musician Quincy Jones. See Ray Charles and David Ritz, *Brother Ray: Ray Charles' Own Story* (New York: Dial, 1978), pp. 97–106.

40. See, for example, *Northwest Enterprise*, May 24, 1928, p. 6; January 11, 1934, p. 2; and February 25, 1938, p. 3.

41. New York led with twenty-seven productions, followed by Boston with sixteen and Seattle with fifteen. Chicago had thirteen productions, Los Angeles seven, and Philadelphia five. See Evamarii Alexandria Johnson, "A Production History of the Seattle Federal Theater Project Negro Repertory Company: 1935–1939" (Ph.D. diss., University of Washington, 1981), pp. 11–12.

42. Ibid., pp. 33, 44–46. For a contemporary description of the Negro Repertory Company locally, see Guy Williams, "Seattle's History-Making Negro Theater," *Federal Theater* 2:1 (1936): 7–9. The black plays staged by the NRC throughout the nation during the Depression are discussed in E. Quinta Craig, *Black Drama of the Federal Theatre Era: Beyond the Formal Horizons* (Amherst: University of Massachusetts Press, 1980). See especially chapters 1, 2, and 13.

43. Johnson, "A Production History," pp. 70–73.

44. Jackson's comments are from her interview in Mumford, *Seven Stars and Orion*, pp. 72–73.

45. Letter to George Hood from the Colored Committee, 1936, Seattle Repertory Playhouse Files, University of Washington Libraries.

46. Shirley Lola Graham, a resident of Seattle since 1916, when her father, Reverend D. A. Graham, came to the city to be pastor of First AME Church, was forty-seven at the time of her marriage to Du Bois in 1951. He was eighty-three. See *Northwest Enterprise*, February 3, 1951, p. 1; Shirley Graham Du Bois, *His Day Is Marching On: A Memoir of W. E. B. Du Bois* (Philadelphia: Lippincott, 1971), pp. 142–46, and Mumford, "Washington's African American Communities," p. 105.

47. Jackson interview in Mumford, *Seven Stars and Orion*, p. 72; Joseph Isom Staton interview, OAHC, p. 27; Johnson, "A Production History," p. 193.

48. Johnson, "A Production History," pp. 51, 59, 98.

49. Ibid., pp. 194, 196. Sara Oliver Jackson entered the theater again in the early 1970s when she joined the cast of *Son Comes Home* for Black Arts West Theater. See Mumford, *Seven Stars and Orion*, p. 76.

50. *Northwest Enterprise*, November 5, 1937, pp. 1 and 4, and November 19, p. 4.

51. Staton interview, OAHC, p. 46.

52. *Northwest Enterprise*, September 5, 1929, p. 6; January 24, 1936, p. 4; and January 31, 1936, p. 4. For a general discussion of the role of baseball and other sports activities in creating a community culture, see Steven M. Gelber, "Working at Playing: The Culture of the Workplace and the Rise of Baseball," *Journal of Social History* 16:4 (Summer 1983): 5–6.

53. Jackson interview in Mumford, *Seven Stars and Orion*, p. 68.

54. Marguerite Johnson interview, ibid., p. 33.

55. See Juana Royster-Horn interview of Robert O'Brien, November 1979, in Royster-Horn, "The Academic and Extracurricular Undergraduate Experiences of Three Black Women," p. 42.

56. John Gayton interview quoted in Royster-Horn, "The Academic and Extracurricular Undergraduate Experiences of Three Black Women," p. 44.

57. Ibid., pp. 44, 55.

6. The Transformation of the Central District, 1941–1960

1. See Carlos A. Schwantes, "The Pacific Northwest in World War II," *Journal of the West* 25:3 (July 1986): 4–19; Neil A. Wynn, *The Afro-American and the Second World War* (New York: Holmes and Meier, 1975), pp. 55–59; Richard Polenberg, *War and Society: The United States, 1941–1945* (Philadelphia: Lippincott, 1972), pp. 116–17.

2. Art Richie and William J. Davis, *The Pacific Northwest Goes to War* (Seattle: Associated Editors, 1949), pp. 13–17, 23–28; Dorothy O. Johansen and Charles M. Gates, *Empire of the Columbia: A History of the Pacific Northwest* (New York: Harper and Row, 1967), p. 529; Schwantes, "The Pacific Northwest in World War II," pp. 4–5.

3. Richie and Davis, *The Pacific Northwest Goes to War*, pp. 23–39; Schwantes, "The Pacific Northwest in World War II," pp. 6–7.

4. The estimated total number of black migrants is based on statistics for various cities. See Charles U. Smith, "Social Change in Certain Aspects of Adjustment of the Negro in Seattle, Washington" (Ph.D. diss., Washington State College, 1950), p. 78; Calvin F. Schmid, *Social Trends in Seattle* (University of Washington Press, 1944), p. 320; Tolbert Hall Kennedy, "Racial Survey of the Intermountain Northwest," *Research Studies of the State College of Washington* 14:3 (September 1946): 170; and James T. Wiley, "Race Conflict as Exemplified in a Washington Town" (M.A. thesis, Washington State College, 1949), p. 14.

5. U.S. Census, *Characteristics of Population, Labor Force, Families, and Housing: Puget Sound Congested Production Area, June, 1944*, Population Series CA-3 (Washington, D.C.: Government Printing Office, 1944), p. 8; Smith,

"Social Change in Certain Aspects of Adjustment of the Negro in Seattle, Washington," pp. 80, 84.

6. See *Northwest Enterprise,* September 26, 1941, p. 1, and July 8, 1941, p. 1; Howard Alan Droker, "The Seattle Civic Unity Committee and the Civil Rights Movement, 1944–1964" (Ph.D. diss., University of Washington, 1974), pp. 8–9.

7. John McCann, *Blood in the Water: A History of District Lodge 751, International Association of Machinists and Aerospace Workers* (Seattle: District Lodge 751, IAMAW, 1989), pp. 23, 86–87.

8. Ibid., pp. 35–37.

9. See Howard A. Droker, "Seattle Race Relations during the Second World War," *Pacific Northwest Quarterly* 67:4 (October 1976): 164; McCann, *Blood in the Water,* p. 48; and Robert C. Weaver, *Negro Labor: A National Problem* (Port Washington, N.Y.: Kennikat Press, 1969), pp. 116–217.

10. Of the sixteen stenographers sent by Idel Vertner of the Phyllis Wheatley YWCA to Boeing to apply for secretarial positions, Spearman was the only person hired by the company. See *Northwest Enterprise,* February 6, 1942, p. 1, and May 22, 1942, p. 1. A Boeing Company memorandum described the hiring of a black male worker as a rivet bucker (riveter's assistant) on April, 16, 1942, and outlined the procedure the company would follow if other employees objected to working with him. The company indicated that it would make three attempts to assign the worker to a riveter. If each of the riveters refused to work with him, they would be discharged for insubordination. However, upon the third refusal, the black worker would also be laid off and the matter taken to the Aero-Mechanics Union. The fate of this unidentified worker is not known, but presumably he was discharged or left the company, since Dorothy West Williams was publicly acknowledged as Boeing's first black production worker. See Boeing Aircraft Company, Staff Committee Meeting Minutes, April 17, 1942, Boeing Company Archives.

11. See also Karen Tucker Anderson, "Last Hired, First Fired: Black Women Workers during World War II," *Journal of American History* 69:1 (June 1982): 83–97. The figures for black employment at Boeing in 1943 are extracted from the minutes of a staff committee meeting. See Boeing Aircraft Company, Staff Committee Meeting Minutes, July 15, 1943, Boeing Company Archives.

12. McCann, *Blood in the Water,* pp. 48–49.

13. *Northwest Enterprise,* June 2, 1943, p. 1. The discriminatory practices of the Aero Mechanics Union lasted throughout most of the war. See Schmid, *Social Trends in Seattle,* p. 320, and McCann, *Blood in the Water,* pp. 49, 87–88.

14. *Northwest Enterprise,* May 19, 1943, p. 1. Karen Tucker Anderson suggests different origins of discrimination against black male and female workers. Black men were feared because they would be rivals for promotion; black women, however, were the objects of social discrimination, such as the objections over sharing bathroom facilities in the Pacific Car and Foundry incident. See Anderson, "Last Hired, First Fired," p. 86.

15. *Northwest Enterprise,* May 31, 1944, p. 22.

16. Lawrence Cramer to Jack Blair, January 29, 1942; Del Castle to Harry Kingman, January 7, June 4, 1944, rolls 107 and 102 respectively, Records of

the Committee on Fair Employment Practices, Record Group 228, National Archives, Washington, D.C.; Richie and Davis, *The Pacific Northwest Goes to War*, pp. 26–28; Frederick C. Lane, *Ships for Victory: A History of Shipbuilding under the U.S. Maritime Commission in World War II* (Baltimore: Johns Hopkins University Press, 1951), p. 276. For a detailed discussion of Portland and Los Angeles shipyard controversies, see Alonzo Smith and Quintard Taylor, "Racial Discrimination in the Workplace: A Study of Two West Coast Cities during the 1940s," *Journal of Ethnic Studies* 8:1 (Spring 1980): 35–54. For a comparison of Seattle and Portland during World War II, see Taylor, "The Great Migration: The Afro-American Communities of Seattle and Portland during the 1940s," *Arizona and the West* 23:2 (Summer 1981): 109–26.

17. Droker, "The Seattle Civic Unity Committee," pp. 35, 46–47.

18. See *Northwest Enterprise*, August 23, 1944, p. 1, and December 20, 1944, p. 1; *Seattle Post-Intelligencer*, August 16, 1944, p. 1; *Seattle Times*, August 18, 1944, p. 2; and Sara Oliver Jackson interview in Mumford, *Seven Stars and Orion*, p. 68. The judge advocate (prosecutor) of the black soldiers was Lieutenant Colonel Leon Jaworski, who would later obtain fame as the federal prosecutor in the Watergate Scandal. See *Northwest Enterprise*, December 6, 1944, p. 1, and December 20, 1944, p. 1; and Leon Jaworski with Mickey Horskowitz, *Confession and Avoidance: A Memoir* (Garden City: Anchor/Doubleday, 1979), pp. 79–80.

19. Remarks of Honorable William F. Devin, mayor of Seattle, "Civic Unity in Seattle," Proceedings of the Ninth Annual Institute of Government, University of Washington, July 24–28, 1944, p. 13, in Seattle Civic Unity Committee Records, 1944–1963, University of Washington Libraries (hereafter cited as CUC Records).

20. See Frederick Dennis Garrity, "The Civic Unity Committee of Seattle, 1944 to 1964" (M.A. thesis, University of Washington, 1971), pp. 7–9; Droker, "The Seattle Civic Unity Committee," pp. 38–39. Lester Granger, an Urban League official surveying similar Civic Unity Committees throughout the United States found fifty-seven spontaneously created committees in 1944. See Granger, "A Hopeful Sign in Race Relations," *Survey Graphic* 33 (November 1944): 455–79.

21. During World War II the *Northwest Enterprise* continuously exposed the names of businesses or public facilities that discriminated against blacks, usually equating the practice with Fascism or Nazism. For examples see *Northwest Enterprise*, March 8, 1940, p. 1, and December 16, 1942, p. 1; See also Pauline Anderson Simmons Hill and Sherrilyn Johnson Jordan, *Too Young To Be Old: The Story of Bertha Pitts Campbell* (Seattle: Peanut Butter Publishing, 1981), pp. 35–38; and Bettylou Valentine, "The Black Homefront in Seattle and King County during World War II," *Portage* 6:2 (Summer 1985): 15; and Eugene V. Dennett, *Agitprop: The Life of an American Working-Class Radical: The Autobiography of Eugene V. Dennett* (Albany: State University of New York Press, 1990), p. 136.

22. *Northwest Enterprise*, March 20, 1942, p. 1.

23. N. P. Dotson, Jr., "Pilot Seattle Urban League Study of the Seattle Negro Community" (June 1948), p. 13, Seattle Urban League Records, University of Washington Libraries (hereafter cited as Urban League Records);

Smith, "Social Change in Certain Aspects of Adjustment of the Negro in Seattle," p. 89; Schmid, *Social Trends in Seattle*, p. 320. See also Valentine, "The Black Homefront in Seattle," p. 15.

24. This account is provided by Irene Burns Miller, the Housing Authority staff member who along with Kay Kerr, wife of Clark Kerr who later became president of the University of California, was responsible for tenant selection at Yesler Terrace. Miller later became the race relations adviser for the Federal Public Housing Authority in Seattle and executive secretary of the Seattle Civic Unity Committee. See Miller, *Profanity Hill* (Everett, Wash.: The Working Press, 1979), p. 63.

25. Arnold Hirsch, for example, asserts that public housing officials' 1943 "deference to the principle of residential segregation," which was assumed to prevent racial conflict, instead led to the creation of the sprawling Chicago black ghetto and generated much of the bitterness and anger that erupted into urban racial violence commonplace in the city in the 1960s. See Arnold R. Hirsch, *Making the Second Ghetto: Race and Housing in Chicago, 1940–1960* (New York: Cambridge University Press, 1983), p. 12. See also Droker, "Seattle Race Relations during the Second World War," pp. 165–66.

26. See *Northwest Enterprise*, January 5, 1944, p. 1; January 19, 1944, p. 1; and February 16, 1944, p. 1. On the rapidly growing black populations in other Pacific Northwest cities, see Robert W. O'Brien, "Seattle: Race Relations Frontier, 1949," *Common Ground* 9:3 (Spring 1949): 18; and Quintard Taylor, "A History of Blacks in the Pacific Northwest, 1788–1970" (Ph.D. diss., University of Minnesota, 1977), pp. 218–23.

27. Seattle NAACP Records, University of Washington Libraries (hereafter cited as NAACP Records); Seattle Urban League Records; CUC Records; and Hill and Jordan, *Too Young To Be Old*, pp. 35–38.

28. Lewis G. Watts, "The Status of Race Relations in the City of Seattle, 1956" (Seattle: Seattle Urban League, 1956), p. 3, in CUC Records; Hill and Jordan, *To Young To Be Old*, p. 37.

29. *Northwest Enterprise*, February 17, 1939, p. 1.

30. The full text of the law appears in *Session Laws of the State of Washington*, 35th Session, 1949, Chapter 183 (Olympia: State Printing Plant, 1949), pp. 506–18. In the late 1940s ten states, beginning with New York in 1945 and including Washington and Oregon by 1949, had passed fair employment practices laws. See Stanley H. Smith, "The Social Aspects of the Washington State Law Against Discrimination in Employment" (Ph.D. diss., Washington State College, 1953), pp. 80, 82, 133; *Washington State Board Against Discrimination, Annual Report, 1951* (Olympia: State Printing Office, 1952), pp. 1–2.

31. See Mumford, *Seven Stars and Orion*, pp. 14–15, 27.

32. Melvina Squires interview, with Howard Droker, May 9, 1973, University of Washington Libraries, transcript, p. 1; *Northwest Enterprise*, March 22, 1944, p. 1; Mumford, *Seven Stars and Orion*, p. 64; Seattle City Councilman Sam Smith to Quintard Taylor, November 20, 1973, Seattle, Washington, author's files. See also Robert E. Colbert, "The Attitude of Older Negro Residents toward Recent Negro Migrants in the Pacific Northwest," *Journal of Negro Education* 15:4 (Fall 1946): 698; Tolbert Hall Kennedy,

"Racial Tensions among Negroes in the Intermountain Northwest," *Phylon* 7:4 (Winter 1946): 359–60.

33. Samson C. Valley interview with Esther Hall Mumford, May 23, 1975, Washington State Oral/Aural History Project, transcript, p. 16. See also Armeta Hearst interview by E. J. Brisker, March 22, 1968, University of Washington Libraries.

34. Sandy Moss to Taylor, December 21, 1972, Seattle, Washington, author's files.

35. *Northwest Enterprise*, March 22, 1944, p. 1. See also Droker, "The Seattle Civic Unity Committee," p. 26.

36. This conclusion is based on a 1946 survey of whites in Spokane concerning their attitudes toward the Japanese and black residents of the city. See Kennedy, "Racial Survey of the Intermountain Northwest," pp. 166, 237.

37. *Northwest Enterprise*, May 22, 1942, p. 1, Audrie Girdner and Anne Loftis, *The Great Betrayal: The Evacuation of the Japanese-Americans during World War II* (New York: Macmillan, 1969), 456; Kennedy, "Racial Tensions among Negroes in the Intermountain Northwest," pp. 237–42. See also John Okada, *No-No Boy* (Seattle: University of Washington Press, 1978), p. 5.

38. See *International Center News* (newsletter of the Jackson Street Community Council), September 12, 1952, p. 1, and "Highlights of the Jackson Street Community Council's Year, 1954–1955," in CUC Papers; and Powell Barnett, "Jackson Street Community Council," n.d., in Barnett Papers, University of Washington Libraries.

39. Cited in Janice L. Reiff, "Urbanization and the Social Structure: Seattle, Washington, 1852–1910" (Ph.D. diss., University of Washington, 1981), p. 1.

40. For a discussion of the continuing expansion of the local economy and its impact on African Americans, see *Boeing News*, January 2, 1947, pp. 1, 4; "First in a Long Line," *Boeing Magazine* 17:1 (January 1947): 7–9; "Rosie Is Back," *Boeing Magazine* 23:9 (September 1953): 15; Andrew Brimmer, "Some Aspects of Fair Employment" (M.A. thesis, University of Washington, 1951), pp. 153, 155; Institute of Labor Economics, *Job Opportunities for Racial Minorities in the Seattle Area* (Seattle: University of Washington Press, 1948), 9; Calvin F. Schmid, Charles E. Nobbe, and Arlene E. Mitchell, *Non-White Races: State of Washington* (Olympia: Washington State Planning and Community Affairs Agency, 1968), p. 53; and Schwantes, "The Pacific Northwest in World War II," p. 14.

41. Thelma Fisher Dewitty, a native of Corpus Christi, Texas, was assigned to teach second grade at Cooper School in West Seattle. Marita Johnson, from Dayton, Ohio, taught household service at Broadway-Edison Technical School. Two years later May Higa, "a Japanese girl," was hired as the first Asian American teacher in the school district. See Doris Hinson Pieroth, "Desegregating the Public Schools, Seattle, Washington, 1954–1968" (Ph.D. diss., University of Washington, 1979), p. 9; and Valentine, "The Black Homefront in Seattle," p. 15.

42. William Owen Bush of Olympia served in the first Washington legislature (1889–90), and John H. Ryan represented Tacoma for three two-year terms between 1920 and 1940. See Quintard Taylor, "A History of Blacks

in the Pacific Northwest, 1788–1970'' (Ph.D. diss., University of Minnesota, 1977), pp. 150, 187. On the earlier campaigns see *Northwest Enterprise,* September 11, 1942, p. 1; May 31, 1944, p. 1; July 19, 1944, p. 1; January 30, 1946, p. 1; April 3, 1946, p. 1; and July 17, 1946, p. 1. State of Washington, *Abstract of Votes, Primary Election, July 9, 1946, General Election, November 5, 1946* (Olympia: State Printing Plant, 1948), pp. 17, 49.

43. See, for example, Warren M. Banner, ''A Survey of Community Patterns Related to the Program of the Seattle Urban League,'' a report of the Seattle Urban League, March 1954, p. 46, in Urban League Records; and Ralph Friedman, ''The Attitudes of West Coast Maritime Unions in Seattle Toward Negroes in the Maritime Industry'' (M.A. thesis, Washington State College, 1952), p. 198.

44. See Dennett, *Agitprop,* pp. 171–72.

45. Banner, ''A Survey of Community Patterns Related to the Program of the Seattle Urban League,'' p. 46; Smith, ''Social Aspects of Washington State Law Against Discrimination in Employment,'' pp. 233–34.

46. Joe W. Trotter, *Black Milwaukee* (Urbana: University of Illinois Press, 1985), p. 118; Evamarii Alexandria Johnson, ''A Production History of The Seattle Federal Theater Project Negro Repertory Company: 1935–1939'' (Ph.D. diss., University of Washington, 1981), p. 32; and *Northwest Enterprise,* April 8, 1938, p. 1.

47. ''Report of the Mayor's Advisory Committee on Police Practices'' (January 5, 1956) in Philip Burton Papers, University of Washington Libraries. See also James E. McIver, President, Seattle Branch NAACP, to Chief James H. Lawrence, Seattle Police Department, April 14, 1955, and James E. McIver to Mayor Allen Pomeroy, n.d., Seattle NAACP Records; and (Seattle) *Puget Sound Observer,* July 16, 1958, p. 1. In 1940 blacks constituted 24 percent of the persons arrested by Seattle police, in 1955 they were 12 percent. See Seattle Urban League, *The Silver Scorecard,* p. 6, in William H. Dixon Collection, University of Washington Libraries.

48. See Lewis G. Watts, ''The Status of Race Relations in the City of Seattle, 1956'' (Seattle: Seattle Urban League, 1956), p. 2, in CUC Records.

49. Thelma Dewitty to Quintard Taylor, January 19, 1973, Seattle, Washington, author's files. Dotson, ''Pilot Study of the Seattle Negro Community,'' p. 13, Urban League Records. Asian homebuyers also frequently faced discrimination as indicated in a 1954 letter from Leonard W. Schroeter, Director of the Washington State Anti-Defamation League of B'nai B'rith, to Bell & Valdoz Builders in Bellevue, Washington, protesting the exclusion of Nisei families from the Eastgate residential housing project. See NAACP Records.

50. Droker, ''The Seattle Civic Unity Committee,'' pp. 195–96.

51. West Seattle resident to Mayor Devin, January 12, 1951, in CUC Records.

52. See CUC Records; Droker, ''The Seattle Civic Unity Committee,'' p. 145; Garrity, ''The Civic Unity Committee of Seattle,'' pp. 41–42.

53. Droker, ''The Seattle Civic Unity Committee,'' p. 148–49.

54. Ibid., p. 150.

55. State of Washington, *State of Washington Enabling Act Providing for Admission of the State, Approved February 22, 1889,* Section 9:1 (Olympia:

Thomas H. Cavanaugh, Public Printer, 1889), p. 26. See also Droker, "The Seattle Civic Unity Committee," p. 74; Schmid and McVey, *Growth and Distribution of Minority Races in Seattle, Washington*, pp. 24–25, 28–29.

56. Quoted in Helen M. Lynd, "Truth at the University of Washington," *American Scholar* 18:3 (Summer 1949): 350.

57. Garrity, "The Civic Unity Committee," p. 35.

58. Brimmer, "Some Aspects of Fair Employment," pp. 203–4, 219–28.

59. See Lenzie Shellman to the *Northwest Enterprise*, May 24, 1950, p. 4. On Gerber's comments see Sidney Gerber Papers, University of Washington Libraries. Howard Droker provided the descriptive commentary of Gerber's interest in minority issues; see Droker, "The Seattle Civic Unity Committee," p. 117.

60. Droker, "The Seattle Civic Unity Committee," p. 117.

61. Bowen and six other individuals were arrested by the FBI on September 17, 1952, for publicly opposing the Korean War. See Leonard Schroeter, Anti-Defamation League of B'nai B'rith to Philip Burton, President, Seattle NAACP, June 3, 1953, NAACP Records; "Isn't There Something Better for Our Boys" (brochure of the Northwest Citizens Defense Committee, n.d.) in Fred P. Woodson Papers, University of Washington Libraries.

62. See Leonard Schroeter, Seattle Anti-Defamation League, to Philip Burton, Seattle NAACP President, June 3, 1953; Philip Burton to Franklin Williams, Regional Secretary NAACP, June 16, 1953, NAACP Records. Despite the contention of the state's anti-Communist crusaders, these new leftist elements may, in fact, have been Marxist radicals with only minimal formal links to the party itself. According to Eugene Dennett, local Communist Party interest in black issues declined rapidly during and immediately after World War II and was not revived before the party went underground during the McCarthy era. See Dennett, *Agitprop*, pp. 135–40.

63. Gerald Horne provides an excellent history of the Civil Rights Congress in his *Communist Front? The Civil Rights Congress 1946–1956* (Rutherford, N.J.: Fairleigh Dickinson University Press, 1988), pp. 13–18. See also David Caute, *The Great Fear: The Anti-Communist Purge under Truman and Eisenhower* (New York: Simon and Schuster, 1978), pp. 178–79.

64. The other defendants were Bill Pennock, a former state legislator, who during the trial allegedly committed suicide; John Daschbach, state leader of the CRC; Barbara Hartle, who became a prosecution witness to reduce her sentence; and labor leader Karly Larsen. Daschbach and Bowen were convicted while Larsen was acquitted. See "Isn't There Anything We Can Do for Our Boys?" and Horne, *Communist Front*, pp. 352–53.

65. Report of Urban League Study Committee" (unpublished paper, May 11, 1946), pp. 4–6 in Urban League Records; Droker, "The Seattle Civic Unity Committee," pp. 119–21.

66. Seattle NAACP Records.

67. Droker and Garrity, in their excellent studies of the Seattle Civic Unity Committee, have delineated the differences in outlook and approach between the NAACP and Urban League and the CUC. While I recognize these differences, I also note that the overall outlook and goals of the organizations and agencies – ending discrimination and promoting integration – were

virtually identical. The similarity of their positions would become readily apparent when in the 1960s black nationalist and black left groups emerged in the Central District to challenge that approach. Interestingly, not all of the various rights "defense" organizations were equally supportive of the concept of mutual identification. Alexander F. Miller, community services director in the national office of the Anti-Defamation League of B'nai B'rith, wondered aloud if Leonard Schroeter's enthusiastic attempts to integrate Central District black and Jewish business owners into the East Madison – East Union Commercial Club to reduce the tensions between the two groups might instead "make a sort of Negro-Jewish axis in Seattle and set those two groups off from the rest of the community?" Miller then warned, "you are not helping the Negro community much but instead you are burdening the Jewish community with some of the same handicaps which the Negroes face," and suggested that white Gentile business owners also be included in the newly integrated organization. See memoranda from Schroeter to Miller, December 16, 1954, and Miller to Schroeter, December 23, 1954, in Anti-Defamation League Papers, Acc No. 2045, box 4, University of Washington Libraries.

68. This designation was coined by the Civic Unity Committee in 1944 after "discovering" that Seattle had far fewer racial problems than eastern and southern cities. See Garrity, "The Civic Unity Committee of Seattle," p. 10.

69. Open letter from Philip Burton, president of Seattle NAACP to civil rights and black community organizations, September 28, 1953, NAACP Records.

70. Ray Charles and David Ritz, *Brother Ray: Ray Charles' Own Story* (New York: Dial, 1978), pp. 108–13.

71. See editorial titled "Narcotics in Extreme," in *Northwest Enterprise*, July 27, 1951, p. 1. See also the editorial "Juvenile Delinquency and Crime," in the *Northwest Enterprise*, April 5, 1950, p. 4.

72. The theme of Seattle as a race relations "frontier," a place where blacks had or were close to achieving complete equality, was explored in scholarly and popular articles such Robert O'Brien, "Seattle: Race Relations Frontier, 1949," *Common Ground* 9:3 (Spring 1949): 18–23, and "New Life in Seattle: In the Biggest, Fastest Growing City of the Northwest, Negroes Have Found a New Frontier," *Our World* 6 (August 1951): 22–25.

7. From "Freedom Now" to "Black Power," 1960–1970

1. The term "open housing" was commonly used to describe one of the major goals of civil rights organization – to end discrimination against blacks in the selling and renting of houses and apartments. See John H. Franklin and Alfred A. Moss, Jr., *From Slavery to Freedom: A History of Negro Americans* (New York: McGraw-Hill, 1988), pp. 452–53.

2. For an assessment of the paradoxical impact of the black power campaign, see Thomas L. Blair, *Retreat to the Ghetto: The End of a Dream?* (New York: Hill and Wang, 1977).

3. Larry S. Richardson, "Civil Rights in Seattle: A Rhetorical Analysis of a Social Movement" (Ph.D. diss., Washington State University, 1975), p.

32. Rillmond Schear describes the Garner family in his article, "The World That Whites Don't Know," *Seattle Magazine* 2:19 (October 1965): 14–15.

4. Schear, "The World That Whites Don't Know," p. 16.

5. Roger Sale, *Seattle, Past to Present* (Seattle: University of Washington Press, 1976), pp. 246–47.

6. Schear, "The World That Whites Don't Know," pp. 16, 18.

7. For a discussion of the intensity and wantonness of such violence in the civil rights era, see David E. Colburn, *Racial Change and Community Crisis: St. Augustine, Florida, 1877–1980* (New York: Columbia University Press, 1985), chapters 1–3.

8. See James Halpin, "Discrimination by Whites Has Kept Negroes Locked in Jobs that Lead Nowhere," *Seattle Magazine* 5:51 (June 1968): 20; Schear, "The World That Whites Don't Know," p. 16; and Seattle Urban League, *Seattle's Racial Gap: 1968*, p. 4.

9. Quoted in Schear, "The World That Whites Don't Know," p. 16; see also Halpin, "Jobs that Lead Nowhere," p. 20.

10. Of the 207 cities surveyed by the Taeubers, only 30 percent had ratings below 79 and more than half the cities were above 87.8. The 79.7 rating indicated that nearly 80 percent of Seattle's black population would have to move to achieve integrated housing. See Karl E. Taeuber and Alma F. Taeuber, *Negroes in Cities* (Chicago: Aldine, 1965), pp. 30–37. For a background discussion of the growing isolation of black Seattle, see Reuel Seeman Amdur, "An Exploratory Study of Nineteen Negro Families in the Seattle Area Who Were First Negro Residents in White Neighborhoods, of Their White Neighbors, and of the Integration Process, Together with a Proposed Program to Promote Integration in Seattle" (M.A. thesis, University of Washington, 1962), pp. 8–12.

11. See Sale, *Seattle*, p. 218.

12. Ericson is quoted in the *Seattle Times*, March 15, 1961, p. 32. Westberg's comments appeared in the same newspaper on August 1, 1963, p. 46. See also Schear, "The World That Whites Don't Know," p. 15.

13. Sale, *Seattle*, p. 219.

14. A typical effort was the campaign to support the Haywood County Civic and Welfare League initiated by the Seattle NAACP and a newly formed branch of CORE in 1961. The two organizations raised money for black sharecroppers and tenant farmers near Brownsville, Tennessee, who had been evicted for registering to vote. See Seattle CORE Newsletter, April 1962. Seattle NAACP Records, University of Washington Libraries.

15. See John Guernsey, "Seattle Works to Widen School Integration," *Portland Oregonian*, October 6, 1963, p. 28.

16. For a discussion of Reverend Samuel McKinney, see *Seattle Times*, January 28, 1968, p. 32. Dr. John H. Adams is profiled in a January 9, 1968, article in the same newspaper (p. 31).

17. Interview of Reverend John H. Adams by Larry Richardson, quoted in Richardson, "Civil Rights in Seattle," p. 77.

18. *Seattle Times*, December 6, 1962, p. 16.

19. See the *Seattle Times*, March 22, 1964, p. 43, and *Seattle Post-Intelligencer*, March 22, 1964, p. 4, for accounts of typical "shop-ins" at local grocery

stores. CORE's newsletter for its January 1963 meeting, held at the East Cherry YWCA, described the organization's ongoing negotiations with the targeted businesses. See "Regular Membership Meeting, Thursday, January 23, 1963," in Seattle Urban League Records, University of Washington Libraries. See also Richardson, "Civil Rights in Seattle," pp. 76–81.

20. On the Nordstrom agreement, see *Seattle Times*, May 16, 1964, p. 1, May 26, p. 16, and Richardson, "Civil Rights in Seattle," pp. 79–80.

21. The other project cited by Meier and Rudwick was the Syracuse, New York, chapter's campaign against the Niagara Mohawk Power Company. See August Meier and Elliott Rudwick, *CORE: A Study in the Civil Rights Movement, 1942–1968* (New York: Oxford University Press, 1973), p. 371.

22. Charles A. Valentine, *DEEDS: Background and Basis, a Report on Research Leading to the Drive for Equal Employment in Downtown Seattle* (Seattle: CORE, 1964), p. 8.

23. Ibid., pp. 19–31.

24. Ibid., p. 44.

25. Ibid., pp. 5, 38–40, 43. See also Report of Seattle CORE Meeting, January 17, 1964, in NAACP Records; *Seattle Times*, October 14, 1964, p. 41.

26. See *Seattle Times*, January 12, 1965, p. 2.

27. See Meier and Rudwick, *CORE*, pp. 184, 227, 241.

28. See, for example, the *Seattle Post-Intelligencer*, October 21, 1964, p. 24, and *The Facts*, November 6, 1964, p. 1, for discussions of the new job training and job placement centers in the Central District.

29. *Seattle Times*, August 28, 1964, p. 12; *Seattle Argus*, September 11, 1964, p. 1.

30. Quoted in *Seattle Post-Intelligencer*, September 8, 1967, p. 1.

31. This example was extracted from Sidney Gerber's personal journal, which he facetiously titled "Diary of a Do Gooder." See Sidney Gerber Papers, University of Washington Libraries. Realtors were professionally committed to racial discrimination until 1950. Although Article 34 of the National Real Estate Board's Code of Ethics, which forbade the introduction of "members of any race or nationality . . . whose presence will clearly be detrimental to property values in that neighborhood," was repealed in that year, over a decade later most Seattle realtors continued to direct potential black homebuyers to Central District listings. See Howard Droker, "The Seattle Civic Unity Committee and the Civil Rights Movement, 1944–1964" (Ph.D. diss., University of Washington, 1974), p. 145.

32. See, for example, L. K. Northwood and Ernest A. T. Barth, *Urban Desegregation: Negro Pioneers and Their White Neighbors* (Seattle: University of Washington Press, 1965), pp. 3–29.

33. NAACP Miscellaneous Records, boxes 1–25, 2–1, 2–32. See also Droker's detailed description of early civil rights efforts through 1964 in his dissertation, "The Seattle Civic Unity Committee," pp. 154–59, and Gerber, "Integrated Housing," in *K-Zam Kazette*, September 26, 1962, p. 6.

34. Droker, "The Seattle Civic Unity Committee," p. 155.

35. This controversial decision stemmed from a dispute between John J. O'Meara and Robert L. Jones over the sale of O'Meara's house. In 1961, O'Meara, a commander in the U.S. Coast Guard, and his wife owned a

single-family residence at 3004 East 70th Street in Seattle. In the spring of that year they placed the house on the market after O'Meara received transfer orders to Washington, D.C. On Sunday, April 19, Jones, a black Postal Service worker, and his wife visited and inspected the O'Meara home. Two days later the Jones's attorney went to the O'Meara home and left a $1,000 down payment with Mrs. O'Meara in anticipation of an "all cash" sale of the home for $18,000. Mrs. O'Meara would later claim that the deposit and an earnest money receipt were left over her protest. One day later Commander O'Meara returned the receipt and check to the attorney. Jones subsequently lodged a complaint with the Washington State Board Against Discrimination, which, after an eleven-hour hearing, found the O'Mearas had discriminated against the Jones family on the basis of color. The O'Mearas, in turn, challenged the WSBAD decision in King County Superior Court. For a fuller discussion see *O'Meara v. Washington State Board Against Discrimination*, Case No. 35436, September 29, 1961, pp. 795–96, and Arval A. Morris and Donald B. Ritter, "Racial Minority Housing in Washington," *Washington Law Review* 37 (Summer 1962): 139–40.

36. *Seattle Times*, July 26, 1963, p. 1. Only two of the nine-member City Council favored the ordinance: Wing Luke, the city's first Chinese American councilman, and A. Ludlow Kramer. Other council members reluctantly voted for the open housing ordinance, anticipating its defeat by referendum. See Droker, "The Seattle Civic Unity Committee," pp. 158–64.

37. Ibid., p. 2; *The Facts*, July 17, 1963, p. 2.

38. Quoted in *Seattle Times*, October 21, 1963, p. 6. For an account of the August march, see the *Seattle Times*, August 28, 1963, p. 1.

39. Philip Bailey, "'Open Housing' the Wrong Approach to Negro Problem," *Argus*, March 6, 1964, pp. 1, 3. See also Droker, "The Seattle Civic Unity Committee," p. 168.

40. Later that night shotgun blasts also ripped the home of Raymond Flavors, a cement finisher who lived three doors from the Green family. The following week Kent experienced another incident when two white youths threw a firebomb onto the front porch of Reverend D. L. Crowder's home. *Seattle Times*, October 27, 1963, p. 1, and November 1, 1963, p. 7.

41. *Seattle Times*, March 11, 1964, p. 1, and *Seattle Post-Intelligencer*, March 11, 1964, p. 1. See also Droker, "The Seattle Civic Unity Committee," p. 170.

42. *Argus*, April 3, 1964, p. 1.

43. For a detailed discussion of the sit-in, see "A Report on Seattle CORE's First 'Sit-in' Demonstration at a Real Estate Office; Picture Floor Plans," March 22, 1964, in Urban League Records.

44. Quoted in the *Seattle Times*, October 22, 1963, p. 29. The Schoenfield letter was reprinted in *The Facts*, November 21, 1963, p. 4. See also Northwood and Barth, *Urban Desegregation*, p. 71.

45. *Seattle Times*, August 17, 1965, p. 6, and August 19, 1965, p. 3.

46. *The Facts*, November 10, 1967, p. 1; *Seattle Times*, November 27, 1967, p. C3.

47. See the *Seattle Post-Intelligencer*, January 14, 1968, p. 2. The Central Area Motivation Program, popularly known as CAMP, was one of the most

remarkable locally initiated antipoverty programs in the nation. CAMP was organized in the spring of 1964, before Congress passed the Economic Opportunity Act, by Central District residents and their supporters in their campaign against poverty in Seattle. CAMP was the first program to receive OEO funding and is the oldest surviving agency launched during that era. Its myriad programs include job counseling and training, family support services, university recruitment, housing rehabilitation, antigang services, community organization, and creative arts. Walter Hundley, after relinquishing the presidency of the Seattle CORE chapter, became CAMP's first executive director. For a history of CAMP, see Ivan King, *The Central Area Motivation Program: A Brief History of a Community in Action"* (Seattle: Central Area Motivation Program, 1990), pp. 5–12.

48. *Seattle Post-Intelligencer,* May 27, 1967, p. 15.

49. Seattle did experience some arson and sporadic violence immediately following Dr. King's assassination. See *Seattle Times,* April 6, 1968, p. 13, and April 7, p. 4.

50. Quoted in the *Seattle Times,* August 11, 1967, p. 6.

51. For a discussion of the Kirkland Fair Housing Organization and Operation Equity, Federal Way Unit, see Seattle City Council, *Seminar on Equal Opportunities and Racial Harmony, March 22 and April 6, 1968: Summary of Proceedings and Recommendations* (Seattle: City of Seattle, 1968), n.p. See also *The Facts,* May 23, 1968, pp. 7–8.

52. For a discussion of the changing spatial demography of black Seattle, see "Racial Migration Stood Out Clearly in Recent Census," *Seattle Times,* June 7, 1981, p. C4.

53. Quoted in the *Seattle Times,* May 13, 1965, p. 53.

54. For a detailed discussion of the Chicago campaign against de facto segregation, see Alan Anderson and George Pickering, *Confronting the Color Line: The Broken Promise of the Civil Rights Movement in Chicago* (Athens: University of Georgia Press, 1986).

55. Quoted in Doris Hinson Pieroth, "Desegregating the Public Schools, Seattle, Washington, 1954–1968" (Ph.D. diss., University of Washington, 1979), pp. 4, 5. Pieroth's dissertation is by far the most comprehensive and the most perceptive of the studies of public schools in Seattle in the 1960s. See also Pieroth, "With All Deliberate Caution: School Integration in Seattle, 1954–1968," *Pacific Northwest Quarterly* 73:2 (April 1982): 50–61.

56. Pieroth, "Desegregating the Public Schools," p. 52.

57. Seattle School District, *Racial Distribution in Seattle Schools, 1957–1968* (Seattle: Seattle School District, 1969), p. 19.

58. Pieroth, "Desegregating the Public Schools," pp. 172–74. For a discussion of Edwards and Keve Bray, another Central District activist opposed to the integrationist thrust of CACRC, see "Black Backlash," *Seattle Magazine* 1:7 (October 1964): 7–8.

59. Pieroth, "Desegregating the Public Schools," p. 170.

60. *The Facts,* August 13, 1964, p. 11.

61. *Seattle Times,* August 29, 1965, p. 12.

62. Walter Hundley interview with Doris Pieroth, "Desegregating the Public Schools," p. 252.

63. Although School Superintendent Forbes Bottomly characterized the boycott as "an illegal thing," the School District attempted no disciplinary action against participants. Moreover, the district increased its efforts to recruit students for the voluntary transfer program and initiated two new programs: a Central District "counseling bank" where parents and schools could take problems involving their children, and recruitment and promotion of black administrators. See *Seattle Times*, April 1, 1966, p. 6, and Pieroth, "Desegregating the Public Schools," pp. 55, 281–82.

64. *Seattle Times*, July 1, 1966, p. 19; *Seattle Post-Intelligencer*, August 25, 1966, p. 7.

65. *Seattle Post-Intelligencer*, April 20, 1967, p. 1; *Seattle Times*, April 20, 1967, p. 5. Civil rights leaders were in a quandary over Carmichael's visit. While they had not opposed it, they also knew that his speech would solidify the evolving opposition to their objectives in the de facto school controversy. The best CACRC could muster in response to Carmichael's presentation was a community meeting at First AME Church, where about one hundred persons turned out to hear California Assemblyman Willie Brown, who warned of the "sophisticated tactics" of northern cities, including Seattle, to maintain de facto segregation. *Seattle Times*, May 20, 1967, p. 12.

66. Pieroth, "Desegregating the Public Schools," p. 336.

67. Ibid., pp. 380–81.

68. *Seattle Times*, December 15, 1967, p. 28.

69. Pieroth, "Desegregating the Public Schools," p. 402.

70. On December 19, 1967, Hundley was appointed Model Cities director by Mayor Braman, with whom he had often clashed as local president of CORE, and as the first director of the Central Area Motivation Program. Eventually recognized as one of the best Model Cities administrators in the nation, Hundley remained head of the agency until it was terminated in 1973. He then became an administrative assistant to Seattle Mayor Wesley Uhlman. See Richardson, "Civil Rights in Seattle," p. 267.

71. Alfred Cowles interview with Doris Pieroth, "Desegregating the Public Schools," p. 404.

72. Pieroth, "Desegregating the Public Schools," pp. 452–53. For a background on the Ocean Hill–Brownsville controversy and the debate over school decentralization, see Alan A. Altshuler, *Community Control: The Black Demand for Participation in Large American Cities* (New York: Pegasus, 1970), and Maurice R. Berube and Marilyn Gittell, eds., *Confrontation at Ocean Hill–Brownsville: The New York School Strikes of 1968* (New York: Praeger, 1969).

73. The Garfield percentages are derived from a report of the Citizens' Committee for Quality Integrated Education. A copy of the report is in the Donald Kazama Papers, University of Washington Libraries. The desegregation controversy that began in the early 1960s would continue to rage through the 1970s and 1980s in a school district that shrank dramatically in enrollment. By 1984–85, Seattle public schools had only 44,000 students, 51.4 percent of whom white, 23.3 percent black, 18 percent Asian American, 4.4 percent Hispanic, and 2.9 percent Native American. In 1978, Seattle adopted an extensive mandatory busing plan, without court order, which, according to a National Education Association report, had by January 1984

"succeeded in eliminating racial and ethnic imbalance in all of the city's schools." The report also noted that the "Seattle Plan" had been adopted despite the opposition of two-thirds of the city's residents. Those residents did indeed voice their opposition in November 1989 when they voted to end the seventeen-year-old mandatory busing plan. See the *Seattle Post-Intelligencer,* November 8, 1989, p. 1; Nand Hart-Nibbrig, "Policies of School Desegregation in Seattle," *Integrated Education* 17:97 (January-April 1979): 27–30; Harriet Elaine Adair, "Trends in School Desegregation: A Historical Case Study of Dayton, Denver, Los Angeles and Seattle" (Ed.D. diss., Brigham Young University, 1986, pp. 303, 306.

74. The March Against Fear was a continuation of the protest march of James Meredith, interrupted when he was shot, and provided the forum for the introduction of the term and subsequently the new militancy titled "black power." Stokely Carmichael, one of the principal leaders, surprised listeners and challenged both the local audience and the nation when he, after describing the pent-up frustration and anger of blacks, called for black power. For a fuller discussion of the origins of black power, see Stokely Carmichael and Charles V. Hamilton, *Black Power: The Politics of Liberation in America* (New York: Vintage, 1967), chap. 2; Clayborne Carson, *In Struggle: SNCC and the Black Awakening of the 1960s* (Cambridge: Harvard University Press, 1981), chap. 14; and William L. Van Deburg, *New Day in Babylon: The Black Power Movement and American Culture, 1965–1975* (Chicago: University of Chicago Press, 1992), pp. 31–34.

75. Seattle reporter Hilda Bryant explored the growing popularity of the black power ideology, particularly among younger Central District African Americans, in her article, "Black Power: Threat or Promise?" *Seattle Post-Intelligencer,* December 27, 1967, pp. 1, 8.

76. Ibid., p. 8.

77. *Seattle Times*, November 13, 1966, p. 45.

78. Ibid., July 19, 1967, p. 34.

79. Ibid., August 26, 1967, p. 12, and September 14, 1967, p. 8. For a discussion of the transformation of the national CORE organization from nonviolence to black power, see Van Deburg, *New Day in Babylon*, pp. 132–40.

80. As early as 1963, Seattle had a "Friends of SNCC" chapter which sponsored educational and fundraising activities for the then integrationist organization whose activities were centered in the South. By 1967, however, SNCC had undergone a transformation, embracing black power and shifting its organizational focus for the first time to northern black communities such as Seattle's Central District. The election of Stokely Carmichael as chair symbolized that transition. For background, see Carson, *SNCC*, pp. 200–203. On the cultural manifestations of black power, see Nancy Giebink, "Bold Experiment in the Ghetto," *Seattle Magazine* 5:51 (June 1968): 11–12, for a discussion of CASPA, and King, *The Central Area Motivation Program*, p. 7, for the origin of Black Arts West. See also returned questionnaires on black Central District organizations included in *Seminar on Equal Opportunities and Racial Harmony,* n.p.

81. *Seattle Times,* August 11, 1967, p. 6, and August 15, 1967, p. 33. See also editorial titled, "Negro Proposals Reasonable," *Seattle Times,* August 14,

1967, p. 10; and Commission on the Causes and Prevention of Civil Disorder, *Race and Violence in Washington State: A Report of the Commission on the Causes and Prevention of Civil Disorder* (Olympia: State Printing Office, 1969), p. 30.

82. *Seattle Times*, September 4, 1968, p. 5; *Seattle Post-Intelligencer*, September 24, 1968, p. 4. See also *Seminar on Equal Opportunities and Racial Harmony*, n.p.

83. Sections of the Panther campaign platform were quoted in *Seattle Times*, July 3, 1968, p. 1. See also July 6, p. 16; July 31, p. 47; the *Vancouver, B.C. Province*, September 7, 1968, p. 5; and Esther Hall Mumford, "Washington's African American Communities," in Sid White and S. E. Solberg, eds., *Peoples of Washington: Perspectives on Cultural Diversity* (Pullman: Washington State University Press, 1989), p. 101.

84. The carefully crafted image the Panthers hoped to promote was challenged by events in late July 1968. On July 29, twelve heavily armed police raided Panther headquarters with a search warrant for a stolen typewriter. When they discovered it, Dixon and fellow Panther Curtis Harris were arrested. But the presence of police officers in riot gear dispatched to search the headquarters and, if necessary, arrest its occupants touched off two consecutive nights of rioting, resulting in the arrests of 101 Central District residents. The violence began with the second of two rallies to protest the arrest of Dixon and Harris. The first, by the Students for a Democratic Society at the downtown police headquarters, was uneventful, but the second, at the Garfield High School playground, resulted in the firebombing of Central District businesses, the burning of vehicles including a firetruck, and rock throwing attacks on the police interspersed with gunfire that continued into the following night and culminated when two black men were shot and wounded by a white Central District resident. While small by the standards of the Detroit or Newark riots of 1967, Seattle had nonetheless experienced its third outburst of urban racial violence in one year. See *Race and Violence in Washington State*, pp. 8, 57–59; Richardson, "The Civil Rights Movement," pp. 249–52; and Pieroth, "Desegregating the Public Schools," pp. 435–37, 453–54. For a recent assessment of the impact and legacy of the Black Panther Party, see Van Deburg, *New Day in Babylon*, pp. 152–66.

85. The spring of 1968 was the apex of racial and political conflicts throughout the United States. In April, Dr. Martin Luther King was assassinated in Memphis, touching off violent confrontations between angry blacks and various public authorities in hundreds of cities across the nation. In Seattle three days of rioting, looting, and arson had followed King's murder. One month later the city still seethed with anger and resentment as both black and antiblack groups predicted violence during the coming summer. This was also a time of escalating student protests over the war in Vietnam, racism on campuses and in the communities, and the role and relationship of universities to the military-industrial complex. At least thirty-four confrontations, beginning with the University of California Free Speech Movement in 1964, had violently disrupted colleges and universities. The largest, the Columbia University protests in April and May 1968, had succeeded in closing the university. Indeed before the end of spring term there would be 2,000 protests on campuses nationwide. See Dianne Louise Walker, "The

University of Washington Establishment and the Black Student Union Sit-In of 1968" (M.A. thesis, University of Washington, 1980), pp. 3–4, 47.

86. See *Seattle Times*, May 21, 1968, p. 5; Walker, "The University of Washington Establishment," pp. 3–4.

87. The university also created an apparatus to assist the incoming black students. The Special Education Project (SEP) was created, headed by Professor Charles Evans. The UW Fund for Disadvantaged Students provided tuition support. To that end, university officials requested of the legislature $1,000 for each minority student brought in under SEP. Graduate students – most of them white – were recruited to provide tutorial assistance. BSU President E. J. Brisker warned them during orientation that SEP students had "enough problems without having to like you." Brisker urged them to be tough and demanding but also to remember how "galling" it is to need help. See Walker, "The University of Washington Establishment," pp. 47, 74.

88. "Diary of a Do Gooder," Gerber Papers.

89. Amy Uyematsu described the growing militancy of young Asian Americans and their organizational and philosophical debt to African American activists of the 1960s in her article, "The Emergence of Yellow Power in America," *GIDRA* (October 1969): 8–11. For a discussion of young Asian activists, see Sucheng Chan, *Asian Americans: An Interpretive History* (Boston: Twayne, 1991), pp. 174–75.

90. Quoted from Donald Kazama, "Chapter Involvement," p. 1, Japanese American Citizens League Records, Acc No.217–6, box 10, University of Washington Libraries (hereafter cited as JACL Records). The JACL was founded in Seattle thirty-four years earlier to advance Japanese American civil rights. Until the creation of the Human Relations Committee in 1964, the organization had ignored the grievances of other groups. But the JACL seemed far ahead of other Asian groups in the city. Although Victorio A. Velasco, a prominent Seattle Filipino American activist, described his involvement in various human rights activities during the 1960s, I could locate no other records of Asian groups or individual Asians that reveal the detail of the JACL Records on the civil rights–black power issue for that decade. See Victorio A. Velasco Papers, University of Washington Libraries.

91. Ibid., p. 3. See also Minutes of Human Relations Committee, October 5, 1965, p. 1, JACL Records.

92. Memorandum from Philip Hayasaka to Pat Okura and Jerry Enomoto, October 19, 1967. See also Minutes of Human Relations Committee, April 12, 1965, p. 3, JACL Records.

93. See Central Seattle Community Council Records, "History," University of Washington Libraries.

94. See letter from Toru Sakahara to George Fugami, President, Seattle Chapter, JACL, August 12, 1968, in JACL Records, box 9; and *Race and Violence in Washington State*, pp. 8, 58–59.

95. Memorandum from Sakahara to Fugami, August 7, 1968, in JACL Records, box 9.

96. Sakahara to Fugami, August 12, 1968, JACL Records. The meetings between the JACL and various black community leaders continued into the fall with speakers such as attorney Gary Gayton who "represented the black

middle class" and Edward Banks, from the Seattle Model Cities office. See *Pacific Citizen*, November 15, 1968, p. 1.

97. For a discussion of Takisaki and the involvement of the Asian and Latino communities in the campaign for jobs in the construction industry, see William A. Little, "Community Organization and Leadership: A Case Study of Minority Workers in Seattle" (Ph.D. diss., University of Washington, 1976), pp. 46, 51, 194–95.

98. Alan Sugiyama, "Co-optation: A New Game?" (editorial), *Asian Family Affair*, May 1977, p. 2.

99. Ibid. See also Uyematsu, "The Emergence of Yellow Power in America," pp. 8–11.

100. Nationally the JACL had an ambiguous record on the subject of black civil rights, just as the NAACP and other predominantly black groups were mostly silent on the grievances of Japanese Americans stemming from their World War II incarceration. While the JACL publicly prided itself on its support for African Americans struggling to gain their rights and pointed to its participation in the March on Washington in 1963, its own survey of chapters in 1967 revealed that only nine of its thirty-six chapters were sponsoring programs on the black civil rights movement or had made any contribution to that cause, and only half of the chapters had members who had individually participated in some activity related to the movement. Thus Seattle's JACL had one of the most active records of involvement during the decade. See Donald Kazama, "Chapter Involvement," box 10, JACL Records.

101. Quoted in David Brewster, "Solidarity Forever! Black Demands for Construction Jobs Have Revived Labor's Old Fighting Spirit – Not on Behalf of All Workers, But *White* Workers," *Seattle Magazine* 6:69 (December 1969): 34. For a discussion of the origins and early progressive influence of Seattle's labor union culture, see Robert L. Friedheim, *The Seattle General Strike* (Seattle: University of Washington Press, 1964), and Dana Frank, "Gender, Consumer Organizing and the Seattle Labor Movement, 1919–1929," in Ava Baron, ed., *Work Engendered: Towards a New History of American Labor* (Ithaca: Cornell University Press, 1991), pp. 273–95.

102. The long struggle of Seattle blacks against organized labor began in the nineteenth century with the generally unsuccessful efforts to prevent complete African American exclusion when labor organizations such as the Cooks and Stewards or the Barbers' Union (the union was finally integrated in 1966) were first established in the city nearly a century earlier. The struggle continued into the early decades of the twentieth century with the focus on the longshore union, which was finally desegregated in the 1934 waterfront strike. In the early 1940s Seattle blacks campaigned against the exclusionary policies of the Aero Mechanics Union, utilizing the labor demands prompted by the rapid wartime expansion of the Boeing Company to establish a foothold in the manufacturing section of what would soon be termed the aerospace industry. See Quintard Taylor, "Black Urban Development – Another View: Seattle's Central District, 1910–1940," *Pacific Historical Review* 58:4 (November 1989): 436–38; and Taylor, "The Great Migration: The Afro-American Communities of Seattle and Portland during the 1940s," *Arizona and the West* 23:2 (Summer 1981): 110–12.

103. William B. Gould, "The Seattle Building Trades Order: The First Comprehensive Relief Against Employment Discrimination in the Construction Industry," *Stanford Law Review* 26 (April 1974): 774–75. See also Little, "Community Organization and Leadership," p. 25.

104. *Seattle Post-Intelligencer,* September 4, 1965, p. 2, Quoted in Richardson, "Civil Rights in Seattle," p. 209.

105. James Halpin related the experience of Howard Lewis and his subsequent decision to file suit against Iron Workers Local 86 in "Jobs that Lead Nowhere," p. 22. See also Gould, "The Seattle Building Trades Order," pp. 785, 787.

106. Many skilled black workers often became "contractors" in order to circumvent union membership restrictions. As independent contractors they did not have to qualify for union membership to work on various construction projects. See Little, "Community Organization and Leadership," pp. 22–23.

107. Scott interview quoted in Gould, "The Seattle Building Trades Order," p. 782. The tactics of the CCA were soon duplicated by African Americans in other cities. In September and October 1969, various groups ranging from Chicago street gangs to Detroit black "hardhats" shut down construction projects with all-white work forces. See, for example, *New York Times,* September 23, 1969, p. 56, and *Detroit Free Press,* October 11, 1969, p. A3. For additional information consult Little, "Community Organization and Leadership," 27–30, 43–51, 120–21.

108. Gould, "The Seattle Building Trades Order," p. 784. See also Brewster, "Solidarity Forever!" pp. 34–41.

109. Gould, "The Seattle Building Trades Order," pp. 785–88.

110. Ibid., p. 799.

111. Writing in 1974, William Gould urged that the remedy applied by Judge Lindberg in the Seattle Plan – quotas and specific programs to ensure implementation – be used to address discrimination in other areas. "Hopefully," he advised, "other courts will follow [Judge Lindberg's] lead and act more quickly against discrimination than they did against school segregation." Gould, "The Seattle Building Trades Order," p. 811. Subsequent court cases involving affirmative action have proved Gould correct.

112. See *Race and Violence in Washington State,* pp. 23–25.

Conclusion

1. See Quintard Taylor, "Black Urban Development – Another View: Seattle's Central District, 1910–1940," *Pacific Historical Review* 58:4 (November 1989): 447–48.

2. Reverend John H. Adams, remarks before the Advisory Committee to the U.S. Civil Rights Commission Hearing, Seattle, Washington, January 20, 1966. Quoted in Larry S. Richardson, "Civil Rights in Seattle: A Rhetorical Analysis of a Social Movement" (Ph.D. diss., Washington State University, 1975), p. 166.

3. The 100,000 figure was projected early in the 1960s and was often quoted by civil rights spokesmen such as Walter Hundley to alert Seattle's

political, civic, and business leadership to the urgent need to address the housing, de facto school segregation, and job discrimination issues facing the city's African American population. See for example the *Seattle Times*, May 13, 1965, p. 53; and Patrick Douglas, "'Yeah, Baby, You Almost Got Burned': Must Act II of Our Negro Revolution Produce as It Did in Watts — a 'Reign of Terror'?" *Seattle Magazine* 4:43 (October 1967): 16.

4. See "The Changing Face of the Central Area," *Seattle Times*, June 7, 1981, pp. C1, C4.

5. By the 1980s numerous neoconservative social theorists, aided by media focus on the spectacular success of well-educated middle-class native or immigrant Asians, began to advance the "model minority" concept, suggesting that African Americans would obtain economic success and social acceptance by emulating their example rather than continuing to pursue the confrontational political and civil rights strategy identified with organizations such as the NAACP. For a discussion of the fallacy of the model minority concept and its potentially negative implications for Asian American and African American relations, see Roger Daniels, *Asian America: Chinese and Japanese in the United States since 1850* (Seattle: University of Washington Press, 1988), pp. 184–85, and Ronald Takaki, *Strangers from a Different Shore: A History of Asian Americans* (Boston: Little, Brown, 1989), pp. 474–79.

6. For a discussion of this rapid diffusion and its implications for the entire city, see "Racial Migration Stood Out Clearly in Recent Census," *Seattle Times*, June 7, 1981, p. C4.

7. For an example of the international dimension of intergroup dynamics in Seattle, see Larry Gossett, "A Perspective on the African American Community in the United States," speech delivered at Kobe, Japan, March 23, 1992, as part of an international forum sponsored by the Sedaka Foundation of Tokyo, Japan. Gossett is executive director of the Central Area Motivation Program, the city's largest and oldest antipoverty agency.

8. The discourse on the origin, size, and particular characteristics of the "underclass" is now entering its second decade with little more agreement on the origin, size, and particular characteristics than in the early 1980s. For a provocative discussion of the history of this debate and a proposed solution to their dilemma, see Roy L. Brooks, *Rethinking the American Race Problem* (Berkeley: University of California Press, 1990), pp. 106–16, 122–24. See also William Julius Wilson, *The Truly Disadvantaged: The Inner City, the Underclass, and Public Policy* (Chicago: University of Chicago Press, 1987), pp. 3–19; and Douglass Glasgow, *The Black Underclass* (New York: Vintage Books, 1981), pp. 3–8, for background on the evolving divisions in the black community prompted by the middle-class flight from the inner city. Seattle sociologist S. Frank Miyamoto describes the impact of the exodus of middle-class, educated Japanese from the postwar Seattle Nihonmachi in "An Immigrant Community in America," in Hilary Conroy and T. Scott Miyakawa, eds., *East Across the Pacific: Historical and Sociological Studies of Japanese Immigration and Assimilation* (Santa Barbara: Clio Press, 1972), p. 240.

9. *Northwest Enterprise*, March 22, 1944, p. 1.

10. Roger Sale in the mid-1970s perceptively anticipated the interclass dynamics inherent in the growing division between successful middle-class

blacks who vacated the Central District for the predominately white city neighborhoods and the suburbs beyond, and the impoverished people left behind. See Sale, *Seattle,* pp. 246–47. For an analysis of the trend nationally and a proposed program of middle-class self-help initiatives to revitalize the inner city, see Brooks, *Rethinking the American Race Problem,* pp. 131–49.

11. See *Seattle Times,* February 26, 1985, p. C2.

Bibliography

Books, Articles, Reports, Government Documents, Theses, and Dissertations

Abbott, Carl. "Regional City and Network City: Portland and Seattle in the Twentieth Century." *Western Historical Quarterly* 23:3 (August 1992): 293–319.

Acena, Albert A. "The Washington Commonwealth Federation: Reform Politics and the Popular Front." Ph.D. dissertation, University of Washington, 1975.

Adair, Harriet Elaine. "Trends in School Desegregation: A Historical Case Study of Dayton, Denver, Los Angeles and Seattle." Ed.D. dissertation, Brigham Young University, 1986.

Altshuler, Alan A. *Community Control: The Black Demand for Participation in Large American Cities.* New York: Pegasus, 1970.

Amdur, Reuel Seeman. "An Exploratory Study of Nineteen Negro Families in the Seattle Area Who Were the First Negro Residents in White Neighborhoods, of Their White Neighbors, and of the Integration Process, Together with a Proposed Program to Promote Integration in Seattle." M.A. thesis, University of Washington, 1962.

Anderson, Alan, and George Pickering. *Confronting the Color Line: The Broken Promise of the Civil Rights Movement in Chicago.* Athens: University of Georgia Press, 1986.

Anderson, Karen Tucker. "Last Hired, First Fired: Black Women Workers during World War II." *Journal of American History* 69:1 (June 1982): 83–97.

Athearn, Robert G. *In Search of Canaan: Black Migration to Kansas, 1879–80.* Lawrence: The Regents Press of Kansas, 1978.

Bagley, Clarence B. *History of Seattle from the Earliest Settlement to the Present Time.* 3 vols. Chicago: S. J. Clarke Publishing Company, 1916.

Baker, Ray Stannard. *Following the Color Line.* New York: Harper and Row, 1964 [first published in 1908].

Barth, Gunther. *Bitter Strength: A History of the Chinese in the United States, 1850–1870.* Cambridge: Harvard University Press, 1964.

Bellson, Ford. "Labor Gains on the Coast: A Report on the Integration of Negro Workers into the Maritime Unions of the Pacific Coast States." *Opportunity: Journal of Negro Life* 17:5 (May 1939): 142–43.

Berner, Richard C. *Seattle, 1900–1920: From Boomtown, Urban Turbulence, to Restoration.* Seattle: Charles Press, 1991.

Berube, Maurice R., and Marilyn Gittell, eds. *Confrontation at Ocean Hill–Brownsville: The New York School Strikes of 1968.* New York: Praeger, 1969.

298

Berwanger, Eugene H. *The West and Reconstruction*. Urbana: University of Illinois Press, 1981.

Bigham, Darrel E. *We Ask Only a Fair Trial: A History of the Black Community of Evansville, Indiana*. Bloomington: Indiana University Press, 1987.

"Black Backlash." *Seattle Magazine* 1:7 (October 1964): 7–8.

Blair, Karen J. *The Clubwoman as Feminist: True Womanhood Redefined, 1868–1914*. New York: Holmes and Meier, 1980.

Blair, Thomas L. *Retreat to the Ghetto: The End of a Dream?* New York: Hill and Wang, 1977.

Blassingame, John. "Before the Ghetto: The Making of the Black Community in Savannah, Georgia, 1865–1880." *Journal of Social History* 6:4 (Summer 1973): 463–88.

Blauner, Robert. *Racial Oppression in America*. New York: Harper and Row, 1972.

Bleeg, Joanne Wagner. "Black People in the Territory of Washington, 1860–1880." M.A. thesis, University of Washington, 1970.

Bodnar, John, Michael Weber, and Roger Simon. "Migration, Kinship, and Urban Adjustment: Blacks and Poles in Pittsburgh, 1900–1930." *Journal of American History* 66:3 (December 1979): 548–65.

Bonacich, Edna, and Lucie Cheng. "Introduction: A Theoretical Orientation to International Labor Migration." In Lucie Cheng and Edna Bonacich, eds. *Labor Immigration under Capitalism: Asian Workers in the United States before World War II*, pp. 1–51. Berkeley: University of California Press, 1984.

Bonacich, Edna, and John Modell. *The Economic Basis of Ethnic Solidarity: Small Business in the Japanese American Community*. Berkeley: University of California Press, 1980.

Bontemps, Arna, and Jack Conroy. *Anyplace But Here*. New York: Hill and Wang, 1966.

Borchert, James. *Alley Life in Washington: Family, Community, Religion and Folklife in the City, 1850–1970*. Urbana: University of Illinois Press, 1980.

Bowles, Samuel S. "Toward Equality of Educational Opportunity." *Harvard Educational Review* 38:1 (Winter 1968): 89–99.

Brewster, David. "Solidarity Forever! Black Demands for Construction Jobs Have Revived Labor's Old Fighting Spirit – Not on Behalf of All Workers, But *White* Workers." *Seattle Magazine* 6:69 (December 1969): 34–41.

Brimmer, Andrew. "Some Aspects of Fair Employment." M.A. thesis, University of Washington, 1951.

Brooks, Roy L. *Rethinking the American Race Problem*. Berkeley: University of California Press, 1990.

Broussard, Albert S. *Black San Francisco: The Struggle for Racial Equality in the West, 1900–1954*. Lawrence: University Press of Kansas, 1993.

Brown, Richard Maxwell. *Strain of Violence: Historical Studies of American Violence and Vigilantism*. New York: Oxford University Press, 1977.

Brownell, Blaine A. *The Urban Ethos in the South, 1920–1930*. Baton Rouge: Louisiana State University Press, 1975.

Bulosan, Carlos. *America Is in the Heart: A Personal History*. Seattle: University of Washington Press, 1973 [first published in 1943].

Butler, Anne M. *Daughters of Joy, Sisters of Misery: Prostitutes in the American*

West, 1865–90. Urbana: University of Illinois Press, 1985.

Campbell, Robert A. "Blacks and the Coal Mines of Western Washington, 1888–1896." *Pacific Northwest Quarterly* 73:4 (October 1982): 146–55.

Carmichael, Stokely, and Charles V. Hamilton. *Black Power: The Politics of Liberation in America.* New York: Vintage, 1967.

Carson, Clayborne. *In Struggle: SNCC and the Black Awakening of the 1960s.* Cambridge: Harvard University Press, 1981.

Caute, David. *The Great Fear: The Anti-Communist Purge under Truman and Eisenhower.* New York: Simon and Schuster, 1978.

Cayton, Horace R. [Jr]. *Long Old Road: An Autobiography.* Seattle: University of Washington Press, 1970 [first published in 1965].

———. *Black Workers and the New Unions.* Chapel Hill: University of North Carolina Press, 1939.

Chan, Anthony B. "The Myth of the Chinese Sojourner in Canada." In K. V. Ujimoto and G. Hirabayashi, eds. *Visible Minorities and Multiculturalism: Asians in Canada,* pp. 33–42. Toronto: Butterworths, 1980.

Chan, Sucheng. *Asian Americans: An Interpretive History.* Boston: Twayne, 1991.

Charles, Ray and David Ritz. *Brother Ray: Ray Charles' Own Story.* New York: Dial, 1978.

Cheng, Lucie. "Free, Indentured, Enslaved: Chinese Prostitutes in Nineteenth Century America." In Lucie Cheng and Edna Bonacich, eds., *Labor Immigration under Capitalism: Asian Workers in the United States before World War II,* pp. 402–30. Berkeley: University of California Press, 1984.

Chin, Art. *Golden Tassels: A History of the Chinese in Washington, 1857–1977.* Seattle: Art Chin, 1977.

Chin, Doug and Art Chin. *Up Hill: The Settlement and Diffusion of the Chinese in Seattle, Washington.* Seattle: Doug and Art Chin, 1973.

Colbert, Robert E. "The Attitude of Older Negro Residents toward Recent Negro Migrants in the Pacific Northwest." *Journal of Negro Education* 15:4 (Fall 1946): 695–703.

Colburn, David E. *Racial Change and Community Crisis: St. Augustine, Florida, 1877–1980.* New York: Columbia University Press, 1985.

Coleman, Willi. "Keeping the Faith and Disturbing the Peace, Black Women: From Anti-Slavery to Women's Suffrage." Ph.D. dissertation, University of California, Irvine, 1982.

Commission on the Causes and Prevention of Civil Disorder. *Race and Violence in Washington State: A Report of the Commission on the Causes and Prevention of Civil Disorder.* Olympia: State Printing Office, 1969.

Cordova, Fred. *Filipinos: Forgotten Asian Americans.* Dubuque: Kendall-Hunt, 1983.

Cox, Thomas. *Blacks in Topeka, Kansas, 1865–1915: A Social History.* Baton Rouge: Louisiana State University Press, 1982.

Craig, E. Quita. *Black Drama of the Federal Theatre Era: Beyond the Formal Horizons.* Amherst: University of Massachusetts Press, 1980.

Crane, Paul, and Alfred Larson. "The Chinese Massacre." *Annals of Wyoming* 12:1 (January 1940): 47–55.

Crew, Spencer. "Black Life in Secondary Cities: A Comparative Analysis of the Black Communities of Camden and Elizabeth, New Jersey, 1860–1920." Ph.D. dissertation, Rutgers University, 1979.

Daniels, Douglas. *Pioneer Urbanites: A Social and Cultural History of Black San Francisco*. Philadelphia: Temple University Press, 1980.

Daniels, John. *In Freedom's Birthplace: A History of the Boston Negro*. New York: Johnson Reprint, 1969 [first published in 1914].

Daniels, Roger. *Asian America: Chinese and Japanese in the United States since 1850*. Seattle: University of Washington Press, 1988.

——. *Concentration Camps, North America: Japanese in the United States and Canada during World War II*. Malabar, Florida: Krieger Publishing Company, 1981.

Daoust, Norma LaSalle. "Building the Democratic Party: Black Voting in Providence in the 1930s." *Rhode Island History* 44:3 (August 1895): 81–88.

Davis, Elizabeth Lindsay. *Lifting as They Climb: The History of the National Association of Colored Women*. Washington, D.C.: National Association of Colored Women, 1933.

DeBow, Samuel P., and Edward A. Pitter, eds. *Who's Who in Religious, Fraternal, Social, Civic and Commercial Life on the Pacific Coast*. Seattle: Searchlight Publishing Company, 1927.

De Graaf, Lawrence B. "The City of Black Angels: Emergence of the Los Angeles Ghetto, 1890–1930." *Pacific Historical Review* 39:3 (August 1970): 323–52.

——. "Race, Sex, and Region: Black Women in the American West, 1850–1920." *Pacific Historical Review* 49:2 (May 1980): 285–313.

Dennett, Eugene V. *Agitprop: The Life of an American Working-Class Radical: The Autobiography of Eugene V. Dennett*. Albany: State University of New York Press, 1990.

Dickerson, Dennis R. *Out of the Crucible: Black Steelworkers in Western Pennsylvania, 1875–1980*. Albany: State University of New York Press, 1986.

Douglas, Patrick. "'Yeah, Baby, You Almost Got Burned': Must Act II of Our Negro Revolution Produce as It Did in Watts – a 'Reign of Terror'?" *Seattle Magazine* 4:43 (October 1967): 16–22, 57–58.

——. "The Family of Two Revolutions: The Gaytons." *Seattle Magazine* 6:58 (January 1969): 21–28, 38–39.

Drake, St. Clair, and Horace Cayton. *Black Metropolis*. New York: Harcourt, Brace, 1945.

Droker, Howard Alan. "The Seattle Civic Unity Committee and the Civil Rights Movement, 1944–1964." Ph.D. dissertation, University of Washington, 1974.

——. "Seattle Race Relations during the Second World War." *Pacific Northwest Quarterly* 67:4 (October 1976): 163–74.

Du Bois, Shirley Graham. *His Day Is Marching On: A Memoir of W. E. B. Du Bois*. Philadelphia: Lippincott, 1971.

Du Bois, W. E. B. "The Great Northwest." *Crisis* 6 (September 1913): 237–40.

Dvorak, Katherine L. *An African-American Exodus: The Segregation of the Southern Churches*. Brooklyn, N.Y.: Carlson, 1991.

Epstein, Abraham. *The Negro Migrant in Pittsburgh.* New York: Arno Press, 1969 [first published in 1918].

"First in a Long Line." *Boeing Magazine* 17:1 (January 1947): 7–9.

Fox, Maier B. *United We Stand: The United Mine Workers of America, 1890–1990.* Washington, D.C.: United Mine Workers, 1991.

Frank, Dana. "Gender, Consumer Organizing and the Seattle Labor Movement, 1919–1929." In Ava Baron, ed., *Work Engendered: Towards a New History of American Labor,* pp. 273–95. Ithaca: Cornell University Press, 1991.

Franklin, John H., and Alfred A. Moss, Jr. *From Slavery to Freedom: A History of Negro Americans.* New York: McGraw-Hill, 1988.

Friedheim, Robert L. *The Seattle General Strike.* Seattle: University of Washington Press, 1964.

Friedman, Ralph. "The Attitudes of West Coast Maritime Unions in Seattle toward Negroes in the Maritime Industry." M.A. thesis, Washington State College, 1952.

Garrity, Frederick Dennis. "The Civic Unity Committee of Seattle, 1944–1964." M.A. thesis, University of Washington, 1971.

Gelber, Steven M. "Working at Playing: The Culture of the Workplace and the Rise of Baseball." *Journal of Social History* 16:4 (Summer 1983): 3–22.

General Statutes and Codes of the State of Washington. Volume 1. San Francisco: Bancroft-Whitney, 1891.

Gerber, David A. "A Politics of Limited Options: Northern Black Politics and the Problem of Change and Continuity in Race Relations Historiography." *Journal of Social History* 14:2 (Winter 1980): 235–55.

Giddings, Paula. *When and Where I Enter: The Impact of Black Women on Race and Sex in America.* New York: Morrow, 1984.

Giebink, Nancy. "Bold Experiment in the Ghetto." *Seattle Magazine* 5:51 (June 1968): 11–12.

Girdner, Audrie, and Anne Loftis. *The Great Betrayal: The Evacuation of the Japanese-Americans during World War II.* New York: Macmillan, 1969.

Glasgow, Douglass. *The Black Underclass.* New York: Vintage Books, 1981.

Glenn, Evelyn Nakano. *Issei, Nisei, War Bride: Three Generations of Japanese American Women in Domestic Service.* Philadelphia: Temple University Press, 1986.

Gottlieb, Peter. *Making Their Own Way: Southern Blacks' Migration to Pittsburgh, 1916–30.* Urbana: University of Illinois Press, 1987.

Gould, William B. "The Seattle Building Trades Order: The First Comprehensive Relief Against Employment Discrimination in the Construction Industry." *Stanford Law Review* 26 (April 1974): 773–813.

Granger, Lester. "A Hopeful Sign in Race Relations." *Survey Graphic* 33 (November 1944): 455–79.

Greenwald, Maurine Weiner. "Working-Class Feminism and the Family Wage Ideal: The Seattle Debate on Married Women's Right to Work, 1914–1920." *Journal of American History* 76:1 (June 1989): 118–49.

Grimshaw, William H. *Official History of Freemasonry among the Colored People in North America.* New York: Negro Universities Press, 1903.

Grossman, James R. *The Land of Hope: Chicago, Black Southerners and the*

Great Migration. Urbana: University of Illinois Press, 1989.

Grossman, Lawrence. *The Democratic Party and the Negro: Northern and National Politics, 1868–1892.* Urbana: University of Illinois Press, 1976.

Gutman, Herbert. *The Black Family in Slavery and Freedom, 1750–1925.* New York: Pantheon, 1976

Hall, Robert L. "Tallahassee's Black Churches, 1865–1885." *Florida Historical Quarterly* 58:2 (October 1979): 185–96.

Halpin, James. "Discrimination by Whites Has Kept Negroes Locked in Jobs that Lead Nowhere." *Seattle Magazine* 5:51 (June 1968): 20–24, 50.

Halseth, James A., and Bruce A. Glasrud. "Anti-Chinese Movements in Washington, 1885–1886: A Reconsideration." In Halseth and Glasrud, eds., *The Northwest Mosaic: Minority Conflicts in Pacific Northwest History,* pp. 116–39. Boulder: Pruett, 1977.

Harris, William H. *The Harder We Run: Black Workers since the Civil War.* New York: Oxford University Press, 1982.

Hart-Nibbrig, Nand. "Policies of School Desegregation in Seattle." *Integrated Education* 17:97 (January-April 1979): 27–30.

Haughland, Marylou McMahon. "A History of the Alaska Steamship Company." M.A. thesis, University of Washington, 1968.

Henri, Florette. *Black Migration, Movement North: The Road from Myth to Man.* Garden City: Doubleday, 1976.

Hershberg, Theodore, and others. *Philadelphia: Work, Space, Family and Group Experience in the Nineteenth Century, Essays Toward an Interdisciplinary History of the City.* New York: Oxford University Press, 1981.

Hill, Daniel G. "The Negro in Oregon: A Survey." M.A. thesis, University of Oregon, 1932.

Hill, Pauline Anderson Simmons, and Sherrilyn Johnson Jordan. *Too Young to Be Old: The Story of Bertha Pitts Campbell.* Seattle: Peanut Butter Publishing, 1981.

Hill, Robert A., ed. *The Marcus Garvey and Universal Negro Improvement Association Papers.* Volumes 2 and 4. Berkeley: University of California Press, 1983–90.

Hirsch, Arnold R. *Making the Second Ghetto: Race and Housing in Chicago, 1940–1960.* New York: Cambridge University Press, 1983.

Hobbs, Richard Stanley. "The Cayton Legacy: Two Generations of a Black Family, 1859–1976." Ph.D. dissertation, University of Washington, 1989.

———, ed. *The Autobiography of Horace Cayton, Sr.* Manama, Bahrain: Delmon Press, 1987.

Horne, Gerald. *Communist Front? The Civil Rights Congress, 1946–1956.* Rutherford, N.J.: Fairleigh Dickinson University Press, 1988.

Hosokawa, Bill. *JACL in Quest of Justice.* New York: Morrow, 1982.

Hynding, Alan A. "The Coal Miners of Washington Territory: Labor Troubles in 1888–1889." *Arizona and the West* 12:3 (Autumn 1970): 221–36.

Ichioka, Yuji. *Issei: The World of the First Generation of Japanese Immigrants, 1885–1924.* New York: Free Press, 1988.

Institute of Labor Economics. *Job Opportunities for Racial Minorities in the Seattle Area.* Seattle: University of Washington Press, 1948.

"Isn't There Anything We Can Do for Our Boys?: The Story of Seven

Northwest Citizens." Pamphlet published by the Northwest Citizens Defense Committee, n.d., pp. 1–7.

Ito, Kazuo. *Issei: A History of Japanese Immigrants in North America.* Seattle: Japanese Community Service, 1973.

Jackson, Joseph Sylvester. "The Colored Marine Employees Benevolent Association of the Pacific, 1921–1934, or Implications of Vertical Mobility for Negro Stewards in Seattle." M.A. thesis, University of Washington, 1939.

Jaworski, Leon, with Mickey Horskowitz. *Confession and Avoidance: A Memoir.* Garden City: Anchor Press/Doubleday, 1979.

Johansen, Dorothy O., and Charles M. Gates. *Empire of the Columbia: A History of the Pacific Northwest.* New York: Harper and Row, 1967.

Johannsen, Robert W. *Frontier Politics on the Eve of the Civil War.* Seattle: University of Washington Press, 1955.

Johnson, Evamarii Alexandria. "A Production History of the Seattle Federal Theater Project Negro Repertory Company: 1935–1939." Ph.D. dissertation, University of Washington, 1981.

Johnson, James Weldon. *Black Manhattan.* New York: Atheneum, 1968 [first published in 1930].

Jones, Jacqueline. *Labor of Love, Labor of Sorrow: Black Women, Work, and the Family from Slavery to the Present.* New York: Basic Books, 1985.

Jue, Willard G. "Chin Gee-Hee, Chinese Pioneer Entrepreneur in Seattle and Toishan." *Annals of the Chinese Historical Society of the Pacific Northwest* 1:1 (1983): 31–38.

Karlin, Jules Alexander. "The Anti-Chinese Outbreaks in Seattle, 1885–1886." *Pacific Northwest Quarterly* 39:1 (April 1948): 103–30.

Katzman, David M. *Before the Ghetto: Black Detroit in the Nineteenth Century.* Urbana: University of Illinois Press, 1973.

———. *Seven Days a Week: Women and Domestic Service in Industrializing America.* New York: Oxford University Press, 1978.

Kellogg, Charles Flint. *NAACP: A History of the National Association for the Advancement of Colored People, Volume I, 1909–1920.* Baltimore: Johns Hopkins Press, 1967.

Kelly, Robin D. G. *Hammer and Hoe: Alabama Communists during the Great Depression.* Chapel Hill: University of North Carolina Press, 1990.

Kennedy, Louise V. *The Negro Peasant Turns Cityward: Effects of Recent Migrations to Northern Centers.* New York: Columbia University Press, 1930.

Kennedy, Tolbert Hall. "Racial Survey of the Intermountain Northwest." *Research Studies of the State College of Washington* 14:3 (September 1946): 163–243.

———. "Racial Tensions among Negroes in the Intermountain Northwest." *Phylon* 7:4 (Winter 1946): 358–64.

Kim, Hyung-chan, and Richard W. Markov. "The Chinese Exclusion Laws and Smuggling Chinese into Whatcom County, Washington, 1890–1900." *Annals of the Chinese Historical Society of the Pacific Northwest* 1:1 (1983): 16–27.

Kimeldorf, Howard. *Reds or Rackets? The Making of Radical and Conservative Unions on the Waterfront.* Berkeley: University of California Press, 1988.

King, Ivan. *The Central Area Motivation Program: A Brief History of a Community in Action.* Seattle: Central Area Motivation Program, 1990.

Kiser, Clyde V. *Sea Island to City: A Study of St. Helena Islanders in Harlem and Other Urban Centers.* New York: Atheneum, 1969 [first published in 1931].

Kitano, Harry H. L., and Roger Daniels. *Asian-Americans: Emerging Minorities.* Englewood Cliffs: Prentice-Hall, 1988.

Klein, Maury, and Harvey A. Kantor. *Prisoners of Progress: American Industrial Cities, 1850–1920.* New York: Macmillan, 1976.

Kusmer, Kenneth. *A Ghetto Takes Shape: Black Cleveland, 1870–1930.* Urbana: University of Illinois Press, 1976.

———. "Black Urban History in the U.S.: Retrospect and Prospect." *Trends in History* 3:1 (Fall 1982): 71–92.

———. "The Structure of Black Urban History: Retrospect and Prospect." In Darlene Clark Hine, ed., *The State of Afro-American History,* pp. 91–122. Baton Rouge: Louisiana State University Press, 1986.

Lane, Frederick C. *Ships for Victory: A History of Shipbuilding under the U.S. Maritime Commission in World War II.* Baltimore: Johns Hopkins University Press, 1951.

Lang, William L. "Tempest on Clore Street: Race and Politics in Helena, Montana, 1906." *Scratchgravel Hills* 3 (Summer 1980): 9–14.

Larrowe, Charles P. *Harry Bridges: The Rise and Fall of Radical Labor in the United States.* Westport, Conn.: Lawrence Hill and Company, 1972.

Larson, T. A. "The Woman Suffrage Movement in Washington." *Pacific Northwest Quarterly* 67:2 (April 1976): 49–62.

Lasker, Bruno. *Filipino Immigration to the Continental United States and Hawaii.* Chicago: University of Chicago Press, 1931.

Laurie, Clayton D. " 'The Chinese Must Go': The United States Army and the Anti-Chinese Riots in Washington Territory, 1885–1886." *Pacific Northwest Quarterly* 81:1 (January 1990): 22–29.

Lee, Rose Hum. *The Chinese in the United States of America.* Hong Kong: Hong Kong University Press, 1960.

Levine, David. *Internal Combustion: The Races in Detroit, 1915–1926.* Westport, Conn.: Greenwood Press, 1976.

Levine, Lawrence E. *Black Culture and Black Consciousness: Afro-American Folk Thought from Slavery to Freedom.* New York: Oxford University Press, 1977.

Lewis, Earl. *In Their Own Interests: Race, Class, and Power in Twentieth-Century Norfolk, Virginia.* Berkeley: University of California Press, 1991.

Light, Ivan H. *Ethnic Enterprise in America: Business and Welfare among Chinese, Japanese, and Blacks.* Berkeley: University of California Press, 1972.

———. "The Ethnic Vice Industry, 1880–1944." *American Sociological Review* 42:3 (June 1977): 464–79.

———. "From Vice District to Tourist Attraction: The Moral Career of American Chinatowns, 1880–1940." *Pacific Historical Review* 43:3 (August 1974): 367–94.

Limerick, Patricia Nelson. *The Legacy of Conquest: The Unbroken Past of the American West.* New York: Norton, 1987.

Little, William A. "Community Organization and Leadership: A Case

Study of Minority Workers in Seattle." Ph.D. dissertation, University of Washington, 1976.

Lyman, Stanford. *Chinese Americans*. New York: Random House, 1974.

———. "The Chinese Diaspora in America." In Chinese Historical Society of America, *The Life, Influence and Role of the Chinese in the United States, 1776–1960*. Proceedings/Papers of the National Conference Held at the University of San Francisco, July 10–12, 1975. San Francisco: Chinese Historical Society of America, 1975.

Lynd, Helen M. "Truth at the University of Washington." *American Scholar* 18:3 (Summer 1949): 346–53.

MacDonald, Norbert. "Population Growth and Change in Seattle and Vancouver, 1880–1960." *Pacific Historical Review* 39:3 (August 1970): 297–321.

Mariano, Honorante. "The Filipino Immigrants in the United States." M.A. thesis, University of Oregon, 1933.

Marks, Carole. "Split Labor Markets and Black-White Relations, 1865–1920." *Phylon* 42:4 (December 1981): 293–308.

Martin, Tony. *Race First: The Ideological and Organizational Struggles of Marcus Garvey and the Universal Negro Improvement Association*. Westport, Conn.: Greenwood Press, 1976.

McCann, John. *Blood in the Water: A History of District Lodge 751, International Association of Machinists and Aerospace Workers*. Seattle: District Lodge 751, IAMAW, 1989.

McLagen, Elizabeth. *A Peculiar Paradise: A History of Blacks in Oregon, 1788–1940*. Portland: Georgian Press, 1980.

Mears, Eliot G. *Resident Orientals on the American Pacific Coast: Their Legal and Economic Status*. New York: Institute of Pacific Relations, 1927.

Meier, August, and Elliott Rudwick. *CORE: A Study in the Civil Rights Movement, 1942–1968*. New York: Oxford University Press, 1973.

Melendy, H. Brett. "Filipinos in the United States." In Norris Hundley, Jr., ed., *The Asian American: The Historical Experience*. Santa Barbara: Clio Press, 1976.

Miller, Irene Burns. *Profanity Hill*. Everett, Wash.: The Working Press, 1979.

Miyamoto, S. Frank. "An Immigrant Community in America." In Hilary Conroy and T. Scott Miyakawa, eds., *East Across the Pacific: Historical and Sociological Studies of Japanese Immigration and Assimilation*, pp. 217–43. Santa Barbara: Clio Press, 1972.

———. *Social Solidarity among the Japanese in Seattle*. Seattle: University of Washington Press, 1984 [first published in 1939].

Modell, John. "Tradition and Opportunity: The Japanese Immigrant in America." *Pacific Historical Review* 40:2 (May 1971): 163–82.

Modell, John, Frank Furstenberg, and Theodore Hershberg. "Social Change and Transitions to Adulthood in Historical Perspective." *Journal of Family History* 1:1 (Autumn 1976): 7–32.

Mohl, Raymond A. *The New City: Urban America in the Industrial Age, 1860–1920*. Arlington Heights, Ill.: Harlan Davidson, Inc., 1985.

Morgan, Murray. *Skid Road: An Informal Portrait of Seattle*. Seattle: University of Washington Press, 1982 [first published in 1951].

Morris, Arval A., and Donald B. Ritter. "Racial Minority Housing in Washington." *Washington Law Review* 37 (Summer 1962): 131–51.

Mumford, Esther Hall. *Seattle's Black Victorians, 1852–1901*. Seattle: Ananse Press, 1980.

———. "Seattle's Black Victorians – Revising a City's History." *Portage* 2:1 (Fall/Winter 1980–81): 16–17.

———. *Seven Stars and Orion: Reflections of the Past*. Seattle: Ananse Press, 1986.

Muraskin, William A. *Middle Class Blacks in a White Society: Prince Hall Freemasonry in America*. Berkeley: University of California Press, 1975.

Murayama, Yuzo. "The Economic History of Japanese Immigration to the Pacific Northwest, 1890–1920." Ph.D. dissertation, University of Washington, 1982.

Naison, Mark. *Communists in Harlem during the Depression*. Urbana: University of Illinois Press, 1983.

Nash, Gary B. *Forging Freedom: The Formation of Philadelphia's Black Community, 1720–1840*. Cambridge: Harvard University Press, 1988.

National Urban League. "Unemployment Status of Negroes." New York: National Urban League, 1931.

Nelson, Bruce. *Workers on the Waterfront: Seamen, Longshoremen, and Unionism in the 1930s*. Urbana: University of Illinois Press, 1988.

Neverdon-Morton, Cynthia. *Afro-American Women of the South and the Advancement of the Race, 1895–1925*. Knoxville: University of Tennessee Press, 1989.

"New Life in Seattle: In the Biggest, Fastest Growing City of the Northwest, Negroes Have Found a New Frontier." *Our World* 6 (August 1951): 22–25.

Nimmons, Julius. "Social Reform and Moral Uplift in the Black Community, 1890–1910: Social Settlements, Temperance, and Social Purity." Ph.D. dissertation, Howard University, 1981.

Northwood, L. K., and Ernest A. T. Barth. *Urban Desegregation: Negro Pioneers and Their White Neighbors*. Seattle: University of Washington Press, 1965.

O'Brien, Robert W. "Seattle: Race Relations Frontier, 1949." *Common Ground* 9:3 (Spring 1949): 18–23.

———. *The College Nisei*. New York: Arno Press, 1978.

Okada, John. *No-No Boy*. Seattle: University of Washington Press, 1979 [first published in 1957].

Osofsky, Gilbert. *Harlem: The Making of a Ghetto, 1890–1930*. 2d edition. New York: Harper and Row, 1971.

Ovington, Mary White. *Half a Man: The Status of the Negro in New York*. New York: Hill and Wang, 1969 [first published in 1911].

Painter, Nell Irvin. *Exodusters: Black Migration to Kansas after Reconstruction*. Lawrence: University Press of Kansas, 1986 [first published in 1977].

Petrik, Paula. *No Step Backward: Women and Family on the Rocky Mountain Mining Frontier, Helena, Montana, 1865–1900*. Helena: Montana Historical Society Press, 1987.

Philpott, Thomas. *The Slum and the Ghetto: Neighborhood Deterioration and Middle-Class Reform, Chicago, 1880–1930*. New York: Oxford University Press, 1978.

Pieroth, Doris Hinson. "Desegregating the Public Schools, Seattle, Washington, 1954–1968." Ph.D. dissertation, University of Washington, 1979.

———. "With All Deliberate Caution: School Integration in Seattle, 1954–1968." *Pacific Northwest Quarterly* 73:2 (April 1982): 50–61.

Pitts, Robert Bedford. "Organized Labor and the Negro in Seattle." M.A. thesis, University of Washington, 1941.

Polenberg, Richard. *War and Society: The United States, 1941–1945.* Philadelphia: Lippincott, 1972.

Pomeroy, Earl. *The Pacific Slope: A History of California, Oregon, Washington, Idaho, Utah, and Nevada.* Lincoln: University of Nebraska Press, 1991 [first published in 1965].

Rabinowitz, Howard N. "From Exclusion to Segregation: Southern Race Relations, 1865–1890." *Journal of American History* 63:2 (September 1976): 325–50.

Ray, Emma J. *Twice Sold, Twice Ransomed: The Autobiography of Mr. and Mrs. L. P. Ray.* Freeport, N.Y.: Books for Libraries Press, 1971 [first published in 1926].

Reiff, Janice L. "Scandinavian Women in Seattle, 1888–1900: Domestication and Americanization." In Karen J. Blair, ed., *Women in Pacific Northwest History: An Anthology*, pp. 170–84. Seattle: University of Washington Press, 1988.

———. "Urbanization and the Social Structure: Seattle, Washington, 1852–1910." Ph.D. dissertation, University of Washington, 1981.

Richardson, Larry S. "Civil Rights in Seattle: A Rhetorical Analysis of a Social Movement." Ph.D. dissertation, Washington State University, 1975.

Ritchie, Art, and William J. Davis. *The Pacific Northwest Goes to War.* Seattle: Associated Editors, 1949.

"Rosie Is Back." *Boeing Magazine* 23:9 (September 1953):15.

Robinson, Armstead L. "The Difference Freedom Made: The Emancipation of Afro-Americans." In Darlene Clark Hine, ed., *The State of Afro-American History: Past, Present, and Future.* Baton Rouge: Louisiana State University Press, 1986.

Romero, Mary. *Maid in the U.S.A.* New York: Routledge, 1992.

Royster-Horn, Juana Racquel. "The Academic and Extracurricular Undergraduate Experiences of Three Black Women at the University of Washington, 1935 to 1941." Ph.D. dissertation, University of Washington, 1980.

Rubin, Lester. *The Negro in the Longshore Industry.* Philadelphia: University of Pennsylvania Press, 1974.

Sale, Roger. *Seattle, Past to Present.* Seattle: University of Washington Press, 1976.

Salem, Dorothy. *To Better Our World: Black Women and Organized Reform, 1890–1920.* Volume 14 of Darlene Clark Hine, ed., *Black Women in United States History.* New York: Carlson, 1990.

Sandmeyer, Elmer C. *The Anti-Chinese Movement in California.* Urbana: University of Illinois Press, 1973.

Schaefer, Richard T. *Sociology.* New York: McGraw-Hill, 1989.

Schear, Rillmond. "The World That Whites Don't Know." *Seattle Magazine*

2:19 (October 1965): 14–16, 18.

Schmid, Calvin F. *Social Trends in Seattle.* Seattle: University of Washington Press, 1944.

———. *Non-white Races: State of Washington.* Olympia: State Printing Office, 1968.

Schmid, Calvin F., and Wayne McVey, Jr. *Growth and Distribution of Minority Races in Seattle, Washington.* Seattle: Seattle Public Schools, 1964.

Schmid, Calvin F., Charles E. Nobbe, and Arlene E. Mitchell. *Non-White Races: State of Washington.* Olympia: Washington State Planning and Community Affairs Agency, 1968.

Schneider, Franz M. "The 'Black Laws' of Oregon." M.A. thesis, University of Santa Clara, 1970.

Schoenberg, Sandra, and Charles Bailey. "The Symbolic Meaning of an Elite Black Community: The Ville in St. Louis." *Missouri Historical Society Bulletin* 33:2 (January 1977): 94–102.

Schuyler, George S. "Black Warriors." *American Mercury* 21 (November 1930): 293–94.

Schwantes, Carlos A. "The Pacific Northwest in World War II." *Journal of the West* 25:3 (July 1986): 4–19.

———. "Protest in a Promised Land: Unemployment, Disinheritance, and the Origin of Labor Militancy in the Pacific Northwest, 1885–1886." *Western Historical Quarterly* 13:4 (October 1982): 373–90.

———. *Radical Heritage: Labor, Socialism, and Reform in Washington and British Columbia, 1885–1917.* Seattle: University of Washington Press, 1979.

Scott, Emmett J. *Negro Migration during the War.* New York: Arno Press, 1969 [first published in 1920].

Seattle Chamber of Commerce. *Demographic Profiles: Seattle-King County.* Seattle: November 1983.

Seattle City Council. *Seminar on Equal Opportunities and Racial Harmony, March 22 and April 6, 1968: Summary of Proceedings and Recommendations.* Seattle: City of Seattle, 1968.

Seattle School District. *Racial Distribution in Seattle Schools, 1957–1968.* Seattle: Seattle School District, 1969.

Seattle Urban League. *Seattle's Racial Gap: 1968.* Seattle: Seattle Urban League, 1968.

———. "The Silver Scoreboard." Seattle: Seattle Urban League, 1955.

———. "What to Tell Them." Seattle: Seattle Urban League, 1935.

Seligmann, Herbert J. *The Negro Faces America.* New York: Harper and Row, 1969 [first published in 1920].

Session Laws of the State of Washington. 35th Session, 1949, Chapter 183. Olympia: State Printing Plant, 1949.

Smith, Alonzo and Quintard Taylor. "Racial Discrimination in the Workplace: A Study of Two West Coast Cities during the 1940s." *Journal of Ethnic Studies* 8:1 (Spring 1980): 35–54.

Smith, Charles U. "Social Change in Certain Aspects of Adjustment of the Negro in Seattle, Washington." Ph.D. dissertation, Washington State College, 1950.

Smith, Stanley H. "Social Aspects of the Washington State Law against

Discrimination in Employment." Ph.D. dissertation, Washington State College, 1953.

Smith, Timothy L. "Black and Foreign Whites: Varying Responses to Educational Opportunity in America, 1880–1950." *Perspectives in American History* 6 (1972): 307–35.

Smurr, J. W. "Jim Crow Out West." In J. W. Smurr and J. Ross Toole, eds., *Historical Essays on Montana and the Northwest,* pp. 149–203. Helena: Western Press, 1957.

Sone, Monica. *Nisei Daughter.* Seattle: University of Washington Press, 1979 [first published in 1953].

Spear, Allan H. *Black Chicago: The Making of a Negro Ghetto, 1890–1920.* Chicago: University of Chicago Press, 1967.

Spickard, Paul R. "The Nisei Assume Power: The Japanese Citizens League, 1941–1942." *Pacific Historical Review* 52:2 (May 1983): 147–74.

State of Washington. *Abstract of Votes, Primary Election, July 9, 1946, General Election, November 5, 1946.* Olympia: State Printing Plant, 1948.

————. *State of Washington Enabling Act Providing for Admission of the State, Approved February 22, 1889.* Olympia: Thomas H. Cavanaugh, Public Printer, 1889.

Stein, Judith. *The World of Marcus Garvey.* Baton Rouge: Louisiana State University Press, 1986.

Stem, Mark. "Black Strikebreakers in the Coal Fields: King County, Washington – 1891." *Journal of Ethnic Studies* 5:3 (Fall 1977): 60–70.

Sugiyama, Alan. "Co-optation, a New Game." *Asian Family Affair* (May 1977): 2.

Taeuber, Karl E. and Alma F. *Negroes in Cities: Residential Segregation and Neighborhood Change.* Chicago: Aldine, 1965.

Takaki, Ronald. *Strangers from a Different Shore: A History of Asian Americans.* Boston: Little, Brown, 1989.

Taylor, Arnold H. *Travail and Triumph: Black Life and Culture in the South since the Civil War.* Westport, Conn.: Greenwood Press, 1976.

Taylor, Quintard. "A History of Blacks in the Pacific Northwest, 1788–1970." Ph.D. dissertation, University of Minnesota, 1977.

————. "Black Urban Development – Another View: Seattle's Central District, 1910–1940." *Pacific Historical Review* 58:4 (November 1989): 429–48.

————. "The Emergence of Black Communities in the Pacific Northwest, 1865–1910." *Journal of Negro History* 64:4 (Fall 1979): 342–51.

————. "The Great Migration: The Afro-American Communities of Seattle and Portland During the 1940s." *Arizona and the West* 23:2 (Summer 1981): 109–26.

————. "The Question of Culture: Black Life and the Transformation of Black Urban America, Seattle's Central District, 1900–1940." *Essays in History: The Journal of the Historical Society of the University of Lagos, Nigeria* 6:4 (December 1989): 13–20.

————. "Slaves and Free Men: Blacks in the Oregon Country, 1840–1860." *Oregon Historical Quarterly* 83:2 (Summer 1982): 153–70.

Thorndale, C. William. "Washington's Green River Coal Company: 1880–1930." M.A. thesis, University of Washington, 1965.

Tolbert, Emory J. *The UNIA and Black Los Angeles.* Los Angeles: University of California Press, 1980.

Toll, William. *The Resurgence of Race: Black Social Theory from Reconstruction to the Pan-African Conferences.* Philadelphia: Temple University Press, 1979.

Trotter, Joe W. *Black Milwaukee: The Making of an Industrial Proletariat, 1915–45.* Urbana: University of Illinois Press, 1985.

————, ed. *The Great Migration in Historical Perspective: New Dimensions of Race, Class, and Gender.* Bloomington: Indiana University Press, 1991.

Tsai, Shih-shan Henry. *China and the Overseas Chinese in the United States, 1868–1911.* Fayetteville: University of Arkansas Press, 1983.

————. *The Chinese Experience in America.* Bloomington: Indiana University Press, 1986.

Tsutakawa, Mayumi. "The Political Conservatism of James Sakamoto's *Japanese American Courier.*" M.A. thesis, University of Washington, 1976.

Tuttle, William, Jr. *Race Riot: Chicago in the Red Summer of 1919.* New York: Atheneum, 1970.

U.S. Bureau of the Census. *Compendium of the Ninth Census.* Washington, D.C.: Government Printing Office, 1872.

————. *Eleventh Census of the United States, 1890, Population,* part 2. Washington, D.C., 1897.

————. *Twelfth Census of the United States, 1900, Population,* vol. 1, part 1. Washington, D.C., 1901.

————. *Twelfth Census of the United States, 1900, Occupations.* Washington, D.C., 1904.

————. *Thirteenth Census of the United States, 1910, Population,* vol. 1. Washington, D.C., 1913.

————. *Thirteenth Census of the United States, 1910, Population,* vol. 3. Washington, D.C., 1913.

————. *Thirteenth Census of the United States, 1910, Occupational Statistics,* vol. 4. Washington, D.C., 1913.

————. *Fourteenth Census of the United States, 1920,* vol. 3, *Population.* Washington, D.C., 1922.

————. *Fourteenth Census of the United States, 1920,* vol. 4, *Occupations.* Washington, D.C., 1922.

————. *Fifteenth Census of the United States, 1930, Population,* vol. 2, *General Reports.* Washington, D.C., 1933.

————. *Fifteenth Census of the United States, 1930, Population,* vol. 3, part 2, *Reports by States.* Washington, D.C., 1932.

————. *Fifteenth Census of the United States, 1930, Population,* vol. 4, *Families.* Washington, D.C., 1933.

————. *Fifteenth Census of the United States 1930,* vol. 4, *Occupational Statistics, Population.* Washington, D.C., 1933.

————. *Sixteenth Census of the United States, 1940, Population,* vol. 1. Washington, D.C., 1942.

————. *Sixteenth Census of the United States, 1940, Population,* vol. 2. *Characteristics of the Population,* part 7. Washington, D.C., 1943.

————. *Sixteenth Census of the United States, 1940, Housing,* vol. 2, *General Characteristics,* part 2. Washington, D.C., 1943.

———. *Sixteenth Census of the United States*, vol. 3, *The Labor Force*. Washington, D.C., 1943.

———. *Characteristics of Population, Labor Force, Families, and Housing: Puget Sound Congested Production Area, June, 1944*. Series CA-3. Washington, D.C., 1944.

———. *Seventeenth Census of the United States, 1950*, vol. 2, *Characteristics of the Population*. Washington, D.C., 1952.

———. *Eighteenth Census of the United States, 1960*, vol. 1, *Characteristics of the Population*. Washington, D.C., 1963.

———. *1960 Census of Population*, vol. 1, *Characteristics of the Population*, part 49, Washington. Washington, D.C., 1961.

———. *1970 Census of Population*, vol. 1, *Characteristics of the Population*, part 49, Washington. Washington, D.C., 1973.

———. *1980 Census of Population*. vol. 1, *Characteristics of the Population*. chapter B, *General Population Characteristics*, part 49, Washington. Washington, D.C., 1982.

———. *1990 Census of Population and Housing: Summary, Population and Housing Characteristics*, Washington. Washington, D.C., 1991.

———. *Negro Population, 1790–1915*. Washington, D.C., 1918.

———. *Negroes in the United States, 1920–1932*. Washington, D.C., 1935.

———. *1980 Census of Population and Housing: Seattle-Everett, Wash. Standard Metropolitan Statistical Area*, Report 329. Washington, D.C., 1983.

Uyematsu, Amy. "The Emergence of Yellow Power in America." *GIDRA* (October 1969): 8–11.

Valentine, Bettylou. "The Black Homefront in Seattle and King County during World War II." *Portage* 6:2 (Summer 1985): 15–16.

Valentine, Charles A. *DEEDS: Background and Basis, a Report on Research Leading to the Drive for Equal Employment in Downtown Seattle*. Seattle: CORE, 1964.

Van Deburg, William L. *New Day in Babylon: The Black Power Movement and American Culture, 1965–1975*. Chicago: University of Chicago Press, 1992.

Wakatsuki, Yasuo. "Japanese Emigration to the United States, 1866–1924: A Monograph." *Perspectives in American History* 12 (1979): 387–516.

Walker, Diane Louise. "The University of Washington Establishment and the Black Student Union Sit-In of 1968." M.A. thesis, University of Washington, 1980.

Wallovits, Sonia E. "The Filipinos in California." M.A. thesis, University of Southern California, 1966.

Washington State Board Against Discrimination: Annual Report, 1951. Olympia: State Printing Office, 1952.

Weaver, Robert C. *Negro Labor: A National Problem*. Port Washington, N.Y.: Kennikat Press, 1969.

Weiss, Nancy J. *The National Urban League, 1910–1940*. New York: Oxford University Press, 1974.

White, Richard. "Race Relations in the American West." *American Quarterly* 38:3 (1986): 394–416.

White, Sid, and S. E. Solberg, eds. *Peoples of Washington: Perspectives on Cultural Diversity*. Pullman: Washington State University Press, 1989.

White, W. Thomas. "Race, Ethnicity, and Gender in the Railroad Work

Force: The Case of the Far Northwest, 1883–1918." *Western Historical Quarterly* 16:3 (July 1985): 265–283.

Wiley, James T. "Race Conflict as Exemplified in a Washington Town." M.A. thesis, Washington State College, 1949.

Williams, Guy. "Seattle's History-Making Negro Theater." *Federal Theater* 2:1 (1936): 7–9.

Williams, Lee. "Concentrated Residences: The Case of Black Toledo, 1890–1930." *Phylon* 43:2 (June 1982): 167–76.

Williams, Loretta J. *Black Freemasonry and Middle-Class Realities*. Columbia: University of Missouri Press, 1980.

Williamson, Joel. *The Crucible of Race: Black-White Relations in the American South since Emancipation*. New York: Oxford University Press, 1984.

Wilson, Robert A., and Bill Hosokawa. *East to America: A History of the Japanese in the United States*. New York: Quill, 1982.

Wilson, William Julius. *The Truly Disadvantaged: The Inner City, the Underclass, and Public Policy*. Chicago: University of Chicago Press, 1987.

Woon, Yuen-fong. "The Voluntary Sojourner among the Overseas Chinese: Myth or Reality?" *Pacific Affairs* 56:4 (Winter 1983–84): 673–90.

Wright, George C. *Life Behind a Veil: Blacks in Louisville, Kentucky, 1865–1930*. Baton Rouge: Louisiana State University Press, 1985.

Wynn, Neil A. *The Afro-American and the Second World War*. New York: Holmes and Meier, 1975.

Wynne, Robert E. *Reaction to the Chinese in the Pacific Northwest and British Columbia, 1859–1910*. New York: Arno Press, 1978.

Zunz, Olivier. *The Changing Face of Inequality: Urbanization, Industrial Development, and Immigrants in Detroit, 1880–1920*. Chicago: University of Chicago Press, 1982.

Manuscripts, Court Cases, and Unpublished Sources

Anti-Defamation League Papers. Acc. No. 2045. University of Washington Libraries.

Nettie J. Asberry Papers. University of Washington Libraries.

Powell R. Barnett Papers. University of Washington Libraries.

Boeing Company Records. Historical Archives. Seattle, Washington.

Philip Burton Papers. University of Washington Libraries.

Central Seattle Community Council Records. University of Washington Libraries.

Coleman, Ronald. "Among the Saints and the Gentiles: Blacks in Utah, 1850–1910." Paper presented at the Blacks in the American West Symposium, University of California, Davis, 1983.

Records of the Committee on Fair Employment Practices, Record Group 228, National Archives, Washington, D.C.

Samuel DeBow Papers. University of Washington Libraries.

William H. Dixon Collection, University of Washington Libraries.

Sidney Gerber Papers. University of Washington Libraries.

Larry Gossett. "A Perspective on the African American Community in the

United States." Speech delivered at Kobe, Japan, March 23, 1992.

Armeta Hearst Interview. University of Washington Libraries.

Japanese American Citizens League Records. Acc. No. 217–6. University of Washington Libraries.

Frank Jenkins Papers. University of Washington Libraries.

Donald Kazama Papers. University of Washington Libraries.

NAACP Branch Files. Manuscript Division, Library of Congress, Washington, D.C.

National Urban League Records. Manuscript Division, Library of Congress, Washington, D.C.

Nicandri, David L. "Washington's Ethnic Workingmen in 1900: A Comparative View." Unpublished paper delivered at the Pacific Northwest History Conference, Portland, Oregon, April 1979, now in the Northwest Collection, University of Washington Libraries.

O'Meara v. Washington State Board Against Discrimination, Case No. 35436, King County Superior Court, September 29, 1961, pp. 795–96.

James A. Roston Papers. University of Washington Libraries.

Seattle Civic Unity Committee Records. University of Washington Libraries.

Seattle NAACP Records. University of Washington Libraries.

Seattle Repertory Playhouse Files. University of Washington Libraries.

Seattle Urban League Records. University of Washington Libraries.

Melvina Squires Interview. University of Washington Libraries.

Victorio A. Velasco Papers. University of Washington Libraries.

Fred P. Woodson Papers, University of Washington Libraries.

Interviews

1. The interviews listed below were part of the Black Oral History Research Project conducted under my direction in the early 1970s. Fifty interviews of black pioneers and their descendants in Washington, Oregon, Idaho, and Montana were conducted by me or my associates between 1972 and 1975. The tapes and their transcripts are housed at Holland Library, Washington State University, Pullman.

Margaret Cogwell	Sandy Moss
Thelma Dewitty	Edward Pitter
Carver Gayton	Sam Smith
Virginia Gayton	

2. The interviews below were conducted by Esther Hall Mumford and her associates in 1975 and 1976 as part of the Washington Oral/Aural History Project sponsored by the Washington State Archives. The tapes and transcripts are at the Washington State Archives, Olympia, Washington, as part of the Washington Oral/Aural History Collection.

Edward Coleman	Mattie Vinyerd Harris
Leonard Gayton	William Henry Lee
Irene Grayson	Sara Oliver Jackson

Rufina Clemente Jenkins
Marguerite Johnson
Sandy Moss
Juanita Warfield Proctor
Mary Ott Saunders

Gertrude Simons
Albert Joseph Smith
Joseph Isom Staton
Samson C. Valley
Robert Wright

Newspapers

Seattle *Boeing News* 1947
Chicago *Defender* 1929
Detroit *Free Press* 1969
New York *The Messenger* 1922
New York *The Negro World* 1923–25
New York *Times* 1969
Olympia *Commercial Age* 1870
Olympia *Standard* 1864
Portland *Oregonian* 1963
San Francisco *Nikkei Shimin* (*Japanese American Citizen*) 1930
Seattle *Argus* 1964
Seattle *Cayton's Weekly* 1917
Seattle *Daily Intelligencer* 1879
Seattle *The Facts* 1964–70
Seattle *Japanese American Courier* 1928–42
Seattle *Northwest Enterprise* 1921–53
Seattle *Pacific Citizen* 1968
Seattle *Post-Intelligencer* 1892–1970
Seattle *Puget Sound Observer* 1958
Seattle *Republican* 1896–1910
Seattle *Searchlight* 1916
Seattle *Times* 1900–1989
Seattle *Voice of Action* 1935
Seattle *Union Record* 1906–20
Vancouver, B.C. *Province* 1968

Index

Carmichael, Stokely, 214, 217, 220, 290, 291
Carpenters Union, 67
Carson, John, 220
Carson, Ron, 222
Carter, W. D., 241
Carter Charity and Benevolent Club, 242
Carter Industrial and Literary Club, 141, 242
Cascade Coal Mining District, 259
Cayton, Horace R.: early years, 19–20; Seattle *Republican*, 19–20, 24, 44; on black migration, 24; on labor unions, 26–27, 66; on intraracial discrimination, 29; community leader, 32; on political patronage, 42; political influence, 43–44, 102; on anti-intermarriage bill, 94; Seattle's frontier past, 99; on Democratic Party, 104; support for Chinese, 125
Cayton, Horace R., Jr.: longshoremen's strike, 52–53, 54; *Long Old Road*, 53; work as steward, 60; on labor unions, 66–67, 257; movie theater sit-in, 82; Urban League, 94; Republican appointment, 103; on community "uplift," 140
Cayton, Madge, 61, 100, 144
Cayton, Revels: unions, 69; Communist Party, 99, 100–101, 102; about his father, 104; candidate for City Council, 176; restaurant discrimination, 261
Cayton, Susie Revels: associate editor, 20; employment, 61; Communist Party, 99–100, 102; community leader, 140, 141; Dorcus Charity Club, 140
Cayton family, 37, 82
Cayton's Weekly, 76
Census data, 258–59
Central Area (Central District): defined, 5; how it developed, 35, 82–83; real estate practices, 82–83; in 1970 (map), 232; no longer center of black Seattle, 236–40
Central Area Civil Rights Committee (CACRC): founding of, 197–98; school desegregation, 211–14, 290; as leadership group, 215, 220; Asian member, 224
Central Area Committee for Peace and Improvement (CAPI), 214, 220
Central Area Community Council, 225
Central Area Motivation Program (CAMP), 207, 288–89
Central Area Neighborhood Development Organization (CANDO), 225
Central Area School Council (CASC), 215
Central Area School of the Performing Arts (CASPA), 220

Central Contractors Association, 227, 230–31, 295
Central District. *See* Central Area
Central District Youth Club, 203
Central Labor Council, 26, 67, 266
Central Seattle Community Association, 180, 181
Central Seattle Community Council (CSCC), 225
Central Washington Finance Holding Corporation, 72
Chamber of Commerce, 77, 201
Chandler, William, 77, 241
Chandler Fuel Company, 77
Change Your Luck, 149
Charles, Ray, 149, 188, 277
Chen Cheong, 111, 113
Cheng Tsao-ju, 112
Cherberg, John, 205
Cherry Hill Baptist Church, 197
Chicago Defender, 156, 175
Children's Home, 140
Children's Orthopedic Hospital, 140–41
Chinatown, 110–16
Chin Chun Hock, 110, 112
Chinese Benevolent Association, 113
Chinese Exclusion Act of 1882, 115
Chinese Garden, 149
Chinese in Seattle: relations with other ethnic groups, 6, 87, 131, 174; in early Seattle, 22, 110–16, 125; violence against, 26, 107, 111–13, 131, 268; and labor unions, 27; population, 108, 245; attitude toward discrimination, 109; credit system, 110; sojourner's attitude, 110, 111; expulsion from Seattle, 112, 251; class structure, 113–15; bachelor society, 114–15; immigration restrictions, 114–15; housing, 115–16; school population in 1959, 182
Chin Gee-hee, 111, 113–14
Christian Friends for Racial Equality (CFRE), 168, 170–71
Churches: early, 36–39; importance of, 138–39; years of founding, 242. *See also individual church organizations*
Church of God in Christ, 242
Citizen's Advisory Committee on Minority Housing, 203
Citizens Against Mandatory Bussing (CAMB), 216
Citizen's Committee for Fair Employment, 183–84
Citizens Committee for Open Housing, 205
Citizens' Committee for Quality Integrated Education, 290
City Council: brothel area confined

93–94, 105, 124; fair employment practices, 171–72, 181–82, 183
Lennox Avenue Follies, 149
Leschi Elementary School, 181, 182
Leschi Improvement Council, 207
Levine, Lawrence, 136, 139
Lewis, Ernie, 154
Lewis, Howard, 229
Lewis, Sinclair, 150
Liberian-West African Transportation and Trading Company, 72, 77
Limerick, Patricia, 113
Lincoln administration, 23
Lincoln Discount Corporation, 72
Lincoln Helping Hand Club, 141, 242
Lincoln High School, 211
Lindberg, William, 231, 295
London Bridge Club, 242
Lone Star Art Club, 242
Long Old Road, 53
Longshoremen's strike of 1916, 52–53, 58
Longshoremen's unions, 52, 53–54, 68, 70, 166, 171, 259
Lopes, Manuel, 16, 17, 25, 28, 249
Los Angeles, 4, 17, 56, 268
Luke, Wing, 204, 224, 288
Lumber industry, 15–16, 17
Lundquist, Hugo, 163–64
Lynch, Lincoln, 218–19
Lysistrata, 150, 151

M

McCarthy era, 184
McClennon, George, 149
McCoy, Sam, 92
McDaniel, James, 184
MacDougall and Southwick, 80
McGraw, John H., 112
Machinists Union, 70, 163–65
McIntosh, Les, 219, 220
McIver, Emmett, 80, 154
McIver, Mrs. William, 95, 96
McKales, Inc., 76
McKinney, Samuel B.: civil rights leader, 197, 198; on open housing, 203, 204, 206; on school integration, 212, 213; on integration, 218
McKissick, Floyd, 219
Madison Street Cable Car, 35
Madison Street Theater, 90
Madrona–Denny Blaine Neighborhood Association, 180, 181
Madrona Elementary School, 182, 213
Magnuson, Warren, 94, 105
Manila Dance Hall, 124
Mann Elementary School, 181, 182, 211, 212
March Against Fear, 217, 291
March on Washington, 204, 210, 294

Mardi Gras club, 148, 149
Marine and Shipbuilding Union, 166
Marine Cooks and Stewards Association of the Pacific (MCSAP), 58, 59, 65, 69–70, 166, 294
Maritime strike of 1934, 68–70
Marks, Carole, 27
Marlborough and Penbrook Hotel, 57
Martin, Clarence D., 98
Martin, Tim, 199
Masonic lodges, 39, 40, 138, 139, 243
Matthews, W. D., 40
Max, Alan, 99
Maxwell, Charles, 144–45
Mayor's Advisory Committee on Police Practices, 178
Means, Donald, 222
Meany Junior High School, 182
Mechanics Union, 64, 259
Medical Lake, 140
Meeting halls, 243
Meier, August, 199
Mercer, Asa, 22
Mercer Island, 202, 209, 238
Meredith, William L., 41, 42
Methodist Church, 137
Metropolitan Theater, 150, 153
Michigan State University, 178
Migration to Seattle: Great Migration, 5, 22; World War II and postwar period, 8, 159–61, 170, 173–75, 187; travelcraft skills, 16; in nineteenth century, 19–20, 22, 24; black recruitment, 22, 24; in twentieth century, 51, 55–56; in 1960s, 190–92
Miliken, Earl, 93–94
Miller, Alexander F., 285
Miller, Carl, 215, 222, 226
Miller, Earl, 197
Miller, Irene Burns, 81, 84–85, 128, 281
Mills, David, 220, 222
Milwaukee, 63, 177, 252, 261
Ming, Ou-yang, 112
Minnehaha Saloon, 30
Minor Elementary School, 182
Mitsui, Sumi, 174
Mittlestadt, Otto, 97, 98
Miura, Tamaki, 118
Miyamoto, S. Frank, 224
Model Cities, 215, 220, 226, 227, 228–29, 290
"Model minority," 296
Monet, Matthias, 29, 30
Montana, 21
Montgomery, "Auntie," 28
Moore, William, 227
Moore Theater, 151
Moran Brothers, 50
Morrison, Edward, 30

Moss, Sandy, 67
Moss, William, 51
Moton, Robert R., 66
Mount Baker neighborhood, 82
Mount Zion Baptist Church, 37, 38, 138, 168, l76, 197, 203, 204, 213, 242
Mumford, Esther Hall, 38, 251, 314
Murray, James S., 27
Musicians Union, 68
Mussolini, Benito, 139
Mystic Night Club, 242

N

Nakamura, "Rhino," 154
Nariaki, Sometani, 117
National Afro-American League, 40
National Association for the Advancement of Colored People (NAACP): Du Bois quoted, 79; in early twentieth century, 80, 82, 87–88, 155–56; Seattle branch founded, 88–90, 241; branch reactivated, 92–94, 98; and Japanese Americans, 131, 294; political club meetings, 136; in late 1930s, 155–56; on segregation, 168; rapid growth during war, 170; fair employment practices, 171; growing black population, 172; on cooperation among blacks, 173; opposed to picketing and boycotts, 184; and Urban League, 186; "establishment," 186–87; in 1960s, 197; open housing, 202, 203, 205; and UNIA, 263
National Association of Colored Women, 141
National Conference of Christians and Jews, 178
National Council of Afro-Americans, 41
National Federation of Constitutional Liberties, 184
National Industrial Recovery Act of 1933, 68
National Institute on Intergroup Relations, 178
National Negro Congress, 88, 98, 99, 184
National Negro Labor Council, 184
National Real Estate Board, 180, 287
National Urban League. See Urban League
National Youth Administration, 161
Nation of Islam, 214, 215, 218
Native Americans: competition with other ethnic groups, 6; attitudes of whites toward, 14, 22; population, 108, 216, 238, 245; freedom schools, 213; JACL meetings, 224
Naturalization laws, 107
Natural Man, 151, 153
Negro History Week, 185
Negro Labor Council, 184

Negro Repertory Company, 149, 150–53, 177
Negro Republican Club, 171
Negro Voters League (NVL), 220
Neuberger, Richard L., 228, 260
Newcastle, 25, 27, 68, 112
New Deal programs, 150
New Harlem Club, 147
Newspapers, 19–20, 21, 72–73, 119, 315
Nicholas, Elva Moore, 84, 172
Nightclubs, 147–49
Nihonmachi (Japanese community): self-sufficiency, 72; "Japantown," 116–17; early twentieth century, 118–21, 133; World War II period, 133, 174; education, 145–46; middle class, 145. *See also* Japanese in Seattle
Nikkei Shimin (Japanese American Citizen), 120
Noah, 153
Noel, Donald, 224
Nordstrom, 199
Nordstrom, Elmer, 199
Norris, Ira F., 104
North American Produce Company, 72
Northern Pacific Railroad Company, 17, 24, 110, 111, 117
Northwest Enterprise: history of, 72–73; on patronage of race enterprises, 73, 75–76; on Lawson case, 98; Communist advertisements, 101; on discrimination, 119, 280; on Japanese evacuation, 126, 174; "Round the Town" column, 148; on theater, 152; and white press, 152; on Executive Order 8802, 163; on segregation, 165, 168; on police, 167; on antidiscrimination bill, 171; on growing population, 172; on cooperation among blacks, 173; editorial cartoon, 173, 239; on growing drug trade, 188–89

O

Oakes, Ira, 219
Oakland, 56
Occupations: in nineteenth century, 24–36; job stereotyping, 24–25, 176–77, 251–52; in early twentieth century, 50–78; occupational categories, 1910–40 (table), 62; of blacks and Asians, 75, 200; occupational data, 258. *See also* Employment; Labor unions
Ocean Hill–Brownsville school controversy, 216
Odd Fellows, 40, 139
Odegaard, Charles, 222–23
Office of Economic Opportunity, 207
Okada, Banzo, 117

Washington Federation of Labor, 171
Washington Junior High School, 182
Washington Natural Gas, 199
Washington Progressive Party, 184
Washington Standard, 23
Washington State Baptist Association, 38
Washington State Board Against Discrimination (WSBAD), 172, 182–84, 186–87, 193, 198, 203
Washington State Supreme Court, 203
Washington Territory, 21–22
Washington Vocational Institute, 273
Waterfront Employers Association, 52, 54, 68, 69
Watsonville, California, 272
Watts riot, 4, 223
Webster, Milton P., 49, 71
Wells, Hulet, 55
We of the Grassroots, 220
Westberg, Arthur, 196
Western Central Labor Union, 26, 252
West Seattle, 169, 179
West Seattle High School, 211
Whalen, Patrick L., 97, 98
White, Frances, 219
White, Richard, 9
White, S. B., 30
White Cooks and Waiters' Union, 26
White supremacy, 20, 22–23
Whitlow, Ernest, 99
Whitman, David, 99
Widow's Mite Missionary Society, 38
Wilder, Douglas, 3
Will Do Club, 242
Williams, Bernard, 99
Williams, Dorothy West, 164, 279
Williams, George, 176
Williams, J. L., 241
Wilson, John L., 42
Wilson, William H. : founder of *Northwest Enterprise*, 72–73; community leader, 77; NAACP, 92, 93; Citizens' Committee,94; Urban League, 95, 96, 98; on intermarriage, 126. *See also Northwest Enterprise*
Wilson, Woodrow, 88
Wing, Sam, 115
Winston, O. H., 89
Women: black employment, 14, 24, 28, 51, 54–55, 57, 60–61, 164–65, 257; on juries, 21; suffrage, 21, 250; Asa Mercer's recruitment, 22; prostitution, 28, 30–31, 34, 253;

pickpockets, 41; competition with men for jobs, 57; in labor unions, 57, 164–65; domestic service, 60–61; Black Cross nurses, 90, 91; census figures, 114; Japanese immigrants, 131; black organizations, 140–42, 242, 243; education, 144–45
Women's Christian Temperance Union (WCTU), 39, 141
Women's Home and Foreign Mission Society, 242
Women's Political and Civic Alliance, 103
Wonder Bread, 199
Woo, Foon, 174
Woods, Henry, 154
Woodson, Irene Frances, 30
Woodson, Zacharias I., 77
Works Projects Administration (WPA), 151
World War II employment, 160–66
Wright, Bonita, 241
Wright, Robert, 147, 148
Wynne, Robert E., 111

Y

Yamaoka, Ototake, 117, 269–70
Yang, Bernie, 215, 227
Yesler, Henry, 15, 17, 28, 35
Yesler-Atlantic Urban Renewal Project, 220
Yesler-Denny Company, 29
Yesler Hill, 81, 84, 87, 169
Yesler-Jackson area, 34–35
Yesler Terrace, 81, 84, 169, 281
Yorita, Miyoshi, 118
Young, Andrew, 197
Young, Mrs. L. B., 104
Young, Whitney, 206
Young, Zoe, 241
Young Communist League, 101
Young Men's Christian Association (YMCA), 136, 137, 215, 220, 277
Young Men's Colored Republican Club, 43
Young Women's Christian Association (YWCA), 77, 94, 126, 137, 142, 144, 171, 279
Youth Opportunity Center, 220
Youth Service Center, 196

Z

Zoot Suit Riot, 167
Zunz, Olivier, 146